If you are interested in knowing what the afterlife looks like to a serious academic studying the available literature from both a scientific and spiritual perspective, there is no better book that I could recommend. Dr. Baruššs approach is thoughtful and well-informed. He is able to integrate masses of data to carefully delineate possibilities in an area that most people find confusing at best.

—**Jeffrey Mishlove, PhD,** Host and Producer, *New Thinking Allowed* YouTube channel

Death as an Altered State of Consciousness: A Scientific Approach is a key contribution to the scientific literature exploring the nature of consciousness. You will be delighted with the way the narrative captures your interest, as well as the clear organization of Barušss arguments. He builds compelling evidence from a variety of research areas, including near-death experiences. This book will be of special interest to caregivers in end-of-life care, offering a new understanding of this highly debated and often misunderstood topic.

—**Marjorie Woollacott, PhD,** Professor, Institute of Neuroscience, University of Oregon, Eugene, OR, United States

Baruš is just one of the few real authorities on altered states. I can't wait to order a copy!

—**Charles T. Tart, PhD,** Professor Emeritus, University of California Davis, Davis, CA, United States; Editor, *Altered States of Consciousness*

Even the most skeptical readers will see *Death as an Altered State of Consciousness*'s relevance to ongoing developments in dissociative identity disorder, fantasy proneness, grief counseling, and psychedelic-assisted psychotherapy and other means of personality transformation. Baruss's lively writing style and his judicious use of intriguing examples make it difficult to put this book down.

—**Stanley Krippner, PhD**, Affiliated Distinguished Professor, California Institute of Integral Studies, San Francisco, CA, United States; Coeditor, *Varieties of Anomalous Experience: Examining the Scientific Evidence*

Perhaps the most important book of our age, and certainly among the most fascinating. Not since Rudolf Steiner, Emanuel Swedenborg, and *The Tibetan Book of the Dead* (Bardo Thodol) have we been treated to such a rich tour of conscious experience during dying and death. And this time with scientific rigor.

—**Allan Leslie Combs, PhD**, Author, *The Radiance of Being: Understanding the Grand Integral Vision; Living the Integral Life* and *Consciousness Explained Better: Towards an Integral Understanding of the Multifaceted Nature of Consciousness*; Coauthor, *Synchronicity: Through the Eyes of Science, Myth, and the Trickster*

Death as an Altered State of Consciousness

Death as an Altered State of Consciousness
A Scientific Approach

Imants Baruss

 AMERICAN PSYCHOLOGICAL ASSOCIATION

Copyright © 2023 by the American Psychological Association. All rights reserved. Except as permitted under the United States Copyright Act of 1976, no part of this publication may be reproduced or distributed in any form or by any means, including, but not limited to, the process of scanning and digitization, or stored in a database or retrieval system, without the prior written permission of the publisher.

The opinions and statements published are the responsibility of the author, and such opinions and statements do not necessarily represent the policies of the American Psychological Association.

Published by
American Psychological Association
750 First Street, NE
Washington, DC 20002
https://www.apa.org

Order Department
https://www.apa.org/pubs/books
order@apa.org

Typeset in Charter and Interstate by Circle Graphics, Inc., Reisterstown, MD

Printer: Gasch Printing, Odenton, MD
Cover Designer: Gwen J. Grafft, Minneapolis, MN

Library of Congress Cataloging-in-Publication Data

CIP Data has been applied for.
Library of Congress Control Number: 2023934129

https://doi.org/10.1037/0000361-000

Printed in the United States of America

10 9 8 7 6 5 4 3 2 1

Imants is not dead,
But merely enchanted lies silent,
Stilled from his exploits,
Dozing beneath Blue Mountain.

Reposing in the golden castle,
His sword does not rust,
Which, shattering iron mail,
Has become like flame.

Once in one hundred years
A tiny dwarf rises
And peers about, to see whether the fog
Has begun to be extinguished round the mountain.

And as long as the blue fog
Cloaks Blue Mountain,
For those thousand years
He is covered by earth.

But once the Sons of Thunder
Detonate shot on that mountain;
Causing all the demons to flee,
His sword he will clutch.

And the Daughters of the Sun shall come
And dissipate the fog;
And voices from the Age of Light
Shall call Imants forth!

–Andrejs Pumpurs, written in 1874
(English translation from Latvian by
Maija Collins and Imants Barušs, 2022)

Contents

Prologue   *ix*
Acknowledgments   *xiii*

1. Studying Death   3
2. Deathbed Phenomena   27
3. Afterdeath Communication   51
4. Mediumship   75
5. Instrumental Transcommunication   99
6. Anomalous Physical Phenomena   125
7. Near-Death Experiences   149
8. Past-Life Experiences   175
9. The Nature of the Afterlife   199
   Epilogue   225

References   *231*
Index   *259*
About the Author   *279*

Prologue

In the past 10 years, a growing number of highly respected scientists from multiple disciplines have begun to question the nature of human consciousness. This small but very influential group has aggressively pushed back against the 100-year dogma in biology and in neuroscience that consciousness is a consequence of, and emerges from, neurochemical trafficking in the brain.
—James T. Lacatski, Colm A. Kelleher, and George Knapp (2021, p. 177)

I had been teaching a third-year, undergraduate psychology course about death as an altered state of consciousness when I made a commitment to write a textbook for that course. A few months later, the COVID-19 pandemic overwhelmed the world, and death was thrust into our collective faces. So, this book has ended up having unexpected significance—not just for my students and scientists with specialized interest in death but for everyone.

Why regard death as an altered state of consciousness? Death brings consciousness to an abrupt end, so its alteration is oblivion. Not interesting. That would be the prevailing materialist ideology. But ideology does not stop you, the reader, or me from examining some unusual phenomena associated with death. In this book, we consider deathbed phenomena, apparent afterdeath communication, mediumship, apparent afterdeath communication through electronic devices, physical phenomena associated with apparent afterdeath communication, near-death experiences, and past-life experiences. One of the things we will find, as we get going, is the occurrence over and over again of anomalous phenomena—in particular, anomalous information acquisition and anomalous physical influencing—which do not fit a conventional materialist interpretation of reality. We could try to explain such anomalies by positing that they are the result of anomalous processes among the living. That is called *living agent psi* (LAP). But can we go one step further? The *survival hypothesis* is the hypothesis that consciousness of some sort survives, at least for a while, after physical death. That death is a nontrivial altered state of consciousness. Is there evidence for survival? Making an argument for survival turns out to be more difficult than it seems it should be. But what this does is set up an imaginary materialist–LAP–survival dial and the question of how far to the right we can turn that dial. We will keep coming back to this scheme as we go from chapter to chapter.

Materialism is entrenched in the academy, so there is considerable resistance to moving the dial at all. We can try to maintain a materialist stance, arguing away each apparently anomalous event on the grounds of poor documentation, misperception, mental illness, hoax, and so on. Materialists have sometimes argued that all materialist explanations must be completely exhausted before entertaining any alternatives because materialism is, after all, the correct interpretation of reality. Given such an agenda, one of my readers said that I should present only the clearest evidence against materialism in favor of survival and leave out the messy cases. Well, I am not doing that. I present some of the clear cases and lots of messy cases because the messy cases represent the way things are, and I want the reader to get a feeling for the richness of the actual terrain of this material and not some eviscerated version of it. Science is not about protecting entrenched ideologies, materialist or otherwise, but about trying to find the theory with the best goodness of fit to the data, so I freely discuss LAP and survivalist explanations throughout. Indeed, the last chapter about the nature of the afterlife is an explication of what the afterlife could be like were the survival hypothesis to be true. That information allows us to explicitly analyze death as an altered state of consciousness.

In keeping with a scientific approach, I do not want readers to believe anything but to evaluate what I say using their own judgment. I am not making some sort of global philosophical argument, although I do point out logical inconsistencies as they appear. And there are lots of those across the spectrum of explanations. Nonetheless, students frequently ask me what I think. As an expert familiar with the nuances of these phenomena and arguments about them, do I think that the survival hypothesis is true? Let me give an answer consistent with the spirit of inquiry in this book. As I worked my way through the details in each chapter, I experienced a slowly dawning realization that the human psyche is far more expansive than any materialist reification could capture. This is a conclusion reached also by many experiencers who frequently undergo a process of self-transformation that leads to transcendent insights about the nature of consciousness and reality, including death.

I open each chapter with an epigraph that comes as close as I can find to capturing the essence of that chapter from the point of view of a believer in survival. But the epigraphs are also meant to be provocative, to pique the reader's interest. So, for instance, a key idea in Chapter 1 is the loss of critical thinking about the subject matter of death due to unwitting adherence to cultural norms. I discuss this using social cognitive ideology. But that is not how Shaman Durek sees it. What he sees is that green gas has emanated from the underworld, coating people so that they become entrained to act in accordance with mass mind. In Chapter 7, we see how near-death experiences can carry over into a person's ordinary waking state, transforming their life. But what exactly can be brought back from an encounter with the unknown? How about a goat? The point here is not to get caught up in arguing about whether the events in the epigraphs really happen but to open another perspective on the phenomenology of these experiences. Lots of discussion about the veridicality of such experiences is within the substance of each chapter. But this brings up another point. There is a stifling atmosphere to much of the academic discussion about death. I want to change that by introducing some levity into the presentation of this subject matter. So, I hope that what I have to say is not only useful, but enjoyable.

The reader may notice that the citation of references is not always in alphabetical order, which is the publisher's usual style. Throughout the book, I cite references in the order of their relevance to what I am saying, with the most significant first.

Acknowledgments

I am grateful to Angie Aristone and Neda Wassie, who have given me permission to use narratives of their experiences to open Chapter 4 about mediumship and Chapter 7 about near-death experiences, respectively. I am grateful to my readers, Monika Mandoki, Carolyn Dillon, Brenda Sanders, Karalee Kothe, Patrizio Tressoldi, Carol Bowman, Julie Beischel, Dee Degard, and Anabela Cardoso, for their feedback on earlier drafts of this book. None of my readers is responsible for any errors or omissions that might remain, nor do they necessarily agree with anything that I say. I thank Shannon Foskett for research assistance, critical comments, and assistance with editing, and Ayla Lyons for assistance with fact-checking. I am grateful to King's University College at Western University for a paid sabbatical leave and research funds that allowed me to write this book.

I also thank Susan Reynolds, my acquisitions editor at the American Psychological Association (APA), for her support over the past 2 decades in getting my books into print. It has been a pleasure working with her. I thank everyone at APA Books who has been part of the editing, production, and sales process for their hard work, patience, and unwavering support for my work.

Finally, I thank my students, colleagues, members of the Consciousness Club, and everyone else with whom I have engaged in vigorous discussions about consciousness and death.

Death as an Altered State of Consciousness

1 STUDYING DEATH

And then there's the green gas. The green gas is the energy the darkness uses to shut down people's synthesis and sever their connection to the spirit realm. This green gas is what allows humans to give up their sovereignty, and to be turned into zombies taking commands from the darkness, and playing out the system's propaganda. They don't realize that their piousness, and their righteousness, and their refusal to consider other points of view are all side effects from this gooey, green underworld toxin that's distorting their system, and shutting down their synthesis.

—Shaman Durek (2019, p. 256)

Just out of medical school in the early 1970s, Bruce Greyson was sitting in a hospital cafeteria eating spaghetti and reading a psychiatry textbook when his pager went off, startling him, so that he ended up spilling spaghetti sauce on his tie. Not having time to change clothes before examining Holly, a young woman who had tried to kill herself, he put on his lab coat and buttoned it to conceal the stain. She was unresponsive. He went down the hallway to talk to her roommate, Susan, who was pacing about but whom

---

https://doi.org/10.1037/0000361-001
Death as an Altered State of Consciousness: A Scientific Approach, by I. Baruss
Copyright © 2023 by the American Psychological Association. All rights reserved.

he managed to settle down sufficiently to get her to sit on a couch. It was hot there, so he moved a fan closer to them and unbuttoned his lab coat. After his conversation with her, he became self-conscious about the stain and rebuttoned the coat before looking in on the unresponsive patient and then leaving the hospital (Greyson, 2021a).

The following morning, Holly was conscious. She said that she knew who he was, that she had seen him the previous night talking to her roommate sitting on a couch—and that he had been wearing a "striped tie that had a red stain on it" (Greyson, 2021a, p. 5). Greyson was confused: "What?" Holly repeated what she had said and "then went on to repeat the conversation [he had] had with Susan, all [his] questions and Susan's answers, along with Susan's pacing and [his] moving the fan, without making any mistakes" (Greyson, 2021a, p. 6). This rattled Greyson, who could not figure out how she could have obtained that information.

Raymond Moody (1975) wrote a best-selling book, *Life After Life*, in which he introduced the expression "near-death experience" (NDE) to the English language and described experiences that people had had at the time they were close to death. In 1976, Moody showed up as a student at Bruce Greyson's hospital, and from Moody, Greyson learned that Holly's experience had not been unique. Other people had had the experience of leaving their bodies and apparently watching what was going on in the environment around them. Greyson went on to carry out research about NDEs, cofound the International Association for Near-Death Studies, and edit the *Journal of Near-Death Studies* (Greyson, 2021a). We return to NDEs later in this chapter and, in greater detail, in Chapter 7.

An *altered state of consciousness* is a state of consciousness that is different from the ordinary waking state along some dimensions of interest. Death is clearly not the ordinary waking state and so, by definition, is an altered state of consciousness. The question is: Is it a state of oblivion, or is there something more interesting going on? The premise that consciousness continues to exist after the death of the physical body is known as the *survival hypothesis* (Baruss, 2020, p. 195). In this book, we consider phenomena associated with death, such as NDEs, and the extent to which they provide evidence for survival.

In this chapter, we create the framework for our investigation and introduce the main issues that arise with this material. I start with some definitions. I then describe the approach that I am taking to the subject matter. Then, I lay out the topics that are covered. At that point, the divergence of ideas about the nature of reality becomes apparent so that we need to explicitly examine beliefs about consciousness and reality and their relevance to a study of death. The problem is that not all contradictory beliefs can be correct. So, to sort them out, we use science—not scientism, but authentic science. And when we do that, we find that there are cases of NDEs in which experiencers have correctly identified events that occurred during the time when their brains were not in a condition that could support sensory processing. That means that there are problems with materialism. But, if so, then why is this not acknowledged more widely in the academy? This leads to a discussion of groupthink. At the end of the chapter, I show that even the best materialist argument against survival is problematic. This will all set the context for our discourse about death.

SETTING THE FRAMEWORK

Let me begin by distinguishing between two definitions of consciousness, which we will use as dimensions of interest for identifying altered states of consciousness: behavioral consciousness and phenomenal consciousness. Behavioral consciousness is a third-person, from the outside, definition of consciousness, whereas phenomenal consciousness is a first-person, from the inside, definition of consciousness. *Behavioral consciousness* refers to an organism's ability to discriminate among stimuli and act in a goal-directed manner. Note that consciousness, by this definition, is not just awareness but has both an input and output aspect to it. An organism could be a living being, such as a human, reptile, plant, and so on; a robot endowed with artificial intelligence; or whatever else might be out there or invented that has the necessary input–output connections to the environment and requisite internal computational ability. Clearly, this criterion for consciousness is a variable from minimal values, such as a plant turning toward the sun, to maximal values of sophisticated interactions with the environment, self-reference, and linguistic articulation by an organism of its own behavior (Barušs, 1987, 2008).

Phenomenal consciousness is about the ongoing experiential stream of thoughts, feelings, images, and so on that go on for a person. And it is not just that there are such contents to our experience but that they have a phenomenal quality to them, called *qualia*. It is "something like" to experience these contents. They have the quality of "raw feels," as philosophers sometimes say. Furthermore, let us use the expression *existential qualia* for the sense that existence as such is going on. So, putting these ideas together, let us say that *phenomenal consciousness* refers to "subjective events suffused with existential qualia that occur privately for a person" (Barušs & Mossbridge, 2017, p. 15). The reader might want to take a few moments to try to identify those psychological features for themselves as an exercise in *metacognition*, the process of directly knowing something about one's own psychological processes (Metcalfe & Shimamura, 1994).

A *state of consciousness* is a stable configuration of consciousness. The *ordinary waking state* is the normative state of an animal that is awake and interacting with its environment. An altered state of consciousness is a stable configuration of consciousness such that either behavioral consciousness or phenomenal consciousness differs from the ordinary waking state. Sleep, in which reactivity to the environment changes and mentation may change or be retrospectively absent, is the prototypical altered state of consciousness. We can also use the expression *alterations of consciousness* as a broader designation to include unstable or slightly altered states of consciousness, such as daydreams or strong emotions. In the context of alterations of consciousness, the ordinary waking state need not be privileged and can be regarded as just one of many alterations of consciousness (Barušs, 2020).

Putting all of this together, to say that death is an altered state of consciousness is to acknowledge that behavioral consciousness has changed so that the organism is no longer interacting in a normative way with its environment. But what happens to phenomenal consciousness? Does it continue or not? If it continues, then what does it feel like? There are three obvious possibilities. First, consciousness could continue with diminished psychological functioning so that, for instance, qualia could be absent, and just some unreflective information field remains. Second, consciousness after death could be equivalent to consciousness as it is experienced during life with perceptual capabilities, memories, and personality dispositions intact so that death is simply the equivalent of removing a meat jacket. Third, consciousness after death could entail enhanced psychological functioning so that we have greater clarity of mind, equanimity of emotions, and so on, than we do while alive (cf. Sudduth, 2016). And if we do continue as the second or third of those possibilities, then is there an environment in which we find ourselves? Heaven perhaps? Or hell (Lorimer, 1984/2017; Bercholz, 2016)? And how are we to find out what awaits? And, in particular, as psychologists and scientists, how would we know?

Perhaps we should not get entangled in the metaphysical and epistemological intricacies of this subject matter right away but lay out the material that is covered in this book and the manner in which I do that. Let me start with the second of those.

As intimated in the prologue, I teach psychology courses about consciousness and altered states of consciousness at an undergraduate, liberal arts, Catholic university college affiliated with one of Canada's largest universities.

Students in my classes bring a broad range of perspectives to the subject matter. We will come back to this range of perspectives in a bit, but it means that I have had to learn to speak as neutrally as possible so as not to alienate my students. My strategy is to use my knowledge to lay out the relevant phenomena with as much transparency as possible, providing students with the evidence they need to develop their own understanding of the subject matter. That is also the strategy for good science writing. "Our aim is to design communications that do not lead people to a particular decision, but help them to understand what is known about a topic and to make up their own minds on the basis of that evidence" (Blastland et al., 2020, p. 363). While I am going to lay out the evidence directly relevant to survival as much as possible, as I do for my students, I cannot do so for the background preparation that is necessary to move into this material. This means that I am making judgments about how much evidence for such background material to include in the text and how much to defer to other sources.

There is another issue. From the little that I have said already, it is likely apparent that the subject matter in this book is controversial. It does not matter how carefully I address this material and how much self-effacement I exercise; friction is likely to arise between my exposition and a reader's own ideas. In my experience, the approach taken by some of my colleagues is to just leave out the controversial material to curry favor with their peers. However, if I know something and I pretend that I do not know it, then that constitutes academic misconduct. I would be withholding knowledge. Academic integrity, on the other hand, requires laying out what I know as carefully as possible.

There is, of course, another way out for the intimidated academic: Namely, ignore the entire field of study and have a more successful career doing something less controversial. And, indeed, whatever the reason, academics have generally stayed away from studying the more interesting phenomena associated with death. The work of those who are left in the ring makes up much of the substance of this book. But the absence of academics has left an informational vacuum. When any person, including an academic, wants to know something about this subject matter, what resources do they have available to them? The vacuum has been partially filled by journalists, who have sometimes done a commendable job of disentangling the intricacies of the subject matter (e.g., Pearson, 2014; Tymn, 2016; Kean, 2017). There are physicians who have written books (e.g., Charbonier, 2012; Long, 2016; Fenwick & Fenwick, 2013) and lots of experiencers who have told us their stories (e.g., Moorjani, 2012; Stavis, 2018; Strieber & Strieber, 2020), including, for instance, experiencers who are physicians (e.g., Kason & Degler, 1994;

Kason, 2019; Medhus, 2015; E. Alexander & Newell, 2017). Indeed, there is a range of material, of uneven quality, by people with differing backgrounds that is available on the internet for anyone to read, listen to, and watch. But this also highlights the need for this book—a book that gives a clear account of what is known amid the reams of confusion that pervade the subject matter of death.

So, what are we going to talk about? I want to start in Chapter 2 with phenomena that occur as a person approaches death, in particular, the occurrence of deathbed visions. The discussion then turns to death itself, including cases of apparently shared death experiences, and *deathbed coincidences*, whereby meaningful, synchronous events occur around the time of someone's death. Chapter 3 is about *afterdeath communication* (ADC), the continuation of anomalous experiences beyond the time of a person's death that suggest that a deceased person is making an effort to communicate with the living. Chapter 4 is about *mental mediumship*, whereby some people, namely, mediums, have the ability to impart correct information that appears to come from the deceased. In Chapter 5, we return to ADC, but this time ADC that occurs electronically, called *instrumental transcommunication* (ITC)—for instance, voices recorded on an audio recorder or text messages received on a cell phone that appear to have originated with the deceased. In Chapter 6, I consider *physical mediumship*, which entails physical phenomena attributed to the deceased, as well as other situations in which anomalous physical phenomena occur. I end that chapter with experiences of possession. Chapter 7 is devoted to NDEs, such as the one that we have already considered. Chapter 8 is about *past-life experiences*, whereby a person, frequently a child, behaves as though that person were living the continuation of a previous lifetime, suggestive of reincarnation. In Chapter 9, I speculate about what an afterlife might look like if the survival hypothesis were to be true and, using that material, explicitly examine death as an altered state of consciousness along 16 dimensions. In the epilogue, I note nine takeaway points from this exposition.

What is the source material for writing about these topics? As much as possible, I rely on recent academic books and papers. If necessary, I go back to older material. Some areas are better covered than others in the academic literature. For instance, there has been considerable discussion about ADC in the context of a continuing bonds model of grief counseling. So, we will summarize some of that research. In other cases, there is almost nothing. For instance, academic research about ITC consists of a handful of studies, mostly by my students and me (Barušs, 2001, 2007a), and, independently, by Gary Schwartz (2021a, 2021b). This means that, in many cases, we need to leave the security of academic publication and roam the reams of confusion to which I alluded previously. However, the split between the academic and nonacademic is not as clean as we might expect in that academic writing cannot automatically be trusted either, thereby introducing its own reams of confusion (B. A. Nosek et al., 2012; Sokal, 1996a, 1996b). And some of what is produced outside the academic environment can be refreshingly free from the types of conceits that pervade the academic environment (e.g., Assagioli, 1965; Kastrup, 2014; Goertzel & Goertzel, 2015). In other words, an academic imprint is no guarantee of credibility, and I need to scrutinize the quality of academic sources just as much as those that are nonacademic.

When I do troll the reams of confusion, how do I know whether a book, video, or web content is worth my time and effort? And at what point does any of that material become suitable for this book? First, there is no algorithm to guarantee the veracity of any of that material. And, years later perhaps, I would not be surprised if some of what I have chosen to use turns out to be nonsense. But that is the price that we pay for academics' avoidance of this subject matter. We cannot have it both ways. We cannot refuse to support research in these areas of inquiry and then complain that the sources of our information are substandard. That is our own fault. The alternative, simply leaving out entire chunks of material, just plays into the avoidance agenda. We learn nothing about those chunks.

Second, I am going to choose material that is intrinsically coherent and meaningful. In other words, what matters is the inherent quality of the material itself rather than any credentials attached to those who produce it. However, third, if necessary, I do pay attention to the credibility of individual authors. This is obviously tricky because it involves making judgments about their integrity and, as such, is an issue that we return to frequently in this book. Clearly, I am trying to present material produced by credible sources.

Fourth, is there any convergence of material from different authors? If so, less weight is placed on each individual source.

Fifth, I have an experiential framework for making the necessary judgments. I have personally witnessed some of these phenomena. In addition, over the course of 45 years of teaching, students have frequently come up to me and said, "I've never told anyone about this before because I didn't want them to think that I was crazy, but . . ." and then proceeded to tell me about unusual experiences that they have had. So, both from my own experiences as well as those of my students, I have some familiarity with different types of anomalous phenomena. Furthermore, when I first started teaching, I regularly taught an undergraduate course in psychopathology, so I have a good understanding of the ways in which human behavior can become dysfunctional. So, in addition to the breadth and depth of my academic knowledge about alterations of consciousness, I have a rich personal context within which to make judgments about the quality of the material that I am using. We return to these methodological issues as necessary throughout this book.

Okay, back to the metaphysical and epistemological issues. Some readers might say that, well, we already know that phenomenal consciousness is produced by the brain, so when behavioral consciousness stops, then so does phenomenal consciousness (cf. Halligan & Oakley, 2021). There is no survival. So, all of that ADC and ITC and everything else in that paragraph is made-up stuff that has perfectly natural explanations, such as misperceptions, misattributions, mental illness, fraud, and so on, which we can call the *usual suspects* (Braude, 2003). There is no point reading further. For instance, given the history of fraud in this domain of research (Dinicastro, 2007), such a reaction would seem to be reasonable. Other readers might react quite differently and say, hey, finally someone is taking survival seriously and talking about all of these really cool things. I cannot wait to read more. What are we to do with such divergent attitudes? It is time to consider the range of perspectives that people bring to this subject matter.

BELIEFS ABOUT CONSCIOUSNESS AND REALITY

In 1986, Robert Moore and I gathered survey data from 334 people who did write or could potentially write about consciousness in the academic literature to see if we could untangle their personal beliefs about reality from the ways in which they conceptualized consciousness. Not surprisingly perhaps, those two are intimately linked so that we ended up just calling them "beliefs about consciousness and reality." We identified a subset of items from the survey to form a questionnaire, which we called the Beliefs About Consciousness and Reality Questionnaire (BACARQ), that could be used for measuring such beliefs in other studies (Barušs, 1990; Barušs & Moore, 1989, 1992).

What Moore and I found is that there exists a material-transcendent dimension of beliefs about consciousness and reality. Some people are *materialists* who think that the universe is a physical place that follows deterministic laws. They would agree with Item Q09 on the BACARQ, which reads: "There is no reality other than the physical universe." Thus, these people are physical monists in that they believe that there is only one type of substance in the universe: physical matter. Hence, phenomenal consciousness is merely a by-product of physical or computational processes. These people tend not to have any religious beliefs and say that science is the proper way to know something. The fundamental idea is that only physical reality exists and that everything can be explained in physical terms.

Moore and I found that those tending toward the transcendent pole of the continuum could be identified with either a moderate or more extreme version of transcendentalism, which we called the "conservatively transcendent" and the "extraordinarily transcendent" positions. There are two defining characteristics of the *conservatively transcendent position*, namely, religiosity and meaning. By religiosity, we mean endorsing ideas such as the importance of a spiritual approach to life and "the existence of an original creator" (Barušs, 1990, p. 120) as well as finding that the participants tending toward this position were likely to choose one of the traditional religions as their religious affiliation. These participants were dualists in that they thought that reality consists of both mental and physical substances so that consciousness is not just something derived from physical matter. Indeed, "the existence of human consciousness is evidence of a spiritual dimension within each person" (Barušs, 1990, p. 121). Meaning is also important for these participants, not just in the sense that they seek purpose in life, but also in a deeper sense that "consciousness gives meaning to reality" (Barušs, 1990, p. 120). Emphasis is placed on meaning, religious ideas, and the importance of phenomenal consciousness.

Those tending toward the *extraordinarily transcendent position* indicated that they had had unusual experiences, such as mystical or out-of-body experiences, and that they had had "experiences which science would have difficulty explaining" (Barušs, 1990, p. 123). They claimed that their ideas had "changed dramatically in the past" (Barušs, 1990, p. 123). They believe that we can know things through extrasensory perception or "modes of understanding latent within a person which are superior to rational thought" (Barušs, 1990, p. 125). Meditation and contemplation are important for them as is inner self-development more generally. These people are mental monists, or "idealists," as philosophers sometimes say, in that they think that there is only one type of substance, namely, consciousness, from which everything else is made. The idea that emerges from these data is that our individual consciousnesses are part of a universal consciousness whose realization is the end goal of self-development through practices in altered states of consciousness.

This is all somewhat dramatic. At one extreme, consciousness is a by-product of physical processes and, at the other extreme, physical processes are by-products of consciousness. As readers are likely aware, there is a bias toward materialism of one sort or another in the academy (Barušs & Mossbridge, 2017), so the first of those beliefs was not unexpected. But the coalescence of the extraordinarily transcendent position with a coherent constellation of characteristics did surprise us. There was no a priori reason why the items defining the transcendent position should group together. Who are these people?

One of my thesis students checked for personality characteristics associated with this beliefs dimension. She gave the BACARQ as well as a comprehensive personality inventory to 75 student volunteers in my classes. The results were interesting. There was a statistically significant correlation of $r = .57$ between the global beliefs scale oriented in the transcendent direction and the personality subscale of Understanding. Understanding is a measure of the degree to which a person has a curious and rational approach to life. We also found a statistically significant negative correlation of $r = -.25$ with Social Recognition, which is a measure of the degree to which a person tries to fit in with others. This surprised us. Those who tend to score in the transcendent direction on the beliefs scale are those who have a more rational approach to life. And they seem to be less concerned about what others think of them than those scoring in the materialist direction so that we have some confidence that these results are not just the product of social desirability (Jewkes & Barušs, 2000).

Understanding is a facet of the personality trait Openness, and there are known positive correlations between Openness and intelligence. Are those with more transcendent beliefs also more intelligent than those with materialist beliefs? Another thesis student checked that by giving 39 students in the psychology participant pool the BACARQ and a timed, restricted intelligence test. Again, the results surprised us. All of the statistically significant correlations were in the direction of a positive correlation between transcendent beliefs and intelligence. In particular, Item Q09 had a correlation of $r = -.48$ with full scale IQ. This means that 23% of the variance in the belief that there is more to reality than the physical universe can be attributed to IQ. In other words, in a small sample of undergraduate psychology students, those who are more intelligent are more likely to score in the transcendent direction on the BACARQ (Lukey & Barušs, 2005).

And what about death? Endorsement of the statement "personal consciousness continues after physical death" is associated with the conservatively transcendent position and disagreement with the materialist position (Barušs, 1990, p. 121). It is consistent with the extraordinarily transcendent position, which also includes endorsement of the statement "reincarnation actually does occur" (Barušs, 1990, p. 124). The absolute rates of endorsement that Moore and I found in the 1986 sample for those two items were 26% and 13%, respectively (Barušs, 1990). In a 1996 sample of 212 participants at an academic consciousness conference, the numbers were 27% and 23%, respectively, for those two questionnaire items (Barušs & Moore, 1998).

In a national poll in the United Kingdom in 1998 with 721 participants, the rates of agreement were 45% and 24% for beliefs in survival and reincarnation, respectively. In 2003, with 1,001 respondents, they were 47% and 23%, respectively (Roe, 2019). For frequencies of more specific beliefs, in a survey conducted in Great Britain in March 2019 with a sample size of 2019 adults, it was found that 28% believed that ADC is possible and 50% believed that NDEs are real (Roe, 2019). For the same sample, 30% thought that they had "communicated or interacted directly . . . with someone who was dead" and 11% claimed that they had had an NDE (Roe, 2019, p. 14).

So, this is the diversity of beliefs that we need to take into account. Clearly, not everyone gets to be right. How are we going to untangle this? Well, the answer, in our Western culture, is to use science to decide. Does that necessarily put us into the materialist camp given that the materialists are the ones who invoke science as their epistemological option? That is the bias in the academy. Those tending toward the extraordinarily transcendent position claim that they have had experiences that fall outside the scope of science. So, is science enough?

One of the things that I have found myself explaining over and over again through the years, not just to students and to members of the wider community but to academics, is the difference between science and materialism. They are not the same. Science is an epistemology consisting of empirical observation and rational thinking. The purpose of science is to know something rather than to just believe things. To that end, a scientist makes observations about the subject matter of interest. They then think about those observations logically. And then they put those thoughts together into a theory that has the best goodness of fit to the observations. In the context of science, materialism is one of a range of theories that can be tested for goodness of fit to the observations (Barušs, 1996).

What frequently happens is that the investigative process of science gets flipped in that materialism is assumed at the beginning as an implicit context within which any investigation is to take place. So, I ask the scientific question: Does consciousness continue after physical death? The next step would be, What would I do to find out? But frequently, that is not what happens. What happens is that there is no second step because the materialist context has already reached an answer: Consciousness is a by-product of the brain, so consciousness without a brain is impossible, so there is no point in looking. Indeed, this can get backed up a step so that there is no point in asking the question in the first place. Within a materialist framework, such a question does not arise. If such a question does not arise, and there is no point in looking, then, for instance, there is no point in giving a scientist a research grant for such a project or access to graduate students to conduct the research (R. G. Jahn, 2001; Barušs & Mossbridge, 2017). When science gets stuck on materialism in this way, then it is sometimes called *scientism* (Barušs, 1996) or *scientistic materialism* (Tart, 2009). And it may be scientism, rather than science, that is associated with the materialist position. Open inquiry could become replaced with belief—belief in materialism.

The reader may ask, What is wrong with any of that? I did not keep track of where this was published, but at one point, one of my critics wrote that "scientism is the true science," or something to that effect. The point is that if materialism is the theory with the best goodness of fit, then why are we getting immersed in all this unnecessary social psychology? We can acknowledge that some smart people can have weird ideas about reality, but that is their problem and does not affect scientific knowledge acquisition, which remains comfortably materialistic.

The short answer to that line of argumentation is that that is not science. Science, by nature, is an open investigation that can include reconsideration of things that we thought we knew. The longer answer is that there are problems with materialism (Koons & Bealer, 2010; Barušs & Mossbridge, 2017; Kastrup, 2014; E. F. Kelly et al., 2015). So, let me give one example of some observations that are difficult to explain using materialist ideology.

AN NDE WITH A TEMPORAL ANCHOR

An *NDE* is an experience that appears to occur when a person is close to death or believes that death is imminent as recounted afterward by that person. In some cases, experiencers describe leaving their bodies at that time and seeing physical events that are occurring in the vicinity of their bodies or at some distance from them (Barušs, 2021). In some cases, the events described by such experiencers match physical events that took place at that time. These are sometimes called *veridical NDEs* (Holden, 2009; Rousseau & Billingham, 2021). In some cases, the veridical perception creates a *temporal anchor* that allows us to match a person's NDE narrative to the sequence of physical events that took place at the time that a person was close to death.

Suppose we make the statement that phenomenal consciousness is caused by neural processes (Halligan & Oakley, 2021). That is a universal statement, which means that to prove that it is true, we need to demonstrate that it is true in all cases. Whenever there is phenomenal consciousness, there must be a neural network of the right sort working the right way to produce it. To show that the statement is false, we need a single counterexample—not some minimal number of cases or some statistical average. Just one. That is just logical.

In the late 1990s or early 2000s, a man was admitted to a hospital for heart surgery. Heart surgeon Lloyd Rudy and his assistant, heart surgeon Roberto Amado-Cattaneo, repaired the heart. But when they tried to remove the patient from the heart–lung machine, they could not do so without losing blood pressure. Eventually, they gave up, pronounced the man dead, and told his wife that the man had died. The lung machine went quiet, the anesthesiologist left, the cleaning staff started cleaning up, and a surgical assistant closed up the body to prepare it for autopsy. The two heart surgeons left the operating room, took off their protective equipment, and then came back into the operating room in short-sleeved shirts and stood at the door discussing whether there could have been anything else that they could have done for the patient (Rivas et al., 2016).

However, no one had turned off the monitoring equipment, including blood pressure monitors and a monitor for an internal ultrasound-probe of the heart. The monitors had been left running and were creating a big pile of paper on the floor. After some 20 to 25 minutes without a heartbeat, just as the surgical assistant had finished closing up the body, the cardiac surgeons noticed that there was some electrical activity. That electrical activity became a heartbeat, and the heartbeat started to generate blood pressure. So, the surgeons called back the surgical staff to resume the surgery. The patient regained consciousness after a few days in the intensive care unit and eventually recovered with no neurological deficit (Rivas et al., 2016).

Over the following 10 days to 2 weeks, when the hospital staff visited with the patient, they were astounded to have him describe that he had been floating around the operating room, ostensibly seeing the two surgeons standing with arms folded in the doorway, seeing the anesthesiologist come running back into the room, and seeing sticky notes stuck to a "TV screen" (Rivas et al., 2016, p. 73). Apparently, the notes had accumulated during the surgery as the nurses wrote down telephone calls that came in for the chief cardiac surgeon on sticky notes that they stuck to a monitor (Rivas et al., 2016).

To my mind, this case has two critical features: the heart monitoring and the veridical perception. First, when the heart stops, within seconds, blood flow to the brain stops, and within 20 seconds, cortical activity in the brain stops (van Lommel, 2013). In this case, the patient could not generate blood pressure, was pronounced dead, a surgical assistant closed up the body pending an autopsy, and output from monitoring equipment piled up on the floor. It is clear from these details that, for 20 to 25 minutes, there was no heart activity and, hence, no brain activity of the sort required for the brain to produce phenomenal consciousness. Second, we have a temporal anchor: the details provided by the patient of events that occurred in the operating room during the time that there was no heart or brain activity. By the patient's account, he perceived these events in the operating room while he was floating around within the time span of those 20 to 25 minutes. It appears that phenomenal consciousness was present while the brain was silent and behavioral consciousness was absent. If that is correct, then we have the single case that we need to falsify the contention that neuronal processing is necessary for phenomenal consciousness.

Is there a way around this interpretation? Possibly. First, we can argue that the documentation is flawed. We have two heart surgeons whose accounts agree on all details, but these are, after all, their memories. Second, the surgeons, including the assistant surgeon closing the surgical wounds, were incompetent and had not noticed the patient's heartbeat during the 20- to 25-minute period. Third, some of the hospital staff may have told the patient details of what had transpired in the operating room, which he then turned into a personal account that he attributed to his own perceptions. Fourth, even though officially dead, the patient might have subliminally noticed what had been going on in the operating room and, afterward, constructed an imaginative account to fit those sensations. Fifth, as a result of his NDE, the patient might have retroactively anomalously perceived what had happened in the operating room.

The first three of these are unlikely given the reputation for integrity of the two cardiac surgeons. For instance, if the patient would have had an opportunity to acquire information through normal means, it is unlikely that the surgeons would have regarded the patient's statements as anomalous. The fourth argument is nonsense—a corpse does not process sensory information—although variations on this argument have been used as explanations for veridical perception with temporal anchors (e.g., Fischer & Mitchell-Yellin, 2016). The strongest argument could be the fifth given that NDEs appear to turn on anomalous abilities. Variations on this argument will haunt us throughout the book in the form of *living agent psi* (LAP), an intermediate position between a materialist interpretation and survival. The reader can decide for themselves whether any of these arguments work or whether these events were truly anomalous.

Let us define *anomalous phenomena* as phenomena that do not fit prevailing ideas about reality. More specifically, in our context, anomalous phenomena are phenomena that do not fit with materialism (Baruš & Mossbridge, 2017; Cardeña et al., 2014). Holly's apparent perception of Greyson's stained tie while she was lying unconscious in another room, a case we considered at the opening of this chapter, and Lloyd Rudy's patient's apparent perception of two surgeons standing in a doorway while he was lying, without a heartbeat, in the same room with the two surgeons are examples of anomalies.

But why should we concern ourselves with something that might or might not have happened years ago in some hospital room? Why should it matter? It matters because anomalous phenomena lead us to the limits of our knowledge and provide an opportunity to learn something that we do not already know. "Empirical anomalies in any scientific sector can be precious indicators of the limits of established wisdom and can open trails to better understanding" (R. G. Jahn, 1989, p. 15). Anomalies are the pathway through which science advances. A patient's knowledge of a stained tie or surgeons standing in a doorway makes no sense if all perception occurs through physical senses in a physical body. So, what explanatory possibilities do such events reveal?

There is good evidence for some types of anomalous phenomena associated with consciousness. These include *remote perception*, the ostensible perception of events occurring outside the range of the physical senses, such as in the examples that we have just seen, and *remote influencing*, the apparent effect of mental influence on physical manifestation without physical mediation. Either of these could be temporally displaced so that, for instance, there could be *precognition*, the apparent anomalous perception of events that occur in the future, or *retrocognition*, which could allow someone to perceive events that had occurred previously.

Much of the book *Transcendent Mind*, which was coauthored by Julia Mossbridge and me (Baruš & Mossbridge, 2017), is spent reviewing the evidence for these phenomena, the arguments against their occurrence, the counterarguments against those arguments, and the reasons why anomalous phenomena have been marginalized within the academy. There have also been other summaries of the evidence for the occurrence of anomalous phenomena (e.g., E. F. Kelly et al., 2007/2010; E. F. Kelly et al., 2015; E. W. Kelly, 2018; Radin, 1997; Cardeña, 2014, 2018). It is remote perception and remote influencing, along with their time-displaced versions, that are the ingredients of LAP in the following chapters.

If the evidence for the occurrence of anomalous phenomena is robust, then why is there still a controversy? Why is this subject matter marginalized? I think there is a clue to this among the characteristics of the extraordinarily transcendent position. Alongside belief in extraordinary ideas, such as extrasensory perception and reincarnation, is agreement with the statement that the participant's "ideas about life have changed dramatically in the past" apparently as a result of having had "experiences which science would have difficulty explaining" (Barušs, 1990, p. 123). It is one thing to read about the robust evidence for anomalous phenomena in the academic literature and quite another to experience anomalous phenomena for oneself. If you are one of the people desperately trying to hold down a woman in a chair who is forcefully rising to the ceiling (Gallagher, 2020), or are an engineer who grasps at a crystal that was just there but has now dematerialized (M. Keen et al., 1999), or are a physician with a stain on his tie that his patient should not know about, then there can be a shift away from materialist toward transcendent beliefs.

GROUPTHINK

I think one of the simplest ways to conceptualize what is happening is to talk about a *boggle threshold*, "the degree to which a person is willing to deviate from normative beliefs" (Barušs & Mossbridge, 2017, p. 24). We find out about something unusual, and the response is that, yeah, clearly, that could not have happened. It is not because the evidence for its occurrence is particularly bad, but just that we already know that those sorts of things cannot happen. Whatever they are. Levitation is impossible. Dematerialization is impossible. Remote perception is impossible. It is beyond our boggle threshold. Until it happens to us. And now we are stuck not being able to tell anyone about it because we know that it will be beyond their boggle thresholds. And we are afraid that they will think that we are mentally ill. Unless the person happens to be a professor who is already talking about these sorts of things. "I've never told anyone about this before because I didn't want them to think that I was crazy, but. . . ." And then we get a chance to tell someone what happened.

Raymond Moody was a philosopher before he became a physician and has used the allegory of the cave from Plato's *The Republic* (Plato, ca. 360 B.C.E./ 1968) as a way of characterizing the impact that NDEs can have on a person (Moody, 1988), and I think that it fits well into our discussion here. Socrates asks Glaucon to imagine a situation in which men have been chained to the floor of an underground cave since birth in such a way that they can only see the back of the cave. Behind the men is a fire. And between the men and the fire is a walkway along which men are walking, sometimes talking, sometimes carrying objects above the level of the wall. The chained men can see none of what is behind them, just the shadows of those objects on the wall in front of them. And the cave has an echo, so the men learn to associate the talking with the shadows of the objects on the wall. Suppose, says Socrates, that one of these men were to be loosed and dragged out of the cave into the light. At first, he would be unable to see anything. However, in time, he would adjust and come to appreciate the real world. And he would pity the men who were left in the cave. And if he were to return to them, his eyes would not immediately adjust to the darkness so that he could not win competitions with the other men about which shadows were doing what, nor would he care to do so. And he would be mocked—that he had left them and come back without his eyes—and that it was better not to even think about leaving and that if anyone tried to loose anyone else, they would "catch the offender, and they would put him to death" (Plato, ca. 360 B.C.E./1968, p. 273).

There are a couple of features of this story that I want to consider. Perhaps the more salient feature is the unity of thinking of the prisoners. *Groupthink* is "a quick and easy way to refer to the mode of thinking that persons engage in when *concurrence-seeking* becomes so dominant in a cohesive ingroup that it tends to override realistic appraisal of alternative courses of action" (Janis, 1971, p. 43). In other words, we have a tendency to go along with whatever it is that we are supposed to think. From the epigraph, for Shaman Durek (2019), such behavior is caused by green gas emanating from the underworld. Whatever we might think of that explanation, more prosaically, what are the dynamics of such unitary thinking?

First, the prisoners have known nothing else since birth. In psychology, we recognize dependence on one's own experience as an example of the *availability heuristic*, whereby judgments are made on the basis of one's access to the relevant data (Colman, 2015). If we have not had an anomalous stained tie experience, then that type of event could well be beyond our boggle thresholds.

Second, there can be considerable pressure to conform to normative ideas, whether they be true or false. Materialism is a normative idea well entrenched in the academy and with sanctions against those who fail to conform. Those sanctions can include exclusion from the academy, lack of promotion, no access to graduate students, denial of research grants, and rejection of papers by mainstream journals. Students can be afraid of thwarting their careers before they have even begun if they choose research projects with anomalous topics. And students have reported reprisals for questioning materialism (Baruss & Mossbridge, 2017). In Plato's allegory of the cave, the penalty for trying to escape the cave is death.

Third, there is an invisible element to this compliance that makes it difficult to apperceive. For Martin Heidegger, we find ourselves in an inauthentic state of being, which has the following three characteristics. *Idle talk* is the unexamined appropriation of information that is circulating within society and passing it on to other people through speech and writing. There is no effort to come to grips with the material in such a way as to open it up to for analysis. Rather, the movement is in the opposite direction so that saying something closes off any further examination. For instance, labeling anomalous phenomena as "pseudoscience" can evoke a feeling of shame on the part of anyone interested in such subject matter and close off further exploration. The net result is that "a person becomes 'uprooted' and floats along unattached in a condition of increasing 'groundlessness' that remains hidden" from them by the "obviousness and self-assurance of the average ways in which things have been interpreted" (Barušs, 1996, p. 8, and Heidegger, 1926/1962, p. 214, respectively). We are not even aware of the situation in which we find ourselves.

Curiosity, the second aspect of an inauthentic state of being as defined by Heidegger, is not the antidote to idle talk but an element of inauthenticity that fuels the uprootedness. *Curiosity* refers to continuous distraction by whatever it is that one is supposed to be interested in as determined by idle talk without actually stopping long enough to examine anything carefully so as to understand it.

The third element is *ambiguity*. When we encounter something, we do not know whether it is the result of an actual investigation or something that is just being carried along by idle talk and curiosity (Barušs, 1996; Heidegger, 1926/1962). Heidegger wrote his monograph in the 1920s, yet the confusion created by discordant media, social media, scientists, and pundits of various sorts is a graphical illustration of inauthenticity. In particular, the reader does not know whether what I am saying is just made-up stuff or the result of an authentic effort to understand death. And they cannot know without stopping any ongoing uprootedness and trying to come to grips with the subject matter themself.

There is a price to pay for inauthenticity. For instance, we are arguably at the beginning of the Sixth Mass Extinction created by global warming and the destruction of the biosphere (Barnosky, 2014; Ward, 2009; Barušs, 2021). We have gotten carried away with our technologized lifestyle and forgotten that we are biological creatures dependent on the natural environment for our existence. Of course, curiosity could bring that to our attention but not long enough to do anything meaningful about it. We regard research about anomalous phenomena as pseudoscience, not because we have engaged in actual research with anomalies or sought out personal experiences to try to understand it but because "scientists," ironically, tell us that this is pseudoscience. And we miss the benefits of expanded knowledge about the nonlocal properties of consciousness. As we can see, science has an inauthentic mode, namely, scientism, based on materialism as an overbelief. Authentic science consists of open exploration based on empirical observation and rationalization (Baruss, 1996). The subtitle of this book—*A Scientific Approach*—refers to authentic science.

There is one domain of human activity, because of its immediate dramatic consequences, in which groupthink is sometimes taken seriously, namely, military invasion. Indeed, the term "groupthink" was appropriated by psychologist Irving Janis as a description of the psychological processes that he had identified which had led the United States into the ill-conceived Bay of Pigs invasion (Janis, 1971).

Similarly, the Israeli government was unprepared for the Yom Kippur War in October 1973. Despite intelligence to the contrary, the Israeli leadership was so enamored with their "Concept" that Egypt would not strike (Kaplan, 2017, p. 5) that they ignored the intelligence reports. The Egyptians attacked on Yom Kippur, and, along with Syrian troops, initially overwhelmed the Israeli military forces. Almost 3,000 Israeli soldiers were killed. Afterward, a commission was struck to investigate how there could have been such an abysmal intelligence failure. The commission found that

> in the days before the war began, the evidence was overwhelming, but because of blind adherence to the Concept, it was not correctly assessed. . . . [T]wo subordinate officers dared to speak up. One was sidelined, and the other faced disciplinary action for telling the truth. (Kaplan, 2017, p. 31)

The commission had a list of recommendations. One of them was the creation of the Tenth Man, whose purpose was "to challenge conventional and received wisdom" (Kaplan, 2017, p. 33). The Tenth Man is "free to obtain any intelligence data it needs and to criticize existing views. Its reports cannot be ignored; they must be considered. Tenth Man reports go directly to the director of military intelligence" (Kaplan, 2017, p. 33). Janis's recommendations also included the policy that "at least one member should play devils' advocate" (Janis, 1971, p. 76). I sometimes feel as though I were the Tenth Man.

To put this in more familiar terms, the antidote to groupthink is science—basing judgments on empirical evidence and reason—or critical thinking more generally. The problem, as Heidegger (1926/1962) pointed out, is that we find ourselves lost in inauthenticity. That that is our initial state. We are unaware of the distortions in our own reasoning processes. In psychology, we call that *bias blindness* (Pronin & Schmidt, 2013). So, we need to undergo a process of self-transformation to recognize our biases and learn to neutralize them so as to approach the subject matter of any investigation in a neutral manner. This becomes particularly relevant when we include first-person data in our research and treat an experimenter as an instrument of observation (Baruš & Mossbridge, 2017). This is also one of the characteristics of the extraordinarily transcendent position. Yet, in my experience, there is rarely any self-development training in graduate school. Rather, there is an opposite pressure to conform to the normative expectations of one's discipline. In psychology, such conformity includes adherence to materialism and rejection of anything that is inconsistent with materialist ideology.

An obvious problem with critical thinking and science is that we cannot know everything. There are limits to our cognitive abilities that restrict the number of academic papers that we can realistically read (Thorngate, 1990). So, when we stop idle talk and investigate the subject matter of some conversation, where does that end? It seems to me that the meta-level of evaluating how one can ground oneself is an aspect of authenticity. In other words, we need to make judgments about the degree to which we can commit ourselves in the evaluation of any information that we receive. And, at some point, we are going to need to depend on the expertise of others. At that point, the probity of those experts becomes an inescapable issue. And that probity will depend, in part, on any relevant self-transformation in which those experts have engaged (Baruš, 1996; Baruš & Mossbridge, 2017).

We have considered the groupthink aspect of Plato's cave allegory. Now, I want to turn to a second feature of that allegory. Self-transformation is an element of the liberated prisoner's experience. In the psychology of religion, we call that a *conversion experience* or a *spiritual transformation*. One of the ways of classifying conversion experiences is to note the time course of the conversion as "sudden" or "gradual" (Hood et al., 2018). An NDE can produce a sudden conversion, although its full impact can take decades to manifest (Atwater, 2011, 1999/2013). Other anomalous phenomena can have a cumulative effect over time, such as *precognitive dreaming*, whereby a dreamer initially wonders about the striking coincidences between a dream and later lived experience and, decades later, after repeated such experiences, realizes that some of their dreams really are precognitive and uses the information in them to anticipate future events (Baruš, 2013). So, psychological transformation, along some dimensions, plays a key role not just for investigators, but experiencers as well, throughout this book.

EPISTEMOLOGY

Let us return to the central question raised at the beginning of this chapter. How would we know whether survival occurs and, if it does, what it would be like? There is an obvious problem: We are not dead. Because we are not dead, we do not have direct empirical access to the state of being dead for the purposes of a scientific investigation. So, anything that happens, here, among the living, could be explained, at least in principle, by the sorts of things that happen among the living.

I think that it is worth considering the following "room allegory" as an adjunct to the cave allegory. Suppose that, since birth, we have lived in a room and that everything that we have ever needed is in that room. The room has a television set. And we watch hockey games on the television set. Of course, because all we know is the room, we assume that the hockey games are produced by the television set. We can prove this to ourselves by playing a disc in a disc player to show that the hockey game is dependent on the television set. But now, I start to wonder whether there might actually be a hockey game going on in some other world. I do not really know what "other world" means because all that exists is the room, but I am no longer convinced, perhaps, that the television set can have that many games in it that it spontaneously produces. But when I mention this to you, you argue that it is obvious that the game is in the television set because you can show me which parts of the television set's electronics are activated when a goal is scored or a save made. And there are different patterns of activation for different players. And if you unplug the television set from the wall, then the games disappear entirely, just to prove your point. Even if the games show up with the television set unplugged from the wall, you can argue that there is some way in which the electronics in the television set could produce the hockey game. It does not matter what argument I propose because all we have access to is the room; we can think of some imaginative way to account for the hockey games even if they do not make sense. So, while we are alive, definitive proof of survival will necessarily escape us.

What the allegory of the room highlights is that any evidence for survival is going to be inferential. One way to put it is to say that it is going to depend on "abductive reasoning and rational judgment about the problems in question, the evidence related to them, and the various interdisciplinary models relevant to explaining them" (Shushan, 2018, p. 245). We are going to need to look at theories of the phenomena that occur and choose the one that has the best goodness of fit to the data. "When our models are contradicted by observation (*falsified*), we discover that they do not accurately map reality, and so must be modified or scrapped altogether as we try to devise more accurate models" (Augustine, 2015a, p. 34). So, now we are talking about probability. More specifically, in our discussion about death, we are going to need to make judgments about whether the balance of probability lies with physicalist, LAP, or survivalist explanations. Given the range of phenomena covered in this book, such as deathbed coincidences, ADC, ITC, mediumship, NDEs, past-life experiences, and so on, it is clear that we are quickly going to run out of conventional physicalist explanations, such as the usual suspects, and are going to need to stretch ourselves into anomalous territory. We are going to find ourselves considering variations of the retrocognition option for Lloyd Rudy's patient's case. Explanations of that type used to be called the *super-psi hypothesis* (Braude, 2003) but are now more commonly known as living agent psi (Sudduth, 2016), the expression that we have already been using.

Of course, the allegories of the cave and the room are themselves models, and we can deny that the evidence supports such models—that there are only shadows on the back of the cave; there is only a single room; reality is entirely physical in nature. So, the following is my version of the general thrust of the materialist arguments against survival.

We can ask ourselves, If phenomenal consciousness arises from neural activity in the brain, then where is that neural activity? Which ones are the neural correlates of consciousness? So, specifically, under what neurological conditions does a perception become part of a subjective experiential stream? More specifically still, can we find the neurological difference between a visual percept of which there is no explicit awareness versus one for which there is explicit awareness? Yes. There has been research that sheds light on those questions. A visual stimulus of which we become aware is associated with neural activity of greater intensity than a visual stimulus of which we do not become aware. "Each phenomenal content (be it visual, auditory, tactile, gustatory, and somatosensory) needs to be analyzed in increasingly sophisticated steps so as to emerge consciously as an object of thought and perception" (Nani et al., 2019, p. 6; see also Mashour & Hudetz, 2018). What is important to note here is that phenomenal consciousness arises as a culmination of intense functioning of the appropriate neural networks.

Now, a materialist argument for the extinguishment of consciousness at death is based on this kind of information, but taking it in reverse. As the brain loses its higher order functioning and defaults to lower levels, we lose phenomenal consciousness along with any linguistic ability to articulate anything that could be going on and the capacity to store any experiences into long-term memory. The progressive deterioration of the brain leads inevitably to the permanent loss of consciousness with death (Weisman, 2015). These sorts of arguments are regarded as

> the strongest case that can be made for personal extinction—empirical evidence of a very tight correlation between mental states and the corruptible brain states that underlie them. . . . This constitutes the strongest available evidence relevant to whether or not we survive death. (Martin & Augustine, 2015, p. xxix)

Exactly how tight are the tight correlations? How strong is the strongest argument?

As already noted, when a person experiences cardiac arrest, within 20 seconds, any meaningful brain activity ceases. From the previous discussion, it should be clear that any subsequent sporadic neural activity cannot rise to the level required for phenomenal consciousness (Chawla et al., 2017; Lake, 2017; Norton et al., 2017; van Rijn et al., 2011; Kramvis et al., 2018; Pana et al., 2016; Parnia et al., 2022). When a person recovers from a period of brain inactivity, there should not be any stories about what happened during that time. And, more to the point, there should not be any stories with temporal anchors into the period of time when the brain was compromised. And yet, as we have seen, such examples exist. The "very tight correlation" between phenomenal consciousness and underlying neural processes has apparently frayed. The strongest argument is not that strong. The reader can decide for themselves what to make of these arguments, one way or the other.

There has been considerable impatience by many of us who study consciousness with such inadequate materialist arguments. For instance,

> the critical rebuttal . . . is not particularly sound, containing many of the same stale arguments that staunchly close-minded skeptics have continuously echoed throughout the years. (Williams, 2021b, p. 39)

There is increasing acknowledgment despite the dominance of materialism in the academy that materialism has become inadequate and that some sort of postmaterialist interpretation of reality is necessary (Baruss, 2007b; Baruss & Mossbridge, 2017; Hoffman, 2019; Hoffman & Prakash, 2014; E. W. Kelly, 2018; Presti, 2018; Klein, 2021; Fields et al., 2018). And such progressive ideas are called for precisely because of the implications of the occurrence of the sorts of anomalous experiences that we have considered.

We need a new story. In that new story, "the chief character (and seeming upstart) is mind-and-consciousness; and this, in opposition to the old story, whose chief agent and narrative star is mindless, measurable matter" (Grosso, 2021, p. 15). This represents a shift from the materialist position regarding beliefs about consciousness and reality to the extraordinarily transcendent position. Another way to think of this is to think of physical manifestation as being a crust that is simply too thin to account for the richness of material to be found in alterations of consciousness. We need an interpretation with more explanatory scope. Actually, the new story is just new to us. It was already prevalent in the 19th century (Noakes, 2019), so we are really just picking up a thread that we laid down for a while (E. F. Kelly et al., 2007/2010; Combs, 2009). And so, in addition to drawing on the old story wherever it makes sense to do so, let us see if we can develop a new story as we go through this material—a postmaterialist story that might be more useful.

Okay. We have a framework for our investigation. Let us now proceed to the first substantive issue raised by death, namely, dying itself.

2 DEATHBED PHENOMENA

There is something about being in the presence of death—not necessarily our own—that can open a portal to a higher world, one that those who are dying can open to those who will go on living.

—Raymond Moody (2010, p. 58)

Let us start with a striking example of the sort of subject matter with which we engage in this chapter. Ian Stevenson, at one time a professor of psychiatry at the University of Virginia, has related the contents of a letter that he received from a woman who had been looking after her dying stepgrandfather in his home. His condition had deteriorated, and he was to be taken later by ambulance to the hospital. As she was waiting, she heard him calling out for help. Then: "Hazel. Hazel," the name of her deceased grandmother, his wife. She went into his room, where she tried to raise him to a sitting position to give him some water but could not lift him. He was still calling out to "Hazel" when she left the room to telephone her mother for help (Theosophical Classics, 2018, minute 39).

---

https://doi.org/10.1037/0000361-002
Death as an Altered State of Consciousness: A Scientific Approach, by I. Baruss
Copyright © 2023 by the American Psychological Association. All rights reserved.

When the step-granddaughter reentered the room, she saw that it was filled with light. Her step-grandfather was sitting with his arms outstretched apparently so as to embrace someone. And then the man's step-granddaughter saw the upper body of her grandmother, Hazel, lit by the brilliant light in the room. The step-granddaughter was certain that the apparition was that of Hazel. What struck her most was the extraordinary sense of peace that she experienced and the smiles on the faces of her step-grandfather and the vision of his wife. Then the man fell back and the specter vanished (Theosophical Classics, 2018, minute 39).

I want to say a bit about fear of death and the physical and psychosocial processes that occur as a person approaches death but then focus for most of the chapter on some of the unique deathbed phenomena associated with dying and the time of death. There appear to be premonitory symptoms of death "for a few days or even weeks before the person finally dies" (Fenwick & Fenwick, 2013, p. 152), during which experiences occur that appear to provide insights into life and death both for the dying and their caregivers (Koedam, 2015), with positive spiritual effects (Claxton-Oldfield et al., 2020) and better outcomes for bereavement (Grant et al., 2020). Such experiences include the timing of death, apparent deathbed communications, dreams, terminal lucidity, shared death experiences, and deathbed coincidences. However, we also consider distressing deathbed phenomena and then discuss explanations for these phenomena. And we get to meet Oscar the cat. Several themes will emerge: the likelihood that some of these phenomena are anomalous, the idea that death facilitates a state of consciousness in which the dying person is in this world and some other world at the same time, and the beneficial impact that these events have on those who experience them as well as those who witness them. What I say here is not meant to be a guide for caregivers. Indeed, I am leaving out explicit guidelines for care. Rather, what I am doing is trying to characterize the dying process so as to allow for a better understanding of the nature of death.

There are terminological and classification inconsistencies when considering phenomena associated with death and the period of time leading up to death, including the naming of the periods of time before death. In each case, I have chosen the most reasonable nomenclature and have alerted the reader if there is alternative language that I think they should know. *Deathbed phenomena* is an expression sometimes used to refer to phenomena "that announce that death is near" (Koedam, 2015, p. xv; see also dos Santos et al., 2017; Fenwick et al., 2010). I use it more generally to refer to events that occur around the time of death for a person who has been progressively approaching death.

ANTICIPATING DEATH

Death is the birthright of everyone who is born. A human being is capable of cognitively anticipating the eventuality of one's own demise. According to *terror management theory*, such realization is accompanied by existential terror, which humans seek to minimize through the adoption of beliefs about reality and corresponding activities whose purpose is to give meaning to life. Such beliefs and activities can include, for instance, beliefs in life after death or reincarnation, and the production of great deeds or progeny. Elements of our civilization amenable to explanation by such a theory continue to grow (Routledge & Vess, 2019). In other words, we are going to die, we know we are going to die, we are afraid of death, and we nonconsciously shape our lives so as to manage the terror associated with death.

I want to distinguish between cognitively anticipating death and confronting the immediacy of death, such as during a terminal illness. The lived inevitability of death forces a confrontation with questions about existence and nonexistence, and can lead to a reexamination of one's spirituality. The possibly resultant "existential distress" has been "recognized as one of the main sources of suffering in patients with advanced illness" (Strada, 2018, p. 145, italics removed). Here, I am simply using the word "existential" to refer to issues concerning existence. The meanings of the word "spiritual" overlap those of "existential" (Lo et al., 2017) but can refer broadly to the ways that people create meaning in their lives (Strada, 2018). However we look at it, there is anxiety associated with death.

Just how afraid of death are we? In one study, blogs kept by 25 patients who were terminally ill from cancer and amyotrophic lateral sclerosis were compared with simulated blogs written by 45 nonpatients who were asked to "imagine that they had been diagnosed with terminal cancer and had created a blog in which they wrote about their experience with this illness" (Goranson et al., 2017, p. 990). A comparison of positive affect words and negative affect words showed that patients used significantly fewer negative affect words than nonpatients. Furthermore, the ratio of positive to negative affect words for patients was consistent with population norms, but not for nonpatients, suggesting that imagining dying as different from everyday living is inconsistent with the actual experience of dying. Furthermore, positive affect words, but not negative affect words, increased as the patients approached death. This study was followed by a second study, using death row inmates as participants, with similar results (Goranson et al., 2017, p. 990). The results of these studies suggest that imagined anticipation of death could be more stressful than the actuality of impending death. But there is another attenuating factor.

As we shall see as we discuss the various anomalous phenomena in this chapter and in this book, those who have experienced such phenomena tend to have an attenuated fear of death. This is perhaps most evident in the case of near-death experiences (NDEs), which are sometimes regarded as "previews of death" by those who have had them (Barušs, 2020, p. 198; Fenwick & Fenwick, 1995). Indeed, sometimes, those who have had an NDE have said that "their fear was completely erased" (Greyson, 2021a, p. 218). And, as a consequence, the disappearance of the fear of death can sometimes also remove the fear of living one's life (Greyson, 2021a). We recall from one survey carried out in Great Britain that 11% of the respondents claimed to have experienced an NDE, so there could be a substantial number of people who do not fear death. With regard to the material in this chapter, the observation has been made that caregivers sometimes undergo a process of self-transformation as a result of being present for people who are dying. Some "gain deep inner knowledge" (Koedam, 2015, p. 113). And "sometimes they lose their fear of death altogether" (Koedam, 2015, pp. 113–114). There are experiences that mitigate the fear of death. Thus, whereas terror management theory could be applicable to large segments of the population, it ceases to be relevant in those cases in which the fear of death has disappeared.

APPROACHING DEATH

The expression *approaching death* has several meanings (Fenwick & Fenwick, 2013; Ohnsorge et al., 2019). Here, I am just using it in a naive sense to refer generally to the approach of death. And what does that approach look like for someone who is dying from a protracted illness?

First, there is the recognition that a person is dying, creating a split between the "dying world" and the "outside world," necessitating the maintenance of "bridging worlds" to connect a dying person to the community around them (Law, 2009, p. 2630). Within the dying world, there is both a visible and an invisible process of dying. The visible process itself can be divided into three segments: "recognizing dying, peripheral shutdown, and imminent death" (Hockley, 2015, p. 166). And those segments can have different trajectories depending on a dying person's illnesses, which can themselves be interrupted by additional medical complications (Strada, 2018).

Typical physical changes that occur during the *recognizing dying* stage, as one enters the dying world, are consistent with an overall loss of energy so that physical activities become progressively curtailed, a person spends increasing time sleeping, and they eventually become bedbound. Eating and drinking decrease. Indeed, in some cases, such as illness from cancer, the body will consume "its own muscle tissue and fat" rather than use nutrients from food for building up the body (Strada, 2018, p. 211). The net result is that a person loses weight and wastes away. Psychologically, a person becomes less engaged with the outside world, including family members, and may appear to be distracted. In some cases, a person might initiate a review of their life and seek to resolve previous problematic situations. In some cases, there can be emotional numbness or sadness that is not experienced as being distressful. Cognitively, there can be decreased ability to concentrate as well as confusion and delirium. This stage can last for several weeks or months (Strada, 2018). With the onset of this constellation of symptoms, it can become clear to caregivers, as well as to the person themselves, that the person is dying (Hockley, 2015).

Peripheral shutdown occurs within days of dying. Blood circulation decreases. Breathing, known as *Cheyne-Stokes respiration* (Hockley, 2015, p. 167), becomes irregular with gaps during which there is no breathing. And a *death rattle* can be heard as air passes through the airways from which the body is no longer capable of clearing secretions (Hockley, 2015; Koedam, 2015). Pain could be present. "Dying is, in itself, not painful; however, dying from a painful disease is, and it should be treated accordingly" (Hockley, 2015, p. 167). So, even though "most people prefer to die at home" (Callanan & Kelley, 1992/1997, p. 23) and the idea is that caregivers engage as human beings with the dying (Hockley, 2015), the process of dying frequently occurs within a medicalized context (Koedam, 2015). Hearing appears to be the last sense to turn off (Hockley, 2015; Diamond, 2019). *Imminent death* occurs within hours of dying. Breathing becomes shallow, and the pulse becomes "thin and thready" (Hockley, 2015, p. 167). And then the heart and breathing stop.

So, that is a sketch of the visible process of dying, the third-person perspective. What about the invisible process, the first-person perspective? In an electroencephalographic study of unresponsive hospice patients, activation of the default mode network was similar to that of activation in responsive comparison groups, suggesting that mind-wandering could continue to occur in the absence of behavioral consciousness (Blundon et al., 2022). But could there be other invisible activities as well? We have been discussing a nonlinear process of entropy, of the disintegration of the coordinated physical and psychological functioning of a human being. But is there also a reverse process, which we could call "negentropic," that breaks through the relentless downward slide to hint at the occurrence of something else, which we do not yet understand?

THE INVISIBLE PROCESS

From the previous description of the visible process of dying, it would seem that death is an inevitable consequence of physiological processes over which the dying have no control. However, "some people can linger at the brink of death for many days or weeks" (Hockley, 2015, p. 169). Others die before their physicians expect them to die (Hockley, 2015). It is possible that those who are dying can "control the time and circumstances of death" (Callanan & Kelley, 1992/1997, p. 15) until their needs are met (Koedam, 2015; Fenwick & Fenwick, 2013). In some cases, this just has to do with timing death so as to die deliberately with relatives present—or relatives absent.

Debra Diamond is a *death doula*, a person who sits with those who are dying. She has related the example of Mr. Buzz, with whom she was sitting, who was apparently unresponsive and close to death. A nurse had come in and explained that the man's son usually came every day at 4:00 p.m. after work, but on that day, he would be coming at 3:30 p.m. "That's in half an hour" (Diamond, 2019, p. 64), the nurse had said to the dying man. As they awaited the arrival of the son, Mr. Buzz stopped breathing. Then started breathing again. Stopped again. Whenever a person stopped breathing, Diamond would count, so she counted now. She got to 39, when the man gasped and then did not "utter another sound" (Diamond, 2019, p. 66). The time was 3:20 p.m., 10 minutes before his son's arrival. The room got colder. Diamond has said that people who are dying "seem to sense" the time of arrival of relatives "and make decisions around it, suggesting there is much more to the mind–body connection than we know" (Diamond, 2019, p. 67). We return for another layer of this case in a bit.

That may not have been a particularly convincing example. Here is another one. An elderly couple had been admitted to a hospital in England following an automobile accident. "The man had been badly injured, but the woman suffered mainly from shock and bruising" (Fenwick & Fenwick, 2013, p. 224). A nurse was told that the man had succumbed to his injuries but that his wife was not to be told yet that he had died. When the nurse went to the wife's bedside, the wife "excitedly" told the nurse "that her husband had just been to see her and told her he would come back at 4 a.m. and they would go home together" (Fenwick & Fenwick, 2013, p. 224, italics removed). Around 3:30 a.m., her blood pressure started to fall. A doctor was called but could not save her. "She was smiling and watching for someone before she passed quickly into spirit . . . at 4 a.m." (Fenwick & Fenwick, 2013, p. 224, italics removed).

Here is another one. Tyrone was approaching 6 years of age when he was readmitted to a hospital in the United States. He had been infected with HIV/AIDS since birth and had outlived his life expectancy by about 3 years. There was optimism among the staff and his foster parents that he would beat the illness yet once again and get to go home. One day, he awoke at 5:00 a.m. and said that "he was going home around 8:00 a.m." (Doka, 2020, p. 46). He told his hospital caregivers that they "needed to pack his stuff and ready his medicines" (Doka, 2020, p. 46). The hospital staff gently tried to tell him that he was not yet ready to be released. He insisted, saying that he was "not going to his foster home but home to Jesus. . . . He died at 8:02 a.m." (Doka, 2020, p. 46).

Another example of timing: In this case, the timing is not with the living but apparently with the deceased. Mrs. Mac, whose husband had died 15 years previously, was in a nursing home. She was receiving a small amount of morphine. One day, she mentioned to a nurse that "she was seeing a whole lot of people in her room" (Hockley, 2015, p. 168). Could the hallucinations be the result of the morphine? The nurse asked whether her husband was one of the people in the room. Mrs. Mac "thought for a while, looking up to where the wall meets the ceiling, and said, 'No, he's not there, and I am not going until he comes!'" (Hockley, 2015, p. 168). Five days later, Mrs. Mac said that her husband was present, and she died that afternoon (Hockley, 2015, p. 169).

Yet one more example of timing: Oscar is a cat adopted as a kitten by the staff at Steere House Nursing and Rehabilitation Center in Providence, Rhode Island. He appears to have the ability to anticipate a resident's death. He ignores residents who are not dying, no matter how deteriorated they are, but instead jumps up on the bed and snuggles with those who do die several hours after his arrival. In this way, he has *"presided over the deaths of more than 25 residents on the third floor of Steere House"* (Dosa, 2007, p. 329, italics in the original). Oscar's behavior is so predictable that the nursing home staff send for a resident's relatives when he acts in this manner (Dosa, 2007).

Of course, it is difficult to know what to make of such synchronicity. Even if the mechanism for Oscar's knowledge of death could be determined, the question remains of why he would be attracted to someone who dies (Fenwick & Fenwick, 2013).

We will consider the different aspects of these examples in more detail as we go along. What comes through from reading the accounts of some caregivers, including physicians, nurses, and volunteers, such as Diamond, is that they think that those who are dying are in two worlds simultaneously. They are part of our world, the "outside" world, but they have also opened to another world to which they are journeying. "The dying person senses that he or she has one foot in the world we know and one foot in another"

(Hockley, 2015, p. 169; Koedam, 2015; Callanan & Kelley, 1992/1997). It could be that both time streams, that of the ordinary world as well as that of the inner world, need to reach the point at which a person can leave (Diamond, 2019), with the implication that the physical condition of a person cannot force one's death until the inner process has been resolved.

There has been considerable discussion about the need for sensitivity to the lived experience of people who are dying. Clearly, as a person's functioning deteriorates, communication with caregivers and family can be impaired. "The attempts of dying people to describe what they are experiencing may be missed, misunderstood, or ignored because the communication is obscure, unexpected, or expressed in symbolic language" (Callanan & Kelley, 1992/1997, p. 13). There are two categories of messages: "attempts to describe what someone is experiencing while dying, and requests for something that a person needs for a peaceful death" (Callanan & Kelley, 1992/1997, p. 14). If caregivers and family members are not listening, or respond with annoyance, or medication, a person who is dying can become bewildered and withdrawn. It is also possible that those who are dying are confused, not because there is organic impairment of their ability to think, but because they are confused by unexpected experiences that they are having. If caregivers and relatives misinterpret the communication of people who are dying, then this just aggravates the confusion (Callanan & Kelley, 1992/1997; Chang et al., 2017).

So, what are the dying trying to tell us? Perhaps the first thing to note is the prevalence of the metaphor of journeying (Koedam, 2015; Diamond, 2019), as we saw in the cases of Tyrone and Mrs. Mac. Those who are dying typically do not come out and say that they will not be here later because they will be dead but, rather, that they are being "collected, are going away, or will be on a journey" (Fenwick & Fenwick, 2013, p. 45). The deathbed phenomena that we are discussing in this chapter appear to prepare a person for this apparent journeying. In other words, the message from the dying is not one of anticipating finality but, rather, of moving into another sphere of activity beyond life as we know it (Fenwick & Fenwick, 2013; Pearson, 2014; Heath, 2017).

Let us consider another journeying example, which includes visions of the deceased. Valerie was nursing her father at home when she heard him talking. Assuming that he needed something from her, she went to his room to inquire. He said that he did not need anything, that he had been talking to her mother. The day that he died, he told her that her mother and brother had "come again" and that he would "go now" (Fenwick & Fenwick, 2013, p. 82, italics removed). She thought that he was talking about falling asleep, but "he lay back on his pillow, still looking at the wall opposite, and just sighed a deep breath and passed away" (Fenwick & Fenwick, 2013, p. 82, italics removed). Valerie assumed that the visions had been the result of the drugs that she had been giving him. However, when she cleaned the room, she found the tablets under the bed. He had not taken them.

So, we see timing that appears to have to do with an invisible process. A person can affect the timing of their death by leaving earlier or later than anticipated. When we listen to those who are dying, they tell us that they are expecting to go on a journey. Those who are dying appear to have opened up to another realm of reality which they foresee entering. We get a glimpse of that reality as these people appear to be in two realms simultaneously. These observations suggest a negentropic process associated with survival.

APPARENT DEATHBED COMMUNICATIONS

I want to focus for a bit on the visions that those who are dying sometimes appear to see, such as in the case presented by Stevenson, Mrs. Mac, and Valerie's father. We need to frame this discussion with some preliminary remarks. The first is that the expression "deathbed visions" is an older term used for these phenomena. The problem with it is that, in addition to sight, these "visions" can include hearing and impressions of being touched or poked. Hence, the terminology "deathbed communications" has been proposed (Shinar & Marks, 2015, p. 251; Lawrence & Repede, 2013, p. 632). However, the word "communications" implies that the objects of the visions are actual beings engaging with the dying person. That is an inference that could be unwarranted. So, to remain neutral, I am using the expression "apparent deathbed communications" for this section.

In keeping with our neutral attitude, in the case presented by Stevenson of the woman tending to her step-grandfather who apparently saw her grandmother, Hazel, we do not know what, if anything, the dying person actually saw or experienced because we have no report from that person. All we have are the observations made by a caregiver. Our assumption is that the dying man saw Hazel, just as his step-granddaughter saw Hazel, but we do not actually know that. This could have been her solitary image shaped to be consistent with his behavior. So, we need to remember that there is a distinction between observations and inferences. That is not to say that the inferences are false, just that their truth-value remains undetermined for onlookers.

There are also methodological inconsistencies. Much of this research has been done by receiving narratives of deathbed phenomena from the public (e.g., Fenwick & Fenwick, 2013; Theosophical Classics, 2018). In other cases, caregivers have been asked to reflect on their prior experiences and to indicate the number of occurrences and characteristics of specific phenomena (e.g., Osis & Haraldsson, 1997; dos Santos et al., 2017). Somewhat more controlled are prospective studies in which caregivers are asked to document these phenomena as they occur (e.g., Lawrence & Repede, 2013). And there are some studies in which reports have been acquired directly from the people who are dying (e.g., C. L. Nosek et al., 2015), although, in general, it becomes less possible to obtain information directly from those who are dying the closer to death that they are. Furthermore, data have been collected from different countries and different settings within those countries, such as hospices and people's homes (e.g., dos Santos et al., 2017). And, perhaps most important, which data are to be collected and regarded as which deathbed phenomena varies from study to study (e.g., dos Santos et al., 2017; Fenwick & Fenwick, 2013). In addition, there are differences between those who witness the reports, so that, for instance, people who are dying appear to be more likely to confide their experiences to nurses rather than other caregivers—and, in some cases, not mention these experiences to their families for fear of upsetting them (Lawrence & Repede, 2013).

Such methodological variances make it difficult to interpret incidence figures. I give some frequencies for some deathbed phenomena toward the end of the chapter. At this point, let us consider a two-part study conducted in the United States. In the first phase, nurses at a hospice agency that provided both inpatient and home care were asked to document the occurrence of deathbed communications in patients' charts. Charts for 60 patients were inspected for the 30 days preceding death to determine the presence of any deathbed communications. Of those 60 patients' charts, "5 (8.3%) were clear descriptions of DBCs [deathbed communications], 5 (8.3%) descriptions of possible DBCs, and 3 (5%) patients who raised their hands up at the time of death" (Lawrence & Repede, 2013, p. 635). Of the five patients with clear descriptions of deathbed communications, it was recorded that three "had a calm and peaceful death" (Lawrence & Repede, 2013, p. 635). The point of noting whether or not a person died a peaceful death has to do with the observation that deathbed communications, and deathbed phenomena more generally, are associated with a reduction of physical suffering (Lawrence & Repede, 2013) and greater psychological well-being (Broadhurst & Harrington, 2016; Masman et al., 2016; Levy et al., 2020).

In the second phase of the study, 75 hospice nurses across the United States responded to a survey. The average number of patients per hospice nurse per month that the nurses said had experienced deathbed communications was 4.8 patients. The average number of patients per nurse who raised "their arms up at the time of death" was 3.3 (Lawrence & Repede, 2013, p. 636). According to 67 (89%) of the nurses, deathbed communications were associated with a calm and peaceful death, with only occasional terminal restlessness or need for additional medication. "None of the nurses said the patients experienced groaning or grimacing if they had a DBC [deathbed communication].... Only 30 (40%) of the nurses said patients not having a DBC had a peaceful and calm death" (Lawrence & Repede, 2013, p. 635). Of the 75 nurses, 84% said that the patients' experience of seeing the deceased "was not distressing or negative" (Lawrence & Repede, 2013, p. 636), and 44% "said the experience was pleasant" (Lawrence & Repede, 2013, p. 636). Fourteen nurses said their patients were unable to communicate the nature of their experiences so that the quality of their experiences remains unknown (Lawrence & Repede, 2013).

The authors of the previous two-phase study have acknowledged problems with it, for example, nurses did not always confine themselves to the 30-day period before someone's death (Lawrence & Repede, 2013). Furthermore, how well can nurses remember whether apparent deathbed communications were associated with a peaceful death? So, these are admittedly wobbly data and not the sort of stereotypical laboratory observations based on physiological metrics that some researchers would ideally like to see. But we cannot wait for an ideal world to manifest. And these data do tell us something. Not frequently, but occasionally, it has come to the attention of caregivers and researchers that people who are dying appear to communicate with deceased beings. In the United States, those deceased beings are usually deceased relatives. And such apparent communication is associated with a more peaceful death.

Some investigators have counted dreams along with apparent deathbed communications that occur during wakefulness. In one study, 59 residents of a hospice in the United States, with a mean age of 75 years, were approached daily and asked to respond to a series of questions about their dreams and visions, if they were capable of doing so. The average number of interviews per person was eight, conducted from 0 to 87 days before death, with a median of 15 days. Eighty-eight percent of the residents reported having had "at least one dream or vision" (C. W. Kerr et al., 2014, p. 298), with 45% of those being dreams; 16%, visions while awake; and 39% reporting the occurrence of both sleeping and waking events. Ninety-nine percent of these events seemed or felt real. Forty-six percent of the dreams "included deceased friends or relatives" (C. W. Kerr et al., 2014, p. 300), and 39% "included a theme of going or preparing to go somewhere" (C. W. Kerr et al., 2014, p. 300). Sixty percent of the dreams and visions were rated as being "comforting or extremely comforting" and 19% as "distressing or extremely distressing" (C. W. Kerr et al., 2014, p. 300). Further analyses revealed that dreams or visions about the deceased or the deceased and living "were more comforting than dreams" just about the living or "other people and experiences" (C. W. Kerr et al., 2014, p. 300). In general, these dreams and visions were personally meaningful experiences for those who had them (C. W. Kerr et al., 2014, p. 300).

The addition of some simple dream analyses supports the information from the waking state experiences. The notion of encountering deceased relatives and friends together with the journeying theme that we considered previously creates a consistent narrative. We can speculate that as a person approaches death, they open up to "another world" into which they are about to enter with the assistance of emotionally meaningful companions. Let us consider that more carefully in a bit. However, at this point, I want to add another important deathbed phenomenon for us to think about.

TERMINAL LUCIDITY

Let me start with an example. Mrs. Adams was a 78-year-old resident of a nursing home who had been severely disabled by a stroke 2 years previously so that she had been unable to speak. Over the course of 2 years, she had not spoken a word her physician or other caregivers could understand and was now deteriorating further. However, in the presence of a caregiver, while her daughter was visiting her, "Mrs. Adams spoke coherently for the first time in two years, saying, 'Remember to take me home.'" She died that evening (Hockley, 2015, p. 170).

Cases of *terminal lucidity* are characterized by the "unexpected return of mental clarity and memory shortly before death" (Nahm & Greyson, 2009, p. 942; see also Lim et al., 2020). It is possible for a person to gradually improve cognitively as physical health declines (Doka, 2020). We are not considering those cases here, just the ones in which there is sudden, unexpected lucidity. The reason why the mental clarity is unexpected is because the brains of the people having these experiences are so compromised by a range of organic pathologies, as evidenced by diagnoses or autopsies, that behavior consistent with mental clarity should not be possible. "Pathologies have included brain abscesses, brain tumors, strokes, various dementias, meningitis, schizophrenia, and possible affective disorders" (Baruš & Mossbridge, 2017, p. 104; see also Nahm et al., 2012). Medical explanations for the phenomenon, such as high fever before death (Nahm & Greyson, 2009; Doka, 2020), are manifestly inadequate. We are back in the same territory as we were in Chapter 1 with the discussion of the sophisticated coordinated functioning of the brain that is necessary for a person to be capable of coherent language and behavior. Thus, the implication with these terminal lucidity cases is that these are anomalous phenomena, that some brain-independent aspect of a person's psyche has the ability to manipulate the body in such a way as to produce these behaviors (Baruš & Mossbridge, 2017).

A worldwide study was carried out over the internet soliciting caregivers of people with dementias to provide information about *paradoxical lucidity*, unexpected lucidity that can include terminal lucidity but need not occur in association with death. This search netted 124 cases with various dementias. Of these cases, 39% had been "unresponsive" and 27% had been "unconscious" for "most of the time" (Batthyány & Greyson, 2021, p. 4) before the occurrence of lucidity. During the lucid episode, 79% were rated as having "clear, coherent, and just about normal verbal communication" (Batthyány & Greyson, 2021, p. 5). The median duration of the episode was between 30 to 60 minutes. The median time of survival after the episode was between 2 and 24 hours. There were two additional observations. Those who were "unresponsive or unconscious prior to the lucid episode tended to have shorter lucid episodes than those patients who had been awake and responsive" and "those whose lucid episodes lasted more than one day tended to live longer after the episode than those whose lucid episode lasted one day or less" (Batthyány & Greyson, 2021, p. 6).

The structure of the data from this study suggests that these lucid episodes occur in close proximity to death, although some of the participants found out about the study through the context of terminal lucidity, which might have increased reports of cases that occurred nearer to death. Nonetheless, this proximity suggests that these phenomena might have something to do with death (Batthyány & Greyson, 2021), such as being made possible, for instance, by a person having entered the process of dying. In addition, the authors noted the parallel with NDEs, which are frequently rated by experiencers as being equally cognitively clear or clearer than waking cognition despite the brain's compromised capabilities. The authors also called for research to determine whether the mechanisms allowing for cognitive clarity during paradoxical lucidity could be harnessed earlier in the course of dementias to reverse them. Again, these are wobbly data, although 17 cases with corroborating material did not differ substantially along critical variables from those without corroborating data (Batthyány & Greyson, 2021).

Terminal lucidity can coincide with apparent deathbed communications, as in the following case. A woman was with her father for the 48 hours leading to his death. Her father claimed to have been able to see people in his room. The nurses told the daughter that these were memories that he was having. Around 3:00 a.m., although the daughter could not see them, her father believed that people had come into his room. She asked him who was present. He named a good friend, an aunt, and her mother, all of whom were already deceased. These people appeared to stay for 3 hours, during which time "he laughed and was very happy" as well as moving an arm "that he had not been able to move for over a year" (Fenwick & Fenwick, 2013, p. 225, italics removed). He waved goodbye and blew kisses to them, his eyes apparently following them out of the door, when they left around 6:00 a.m. They apparently reentered the room and stayed for an additional hour before departing again. The woman's father died at 2:15 p.m. that afternoon. In this case, there is muscle coordination and limb movement present that had apparently been absent for more than a year.

Terminal lucidity opens another window into the possibility of a state of being in which some other aspect of reality merges with physical manifestation in such a way as to superimpose its agenda on physical manifestation. It is not just the timing of death or the apparent presence of discarnate beings, but the apparent activation of cognitive coherence and physical functioning that appear to be impossible given a person's deteriorated physiological condition. But this opening up is not always experienced in a positive way.

DISTRESSING DEATHBED PHENOMENA

In the dream study with hospice residents, 19% experienced distressing events. That is not surprising because dreams can frequently have dysphoric content. In the case of dreams, we can think of such material as arising from the *shadow*, a part of our psyche that we do not wish to be. We can adopt an instrumental approach to try to prevent the occurrence of such experiences, or we can embrace them and seek to transform and integrate them (Barušs, 2020; Naiman, 2014). We could adopt the same rationale to any dysphoric content, including events that occur as one approaches death. But let us look at the specifics of the types of distressing events that occur.

In a historically significant study of apparent deathbed communications observed by caregivers, there were 471 cases of apparitions, 216 of which were reported from the United States and 255 from India. Whereas for the U.S. sample, there were more visions of deceased people, usually relatives, than the India sample, the India sample had more visions of religious figures, such as Yama, the god of death, or "one of his messengers" (Osis & Haraldsson, 1997, p. 66), which was reported 93 times. In addition, in the

India sample, the purpose of the visit "to take patient away, without consent" (Osis & Haraldsson, 1997, p. 234) occurred 53 times, but only once in the U.S. sample. In the India sample, 91 patients had a negative emotional reaction to their experience, whereas that number was only 33 in the United States. For instance, an Indian woman "saw people coming to take her away" (Osis & Haraldsson, 1997, p. 70). She resisted, calling out that she did not want to go, and held her daughter-in-law's hand tightly. Furthermore, it is not difficult to see that negative emotions, such as "depression, fear, and anxiety" (Osis & Haraldsson, 1997, p. 71), would arise when a messenger of death shows up.

Religious ideation can contribute to dysphoric feelings at the end of life. For instance, sometimes people who are dying feel that they have not been good enough and that they will be punished at the time of death. Sometimes hearing about positive deathbed visions can relax people who are struggling. A caregiver has given the example of woman who was frightened because "she was sure she wasn't good enough to go to heaven" (Koedam, 2015, p. 71). The caregiver told the woman the story of her grandmother with dementia who had asked her children to get her coat because Jesus was coming to collect her. This story appeared to help the woman to relax into a peaceful sleep (Koedam, 2015).

Distressing experiences can carry over from worrying to dysphoric apparent deathbed communications. In one case, BT, a 68-year-old man in a hospice unit in a U.S. hospital, had a "vision of the devil, standing at the foot of his hospital bed, rubbing his hands in glee in anticipation of taking BT to hell," followed by a second apparent deathbed communication in which his relatives and deceased ex-wife were "standing in a ring around his bed, with their backs to him" (Shinar & Marks, 2015, p. 252). When he tried to communicate with them, they would not acknowledge him. He told a social worker, "I've done bad things; I know where I'm going," and died 2 days after the second vision (Shinar & Marks, 2015, p. 252).

As noted at the beginning of this chapter, there is a more basic issue here. Given that approaching death forces a person to resolve issues about their existence and nonexistence, it is not surprising that dysphoric states occur. Some people are able to do this successfully, as in the case of those writing blogs about dying, as we saw at the beginning of this chapter. And other people do so less successfully, such as the participants in the India study of deathbed visions.

One idea is that those who are approaching death can go through a process of transformation in such a way as to lose their egoic conceptualization of their being "into a completely new, ego-distant mode of perception, which seemed accompanied by less or no fear/struggle/denial" (Renz et al., 2018, p. 479). This theory was tested in a study of 80 hospice residents in Switzerland who were expected to die within 2 weeks. Residents with dementia or psychosis or who could not answer questions during the admission process were excluded from the study. The residents were observed daily, up to eight times a day, to track their experiences of dysphoric emotions, spirituality, altered spatiotemporality, and altered social connections. Spirituality appeared to be loosely understood as comprising religious events, such as speaking about angels, or mystical events, such as those that occur during NDEs (Renz et al., 2018, p. 479).

In the transformation study, 94% of residents showed fear and pain at some point, 53% "underwent denial" (Renz et al., 2018, p. 481), 31% experienced darkness or ambivalence, and 90% had "spiritual experiences" (Renz et al., 2018, p. 481). Overall, 17.5% of residents "died amid distress," although 57% of those had "had long periods of peace before" death (Renz et al., 2018, p. 483). "*No trajectory* displayed uninterrupted distress" (Renz et al., 2018, p. 481). In 58% of cases, there was a clear association between the occurrence of spiritual experiences and peace; in 29% of cases, the association was partial. A "transformation of perception" occurred in 86% of cases (Renz et al., 2018, p. 482). In other words, the investigators' notion that there is a process of self-transformation as death approaches was supported. Distress occurs with the threat of losing one's self-identity and through the process of releasing one's attachment to oneself. Peace lies on the other side of the transformation. The investigators have speculated that the ability to surrender to death could be the key to negotiating the transition to a new perspective. "The point may be that *open-mindedness of believers* supports dying: letting go and finding a new dimension" (Renz et al., 2018, p. 487).

The transformations associated with dying that were identified in the previous study are reminiscent of the death and rebirth themes that can emerge during intoxication with psychedelic drugs. Indeed, psychedelics, particularly LSD and psilocybin, have been successfully used in palliative care. The idea is that the mystical-like experiences that can occur with these drugs can open a person to an apparently greater reality in such a way as to lose the importance attached to the individual self. With such experiences, a person becomes reconciled to their own death (Barušs, 2020; Richards, 2016). Deathbed phenomena could have an effect similar to that of psychedelic drugs, including the occasional occurrence of dysphoric experiences. So, it would seem that those who are dying can initially experience a range of emotions that can resolve themselves into feelings of peace as a result of transformations that occur, in part, as a result of adaptive responses to anomalous deathbed phenomena.

SHARED DEATH EXPERIENCES

While still a medical student, Raymond Moody was approached by a professor of medicine who shared with him what had happened when her mother had died. The professor said that she had been raised without religion and had not thought about the afterlife. She said that several years previously, she had been visiting her mother, when her mother had gone into cardiac arrest. The professor had tried to resuscitate her mother, but realized, after about 30 minutes of effort, that her mother was dead. At that point, she felt that she left her body and was looking down at it and the body of her mother. And as she tried to orient herself, she became aware that her mother was hovering next to her. She "calmly said good-bye to her mother, who was now smiling and quite happy, a stark contrast to her corpse down below" (Moody, 2010, p. 7). She also saw that there was a "breach in the universe" (Moody, 2010, p. 7) in the corner of the room from which light was pouring. And out of the light emerged deceased friends of her mother's. And, as she watched, "her mother drifted off into the light" (Moody, 2010, p. 7) together with her friends. Then the breach closed, the light was gone, and she "found herself back in her body, standing next to her deceased mother" (Moody, 2010, p. 7). The professor asked Moody what he made of the story. He told her that he had no idea, just that she had had a *"shared death experience"* (Moody, 2010, p. 8).

A *shared death experience* is an experience in which a person who is present with a person who is dying appears to share the dying person's experience of dying. We saw something like this right at the beginning of this chapter, when a dying man's step-granddaughter apparently saw the man's wife lit by a bright light that had showed up in the room. The dying man had not died at that point, but there is the same notion that a person who is present with someone who is dying is somehow drawn into the dying person's experience.

Here is another example. Four children and an in-law were sitting with their mother who was near the end of her life. She had not spoken for several hours, and her breathing had become irregular. Then all five saw a light in the room that surprised and frightened them. At that point, their mother died. They then saw lights in the room that formed into what appeared to be an entranceway. Then they saw their "mother lift up out of her body and go through that entranceway" (Moody, 2010, pp. 13–14, italics removed). They experienced a feeling of joy as this transpired, and one of them "heard beautiful music" (Moody, 2010, p. 14, italics removed). When they told the hospice nurse their story, the nurse told them "that it was not uncommon for the dying process to encompass people nearby" (Moody, 2010, p. 14, italics removed).

One more example, this one with a life review: A woman was holding the hand of her 15-year-old son when he died. She says that she felt a surge or vibration as he died, "the shape of the room changed" into a "field of intense light," and there was a vision of everything that her son had done, with her son "right in the middle of it, beaming a bright smile of joy" (Moody, 2010, p. 93, italics removed). The vision revealed events about which the mother had forgotten as well as events for which she had not been present, such as her son playing with his toys or talking on the telephone. Some of the material was blurred out so that it could not be seen—not, she thought, because they revealed anything bad that had happened but because "this was not the occasion for it to surface" (Moody, 2010, p. 94, italics removed).

Let us turn to the results of a systematic study of shared death experiences. Investigators conducted structured interviews between 2018 and 2020 of people who thought that they had "participated in a dying person's transition to a post-mortem existence" (Shared Crossing Research Initiative, 2021, p. 1480), yielding a total of 164 usable cases from 107 participants. Additional death-related phenomena were reported by 79% of the participants, most commonly visions of the deceased and afterdeath communication. Content analyses revealed four types of participation: "remotely sensing a death, witnessing unusual phenomena attributed to a death, accompanying the dying in a visionary realm, and assisting the dying in transitioning" (Shared Crossing Research Initiative, 2021, p. 1480). The first of these types can also be classified as deathbed coincidences, which we consider separately in a bit, along with some examples. The second type, unusual phenomena accompanying death, in deceasing frequency included

> a vision of the dying [person], . . . appearance of a transcendent light, . . . sensing energy, . . . alterations in time and space, . . . encounters with nonhuman beings, . . . seeing light or material believed to be the spirit leaving the body, . . . presence of previously deceased loved ones, . . . visions of otherworldly or heavenly realms, . . . appearance of tunnels or gateways, . . . life reviews [of the] lives of the dying. (Shared Crossing Research Initiative, 2021, p. 1482)

For the third type, in 15% of the accounts, the participant found themselves accompanying the dying person in a visionary realm consisting of "gardens, castles, otherworldly regions, or a void" (Shared Crossing Research Initiative, 2021, p. 1482). "Otherwise inaccessible or indescribable" knowledge about the nature of reality became available to them in this realm. In 11% of cases, there was a boundary beyond which they were not able to go. The fourth type of interaction involved a participant believing that their assistance was required by the dying person to be able to transition to the postmortem realm. In one example, a woman felt that she had lent her energy to the dying person to propel him upward, allowing him to pass over (Shared Crossing Research Initiative, 2021).

These are inadvertent shared death experiences. But can they be cultivated? Can a person learn how to track what is happening for a person who is dying? Perhaps. There are those who claim to be able to facilitate shared death experiences (Hogan, 2021). But there are also people who already ostensibly have the ability to perceive the deceased, as occurs apparently in some cases of mediumship. Debra Diamond, the death doula, is one such medium, so let us return to the example of Mr. Buzz.

Recall that the nurse had told Mr. Buzz that his son was coming at 3:30 p.m., before leaving him alone in the room with the death doula. Diamond could see his deceased family members in the room. They told her that they were keeping the "connections alive" (Diamond, 2019, p. 65, italics removed). She could see that when Mr. Buzz stopped breathing, he moved away from his body, whereas breathing corresponded to a pause in the outward movement. She saw that his "aura" began to glow intensely and extend upward. He seemed to be slowly getting himself ready to leave and that "most of his consciousness [had] left" (Diamond, 2019, p. 65), yet he continued to breathe softly. Diamond checked her watch: 3:15 p.m. "He must be waiting for his son" (Diamond, 2019, p. 66), she thought. But she could see him moving away from his body. He gasped, and then he was gone. It was 3:20 p.m. Diamond felt that he was called back. "Freshly out of his body, Mr. Buzz's ancestors [were] lining up for him in the afterlife" (Diamond, 2019, p. 66). The temperature in the room dropped. There was a sense of "sacred energy" (Diamond, 2019, p. 66) that had not been present a moment previously. Diamond was deeply affected by what she had seen. Depending on one's boggle threshold, this account is either ridiculous or meaningful or something to be noted for future reference.

With shared death experiences, we have added possible witnesses among the living to the invisible process of dying. It is also notable that shared death experiences have common elements with NDEs, which we consider in detail in Chapter 7. We have seen out-of-body components, the perception of light, feelings of joy, encounters with discarnate beings, life reviews, and even a boundary beyond which an experiencer is unable to go. It is possible that both shared death experiences and NDEs occur at the conjunction of this world and another world, allowing a glimpse into a postmortem domain of reality.

DEATHBED COINCIDENCES

Deathbed coincidences refers to events that coincide with a person's death for which there do not appear to be readily available causal explanations. The behavior of Oscar the cat is an example of a deathbed coincidence. Sometimes the category of shared death experiences is expanded as *perceptions connected to death* to include shared death experiences that occur at a distance from the dying person (Charbonier, 2012; Shared Crossing Research Initiative, 2021). Those could also be regarded as deathbed coincidences (Fenwick & Fenwick, 2013).

Let me start with an example of such an experience. A man in the United Kingdom went home to visit with his father who was seriously ill with lung cancer in a hospital. After visiting with him, the man went home and fell asleep. He woke with pain in his chest and difficulty breathing. Because of the pain, he was unable to turn on the light but thinks that the time was 4:15 a.m. by his clock. The pain was unbearable but then suddenly subsided, and he "was overwhelmed with feelings of great peace and love" (Fenwick & Fenwick, 2013, p. 56, italics removed). He wanted those feelings to continue and did not want to come back to his body. He was awakened at 7:00 a.m. by a knock on the door by his neighbor to tell him that his "father had passed away during the night" (Fenwick & Fenwick, 2013, p. 56, italics removed). There was nothing wrong with his own health. What is noteworthy here is the apparent shift from the experience of pain to that of peace, which commonly occurs in NDEs (Fenwick & Fenwick, 2013).

A somewhat less somatic but equally dramatic deathbed coincidence involves an apparent visit by a person who is dying. Katherine in Canada was seriously ill and could not sleep. Around 4:30 a.m., she had an "amazing spiritual experience" lasting about 2 hours, during which she "felt nothing but joy and healing" (Pearson, 2014, p. 3). She said that she "felt hands on [her] head, and experienced vision after vision of a happy future" (Pearson, 2014, p. 3). The following day she found out that her father had died unexpectedly that night. She did not prevaricate. She said outright that she knew that that had been her father who had come to comfort her (Pearson, 2014).

When it was her turn to die several months later, Katherine herself appeared to be content. She had "whispered conversations" (Pearson, 2014, p. 12) with a person her caregivers could not see. And she would stare at the ceiling with a range of expressions on her face as though she were watching a show. She woke up one morning and said that she did not know how to leave. She pointed at the garden and complained about the flight attendants. "What's the situation?" she asked. "When do I leave?" (Pearson, 2014, p. 14). She died that night. And her mother and godmother, 3,000 miles distant from her, "awoke in their beds" (Pearson, 2014, p. 15). So, here, we see elements that we have seen previously as a person approaches death as well as awakening by others around the time of death. *Sudden awakenings* are a common type of deathbed coincidence (Fenwick & Fenwick, 2013).

Are these coincidences just coincidences? Peter Fenwick and Elizabeth Fenwick have devised a Coincidence Scale consisting of 11 items that can be used to help to make judgments about whether a coincidence is just a coincidence or whether something meaningful is occurring. The items are concerned with the emotional connections between the people involved, just what the experiencer knew about the dying person, the intensity of the events that occurred, and their statistical rarity. A high score is indicative of the occurrence of an actual deathbed coincidence (Fenwick & Fenwick, 2013).

A prototypical deathbed coincidence is that of clocks stopping at the time of a person's death. Here is an example. A man's father died at 3:15 a.m. In the morning, the man went to see his uncle, who had been close to his father. When his uncle opened the door, the uncle said that he already knew, not because anyone had told him, but because all of his clocks had stopped at 3:15 a.m.—the clock on his mantle, his wristwatch, the clock at his bedside, and all of the other clocks in the house (Fenwick & Fenwick, 2013). In a collection of 178 cases of anomalous physical effects, 37 involved clocks stopping or starting at the time of someone's death (Rhine, 1963). It is not just that clocks are affected at the time of one's death, but electronic and mechanical devices, and physical manifestation more generally (Fenwick & Fenwick, 2013; Rhine, 1963), as we see in the following example.

A nurse sat at the end of the bed with the sister of a "special lady" who was dying. "Just as she was about to die, her bedside table rose off the floor" (Koedam, 2015, p. 43). The nurse nudged the sister to draw her attention to it. "It sank back to the floor and it was as though nothing had happened" (Koedam, 2015, p. 43). The room was serene and calm. The nurse did not know what to make of the incident and never spoke about it with the sister again. It is not clear how this is possible, but such is the account given by a participant in a study of hospice caregivers carried out in the Netherlands (Koedam, 2015). We usually think that physical manifestation is separated from the psychological world, but as we look at phenomena associated with death, we see that there are meaningful coincidences suggestive of negentropic processes associated with death.

Another connection that death has with the dying is through animals, as we have seen already with Oscar the cat. Usually, cats and dogs appear to be disturbed when those to whom they are connected die. "Dogs bark or howl, the cats' fur stands on end" (Fenwick & Fenwick, 2013, p. 144). In Chapter 9, we encounter a dog who cannot tell whether he should pay attention to the corpse or discarnate presence of his owner, which have become disconnected from one another. But here is a somewhat different story. In a British study, a woman reported that when she had been a child, her mother had kept a jackdaw, a gray-headed type of crow. She had never had one at her house except for the day that her grandfather had died. That day, a jackdaw showed up, walked through the garden, "into the kitchen . . . past the cat," which ignored it, looked at her mother, squawked, "and then left" (Fenwick & Fenwick, 2013, p. 147, italics removed). There appears to be a coincidence between the time of death of the woman's grandfather and the unusual behavior of the jackdaw. Indeed, birds and butterflies frequently appear as apparent representatives of those who are deceased (Koedam, 2015), as we shall see in the following chapters.

EXPLANATIONS

How are we to explain the phenomena discussed in this chapter? We have already suggested that deathbed phenomena could be induced by drugs that have been given to those who are dying. A second explanation that we have noted is the possible presence of a high fever. Third, we can note that delirium can occur in up to 85% (Strada, 2018) or even 90% (Szarpa et al., 2013) of people in the last weeks or days before death. *Delirium* is a condition in which attention and cognition are impaired, including, for instance, altered perception, that cannot be accounted for by preexisting dementias (Strada, 2018; Breier et al., 2018; Depner et al., 2020).

In a study of 133 health care providers in Brazil, the following are the frequencies of some of the types of deathbed phenomena that caregivers had encountered within the previous 5 years: 88% reported "visions" by the dying person "of dead relatives or religious figures 'taking away' the dying person"; 53% agreed that "patient reports a sense of going back and forth from a different reality during the dying process"; 46% had witnessed "experiencing a radiant light that envelops the dying person"; 41% said yes to "a symbolic appearance of an animal, bird, or insect near or at the time of death"; for 30%, "at the time of death, coincidental events occur, such as clocks stopping"; and, for 60%, "a comatose patient suddenly becomes alert enough to coherently say goodbye to loved ones at the bedside" (dos Santos et al., 2017, p. 430). As for explanations, 15% agreed that deathbed phenomena "have little significance beyond a chemical change in the brain"; 18%, that they are "hallucinations induced by medications or fever"; and 9%, that they are "just manifestations of the imagination" (dos Santos et al., 2017, p. 431). On the other hand, 69% of health care professionals agreed that deathbed phenomena "differ from drug- or fever-induced hallucinations"; 70% agree that they consider deathbed phenomena to be "profound spiritual events"; 77% agree that deathbed phenomena are "often a source of spiritual comfort for the dying"; and 60% agree that "patients who experience a DBP [deathbed phenomenon] have a peaceful death" (dos Santos et al., 2017, p. 431). It appears that caregivers can usually tell delirium apart from meaningful deathbed phenomena.

To further clarify these distinctions, drug- and fever-induced hallucinations can include "children running in and out of the room" or "insects moving in wall-paper" (Fenwick & Fenwick, 2013, p. 81). Patients themselves question the reality of drug-induced hallucinations. On the other hand, deathbed phenomena are typically characterized by mental clarity, engagement, and comfort, as in the case of deathbed dreams and visions (Depner et al., 2020). Those who are dying can experience fluctuations of both delirium and meaningful end-of-life dreams and visions. This distinction is regarded as being critical, given that medicating end-of-life dreams and visions "mistakenly perceived as delirium may remove the dying patient from comforting experiences inherent to the dying process" (C. W. Kerr et al., 2014, p. 302; Broadhurst & Harrington, 2016; C. L. Nosek et al., 2015; Chang et al., 2017).

The beneficial effects of deathbed phenomena can carry over to those who witness them but are not, themselves, dying. In the shared death experience study, 87% of participants "stated that their experience had left them absolutely convinced of the reality of a benevolent afterlife" (Shared Crossing Research Initiative, 2021, p. 1483). For 69%, their grief was ameliorated; 52% reported attenuated fear of death; 43% found new meaning in life; 36% became "more spiritual" (Shared Crossing Research Initiative, 2021, p. 1483) as a result of their experience; and 24% said that there had been continued communication with the deceased, usually through "direct mental contact" (Shared Crossing Research Initiative, 2021, p. 1484).

Importantly, many of these deathbed phenomena are experienced not just by people who are dying but also by those who are not dying, such as in cases of shared death experiences and deathbed coincidences, which can be witnessed by more than one person. In such cases, arguments about delirium, drug effects, and high fevers are less plausible, given that such witnesses are unlikely to have been in such compromised states of mind at the time of the occurrence of the deathbed phenomena. If those who are not dying have similar experiences to those who are dying, then the experiences of those who are dying could have the same mechanisms underlying them, which is to say that they are not just due to high fever, drugs, and delirium. In other words, in the midst of disintegration, coherent negentropic experiences can arise as a person is dying that could be essential for preparing them for death itself.

Terminal lucidity appears to be truly anomalous. Despite brain damage from a wide variety of etiologies, a person who is close to death regains sufficient memory, clarity of mind, and motor activity to speak and behave in a lucid manner with those around them. There is no conventional way to explain it except to say that a person for whom it occurs must have been misdiagnosed or that what happened simply did not happen. The documentation for terminal lucidity is good, so neither of those explanations is credible. But then what? One way to think about this is to suggest that, somewhere, at least parts of the psyche of a dying person are still intact, and, in some cases, those parts have the ability to reanimate the physical body. It is not clear what the mechanism for such reanimation would be, except to say that it is clearly not through the ordinary use of the brain. Perhaps whatever rules apply to a bedside table that rises by itself apply in cases of terminal lucidity. Of course, engaging such anomalous mind–matter mechanisms could be inherently difficult so that terminal lucidity and physical deathbed coincidences rarely occur; one needs to be a "special lady," whatever that might involve, to produce such manifestations. But the result is that another level of reality intrudes into physical manifestation in such a way as to effectively override ordinary physical processes. This is an important observation and takes us away from materialist explanations toward living agent psi and survival.

If we look at the variety of phenomena that we have considered in this chapter, then we see that it is consistent with the survival hypothesis. As a person approaches death, they begin to gain access to a dimension of reality within which their psyche already exists but is usually occluded while a person is alive. This can include perceptions of vistas and people known or unknown to a dying person colored, to some degree, by the dying person's expectations. Events in those dimensions are not separated by physical space so that, as a dying person becomes freed from their physical body, interactions with other people or animals at a distance become possible. Furthermore, the process of dying could be such that it can be shared by other people who also open up to the domain of activity within which those who are dying are beginning to function so that they, too, can perceive the events or beings that those who are dying can perceive. In this way, as Raymond Moody noted in the epigraph to this chapter, those who are dying can open a portal to those of us who go on living. Perhaps, we, too, can get an insight into other dimensions of reality. But do those portals close? Can they be opened from the other side? Let us turn to ostensible communication coming back to us from the afterlife.

3 AFTERDEATH COMMUNICATION

A voice speaks: birth and death are sisters. I am forever healed.
—Jennifer Hill (2011, p. 7)

Karen McCarthy lost her fiancé, Johann, when he died unexpectedly. Barely able to function as a result of her grief, McCarthy accepted an invitation to house-sit in the Chesapeake Bay area, bought a cheap car, and drove out to the house. She alternated between sleeping and splitting headaches. Then:

> I wished the world would die. . . . Something caught my eye. . . . Something was moving on the bed—small, round indentations were tip-toeing up the duvet like the imprints of invisible animal paws. (McCarthy, 2020, p. 5)

They stopped close to her head. And did not restart. Over the next several weeks, she heard knocking sounds and creaking floorboards; smelled Johann and, on several occasions, tobacco smoke; felt someone heavy sitting on her bed; felt sensations of having her forehead brushed, hair tugged, heat between her shoulder blades, and right shoulder squeezed; saw a solid-black figure standing in a doorway, and then perceived the apparition disappear;

---

https://doi.org/10.1037/0000361-003
Death as an Altered State of Consciousness: A Scientific Approach, by I. Barušs
Copyright © 2023 by the American Psychological Association. All rights reserved.

saw a spinning pine needle; felt a change in the air; and saw her cell phone and computer act up. One morning, while asleep, she felt Johann lying beside her in bed, his arm across her waist, his breath on her neck. "It felt so real, and he felt so present that it didn't feel like a dream" (McCarthy, 2020, p. 31).

McCarthy was a skeptic. Sure, strange things were happening. These could be due to some sort of feedback from a global consciousness cauldron into which Johann had melted. How did she know that Johann, as a separate personality, was still intact, out there, somewhere beyond physical apperception? There had been butterflies all over the place. The cat that came with the house had been swatting at a butterfly in the morning, then one had flown alongside her head as she had walked down to the beach. Sightings of butterflies are common afterdeath coincidences, but, so thought McCarthy, not something that Johann, with his dry sense of humor, would have orchestrated. Then, a large butterfly crashed into her head. No, of course not. He would send her hundreds. So, she put this to the test and asked him:

> *Are you sending me butterflies?* . . . A monarch butterfly fluttered along, landed on my foot, and sat there with wings erect, quivering in the ocean breeze. . . . I sat there staring at this pretty insect on a beach at dawn in some tiny town where I'd hid and cried and wanted to be dead and searched for meaning and answers and found none. Till now. . . . *It is you! Holy freaking shit!* (McCarthy, 2020, p. 73)

In Chapter 9, we consider how such insect events could be orchestrated. Overall, McCarthy counted 57 unusual encounter experiences while she was house-sitting for 2 months. She went on to apparently communicate telepathically with Johann and then become a medium (McCarthy, 2020).

In this chapter, I want to set the context for this discussion by clarifying terminology, introducing a taxonomy, and noting the frequency of these types of experiences. Then, we describe the characteristics of afterdeath communication (ADC) and provide examples, including cases of shared experiences and those in which new information is acquired. Those two features of ADCs have been used to argue against materialism for living agent psi (LAP) or survival as explanations. We talk about ADCs in dreams. Then, we examine the contention that these experiences are symptoms of psychopathology. We move on to their role in the continuing bonds approach to grief counseling. This leads into two different techniques that have been used for inducing ADCs. After that, I switch to a different set of cases, those in which an organ transplant recipient has acquired some of the donor's psychological dispositions and memories. We then reflect on the material in this chapter and consider more carefully our explanations. The conclusion? "ADCs could provide deep reassurance of a peaceful, joyful, and amazing afterlife, which in turn could substantially reduce fear of death, provide hope and comfort after loss, and perhaps even make the universe itself seem brighter and more welcoming" (Exline, 2021, p. 172).

CHARACTERISTICS OF AFTERDEATH COMMUNICATION

Let us use the expression *afterdeath communication* to refer to apparent interactions with the deceased, such as those of McCarthy. Again, we need to be careful, so we can think of this as ostensible communication. Unlike our terminology in the previous chapter in which we prefixed the word "apparent" to "deathbed communications" to make it more precise, the word "apparent" is implicit in the expression "afterdeath communication" (Hastings, 2012). Another way around the problem of the source of ADCs is to call these "afterdeath communication experiences" and to assume the word "experiences" to be present when using the abbreviation "ADCs" (Beischel, 2019, p. 3). Other names that have been used for these experiences include "post-bereavement hallucinations" (Elsaesser et al., 2021, para. 1), "post-bereavement hallucinatory experiences" (Castelnovo et al., 2015, p. 266), "encounters with the dead" (Elsaesser et al., 2021, p. 1), and "extraordinary experiences, ideonecrophic experiences, reunion experiences, post-death encounters, grief apparitions, afterlife encounters, and post-death contact" (Beischel, 2019, p. 4). Given that the word "hallucination" has negative associations (C. Keen et al., 2013), the expression "sensory and quasi-sensory experiences of the deceased" (Kamp et al., 2020) has also been used as a more neutral term. We will look at the notion of hallucination more carefully in a bit. But this is not the end of terminology. One source lists a table of 25 expressions that have been used to refer to these experiences (Kamp et al., 2020). I also use the terms *experiencer* and *percipient* for the person who is experiencing ADC and *apparition* to refer to the perceived entity with which a percipient appears to be communicating (cf. E. W. Kelly, 2018).

Using Julie Beischel's taxonomy, there are four types of ADCs: spontaneous, facilitated, assisted, and requested (Beischel, 2019). All but the last of McCarthy's experiences fall in the first category of spontaneous ADCs. For the second type, there are ways of inducing ADCs under the guidance of trained facilitators, two of which are discussed in this chapter. The third type, assisted, is mediumship, which is taken up in Chapter 4. The fourth type, requested ADCs, involves engagement in practices whose purpose is to evoke apparent communication with the deceased. This can be as simple as "inviting the deceased to communicate" (Beischel, 2019, p. 15) or using electronic equipment to do so, known as instrumental transcommunication (ITC), which we consider in Chapter 5. In Chapter 6, we discuss apparent communication that involves more dramatic physical phenomena. The last of McCarthy's experiences, described earlier, is an example of a requested ADC, given that she put the question of Johann's survival to the test and deliberately asked him if he were responsible for the proliferation of butterflies.

Notably, most of the academic discussion of afterdeath experiences has been in the context of bereavement and, in particular, the *continuing bonds approach to grief counseling*, whereby a bereaved person accepts an ongoing role of a deceased person in their life. We talk about that approach in this chapter. We saw the impact of grief in McCarthy's account. She was devastated by the loss of her fiancé. However, one need not be grieving to experience these types of phenomena. They can also occur for those who are not emotionally affected by a person's death (Barušs & Mossbridge, 2017; Barušs, 2021). For instance, Charles Lindbergh, during the first successful solo transatlantic flight in 1927, sensed the presence of beings that appeared and disappeared from the cockpit of his airplane, speaking above the roar of the engine, and helping him with the flight (Lindbergh, 1953). More generally, solo travel has sometimes entailed sensed presences (Barušs, 2020).

I also want to note at the outset the transformational effect that ADCs can have (Kason, 2019; Bolsheva, 2014). McCarthy starts out as a disbeliever, then turns into a skeptic, then becomes convinced that she really is communicating with a particular person, and, later still, loses her fear of death (McCarthy, 2020). Whatever an academic discussion might reveal about the survival hypothesis, as we see over and over again, those for whom experiences such as these occur, including academics themselves, frequently end up feeling convinced that the dead do survive death (see also Cooper, 2017). In that sense, ADCs and many of the other phenomena discussed in this book fall within the larger class of spiritually transformative experiences (Kason, 2019; Barušs, 1996, 2021).

How frequently do these apparent contacts with the deceased occur? The answer is, perhaps surprisingly, that they occur fairly often. Prevalence statistics have been reported for representative samples as well as for samples drawn from those who are bereaved. In a 1974–1975 representative sample of 902 people in Iceland by Erlendur Haraldsson, to which we refer several times in this chapter, 31% claimed to have been "aware of the presence of a deceased person" (Haraldsson, 2012, p. 1). In a 1984 National Opinions Research Council Poll in the United States, 42% of respondents had ostensibly had contact with the dead (Greeley, 1987). The numbers are higher among the bereaved, ranging from 35% to 97% across different studies (Beischel et al., 2017). Although inconclusive, it appears that more women than men report ADCs, and, unsurprisingly perhaps, the occurrence of ADCs among widows and widowers is correlated with marital satisfaction. There appear to be no ethnic, religious, regional, educational, or socioeconomic covariates (Castelnovo et al., 2015; Beischel, 2019), although more diverse and fine-grained sampling could reveal cultural differences (e.g., Elsaesser et al., 2021). In one study, 69% of participants found it helpful to reexperience the deceased; for 26%, it was "neither helpful nor unpleasant" (Castelnovo et al., 2015, p. 270); and 6% found the experiences unpleasant. So, overall, ADCs occur frequently and are usually experienced as being positive.

It is generally acknowledged that ADCs are underreported (Castelnovo et al., 2015; Cooper, 2017). More than 50% of bereaved people do not report these experiences to others. The reasons vary, but a salient reason is fear of rejection by others who could regard these experiences as signs of mental illness (Castelnovo et al., 2015; Elsaesser et al., 2021; C. Keen et al., 2013). In particular, percipients are reluctant to report these experiences to caregivers. Despite the significance and potentially transformative nature of these experiences for those who have had them, caregivers typically lack formal training for appropriate ways of assisting people with them (Beischel, 2019). In one study, 62% of counseling experiences by people who claimed to have sensed the presence of the deceased had been "totally unsatisfactory" (Taylor, 2005, p. 60), and the percipients had felt "unaccepted, abnormal, not understood, unable to connect to counsellors, and that they had received no empathy" (Taylor, 2005, p. 60). From the point of view of percipients, interactions with caregivers frequently have not gone well.

Sensed presence or *felt presence* (Castelnovo et al., 2015) refers to an impression that a deceased person is present without the occurrence of specific sensory concomitants. These are sometimes described as "'quasi-sensory' feelings of non-specific awareness of the deceased" (D. R. Jahn & Spencer-Thomas, 2018, p. 4). It is not clear what this state is neurologically or even phenomenologically (Castelnovo et al., 2015). An example of sensed presence from the Icelandic study involves a man whose grandfather lived in a room in the basement in which he eventually died. One evening, 9 years after the grandfather's death, the man was making bookshelves in that basement room when he "suddenly felt such a presence that [he] stopped and left" (Haraldsson, 2012, p. 39). This feeling was accompanied by fear, although this sensed presence recurred frequently thereafter without the feeling of fear. "I really felt he was there at my side," the man said (Haraldsson, 2012, p. 39).

In some studies, it has been found that sensed presence is the most common type of ADC; in two separate studies, 32% and 52%, respectively, of those having had an ADC had a feeling of sensed presence (Castelnovo et al., 2015). That number was 11% in the Icelandic study for sense of presence without the involvement of other sensory modalities (Haraldsson, 2012). Visual impressions were second at 79%, 26%, and 67% respectively; auditory, at 50%, 30%, and 28%; and tactile, at 21%, 6%, and 13%. Olfactory sensations occurred for 5% of participants in the Icelandic study. More than one modality was involved in 46%, 64%, and about 20% of cases, respectively (Castelnovo et al., 2015, Haraldsson, 2012), with 10% of ADC accounts in the Icelandic study involving sight and sound (Haraldsson, 2012). When encounters during sleep have been included in relative frequencies, those are found to be the most common form of ADCs (Elsaesser et al., 2021). We saw in McCarthy's case an example of apparent contact with the deceased during sleep.

Let us consider a 194-item online survey of ADCs carried out during 2018 and 2019 by Evelyn Elsaesser and colleagues. The survey, in English, French, and Spanish, netted 991 completed questionnaires, mostly by women (85%; Elsaesser et al., 2021). We just referenced that study in the previous paragraph. Here, I want to consider the tactile component of ADC apparitions. In the Elsaesser database, 48% of 991 respondents claimed to have felt physical contact that had been initiated by the apparition—for instance: "She felt like a living person when we embraced in a hug, I felt her clothes, her frail body, and hair" (Woollacott et al., 2022, p. 428). For 55% of those cases, the sensations that had been evoked were characteristic of the deceased—for example: "His hand suddenly grabbed my lower leg, ankle area. . . . reminiscent of what he used to do when we were kids and growing up" (Woollacott et al., 2022, p. 428). When asked about trying to touch the apparition, 26% said yes, and, of those, 43% agreed that they could "grasp the deceased" or feel "resistance/matter" (Woollacott et al., 2022, p. 427). In a few cases, the apparitions evaded being touched. Of those who experienced being touched, 80% agreed that touching was a message—for instance: "He was letting me know that he was there, and I was not imagining it" (Woollacott et al., 2022, p. 428).

Here is another example of the occurrence of physical events that were interpreted as a message. A woman said that she had been at the funeral of her husband's step-grandmother, when flowers rose from a tall, thin basket in which they had been placed, separated into clumps of three, and then "shot fast to the ground" (Glazier et al., 2015, p. 251). The basket they had been in had tipped over but then righted itself without falling. The participant's explanation was that there had been three relatives who had been disrespectful toward the deceased and that the crashing flower incident was retribution toward them, given that it was their donated flowers that had flown from the basket (Glazier et al., 2015, p. 251). We could perhaps link this back to the levitating bedside table deathbed coincidence in the previous chapter. In this case, there was no apparition, just events that suggested to some of those who were present that they had received a message from the deceased.

One taxonomy of ADCs found four themes. The first is that of *reassurance*: The deceased is fine, and the living no longer need to be concerned about them. The second is that of *resolution*: The afterdeath contact allows for the completion of unfinished business, settling conflicts, and providing closure. The third is *reaffirmation*: the continuation of emotional bonds, expressions of love, and assurances of future reunion. And with the fourth, *release*, grief terminates and life resumes, allowing the deceased to move on (Elsaesser et al., 2021). Other researchers have noted as well the theme that ADCs can help to solve everyday problems (Kamp et al., 2020). We saw this in the case of Lindbergh's transatlantic flight and will see that again in the next couple of examples.

EXAMPLES OF AFTERDEATH COMMUNICATIONS

Let us consider five quite different examples. In the first, an experiencer received information from a deceased friend about the location of a key that was in the house in which the friend had lived. The information was passed on to that deceased man's wife, who ostensibly said, "I have been looking for that key all weekend!" (Woollacott et al., 2022, p. 429). The key was for a cupboard containing a gun that she wanted to have taken away. This information acquisition appears to be anomalous but could be the result of LAP rather than survival.

In a second example, the last time that a man had seen his wife alive, she had been wearing a blue nightgown in the hospital. As he was selecting the hymns to be sung at her funeral, he suddenly saw his wife standing in front of him "bathed in an oval of white light" (Haraldsson, 2012, p. 200). She was holding the collar of a fancy pink nightgown that she was wearing but had rarely worn while alive. He became startled, and the apparition disappeared. He found out later that this was the nightgown his daughter-in-law had chosen for his wife's burial.

The third example is one of apparent protection provided by a deceased person. In this case, a man said that his father had been an alcoholic. Early one morning, the father had sat down on his wife's bed to beat her. But his arm had stopped short of actually striking her. His son had seen "a man in a sea officer uniform grasp [his] father's hand" (Haraldsson, 2012, p. 162). The father had tried several more times to strike his wife but, each time, had been unable to land the blow. An apparition was preventing the living husband from assaulting his wife. When the son later mentioned this to his mother, she told him that the apparition had been a friend, a naval officer who had been killed during the war.

In 174 of 349 cases in the representative Icelandic sample, the participants had indicated that another person had been present during their experience. Haraldsson was able to track down 32 such witnesses, 29 of whom confirmed that they had perceived the same apparitions as the participants (Haraldsson, 2012). Having multiple witnesses to an event helps to establish that the event is objective to any given witness.

Here are a couple of those cases. In our fourth example, a well-known Icelandic lawyer had been coming home from a dance at about 4:00 a.m. in the morning, by which time it was already light out. He had not been drinking. He saw a slightly stooped woman wearing a shawl coming toward him. He greeted her, but she did not respond. Then he noticed that she was following him. When he stopped, she stopped. When he got home, which was on the grounds of a psychiatric hospital, his brother awakened and asked why the old woman was with him. The lawyer went from the room and, when he came back, his brother asked the same question. The lawyer did not see the woman at those times, and he told his brother not to talk such nonsense. That day at lunchtime, the lawyer challenged his brother about what he had said during the night. His brother confirmed that he had seen an old woman come into the room with him. Their father, who worked at the hospital, said that one of the psychiatric patients had died at 3:00 a.m. and that the details of the lawyer's description matched the woman who had died. When contacted by Haraldsson, the lawyer's brother said that he had seen "the outlines of some woman . . . but not clearly" (Haraldsson, 2012, p. 202).

In our fifth example, a doctor, along with his wife, were visiting with an Icelandic relative living in Germany with his German wife. They were eating, with the German wife's mother present as well, when there was a man suddenly standing in the room. The doctor said that the man appeared to be a relative because of his resemblance to his relative's German wife. He suspected that it could be her deceased father, a picture of whom he had once seen. He was well groomed. The doctor looked down and then up again, and the apparition was still there. It persisted for quite a while before disappearing. When the doctor's wife was contacted, she confirmed that she had also seen the apparition, commented on the immaculate grooming and his resemblance to the German wife, and said that "he walked back and forth and was acting very loving towards his wife, daughter and grandchildren" (Haraldsson, 2012, p. 86).

AFTERDEATH COMMUNICATION IN DREAMS

We can analyze the dreams of the bereaved to see if they reveal anything interesting (Wright et al., 2014; Liu & Field, 2022). Sometimes dreams about the deceased are counted as ADC (Barbato et al., 1999; Elsaesser et al., 2021). When dreams are counted, those are the most frequently reported ADCs. Readers undoubtedly will have different attitudes toward the significance of dreams. So, if dreams are regarded as insignificant, why should they reveal anything interesting about the deceased? The answer has to do with this: The dreams that are interpreted as visits from the deceased are perceived as being different in quality from dreams that are just about the deceased. Also, external agency on the part of the deceased is attributed to the deceased for dreams that are regarded as visits. In one study, 37% of respondents who had dreamed about the deceased asserted that there was a difference, including those who had had both dreams just about the deceased and dreams that seemed to be visits from the deceased (Elsaesser et al., 2021).

A *lucid dream* is one in which the dreamer knows that they are dreaming. These dreams can sometimes feel more real than ordinary reality, and there can be a greater degree of control over the dream events in lucid dreams (Baruš, 2020). In one study carried out in 2014 and 2015, frequent lucid dreamers were recruited through personal contacts and word of mouth to try to dream about a deceased person of their choice. There was no intention to try to determine the objective reality of the resulting lucid dream figures, just to get some sense of the degree to which such figures appeared to be real to the dreamers. Other dimensions of the dream experience were of interest to the researchers, too. Participants were provided with instructions for the induction of lucid dreaming as well as suggestions for having conversations with dream figures. There ended up being 28 lucid dreamers who provided 80 lucid dreams, 63 of which occurred prospectively during the study period, with the remainder being accounts of previous experiences that the dreamers had had (Puhle & Parker, 2017).

In the lucid dream study, it was found that 90% of the deceased dream figures were relatives. In some cases, several deceased figures appeared.

Usually, the appearance was spontaneous. However, 29% of the time, some effort was made by the dreamer to encounter the dream figure. In 43% of cases, the appearance of the dream figure matched that of the deceased before their death, whereas in 16% of cases, they appeared unusual or did not look like themselves. In 54% of cases, the deceased had been dead for several years. Perhaps one way of distinguishing just dreams from apparent dream visits by the deceased is to consider whether the dream figures are aware that they are deceased. There were 15 cases in which such awareness occurred. Katharina said that, in her dream, she had come into the kitchen of her parents' house, where she had seen her father standing. She had asked him what it is like to be dead, and he had smiled and had told her that it was not so bad (Puhle & Parker, 2017).

Furthermore, in the study, in 10% of the cases, information was ostensibly provided to the dreamer by the dream character that was unknown to the dreamer. For instance, Sylvia asked a deceased preacher what message he would like her to convey to his wife. He told her to tell his wife that "if she has the big picture of me, it is not me" (Puhle & Parker, 2017, p. 155). The following morning, Sylvia telephoned the preacher's wife with the message. The wife started crying and explained that she had a big picture of her husband that had been in the church and that "she had been crying and trying to pull him from the picture" (Puhle & Parker, 2017, p. 155). The message appeared to have been that the image in the picture is no longer who the preacher is. These types of cases suggest the possible correspondence with physical circumstances of some dream events (Puhle & Parker, 2017).

In her capacity as an events planner for the U.S. Army, Amanda sometimes interacted with Wink, who was a chaplain's assistant. She started having unusual dreams and had a compulsion to tell Wink because she thought that he could verify some of the details of the dreams. Here is one of them. In the dream, Amanda was in a helicopter flying over a canyon with a river and a large bridge crossing it. She could see a U.S. military truck driving on a road along a cliffside toward the bridge and hear the conversation between the soldiers in the helicopter and those in the truck. Wink was manning a gun mounted on the truck. When he received the command, he fired at the bridge. In her dream, Amanda saw that the bridge was a drawbridge that was raised in the middle to create a second level above a lower level. She saw the symbol *pi* (π) in the middle of it. The round from the gun hit the top of the drawbridge, which fell onto the men below it who were trying to blow it up. Once that had happened, she saw divers in wetsuits, whom she knew to be U.S. Navy SEALs (i.e., Navy Sea, Air, and Land teams), who jumped into the water to pull out the bodies. When Amanda told Wink about her dream, Wink said that the dream referenced a mission he had been on with Nick, a SEALs member. Nick had survived that operation but perished during a later mission in which he had lain on top of a grenade to protect Wink and his other comrades. The *pi* symbol was actually the Roman numeral II that really was on a drawbridge of that description, which is how Wink said that he knew which mission was being referenced in the dream. The implication is that this was a dream created by Nick. Amanda believed that through her dreams, Wink's deceased comrades were reaching out to him to "tell him that they are fine and not in the condition in which he last saw them" (Krippner, 2017, p. 186).

AFTERDEATH COMMUNICATION AS PATHOLOGICAL

What is going on? Are these postbereavement hallucinatory experiences or encounters with the dead? Or something else? Experiencers frequently report that caregivers treat them as though there were something wrong with them. Within academia, we engage in *pathomorphism*, the pathologization of states of consciousness that we do not understand (Barušs, 2000, 2020). So, experiencers are correct when they sometimes feel as though their experiences are inspected through a pathologizing lens (Exline, 2021). Some caregivers believe that experiencers really are mentally ill or stupid (Hall, 2014). So let us consider the postbereavement hallucinatory experiences perspective for a bit.

Defining what we mean by "hallucination" turns out to be more difficult than it seems initially that it should be. I have previously defined *hallucinations* as "perceptions that do not correspond to physical reality" (Barušs, 2020, p. 4). In the context of psychopathology, "*Hallucinations* are perception-like experiences that occur without an external stimulus" (American Psychiatric Association, 2013, p. 87; see also Kamp et al., 2020). I find that somewhat muddier. What counts as "perception-like?" And what exactly is "external?" For instance, are dreams classified as hallucinations? Are shared death experiences external? Or just "objective?" Or just "subjectively objective?" Does our worldview allow for such possibilities, or do we draw a hard physical line prohibiting ourselves from thinking that such experiences can occur?

There is also the matter of reality-testing so that a hallucination has two ingredients: a subjectively generated perception and a mistaken judgment that the subjective perception is objective (Castelnovo et al., 2015). In other words, seeing our deceased Aunt Matilda sitting on the bed beside us is only an issue if we mistake the subjective impression for an objective one and think that the deceased Aunt Matilda really is sitting beside us. But how do we know that our impression is mistaken? It is only necessarily mistaken in a materialist framework in which deceased Aunt Matilda has ceased to exist. If we reject that interpretation and consider that Aunt Matilda is deceased and alive and sitting on our bed, then is she still a hallucination?

We have to acknowledge that we can process through our physical sensory modalities only a tiny fraction of the physical reality that goes on around us. The visible spectrum of light is the prototypical illustration of our narrow perceptual window on reality (Barušs, 2020). We cannot see into the infrared or ultraviolet without technologies that translate those frequencies into ones that are within the visible spectrum. So, are there circumstances, such as bereavement, in which our ability to penetrate into the unseen is enhanced? Or, conversely, are there circumstances in which the material from those unseen aspects of reality can emerge into the narrow spectrum within which we can make sensory observations? In either case, is it possible to suddenly perceive that which was previously invisible?

So, which is it? Going back to my original definition of hallucination, are ADCs veridical hallucinations in that their content is objectively present, if not necessarily available, through the physical senses? Or mistaken hallucinations? Two criteria have been suggested for resolving this ambiguity, although both are philosophically problematic. First, is the hallucination solitary or is it shared? Do others perceive the same hallucination (Cooper, 2017)? Consider the following example: "I felt my dad physically present. My cat literally doubled in size with all her hair sticking up" (Woollacott et al., 2022, p. 425). Are owner and cat both sensing a presence? The second criterion is that of the acquisition of new information. Does information emerge that would have been known to the deceased, but not the person having the experience, and that was subsequently verified to be correct (Cooper, 2017)? Of course, such information could result from remote perception and does not necessarily imply survival. We have already seen examples of both of these types of ADCs.

Sometimes a distinction is made between splitting and lumping explanations of pathological ADCs. *Splitting* refers to the idea that the afterdeath experiences of people who are mentally healthy are not the same experiences as those of people who are mentally ill. A diagnosis of "persistent complex bereavement disorder" can be made in cases in which there are "severe and persistent grief and mourning reactions" (Castelnovo et al., 2015, p. 267), which can include the presence of hallucinations of the deceased. This syndrome has a prevalence around 2.4% to 4.8%, which is well below the frequencies of ADCs that we reviewed previously. In other words, we are not talking about the same experiences.

Lumping refers to the idea that afterdeath experiences are all alike, but it is only once they cross a particular threshold of intensity that they become pathological. "Pathology is determined by variables such as frequency, content control, subjective distress, objective impairment and co-occurrence with other symptoms" (Castelnovo et al., 2015, p. 272). In this case, it does not particularly matter whether the source of the apparent communication is internal or external; if it causes psychological impairment, then it is a problem that can come to the attention of mental health professionals (Castelnovo et al., 2015). The occurrence of ADCs has been associated with levels of distress, such as "anxiety, depression, and loneliness" (Kamp et al., 2020, p. 1375). However, the meaning of that relationship is unclear. In particular, it is not clear that ADCs should themselves be regarded as symptoms of psychopathology, particularly given that only some individuals with persistent complex bereavement disorder "are reported to have hallucinatory experiences" (Castelnovo et al., 2015, p. 267). Thus, we see the struggles of trying to place ADCs in the context of psychopathology.

Overall, the tendency has been not to regard ADCs as pathological in and of themselves (Elsaesser et al., 2021; Beischel et al., 2017; Bolsheva, 2014; Dannenbaum & Kinnier, 2009), although that is one lens through which they can be addressed (Exline, 2021).

CONTINUING BONDS APPROACH TO GRIEF COUNSELING

Apparently there is a pessimistic attitude in some of the bereavement literature that grief counseling is ineffective or even harmful. Historically, a psychoanalytic perspective has been used, whereby the bereaved are encouraged to sever their ties to the deceased as a way of resolving their grief. Failure to do so could be regarded as pathological (Beischel et al., 2017; Pearson, 2021). From this view, ADCs themselves are problematic because they are symptomatic of insufficient severing. So, reports by experiencers that mental health professionals regard their experiences as abnormal are not unfounded. But do such theories adequately fit today's bereavement process for the resolution of grief?

From a continuing bonds model, based in part on attachment theory, it is important to allow a person's relationship to the deceased to play out in new ways after their death so as to achieve a meaningful resolution (D. R. Jahn & Spencer-Thomas, 2018). It is not up to caregivers to impose their beliefs about the afterlife onto the grieving. Rather, there should be an emphasis on the development of personal meaning (C. Keen et al., 2013; Bolsheva, 2014). And normalizing ADCs prevents additional suffering to the bereaved person having such experiences (Beischel, 2019).

Continuing relationships can be maintained at two levels. The first is that of *mental representation,* whereby a connection to the deceased is maintained through reflecting on memories of the deceased and possibly engaging in memorial projects that honor the deceased person's life trajectory. The second is an *interactive connection,* whereby the deceased person is regarded as a separate being and with whom some events can be experienced as though they were initiated by the deceased (D. R. Jahn & Spencer-Thomas, 2018). Instances of these connections are sensed presences, perceptions, and the anomalous phenomena of ADCs. Experiencers frequently insist that the deceased can hear them (DeGroot, 2018). And we have also had examples of events that appear to have been initiated by the deceased, such as the butterfly landing on McCarthy's foot, the floating flowers dashed to the floor, and the restrained strikes.

Does continuing bonds with the deceased work? Is that helpful? That appears to be true in some cases. They can "provide reassurance, encouragement, and consolation" (Beischel, 2019, p. 5). And "ADCs have been associated with reduced susceptibility to adverse consequences of bereavement such as loneliness, sleep problems, loss of appetite and weight loss" (Elsaesser et al., 2021, p. 2). The ability to integrate ADC experiences—for instance, by using a spiritual framework—is associated with greater benefits (Elsaesser et al., 2021, p. 2). However, the point has been made that afterdeath experiences must be respected as being real by caregivers if there is to be any improvement in grief therapy (Pearson, 2021).

In the Elsaesser database, investigators found that participants typically regarded their ADCs as meaningful; 73% agreed that their experiences had "brought them comfort and emotional healing," 68% "considered it to be important for their bereavement process" (Elsaesser et al., 2021, p. 3), 71% said that they "treasured" the experience, and a further 21% stated that they "were very glad it had happened" (Elsaesser et al., 2021, p. 3). Only 12% felt that their experience had made the physical absence of the deceased "more painful" (Elsaesser et al., 2021, p. 3). For 60%, the fear of death had "decreased or even disappeared" (Elsaesser et al., 2021, p. 3), and belief in an afterlife had increased from 69% to 93% (Elsaesser et al., 2021). So, overall, ADCs appear to be helpful in the bereavement process.

INDUCED AFTERDEATH COMMUNICATION

Suppose we decide that ADCs are a good thing. Can we help people to experience them? Four main ways of inducing ADCs have been discussed in the literature: psychedelic drugs, eye-movement desensitization and reprocessing

(EMDR), mirror gazing, and ITC. We will leave ITC for Chapter 5. Psychedelic drugs are not usually ingested for the purpose of contacting the deceased in Western cultures, although beings of various sorts can show up during psychedelic experiences (Baruss, 2020). In particular indigenous cultures, however, the aim of some psychoactive substance use, such as ayahuasca, is explicitly that of contacting one's ancestors (Beischel, 2019). Some data concern the use of psychedelics in the context of bereavement, however, there is no indication that those data were obtained from the legal use of psychedelics rather than illicit use, and, therefore, that information is not being included here for ethical reasons. That leaves us with EMDR and mirror gazing.

The use of EMDR to induce ADC was inadvertently discovered by Allan Botkin, who was using that technique as a treatment for posttraumatic stress disorder among war veterans when he found that it could also evoke images of the deceased. The EMDR procedure consists of moving a wand laterally in front of a person's face at eye level. The person recalls a disturbing memory while tracking the movement of the wand with their eyes. The idea is that the emotional charge associated with distressing thoughts is thereby removed, rendering the memories more abstract.

Botkin had administered the EMDR procedure several times to a Vietnam War veteran, who was still grief stricken by the death of a young Vietnamese girl during a firefight. He asked the veteran to close his eyes, and on doing so, the veteran saw the girl "as a beautiful woman with long black hair in a white gown surrounded by a radiant light" (Botkin, 2014, p. 13), and they apparently expressed mutual appreciation toward one another. For the veteran, this had been an experience of actual communication with the deceased. Botkin was puzzled by what had occurred. He tried the same strategy with other veterans and found that they, too, had impressions of the deceased. At the end of EMDR sessions, he asked them to stay in a receptive state of mind and to think of what they would say to the deceased if they could. Then he had them repeat the eye movements and, then, close their eyes. On closing their eyes, the veterans would experience images of the deceased. According to Botkin, that worked 98% of the time (Botkin, 2014; Baruss & Mossbridge, 2017). Other psychotherapists claim to have had similar success with this technique and that it works better than traditional approaches they have used (Beischel, 2019).

Here is another example of the use of the EMDR procedure. Julia Mossbridge's college friend had died in a car accident on his way to a dance at her college to which she had invited him. She went to see Allan Botkin to try to resolve her residual grief over her friend's death. She was skeptical of the blue marker cap at the end of a white stick that Botkin waved in front of her face. Nonetheless, as she was encouraged to experience her grief, images arose of her last interactions with her friend. She cried and then had a happy memory of her friend—and then an ADC:

> Simply, without pretense, I saw Josh walk out from behind a door. My friend jumped around with his youthful enthusiasm, beaming at me. I felt great joy at the connection but I couldn't tell whether I was making the whole thing up. He told me I wasn't to blame and I believed him. Then I saw Josh playing with his sister's dog. I didn't know she had one. We said good-bye and I opened my eyes, laughing. (Mossbridge, 2003, para. 8)

Subsequently Mossbridge learned that her friend's sister had had a golden retriever, which was the same breed of dog that Mossbridge had seen in her vision. So, if Mossbridge's account has been correctly remembered, we have an experience of induced ADC in which there was both a reduction in grief as well as apparently correct information that had previously been unknown to Mossbridge (Baruš & Mossbridge, 2017).

In general, altered states of consciousness are conducive to anomalous phenomena, including anomalous phenomena associated with death. We have seen that already in this chapter with sleep. *Sensory restriction*, also sometimes called *sensory deprivation* or *restricted environmental stimulation technique*, entails the attenuation of sensory input or substantially removing its variability so as to create a homogeneous sensory field. Over time, researchers have found multiple benefits of sensory restriction, including the reduction in addictive behaviors and improved athletic performance (Baruš, 2020). But there has been more. John Lilly invented a floatation tank in which a person can float in a solution of Epsom salts with the tank itself placed in a dark and quiet room. But then, as he used the tank himself, he felt that people whom he knew as well as "strange and alien presences with whom he had had no known previous experience" (Lilly, 1978, p. 103) showed up as "apparent presences" (Lilly, 1978, p. 103). At the time when these events first occurred, he assumed that they were produced by his imagination or some "unknown sources" (Lilly, 1978, p. 103) that were programming his brain. Such sensed presences have been observed in the context of sensory restriction (Baruš, 2020). Importantly, the occurrence of sensed presences during sensory restriction is a description of occurrent phenomena and not an explanation for them. We still need to determine their cause.

Mirror gazing is an example of sensory restriction that has been used in the context of bereavement counseling (Beischel, 2019). Raymond Moody, whom we met in previous chapters, became interested in mirror gazing and led people to experience what he called *facilitated apparitions* (Moody, 1993,

p. xxi) that included seeing and conversing with the deceased in a way that led participants to believe that these had been actual interactions. Having seen others have powerful experiences that they interpreted as being real, Moody decided that he would try this for himself because he felt that he would not be fooled into thinking that what transpired was real. He chose to try to connect with his maternal grandmother for whom he had strong positive feelings because she had been a powerful influence during his upbringing.

In preparation for his effort to communicate with his maternal grandmother, Moody spent many hours recalling memories of her and going through old photographs. Then he entered what he called the "apparition booth" (Moody, 1993, p. 24), where he sat in dim lighting gazing "into the depth of a large mirror, offset in such a way that [he] gazed into a sort of three-dimensional clarity" (Moody, 1993, p. 24). After doing this for "at least an hour" (Moody, 1993, p. 24), Moody decided that he was not capable of having these experiences and left the booth.

As Moody was sitting alone in a room afterward, a woman walked in. It took him almost a minute to recognize who this was. It was his deceased paternal grandmother with whom he had not had a warm relationship because she was cranky and frequently warned him that he would go to hell if he did not behave as she believed he should. Moody threw his hands up toward his face and exclaimed, "Grandma!" (Moody, 1993, p. 25) to which she responded by addressing him using a nickname that only she had used. Memories rushed into Moody's head. But his grandmother had apparently changed. He experienced her as younger than she had been when he had been a child. She was warm and loving and "confidently humorous, with an air of quiet calm and joyfulness about her" (Moody, 1993, p. 26). They discussed their relationship and specific incidents, including ones that Moody had forgotten. She told him something about his family circumstances that he had not realized but that was useful to him going forward.

During his ADC, Moody heard his paternal grandmother's "voice clearly, the only difference being that there was a crisp, electric quality to it that seemed clearer and louder than her voice before she died" (Moody, 1993, p. 27). At times, the communication was telepathic in that he and she both appeared to know what the other was thinking without the use of words. She was physical in appearance, indistinguishable from living people, except that there "appeared to be a light or an indentation in space, as if she were somehow set off or recessed from the rest of her physical surroundings" (Moody, 1993, p. 28). When Moody reached out to touch her, she put up her hands and motioned him to step back. Moody does not know how long this visionary experience lasted, possibly several hours, but, at some point, he just said, "Good-bye" (Moody, 1993, p. 28) and left the room. When he returned, she was gone.

For Moody, his relationship with his paternal grandmother was healed. He now appreciated her humor and the struggles that she had faced during her lifetime. And he now knew that "death is not the end of life" (Moody, 1993, p. 28). Furthermore, this experience was contiguous with experiences in his ordinary waking state so that he reached the conclusion that if he were to regard this experience as hallucinatory, then the rest of his life was also a hallucination (Moody, 1993, p. 29). I will let the reader make up their own mind about this case. I want to add that, according to Moody, his family had had him "put into a mental hospital" because of his mirror-gazing research (Barbell, 1993). I have included his experience here because he is an iconic figure and because the details of his experience are consistent with the experiences of others, not just in a mirror-gazing setting, but ADC more generally.

Several features of this example are important to note. The first is that the apparent encounter took place after at least an hour of mirror gazing rather than during the time that Moody was sitting in front of the mirror. In his later research, he found that about 10% of the time, the experiencer enters the mirror, where the deceased are then encountered; 10% of the time, an apparition leaves the mirror and enters the surrounding environment; and in about 25% of cases, the apparitions occur for a person when the person has left the experimental setting, as occurred in Moody's own case (Moody, 1993). This calls into question the role that a mirror plays in facilitating these events. Second is that Moody did not encounter the person with whom he had hoped to engage. He found that that occurred in 25% of cases with the participants in his studies (Moody, 1993). We see this with ADCs more generally, and it is not always clear why the person who is experienced is the one to show up. Third is the feeling of reality associated with the occurrence of the apparition. I think that it is natural for us as readers to crinkle our brows and wonder just what Moody thinks is happening. There is a disconnection between the way that we usually experience our physical world and the implication that physical events such as this encounter can just somehow be inserted into our ongoing waking experience. Because experiences of anomalous physical manipulation challenge our boggle thresholds, it is tempting to simply not mention them. However, it is important to reflect what is actually in the literature rather than censor out the parts that we find unpalatable. Whatever we make of them, it is important to realize that physical phenomena recur over and over again in the accounts of experiences that are associated with death.

Following his experience, Moody went on to create a *psychomanteum*, a room dedicated to mirror gazing, which he used for conducting his research (Moody, 1993; Wehrstein, 2017). However, let us consider a different study in which a *psychomanteum* booth was used in the context of bereavement counseling. In that study, a participant sat in a reclining chair in the booth, looking at a mirror that was tilted so as not to reflect the person's face. They had access to a dimmer, which could be used to adjust the indirect lighting in the booth. Their instructions were to gaze into the mirror for about 45 minutes and reflect on a deceased person of their choice. A facilitator was available if necessary. Based on a self-report questionnaire item, participants appeared to have been in an altered state of consciousness. Some also reported altered time perception. Otherwise, the features of that state of consciousness were not further explored (Hastings, 2012).

Of the 100 participants in the study, 63 claimed to have had contact with the deceased, with 34 of 100 reporting the presence also of others who appeared. There was a statistically significant improvement on a 20-item bereavement measure with the greatest changes for "need to communicate, followed by sadness, loss, peacefulness, and anger" (Hastings, 2012, p. 8). There was no relationship with the time that had elapsed since death, suggesting that it was the intervention itself rather than some stage in the grieving process that was responsible for the positive results. Qualitative analyses of participants' written data revealed that there were no universal themes, although there were some common elements. These included "meaningful imagery, mental conversation with the deceased, feelings of gratitude" (Hastings, 2012, p. 11); synchronicity; shift toward feeling peace; messages from the deceased as well as visual, auditory, and psychosomatic sensations and positive feelings of "gratitude, love, peacefulness, calm, relief, forgiveness, tears, and reassurance" (Hastings, 2012, p. 14); and negative feelings of anger, disappointment, and regret. Most participants accepted the possibility that they could be communicating with the deceased, and only a few questioned whether they were imagining it. The 27 participants who indicated that they had not made contact and 10 participants who left the item blank had the same sensory events as those who did have contact, but their session was one-sided without an apparent response from the deceased. However, even without an apparent response, "participants often reported insights or resolution of feelings from the experience" (Hastings, 2012, p. 15). In other words, there were likely different mechanisms through which bereavement was improved, some of which involve apparent contact with the deceased and others of which do not. No effort was made in this project to determine whether the apparent contacts were veridical.

TRANSPLANT CASES

The Society for Psychical Research was founded in 1882 in England for the purpose of investigating unusual psychological phenomena, including phenomena suggestive of life after death. The phenomena they investigated, such as apparitions and mediumship (West, 2015), still form much of the discussion of the survival hypothesis today. However, because of advances in technology, researchers can now scrutinize phenomena that simply did not exist in the late 19th century. Most obvious, perhaps, is ITC, which has been brought about by the development of electronics and which we consider in Chapter 5. Another example is the occurrence of anomalies associated with organ transplantation (Braude, 2017). In particular, heart transplant recipients frequently begin to express elements from their heart donors' lives. These elements can include "changes in food, music, art, sexual, recreational, and career preferences, as well as specific instances of perceptions of names and sensory experiences related to the donors" (Pearsall et al., 2000, p. 65). The following is an example that emerged from a study in which reports were obtained from transplant donors and recipients as well as their family members.

A police officer was killed when he was shot in the face as he tried to apprehend a drug dealer who looked like iconic religious images of Jesus. His heart was received by a college professor, who started to have disturbing dreams several weeks after transplantation and, later, daydreams as well as the dreams. He would see a "flash of light right in [his] face" (Pearsall et al., 2000, p. 71). Then his face would get very hot. And just before these impressions, he "would get a glimpse of Jesus" (Pearsall et al., 2000, p. 71). The recipient's doctors told him that these flashes were "probably a side effect of the medications" (Pearsall et al., 2000, p. 71) that he was taking. However, there appears to be a correspondence between the donor's manner of death and the recipient's traumatic images.

Let us consider a second example that could perhaps help us to understand the psychological dynamics that might be at play here. The donor, Jerry, was a "16-month-old boy who drowned in a bathtub" (Pearsall et al., 2000, p. 67). The recipient, Carter, was a 7-month-old boy. The donor's and recipient's families were introduced when Carter was 6 years old. At that time, Carter ran up to Jerry's mother and rubbed his nose against her, which, according to her, was what Jerry used to do. In addition, at the time they met, even though Carter was 6 years old, he used the same baby talk that Jerry had used. When they went to church together, Carter, who had not yet met Jerry's father, spontaneously identified and ran up to him in church, "climbed on his lap, hugged him and said 'Daddy'" (Pearsall et al., 2000, p. 67). When asked why he had done so, Carter had responded that he had not done that, that Jerry had done it, and that he, Carter, had just gone with him. In this case, we appear to have a subjective interplay of two psyches, that of Jerry and Carter, who are using the body at different times. Is that even possible?

What is going on here? The most common explanation for these phenomena is the cellular memory theory, whereby information stored in the donor's heart becomes available to the recipient (Braude, 2017). In other words, this has nothing to do with survival because the donor's heart is still physically alive. The problem with this theory is the lack of evidence that cellular memory exists and includes such specific information as we find in these cases. There are also the usual suspects of malobservation and deceit to consider. The most popular of those is the hospital grapevine theory, whereby patients, even when anaesthetized, hear details about the donor from hospital staff, which they then later repeat. That clearly cannot account for either of the cases we are considering here, even were hospital staff to know idiosyncratic details about the donors.

Perhaps we can apply the LAP hypothesis more successfully to explain transplant cases. There is an emotional need, perhaps, on the part of the families of donors to continue to have a relationship with the donors so that they telepathically and psychokinetically influence the recipients. Perhaps. According to the *hover hypothesis*, some aspect of the donor's psyche, and possibly the entire personality, remains in close proximity to the donor's physical heart so that it can influence the recipient in ways that are characteristic of itself (Braude, 2017). Of course, that also requires telepathy and psychokinesis, this time on the part of the deceased donors. This is what makes the Jerry/Carter case instructive: Some residue of Jerry appears to be using the body at times while Carter relinquishes control. This is reminiscent of *dissociative identity disorder*, whereby different alters appear to take turns using a body (American Psychiatric Association, 2013; Barušs, 2020). These also start to resemble possession cases, which are difficult to distinguish from dissociative identity disorder, and which we consider more fully in Chapter 6.

REFLECTIONS

It is important to distinguish two questions with regard to the experiences discussed in this book. The first is, What is happening? And the second is, Are these experiences meaningful? The first is an ontological question, and the second is pragmatic. The first is difficult to answer, so most researchers cited in this chapter did not even try. They simply bracketed the issue—for instance: "This research did not engage in the question of the ontological nature of the contacts—whether they were really some form of survival after death" (Hastings, 2012, p. 3). Rather, emphasis is placed on the second of those questions so that "the analytic goal is not to explain away or corroborate participants' claims or experiences but to understand in more detail their significance as psychological, social, and cultural events" (Murray & Wooffitt, 2010, p. 2; Steffen & Coyle, 2017). That way, we try to get on with examining anomalous experiences without getting mired in conflicting ideologies.

The answer to the second question is yes, ADCs are usually meaningful (C. Keen et al., 2013; Beischel, 2019). Having said that, it is important also to acknowledge the need to explore the meanings and transformational aspects of negative ADCs (Beischel, 2019). But there is an odd catch here in that the pragmatic attitude cannot be cleanly severed from the ontological abyss. One reason why afterdeath experiences work in the context of grief counseling is precisely because the bereaved accept these as genuine encounters with the deceased (Pearson, 2021). So, we get pulled right back into having to acknowledge the first question, whether we want to or not. So, if we are strict materialists, we are back to our research program of showing how people come to have counterfactual beliefs (cf. Lange & Houran, 2015; Lange et al., 2019).

To address the ontological question, I want to return to the representative Icelandic study carried out by Erlendur Haraldsson (2012). He identified six critical features of ADCs that suggest that these experiences are not just products of the imagination. First, 28% of the people whose apparitions were perceived had died violently, whereas the baseline rate of violent deaths in Iceland was only 8%. In many of these cases, experiencers did not know that the deceased had died at the time of the apparitions. The idea is that the possible need to say goodbye and complete unfinished business on the part of the deceased means that we could attribute motivation to the deceased at least in some cases. A similar argument is made with Haraldsson's second point, that for 14% of the sample the afterdeath event occurred within 24 hours of a person's death, again, frequently when the experiencer did not know that the person had died or was close to death. Third, occasionally these experiences are shared so that there are multiple witnesses, making it less likely that the experiences could just be products of the imagination. We have seen several examples of such ADCs. Fourth, in some cases, a deceased person unknown to the percipient was encountered but only later identified. We also have seen some examples of that as well as an example involving a dog. Fifth, in some cases, information was relayed by the deceased that was not known to the experiencer but was later verified to be true. And we have seen those examples as well. Sixth, in some cases, apparent encounters with the deceased appeared to be deliberate efforts on the part of the deceased to assist the experiencers. Information about a lost key and apparent intervention by a naval officer are examples of such ADCs.

Two of these criteria are sometimes regarded as being evidence of actual contact: the communication of correct information unknown to the experiencer and the presence of multiple witnesses (Cooper, 2017). Both establish that, in those cases, the visionary experiences are not just a product of an individual's imagination. But that does not necessarily establish survival of the entities associated with those events. These could just be instances of LAP. That is where the third ingredient, motivation on the part of the deceased, becomes important. If the most reasonable source for a phenomenon is the deceased themselves, then that has been used as an argument for survival (Baruss & Mossbridge, 2017). Of course, establishing motivation on the part of those involved is not unproblematic either.

Several systems have been proposed for distinguishing explanations of ADCs (e.g., Kamp et al., 2020; Kwilecki, 2011), but let us keep this simple and return to our materialism–LAP–survival dial (cf. Woollacott et al., 2022). First, these phenomena could have a strictly physicalist explanation; second, they could be due to LAP; and, third, there really is something external out there, whatever that might mean, possibly constituting evidence for survival. We have already considered some of the variations on the first of these hypotheses, particularly in the discussions about hallucinations and the pathological nature of these phenomena. However, there are simply too many examples of breaches of strict physicalism to be able to squish everything back into the materialist bag without residue. The second of these, LAP, is clearly applicable. However, there is a similar problem as that with strict physicalism. For instance, in the case of the apparitions seen by the Icelandic lawyer and his brother, what reason was there on their part to produce apparitions whose appearance matched that of a psychiatric patient who died that night? That question could have an adequate answer but would require considerable work to produce. That suggests the probability of the third option, at least in some cases, that there is something external with which percipients are coming into contact. Now, that does not necessarily entail survival. For instance, there are *residue theories* in which it is posited that, in some cases, a pattern of events gets somehow imprinted onto a location that then plays itself out from time to time and creates haunting phenomena (Massullo, 2017). However, if there appears to be sufficient intelligent agency on the part of the person associated with an apparition or coincidence, then perhaps we are interacting with the deceased who continue to exist in some form. This argument for the presence of intelligent agents resurfaces again and again as we go through the material in this book.

Can we make our judgments about the position of the needle on the materialism–LAP–survival dial more precise? For instance, can we quantify the presence of an intelligent agent? With a little imagination, we can quantify anything (e.g., Sudduth, 2016). But the quantification would only be as valid as the data on which it were based, and that is so wobbly at this point that quantification seems premature.

Perhaps one of the surprising features of some ADC experiences is their physicality. We saw this with the naval officer, Moody's grandmother, and the tactile nature of the apparitions from the Elsaesser database. At some point, the distinction between the corporeal person before death and the apparent corporeality of the person after death disappears. We run into a similar problem with life reviews during near-death experiences that are indistinguishable from living life itself. As we make those comparisons, not only are our ideas about the afterlife challenged but so are our assumptions about the nature of physical manifestation. Not only does death come apart, but so does life. And it leads us to reflect whether life is really that different from death.

4 MEDIUMSHIP

Measuring the effects on a physical body of the channeling experience is quite akin to the idea of being in the caboose of a mile-long train and attempting to imagine where the engineer is headed.
—Joyce Anastasia, Helané Wahbeh, Arnaud Delorme, and Jennifer Okonsky (2020, p. 233, italics removed)

Angie Aristone is a medium whom I brought into my classes for 9 years to describe her experiences of mediumship and to demonstrate what she does. She was a popular guest speaker among the students, who were understandably disappointed when the academic dean put a stop to her class demonstrations. It is one thing to be exposed to mediumship research but quite another to hear a medium tell you your uncle's pet name in Italian or tell you that your mother was one of 17 children in the family or correctly imitate idiosyncratic gestures made by your grandfather while he was still alive (Barušs, 2013). "I had no idea that this really happens," was a common reaction by students, who subsequently had a greater appreciation for the occurrence of anomalous phenomena.

---

https://doi.org/10.1037/0000361-004
Death as an Altered State of Consciousness: A Scientific Approach, by I. Barušs
Copyright © 2023 by the American Psychological Association. All rights reserved.

I asked Aristone to share one of my favorite of her experiences with the readers of this book. This is the narrative in her own words:

> I ran into my old friend JT, whom I hadn't seen in well over a decade, on my way out of a restaurant down town. He wanted to chat but I couldn't stay, so I gave him my card and told him to call me sometime so we could catch up. That night, while trying to fall asleep, a dead acquaintance, I'll call Michelle, showed up in my thoughts, interrupting me as I was trying to fall asleep. She wanted me to call JT, which seemed absurd to me. I ignored her and went to sleep. Michelle persisted for the following three nights. Annoyed by her persistence, my husband and I laid in bed discussing the ethics of pouncing on unsuspecting strangers or old friends with unsolicited messages. I concluded that it was beyond rude to do so, and that I wasn't open to getting involved.
>
> On the fourth night she was back. This time I put my foot down. I sat up in bed and told Michelle out loud that I was not going to call JT. I went on to say that if she wanted to talk to him, she would have to get him to call me since he had my number and I didn't have his. I lay back down to sleep. Five minutes later, at nearly 1:00 a.m., the phone rang. JT, as bewildered as I was, apologized for calling so late, and explained that my card had just fallen out of his closet all by itself, so he figured he should call. I decided to give him a reading even though he didn't know that I was a medium. It turned out that Michelle and JT had not only known each other but had dated in their late twenties. Michelle had ended her own life shortly after their relationship had ended; an unrelated event at the time. In their grief, Michelle's family blamed JT, and the guilt had weighed heavily on him for years. Michelle had insisted I call JT for four days because she saw an opportunity and wanted to let him off the hook, which she unequivocally did that night. (A. Aristone, personal communication, February 22, 2022)

Aristone and her husband, on discussing possible explanations for this series of events, concluded that Michelle had organized them so as to alleviate her former boyfriend's guilt. In other words, these events suggest that mediums, such as Aristone, are not just obtaining correct information through anomalous means but also that the deceased are still acting with some of the same capacities that they had while alive.

Three types of information appear to be commonly conveyed by mediums to those who seek them out. The first has to do with identifying the deceased person. This can include a person's physical appearance, manner of speech, style of clothing, personality, "favorite activities, foods, events, places, etc." (Beischel et al., 2017, p. 180). Second, a deceased person appears to convey information through a medium about matters that would have been of interest to the deceased but that occurred after their death. For instance, at one point, Aristone told me that my deceased colleague, whom I replaced in the department when he retired, did not like the new classroom building going up on campus because it spoiled the view from the front entrance of the mansion where his and my offices were located. The third is to give messages, such as the ones that occur during afterdeath communication, to those who are grieving the loss of the deceased person. These can be messages of inspiration, love, forgiveness, reprimand, encouragement, and so on. It is as though the relationship between the living and the dead continues with the interplay of communication that takes place between people who are emotionally close to one another (Beischel et al., 2017).

Before laying out the structure of this chapter, let me just give another example with a different medium. A couple arrived in a bookstore where the medium was interacting with clients. The medium said that three male figures were coming through, one of them laughing, with a name like "Kerry"; then, a "tall blond man projecting the image of a St. Christopher medal" (Anthony, 2021, p. 65), which the medium said could be a trigger for the name "Christopher"; and a guy who eats beans and passes wind. The medium cringed as a shock went through his body and explained that when that occurs, it means an abrupt death, accompanied in this case with the sense of a metallic tank and a loud sound "like an explosion" (Anthony, 2021, p. 66). It turned out that the man from the couple had been the commander of a special operations force in Afghanistan, when the Humvee they were in hit an improvised explosive device, killing Kenny, Christopher, and Todd, the wind-passing soldier (Anthony, 2021). I want to draw attention to the dynamics of the way in which the medium articulated the information that he appeared to be receiving anomalously, including not getting some of the details quite right by saying, "Kerry," rather than "Kenny." This example is fairly characteristic of successful mediumship activity.

So, as usual, let us start by setting the context, in particular, clarifying terminology, which will reveal the landscape of the subject matter. Next, we consider conventional approaches to mediumship: that there really is nothing interesting happening. Then we establish that good mediums sometimes get correct information, such as in the earlier examples. Usually when people are presented with such knowledge, they assume it means the correct information is coming from the deceased. However, that need not be the case. Mediums could just be really good at drawing information from existing physical sources, including the minds of other people; in other words, this could just be living agent psi (LAP). As Aristone has said to my class, "Some days I just think I'm a really good guesser" (Barušs, 2013, p. 97).

In this chapter, we consider more details than we have previously about moving away, not just from materialist explanations, but also moving away from LAP explanations. The critical features of mediumship that allow us to do that include the nature of the interaction with the ostensibly deceased and making attributions about the source of motivation, such as we saw with identifying Michelle as the source of the information in the opening example. We return to one of our common themes, that of psychopathology, and also look at some psychological and physiological parameters of mediumship. We open the discussion into a greater concern for supporting the mental health of mediums and their process of development. An overarching theme of this book is to see how far to the right we can move our materialism–LAP–survival explanatory dial, but we are also familiarizing ourselves with the relevant phenomena for the sake of understanding them better to inform both research and mental health practice.

TERMINOLOGY

As usual, we have a terminological knot to untangle to get this discussion underway. The basic idea is that there exist dimensions of reality outside the range of our physical senses that are populated with entities of various sorts which we can access under some conditions. The people who can access and bring something through, including information, from those dimensions of reality are called *mediums*. So, I use the word *mediumship* to refer to the activity of being a conduit for whatever is "out there" that we cannot access through our physical senses (Baruss, 2014, 2020). In general, "mediumship" was an expression used in the late 19th century, then replaced recently by the word "channeling." And, still more recently, the word "mediumship" has been resuscitated and brought back into wider use (see E. W. Kelly, 2018; Heath & Klimo, 2010; Maraldi et al., 2019).

I used the expression "entities" in the preceding paragraph. Who knows what exists apart from the individual mind that most of us cannot see? Deceased people are only one of many options. We could also channel wise parts of our own psyches, angels, djinn, demons, interdimensional aliens, mythological beings, animals, and so on (Baruss, 2014; Maraldi et al., 2019), hence my use of the term "entities" and sometimes "discarnates" (cf. Beischel, 2007). Sometimes the word "mediumship" is reserved for communicating with the deceased (Sarraf et al., 2021) and "channeling" is used more broadly for bringing through not only the deceased but entities other than the deceased (Maraldi et al., 2019). I use "mediumship" and "channeling" interchangeably. In the definitions, I also used the expression "bring something through" because I do not want to restrict interactions with unseen entities to just communication. Something else could be brought through, such as "energy" used for the purpose of healing. *Energy* is used loosely here as a descriptor for dynamic elements of liminal phenomena (cf. Krippner & Achterberg, 2014).

A dimension of mediumship that we need to consider is the degree of incorporation of an entity by a medium. At one end of the spectrum, there is no incorporation. A medium has the experience of interacting with an entity in the same way that they would interact physically with a person. An entity communicates telepathically or through a medium's senses to convey information. For instance, a medium could have a visual impression of a woman holding a red apple with green and yellow stripes. Or, a medium might notice that there is a cat rubbing against their left leg while they are sitting and meditating and, on "looking" down, see that it is a black, adult, male cat, with a sweet disposition, about two-thirds the size of a normal adult cat, with its tail sticking straight up, the tip of which is pure white. Both are examples of impressions that occur in the imagination. However, both could also correspond to meaningful physical events, such as—in the first case—the last meal eaten by the deceased person holding the apple and—in the second case—a deceased cat whose owner was grieving its recent loss. There is no incorporation in these cases; rather, these are experienced in the imagination as interactions with a person and an animal. Let us call this mental mediumship (Barušs, 2020; Wahbeh et al., 2018; Sudduth, 2016), although other investigators have used that expression to refer to the communication of information more generally (Beischel & Zingrone, 2015).

At the other extreme, we have complete incorporation, whereby a medium has been displaced, and an entity is temporarily apparently using the medium's body. In this case, the term *possession* can also be used, although that expression is sometimes reserved only for involuntary and distressing incorporation (Maraldi et al., 2019). For instance, the British medium Stewart Alexander has said that when the entity White Feather approached him, Alexander found that his "left hand would immediately begin to curl in upon itself as if grossly deformed, and then the remainder of the entrancement process would quickly and forcefully follow." His conscious self would become "submerged and dissociated from [his] body," and when White Feather spoke, Alexander could "hear his words, seemingly from a distance, but [Alexander] was quite unable to interfere with their flow and [Alexander] could exert no influence in any way upon what was taking place" (S. Alexander, 2010/2020, p. 11). This is a case of complete incorporation, with the medium's still retaining consciousness "outside, behind and to the left of [his] body" (S. Alexander, 2010/2020, p. 10) during the first time that the incorporation occurred. In other cases, the dissociation is so profound that there is no memory for what occurred during the time of incorporation. In some cases, incorporation can be accompanied by other anomalous physical phenomena, such as the extrusion of so-called ectoplasm, ringing of bells, and the apparent presence of materialized hands or entire bodies (S. Alexander, 2010/2020; M. Keen et al., 1999). Let us call this extreme end of embodiment *physical mediumship* (S. Alexander, 2010/2020; Sudduth, 2016).

Between these two extremes of dissociation, we can think of the medium as being in more or less of an altered state of consciousness, usually called *trance* (Luke & Hunter, 2014), which can include some degree of incorporation. For instance, a medium can be in a state of heightened absorption focused on perceiving the substance of the communication (Bastos et al., 2016). There can be partial incorporation, such as in the case of *automatic writing* or *psychography*, whereby a medium allows their hands to write or type text without volitional control, as was the case with the medium Robert Rollans (Eisenbeiss & Hassler, 2006), or *artistic mediumship* or *mediumistic painting*, whereby a medium paints works in the style of deceased masters (Maraldi et al., 2014, 2019). Sometimes the trance can be so light as to not look like an altered state of consciousness to those in the medium's presence (Tomlinson, 2019). In some cases, the expression *conscious channeling* is used for mental mediumship during which a medium acts with volitional control, and *trance channeling* is used to refer to channeling with at least some loss of control (Barušs, 2020; Wahbeh & Butzer, 2020). We need to be a bit careful with the notion of volitional control because, even in the case of conscious channeling, "control" refers to the overall process and not to the content of anomalous information, which typically arises spontaneously in the experiential stream of a medium (Barušs, 2007b, 2020). If we call the intermediate states *trance mediumship*, then we roughly have a spectrum from mental mediumship through trance mediumship to physical mediumship (Sudduth, 2016). We can also extend the notion of trance and use the expression *full trance mediumship* for physical mediumship. In this chapter, we are concerned mostly with mental mediumship and some trance mediumship, with only a few references to physical mediumship, which is taken up more fully in Chapter 6.

Here are a few more terms. We have already seen the expression *reading* in Aristone's account, which refers to a medium's production of communication with an entity for someone. The person for whom the communication is intended is called a *sitter* (Tressoldi et al., 2022). A *proxy sitter* is someone who has been substituted for the real sitter, while the real sitter is not in a medium's presence. Proxy sitters have been used in some mediumship research (E. W. Kelly, 2018; Sudduth, 2016). A *spirit guide* or *control* is an incorporeal entity ostensibly assisting a medium from the other side (Everist, 2018). And *twaddle* refers to silly things that mediums sometimes say that have no meaningful connection to anything at all (cf. Barber, 2004).

These terminological nuances suggest only some of the diverse manifestations of mediumship that exist both in terms of the cultures within which it occurs and the forms of expression that it can take (Luke & Hunter, 2014; Luhrmann et al., 2021). For instance, *shamanism*, within Indigenous cultures around the world, is apparently concerned with interactions with spirits, both by having a shaman travel into the domain of the spirits and by allowing incorporation by spirits (Luke & Hunter, 2014; Barušs, 2020). In some cases, these interactions are facilitated with the use of psychedelic substances (Barušs, 2020). As another example, considerable mediumistic activity takes place over the internet. For instance, some social media sites provide a venue for mediums to meet and develop their mediumship skills. And there are opportunities to give and receive online readings (Ryan, 2014).

CONTEXT

We have three categories of explanations for many of the phenomena discussed in this book: materialism, LAP, and survival. Some of the materialist explanations are helpful up to a point, so let us start with those. However, it is fairly straightforward to show that good mediums get correct information through anomalous means. We review that evidence. And, for many people, hearing correct information from a medium is all that is needed for them to be convinced that they are receiving messages from the deceased (cf. Tomlinson, 2019). However, logically, all that producing correct information does is to get us from materialism to LAP. The problem is the next step to survival. So, in addition to correct information, imitations of the deceased's behavior, agency on the part of the deceased, and skills unique to the deceased have been used to argue for survival (Barušs & Mossbridge, 2017). We have already mentioned imitative behavior and given an example of apparent agency on the part of the deceased. Later in this chapter, we consider the chess match between Victor Korchnoi, who was alive, and Géza Maróczy, who was dead, as an example of a skill that can be attributed to the deceased. We can also take into account a medium's sense that they are interacting with a person, albeit deceased. Let us see if all of that is enough to move the needle from LAP to survival.

From a conventional point of view, life ends at death (Moreira-Almeida, 2012), so whatever it is that mediums do is necessarily the result of misperception, mental illness, fraud, or something along those lines. And it is not difficult to find such examples in the historical record (Larsen, 2015). A common skeptical approach is to suggest that mediums obtain information from sitters through *cold reading*. In other words, a medium can start with vague statements or more specific statements suggested by a person's name, ethnicity, style of dress, and so on, and see how a sitter responds to them, both verbally and through body language, thereby getting feedback from the sitter regarding the accuracy of their statements. A medium can keep improvising in this way and fish for additional information that could be correct. Sitters can have selective memory for correct statements and display confirmation bias by interpreting ambiguous statements as being factual, thereby becoming convinced that a medium is actually speaking to the deceased. A medium could also resort to *hot reading*, whereby information about a sitter is gathered through social media, overheard conversations before the reading, and other sources of information about a sitter that are then recycled as messages from the deceased (Augustine, 2015a).

To understand what is happening, it might be helpful to establish the historical context for much of contemporary mediumship. A movement called *Spiritualism* originated in 1848 with two sisters, Margaretta and Catherina Fox, about 14 and 11 years of age, respectively, at the time, when rapping noises were heard every night throughout the house in which they lived in Hydesville, New York. Margaretta Fox asked that if a spirit were creating the noises, then that spirit should produce two sounds. Two sounds followed. She asked to hear one sound if it were an injured spirit, and one sound ensued. In this way, the sisters had ostensibly established a means of communication with spirits. In addition to the knocking sounds, in the presence of the sisters, "tables moved, doors opened and shut, people present felt touches from cold hands, and there was a sound of dancing in clogs" (Wehrstein & McLuhan, 2018, para. 11). Such physical phenomena associated with a person or place have sometimes been called *poltergeist phenomena* (Colvin, 2015). In this case, attention from visitors ensued and continued to grow until the sisters were giving demonstrations of these phenomena in Rochester, New York, and then, later, in other cities, with the purpose of demonstrating the survival of death. Pamphlets, periodicals, and books were written, and *sitting circles* were formed across the United States to engage in similar mediumistic activity (Wehrstein & McLuhan, 2018). Whether the phenomena associated with the Fox sisters were genuine or fraudulent (Wehrstein & McLuhan, 2018), or a mixture of both, Spiritualism continued to grow, adopting "ideas from other movements, including mesmerism, Swedenborgianism, and transcendentalism" (Tomlinson, 2019, p. 483). It has become a global movement consisting of international organizations with their own local chapters.

Poltergeist phenomena have become less visible in contemporary Spiritualism. There has been a variation of trance mediumship, whereby mediums alter the qualities of their voices to match those of a deceased person.

A variation on that is *trance lecturing*, giving a lecture about subject matter that would be attributed to the deceased about which a medium themselves would not be knowledgeable. None of these is popular today. Rather, Spiritualist mediums typically engage in mental mediumship so that they are seeing visions, hearing sounds, feeling sensations, smelling smells, tasting tastes, and experiencing "unexpected mental impulses" (Tomlinson, 2019, p. 484). The idea is for the medium to be in a light trance so as to engage in a *"hinged dialogue"* (Tomlinson, 2019, p. 483, italics added), being able to perceive what they are sensing at the same time as interacting with an audience to tell listeners what the medium is experiencing. And "in dialogue with audience members, mediums and 'recipients' usually arrive at an understanding of who is sending these signals to the medium. It is nearly always the recipient's deceased friend or family member" (Tomlinson, 2019, p. 484). A medium speaks casually, "directly but tactfully, clearly and confidently . . . without altering her voice qualities" (Tomlinson, 2019, p. 484).

In Spiritualist settings, audience members typically do not question a medium's genuineness. They are prepared to cooperate with a medium to have a successful session. Here is an example from a Spiritualist meeting in Australia in 2017. The medium, Jane, was talking to Patty, one of 17 people in attendance that day. Jane had felt a "gentleman that's drawing close" (Tomlinson, 2019, p. 489) who had paid attention to detail earlier in life but lost that ability later, did not do a good job of shaving, and possibly had some military connections. Eventually, Patty affirmed that it was her father, even though she questioned some statements made by the medium. And then "Jane mentions boys and girls, and Patty responds that in her family there are only girls 'that we know of'" (Tomlinson, 2019, p. 490), and both medium and sitter appear to agree that the spirit world has provided evidence of an extramarital affair (Tomlinson, 2019). I think what is significant here is the interactive nature of the reading. In this example, is the medium sifting through possible meanings of the information that she is receiving? Is this just twaddle? Is she inadvertently or deliberately cold reading? Is there too much noise in the connection? Is it some of each of those? Examples such as this one are sufficiently wobbly to question just what it is that is going on in some mediumship readings.

VERIDICALITY OF MEDIUMISTIC ACTIVITY

For all the prevarication that accompanies some readings, there is no shortage of examples of utterances and behavior by mediums that are strikingly accurate. Materialists sometimes focus on criticizing the weak cases and disregarding the strong ones. As an example of accuracy, a medium referenced a sitter's mother or grandmother who could "strangle a chicken" (E. W. Kelly, 2018, p. 74). And, indeed, the sitter called her grandmother the "chicken killer" because she really did kill chickens (E. W. Kelly, 2018, p. 75). I already alluded to an experience with Aristone, whereby she turned to a student in the class and told her that her mother was one of 17 children in the family before she had heard anything from her (Barušs, 2013). And we have seen other examples and will see more as we go on. So, what do we need to do to demonstrate that good mediums really do convey correct information? Well, we could do the obvious: simply check to see how much of the information is correct.

The Brazilian medium Chico Xavier channeled a letter on September 29, 1973, ostensibly written by the deceased José Roberto Pereira da Silva, who died on June 8, 1972, as a result of a train crash. The letter had 29 individual items of information that could be verified against existing documents and interviews with relatives. For instance, Xavier had written, "A career in medicine was waiting for me," and the deceased was a medical student (Paraná et al., 2019, p. 501). Also, Xavier had written, "My preoccupation with time would make me write dates on everything," and, in fact, da Silva did "write his name and dates on personal objects, papers, newpapers [sic], and other small objects" (Paraná et al., 2019, p. 501). All 29 items were evaluated as having a "clear and precise fit" (Paraná et al., 2019, p. 497). Furthermore, alternative hypotheses, such as "fraud, information leakage, chance, and cold reading" (Paraná et al., 2019, p. 503), were judged to be unlikely.

How about a prospective study? I want to talk about some of the work done by Julie Beischel because I have discussed the details of her research with her on several occasions. Her idea was to obtain a reading from a medium for a sitter, then have the sitter score that reading for accuracy and to also have the sitter score a reading for a different sitter. If a medium is obtaining correct information, then the score for the reading intended for a sitter should be higher than the score for the reading intended for someone else. Given that this is the strategy, then it is helpful to choose sitters whose deceased relatives have distinctive features. For instance, if the deceased died of a heart attack in both cases, then that information cannot distinguish between the readings (Beischel, 2007). It has been said of the use of this strategy that the investigators "essentially rigged the experiment to produce the result that they wanted" (Battista et al., 2015, p. 625). It is not clear how this is even an argument, given that mediums would still need to produce correct information whether that information is for two people who died of heart attacks or two people who died of different causes. It is just that there is more statistical power for finding a difference between the two readings if the causes of death are different. If mediums produce nothing but twaddle, then it does not matter whether the causes of death are the same or different; different causes of death cannot "rig" the study. There is no argument.

When starting on a line of investigation, such as trying to see whether mediums can produce correct information, a researcher just wants to see if there is an effect. If an effect is found, then more experimental controls are introduced in subsequent studies, and improvements are made to the methodology. To study mediumship, an experimenter needs to set up a procedure that allows them to rule out information leakage to the mediums. So, for instance, Beischel has used a "quintuple-blind protocol" (Beischel, 2007, p. 48) to eliminate all ordinary sources of information. As one of the aspects of blinding, during a reading, the medium interacts with an experimenter who does not know anything about the sitter or target discarnate except for the target discarnate's first name. Another aspect of blinding is having a different experimenter interact with the sitters and having them score two of the transcripts from the readings without knowing anything about the discarnates or mediums, and so on. Furthermore, the orders of what happens are randomized—for instance, the orders of names provided to mediums (Beischel, 2007).

In this protocol, mediums are given only the first name of the target deceased person about which the medium is to receive information. Given that providing first names has been criticized as giving information for cold reading to mediums (Battista et al., 2015), the pairs of names intended for two sitters are scrutinized to rule out the possibility of obtaining meaningful information from the first names alone. So, for instance, "actual names of discarnate pairs chosen for recent studies . . . include: Ron and Brandon, Cindy and Joan, Daniel and Larry, Vicki and Eleanor" (Beischel, 2007, p. 41). In other words, any differences in meaningful cold reading clues have thereby been eliminated. It seems to me that if the argument for achieving statistically significant results in mediumship research hinges on cold reading based solely on differences in the first names of discarnate entities, then the debate is over. There is no ground for argument.

Beischel added another methodological twist in that she prescreened the mediums who participated in her research. Suppose that I want to know whether it is possible for anyone to play the *Toccata and Fugue in D Minor* by Johann Sebastian Bach on a pipe organ. So, I pull people randomly off the street, sit them in front of a pipe organ, put the sheet music in front of them, and ask them to play. Maybe some of them thought they could play the organ or read sheet music, but I will find out quickly enough if they can or cannot. Now suppose that I had 10 people sit down at my organ, and the best that anyone could do was to plink out a few notes on one of the manuals. My average would be statistically zero, and I would have failed to have found support for my hypothesis. And if I were using Bayesian statistics, then I might even find evidence against the ability to play. Well, what can I do? The answer is obvious: Start with people who can already play the pipe organ.

That is what Beischel did. She set up an eight-step certification process that involved prospective mediums' responding to a questionnaire about themselves, taking psychological tests, being interviewed on the telephone by other mediums and by investigators, and undergoing research participant and grief training. In addition, each medium needed to obtain a minimal score for two blinded readings that they were required to do over the telephone. In other words, Beischel screened mediums to ensure that they could actually receive correct information anomalously and that they were suitable and properly trained for mediumship research. Mediums who successfully passed through all of the steps were designated as "Windbridge Certified Research Mediums" (Beischel, 2007, p. 52).

So, Beischel carefully selected and paired sitters, introduced sufficient blinding to rule out information leakage, and prescreened mediums. She also clarified the questions that mediums would be asked about discarnates and rationalized and formatted the scoring. Using such a protocol, in a study with 20 certified mediums doing 58 telephone readings, in the forced-choice task, the target reading was chosen by a sitter over the control reading 65.5% of the time, which was statistically significant. In addition, global accuracy scores and hits versus misses scores were statistically significantly higher for target readings (Beischel et al., 2015).

In a separate study by different investigators using a modified version of Beischel's protocol, nine mediums produced 38 readings for sitters who selected their target readings correctly 65.8% of the time, which was statistically significant (Tressoldi et al., 2022). The mediums were not prescreened but were offered public recognition if they performed at a preset minimal level of accuracy during the experiment (P. Tressoldi, personal communication, November 19, 2021).

Not all studies support the anomalous acquisition of information. In a Brazilian investigation, nine mediums produced 78 psychographic letters for a pool of 94 sitters under blinded conditions with proxy sitters. Mediums were given a printed photograph of the target discarnate along with the discarnate's first name written at the bottom of the photograph. The first name of the sitter had been written on the back. Sitters evaluated the accuracy of six letters, one of which was the letter ostensibly written by the target discarnate for them. There were no statistically significant differences in accuracy scores between target and control letters. In fact, 71% of sitters scored their target letter as zero, which is to say, *"I'm certain this is not the letter attributed to my relative/friend"* (Freire et al., 2022, p. 85, emphasis in original), and "17% of participants thought the [target] letters were certainly or probably authored by their deceased relative/friend" (Freire et al., 2022, p. 86). I think the issue here is the lack of prescreening of the mediums. Indeed, it was difficult to find mediums who were willing to engage in the psychographic letter-writing task. And the ones who did participate had not been "tested under controlled protocols" (Freire et al., 86, p. 5).

There have been two meta-analyses of mediumship accuracy. In one of those, eight studies published in seven papers were reviewed, finding no overall effect. Degree of blinding was not a factor (Rock et al., 2021). This meta-analysis has been criticized for being insufficiently comprehensive because of the use of "selective inclusion criteria" (Sarraf et al., 2021, p. 397). In a second study in which 18 experiments published in 14 papers were reviewed, an anomalous result was found using both frequentist and Bayesian statistics. Furthermore, in the second study, there was some support for the notion that "mediums selected on some basis for their mediumistic skills outperform, as expected, those recruited without such a selection process" (Sarraf et al., 2021, p. 399). Again, degree of blinding does not appear to covary with accuracy. This suggests that information leakage is not the explanation for anomalous effects, even in studies with low levels of blinding. In other words, if increasing blinding does not make the effects disappear, then information leakage was not the explanation for the results in the first place (Sarraf et al., 2021). I think that the critical parameter in these studies is the ability of individual mediums to produce correct information in research settings. In the first meta-analysis, only two of the studies used prescreened mediums—the two by Beischel and her colleagues. If we want to hear music, then we need to start by inviting musicians to the performance (cf. E. W. Kelly, 2018).

LIVING AGENT PSI VERSUS SURVIVAL

Good mediums obtain correct information. I have provided considerable detail about the formal studies to make that point. A person could also follow a good medium around for a while and watch them do their thing until it becomes clear that the medium is obtaining correct information. Or, a person could try to become a medium themselves, something to which we will return at the end of this chapter (e.g., Heath & Klimo, 2010). Once we realize that good mediums obtain correct information, we are faced with the question, What is the source of that information? The evidence for anomalous information transfer, as such, is robust with a number of good reviews available of the relevant research. For instance, Julia Mossbridge and I have summarized the relevant research findings and explicitly addressed counter-arguments, including potential problems raised by questionable research practices, in Chapter 2 of *Transcendent Mind* (Barušs & Mossbridge, 2017). Anomalous information transfer occurs. So, are good mediums just good at extracting needed information from physically available sources? In other words, are we just seeing LAP? Do we have any support for the survival hypothesis?

A critical position has sometimes been taken that there is no need to distinguish between the survival hypothesis and LAP. The idea is that both hypotheses refer to putative paranormal phenomena with "shaky" empirical support (Augustine, 2015a, p. 35). Moreover, the argument is that there are no "observational consequences" that could be used to differentiate them (Augustine, 2015a, p. 35). Thus, they are "operationally equivalent" (Augustine, 2015a, p. 35). I get the feeling that what is behind this argument is the notion that, for a materialist, both hypotheses refer to impossible events and that all impossible events are equivalent by virtue of the fact that they are impossible. So, restoring possibility to the impossible, let us proceed and see what we can do to differentiate between LAP and survival.

There are two versions of LAP for mediumship. The first of those is a *multiple-process hypothesis*, whereby a medium engages in a constellation of precisely timed remote perception tasks to extract information from the sources where it can be found, such as the minds of sitters, documents, physical events from the past or future, and so on. Or, perhaps sitters and other relevant living individuals are telepathically impressing correct information on mediums for their readings. The second version is the *magic wand hypothesis*, which is the notion that a desire to obtain correct information is all that is required to engage whatever the relevant mechanisms are that are necessary for producing correct information (Braude, 2003, p. 11). The arguments for taking these hypotheses seriously are philosophically complex, and trying to eliminate them on their own terms using the existing data about anomalous information transfer is notoriously difficult (Braude, 2003; Sudduth, 2016). But it is not necessary to do so. We can adopt a more effective approach, one to which we have already alluded.

Are there phenomena that suggest actual interaction with an entity? Yes. These would include apparent interaction with a deceased person, a medium's imitation of gestures made by the deceased while alive, motivation on the part of the deceased, and skills demonstrated by a medium that cannot be attributed to the medium. We have seen some examples of these already. For instance, the apparent interaction with Michelle described by Aristone is an example of motivation on the part of the deceased. But let me move to the skills argument by describing an interesting chess match.

In 1985, Wolfgang Eisenbeiss, an amateur chess player in Switzerland, initiated a chess match between a living grandmaster and a dead one. Viktor Korchnoi, at the time ranked third in the world, agreed to play against a deceased grandmaster. Eisenbeiss asked Robert Rollans—who channeled using automatic writing, who had an impeccable reputation for honesty, and who did not know how to play chess—to find a deceased grandmaster from a list that Eisenbeiss gave him to play a game with Korchnoi. On June 15, 1985, through automatic writing, first in Hungarian and then in German, Géza Maróczy, a deceased Hungarian grandmaster ranked third in the world around 1900, agreed to play, noted that he would be a poor opponent because of his lack of practice for a long time, and opened the game. Rollans relayed the information that he received to Eisenbeiss, who gave it to Korchnoi. Korchnoi gave his countermoves to Eisenbeiss, who gave them to Rollans, who made the countermoves on a chessboard. In this manner, the game was played for 7 years and 8 months until February 11, 1993, at which point, the ostensible Maróczy resigned at move 48 (Eisenbeiss & Hassler, 2006; Neppe, 2007).

With that much time to play the game and the lack of controls, is there any reason to take this chess match seriously? Well, the question is, What is the source of the chess moves? The game was played at a master or possibly low grandmaster level (Neppe, 2007). There are interesting features to the game. Moves 7, 10, and 12 against the French defense by the ostensible Maróczy were appropriate for Maróczy's time period but regarded as weak moves in the 1980s as a result of advances in opening theory. But, the Maróczy player finished strong, a characteristic of the living Maróczy's play (Neppe, 2007). At the 27th move, Korchnoi apparently commented that he was not certain that he would win the game (Eisenbeiss & Hassler, 2006), although that should have been clear to him after the earlier weak moves (Neppe, 2007). Whoever was playing was mimicking Maróczy's style.

Computers can be ruled out given that they could not play at that level during the course of this game (Neppe, 2007). Also, given that the game was played against the world's Number 3 ranked player, there were not many chess players in the world who could have taken on the grandmaster.

A consortium, perhaps—but then we would need to assume that the moves were given to Rollans by such a consortium to fake as automatic writing, unless there was a broader conspiracy to perpetrate a fraud in which Rollans was complicit. The point is that the level of skill required to play the game would have been difficult to surreptitiously mimic by the living—skill that the deceased had while alive. We can also flip this. If we can imagine a consortium of living players aligned against Korchnoi, we can also imagine a consortium of deceased players aligning against Korchnoi. Why did Maróczy not consult with deceased grandmasters, perhaps those fluent in opening theory, who could have advised him against the weak moves and, perhaps, eked out a win? In fact, how do we know that Maróczy was playing on his own? Or that a deceased grandmaster was not imitating Maróczy's style? Or some other variation?

There is something else to this case. Prior to move 27, the ostensible Maróczy was asked for a report about his life, particularly with regard to his chess playing. The following day, on July 31, 1986, Rollans wrote out a 38-page text. This text was broken down into 91 individual items of information, which were then checked by a Hungarian historian who was not made aware of the source of the information. Of the ones that could be solved, 88% were judged to be correct (Eisenbeiss & Hassler, 2006). A later reexamination of the data led to the conclusion that 97.5% of the 81 solved items were correct, some of which were concerned with information that was difficult to track down (Neppe, 2007). So, in this case, in addition to the chess-playing skill set, we have correct information about Maróczy that was received by the medium through automatic writing. So, we have two of the qualities of mediumship that are indicative of survival: anomalously acquired correct information and the demonstration of a skill that was specific to the deceased.

There is a more direct way of approaching the LAP versus survival issue. For some mediums, the deceased communicator shows up in the same way that a physical person would. For instance:

> When I receive communication, it is a lot like having a good friend come to my house, knock on the door to get my attention, and then walk in. I see them like they are in the room with me and they talk to me like a living person would. . . . As the communication begins, it is a very intense awareness of the person who is standing next to me, like someone is in my personal space bubble. (Beischel, 2014, p. 21)

As another example, the medium Jamie Butler has described how the deceased Erik Medhus would show up early before his mother would call for a reading and turn Butler's computer off and on, open programs, play music from her iTunes, or turn her cell phone on. Butler said,

I have learned to ask Erik before the session to please not mess with the equipment. He normally just gives me a cute smile and shakes his head of messy hair, reminding me that it's okay to lighten up and laugh a little. . . . [Once the reading starts, he] sits on the back of my chair or on the couch with his feet on the cushion to do his confessional-style sharing. (Medhus, 2015, p. 196)

One of my graduate students went to Lily Dale, New York, a hotbed of American Spiritualism, to interview and gather self-report data from mediums after witnessing them doing readings. What struck me about her results was the emergence of data about mediums who reported apperceiving discarnate communicators through their physical senses (Ali, 2018). If a medium perceives an interaction with a deceased person as analogous to an interaction with a physical person, then not only does survival seem plausible to that medium, but so does survival in a form similar to that when alive.

But how do we determine the presence of a person in the first place, dead or alive? The obvious answer is that we make judgments about the presence of a person on the basis of their characteristics. In particular, memory, skills, and personality traits have been suggested as markers for the presence of a person (Moreira-Almeida, 2012). So, first, does a deceased presence reproduce facts that the person would have known during their lifetime? In the case of the ostensible Maróczy, that would be the information about Maróczy's early life, chess matches that he had played, and similar information. For Erik Medhus, it would be recalling his manner of death by suicide. Second, skills could be languages, writing, artistic or musical abilities, expert virtuosity in some domain, and so on. For Maróczy, that would clearly be the ability to play chess at a master level. Third, people have individual personal styles of living and interacting with others. In Medhus's case, he liked to play pranks on people while alive and continued to prank them after death—for instance, by fooling around with Butler's electronics. So, if the qualities of the entity with which we seem to be interacting in some way match those of a person while living, then we could have the same basis for making a judgment about their presence as we did when they were alive. This is a pivotal argument. If people who are dead show up in our lives with the same characteristics as people who are alive, then it makes sense to attribute personhood to the dead on the same basis as we attribute personhood to the living.

MEDIUMS' MENTAL HEALTH

As I was preparing to write this book, I emailed several mediums whom I did not already know, told them that I was writing this book, and asked if I could speak to them to hear what they thought readers should know.

I did not hear back, or I was told that the medium was too busy. The one medium who did respond said that they had been warned to stay away from me because I was an academic. So, on the basis of my limited experience, I can attest that academics have such a bad reputation that mediums, as well as other experiencers, just stay away from us. Why? Well, I suspect that the problem is our collective arrogance; our certitude that whatever experiencers tell us happened obviously did not happen; and that the only reason experiencers think it happened is because of misperception, deception, and mental illness on their part. It is such pathomorphism that cuts off communication with experiencers. Clearly, such an attitude is not useful if we want to learn anything (Barušs & Mossbridge, 2017). And it is not just academics. Mediums have frequently expressed a lack of empathy and support from mental health professionals (Wilde et al., 2019).

So, what about the mental health of mediums? Perhaps the place to start is to note that there is no single psychophysical state that can be designated as "mediumship," nor is it possible to find consistent neurophysiological markers of mediumship (Maraldi et al., 2019). For instance, in a study in California in which 13 full trance mediums were monitored using electroencephalogram (EEG), electrocardiogram, and other physiological measures, there were no differences on those measures during channeling versus non-channeling intervals. The only differences occurred when mediums were asked to read a story either while channeling or not channeling, with story reading being slower during channeling sessions (Wahbeh et al., 2019). In a separate study in the United States, there were no differences in blood chemistry or other physiological measures, such as heart rate variability, between a mediumship reading and control condition for five Windbridge Certified Research Mediums (Beischel et al., 2019). In a Brazilian study, no differences were found for levels of the endogenous psychedelics dimethyltryptamine and bufotenine between five Spiritist mediums after mediumistic activity versus five control participants taken from the staff of a medical center (Bastos et al., 2018). As another example, in a study seeking neurophysiological markers for differences between channeling versus other tasks and greater versus lower accuracy of readings, EEG differences were found, but they were deemed to be the result of facial muscular activity (Delorme et al., 2013).

There has been considerable agreement that mediumship as such in psychologically healthy individuals is not a mental disorder (Menezes & Moreira-Almeida, 2011). Incidentally, genuine mediumship can also exist in people with psychological challenges, although mental illness overshadows a person's other attributes so that we just assume that any mediumship they experience must also be part of a mental disorder (Barušs, 2000). The following is one list of reasons given for why mediumship should not be regarded as a mental disorder. First, a medium is not subjugated to their mental states in such a way as to produce suffering. Second, the course of everyday life, such as one's social life, is not impaired. Third, the experience is not continuous but only occurs intermittently. Fourth, there is a self-critical attitude toward one's own experiences. Fifth, mediumship experiences are compatible with some cultures within which they are accepted and supported. Sixth is the "absence of co-morbidities" (Menezes & Moreira-Almeida, 2011, p. 111). Seventh is the control over the occurrence of mediumship. Eighth: Mediumship makes life more meaningful. Ninth: A medium is engaged in prosocial behavior (Menezes & Moreira-Almeida, 2011).

Because of the role of trance in mediumship, one of the relevant psychological parameters that has been proposed is dissociation (Wilde et al., 2019). There are degrees of dissociation, with dissociative identity disorder (DID) at the extreme end. *DID* is characterized by "the presence of two or more distinct personality states or an experience of possession" (American Psychiatric Association, 2013, p. 292). Such a characterization is certainly applicable to the behavior of some mediums, as we have seen. Later in this chapter we consider a case in which a diagnosis of DID was applied to a person who went on to become a medium. But does it mean that the mind is closed and that the alters and possessing entities are parts of a person's psyche? We can flip this around. In a study of 236 people with DID, 21% had a "personality identified as a dead relative," and 29% had an alter that was "identified as a demon" (Ross et al., 1989, p. 415). Which way round is it? Are trance mediums expressing nonconscious aspects of themselves, perhaps with a little help from LAP? Or, are people with DID actually trance mediums? Or, can either or both occur (Barušs, 2020)?

It is important to note that there can be both pathological and adaptive expressions of dissociation (Menezes & Moreira-Almeida, 2011; Maraldi et al., 2019). Indeed, it could be argued that DID itself is an adaptive psychological response to unacceptable childhood trauma (Barušs, 2020). The degree to which dissociation is considered maladaptive depends, in part, on allegiance to either a biomedical or sociocultural model. The biomedical model has been criticized for an insufficiently comprehensive ideological integration of psychosocial and cultural factors in the understanding of dissociation. This allegiance is paralleled by a trait versus state distinction. A person could have an innate tendency to dissociate, or they could express functional dissociation in culturally sanctioned circumstances, such as that of mediumship (Maraldi et al., 2019). In other words, there could be varying types and degrees of dissociation constituting mediumship (Maraldi et al., 2019, p. 187). Also important to note is that there are substantial background rates of trait dissociation in the general population that are not regarded as pathological, with one study finding that rate to be 13% (Menezes & Moreira-Almeida, 2011).

Several studies support some of these observations about dissociation. In a Brazilian study with 10 female Spiritist mediums and 10 female support staff as controls, EEG readings were taken before, during, and after mediumship sessions. Greater beta and theta power was noted for some electrodes for the mediums, but not the control participants, indicative of the engagement of attentional systems for meeting task demands. There were no within-subject changes during the mediumship readings. The EEG results did not support the presence of pathological dissociation or hypnosis (Bastos et al., 2016). In another Brazilian study, there were no differences in hypnotizability noted between 16 female Spiritist mediums and 16 female control participants drawn from a Masonic lodge, with six mediums and four lodge members scoring in the highly hypnotizable range (Bastos et al., 2022). In a California study of five full trance mediums, personality scores were within the normal range. None was fully unconscious while channeling, suggesting that, even in some cases that are identified as full trance channeling, the full trance does not involve complete dissociation with amnesia (Wahbeh et al., 2018). So, although different types and levels of dissociation are present in mediumship, such presence is either clearly not pathological or does not need to be regarded as pathological.

The other obvious psychological parameter that enters the discussion about the mental health of mediums is the presence of hallucinations, which raises an alarm for mental health professionals. We jump to *schizotypal personality disorder*, which is characterized by strange beliefs, such as beliefs in the occurrence of anomalous events and the presence of "unusual perceptual experiences" (American Psychiatric Association, 2013, p. 655). Okay, that fits mediumship. But does this mean that we have found mediumship to be pathological, or are we just overreaching again? We need to keep a couple of facts in mind.

The first fact to consider is the baseline rates of hallucinations in the general population. These have been recorded since the late 19th century and range from around 10% to 25%. So, the ratio of those who have unproblematic hallucinations to those with hallucinations in the context of psychiatric diagnoses is at least 10 to 1. The majority of people who hallucinate are not mentally ill (Menezes & Moreira-Almeida, 2011). Second, schizotypy has two separable factors: unusual experiences and dysfunctional behavior.

A person who exhibits the unusual experiences without the dysfunctional behavior is called a *happy schizotype* (Cardeña et al., 2014, p. 413). And the unusual experiences without the dysfunction can spur self-development toward exceptional functioning, the opposite of dysfunction (Barušs & Mossbridge, 2017; Claridge, 1997; Kason, 2019). In other words, although dissociation and hallucinations can be present in mediumship, in many cases, they need not be regarded as pathological.

DEVELOPMENT OF MEDIUMSHIP

Let us turn this discussion around. What can psychologists and mental health professionals do to help mediums to be psychologically healthy as they develop and practice their mediumship skills? In addition to stressors faced by the general population, mediums face unique challenges. One is that mediums appear to experience a higher disease burden than nonmediums. In an online survey of 125 self-identified mediums versus 222 nonmediums, all of whom were "citizens or permanent residents of the United States" (Beischel et al., 2019, p. 130), it was found that mediums were more likely than the nonmediums to have been "diagnosed with at least one autoimmune disease" (Beischel et al., 2019, p. 131). Furthermore, mediums reported having a "statistically significantly greater number of health issues than did non-mediums" (Beischel et al., 2019, p. 130).

Another challenge mediums face, which was identified from interviews with 14 practicing mediums in England's North West, is the trauma associated with the emergence of their abilities during childhood. For instance, one participant said that the appearance of her abilities made it difficult for her to fit in with other children and that it was when she simply accepted her abilities that her life became easier. "It is what it is and I talk to dead people, I see them, I hear them, I interact with them and when necessary I deal with them," she said. "That's what I do, that's who I am" (Wilde et al., 2019, p. 267). Another participant related the difficulty during her childhood of dealing with "psychic experiences that could not be explained, with no one to confide in about them, feelings of isolation, alienation, and being 'bullied all the way through school'" (Wilde et al., 2019, p. 267).

We need to keep in mind that mediums are ostensibly interacting with the deceased, which, by its nature, can be traumatic. For instance, mediums sometimes report feeling the cause of a deceased person's death in their own body as the deceased is purportedly trying to show the medium how they died (Beischel, 2014; Wilde et al., 2019). We already saw the apparent occurrence of this as a deathbed synchronicity with the example of a dying man's son who experienced excruciating chest pain and difficulty breathing in the middle of the night as his father was dying in the hospital. Furthermore, mediums are interacting, frequently, with a sitter who is suffering from grief so that they are interacting with distressed individuals frequently without the training that grief counselors would have had (Wilde et al., 2019). So, they need mental health support for the undercurrent of trauma that runs through their practice.

Mediums also face ethical dilemmas. If, as a medium, you feel that you have received sensitive information from a discarnate, what responsibility do you have to pass that information to a sitter? Should you say anything? Or keep your mouth shut? For instance, suppose that a grieving widow wants reassurance from you that their spouse, whose last days were spent in considerable suffering, is now at peace. And when you check in on the person's spouse, you see that they are angry and upset. So? What do you say? Remember the self-critical aspect associated with mediumship. As a medium, you realize that you could be wrong, that the signal coming through the glass darkly could have become corrupted. But your impression is consistent with other information that had the same veridical feeling and turned out to be correct. You would qualify what you say—for instance, "When I look at your spouse, they are really upset. And here's what it looks as though they are upset about." Negotiating such ethical dilemmas is not easy, and there is no standardized mediums' manual for resolving them. More generally, mediums can try to find ways of speaking to sitters so as to make the messages understood while helping sitters improve their sense of well-being (Wilde et al., 2019).

How does mediumship emerge in the first place? Can anyone be a medium? The assertion that mediumship is a skill that could be developed by anyone with appropriate training is the *developmental hypothesis* (Maraldi et al., 2019, p. 183). However, there have not been any longitudinal studies to test this contention. As with most human skills, it is likely to be a combination of natural ability and development (Maraldi et al., 2019). However, we can consider the notion of development more broadly in the sense of *self-development*, whereby a person undergoes a process of self-transformation as they engage in strategies to lead a more meaningful life. In that context, how does a person begin the process of development to become a medium, and what are some of the milestones of such self-development?

Six Windbridge Certified Research Mediums were interviewed about the origins and development of their mediumship. All six participants "described their initial mediumship experience as being an encounter with a discarnate being(s)" (Everist, 2018, p. 23), with four of those incidents having occurred during childhood. Two of the six regarded the initial contact as being frightening, "were later diagnosed with a mental disturbance" (Everist, 2018, p. 24), and were afraid to talk about their experiences with their mothers. For instance, Participant 3 had the experience of smelling the rotting flesh of a deceased pirate, hearing it breathe, and feeling "water droplets on her head" (Everist, 2018, p. 25), and she could "see people walking through walls and coming out of the ceiling" (Everist, 2018, p. 24). She assumed that there was something mentally wrong with her but tolerated her experiences. She heard voices at the age of 21 and was diagnosed with what is now called DID. She gained an understanding of her experiences through reading metaphysical books during her late teenage years and later became convinced during a "group therapy experience that she had been misdiagnosed" (Everist, 2018, p. 24). She went on to work as a professional medium.

Not everyone has had a rocky transition to mediumship. Participant 5 thought that she may have had visits from spirits during childhood but only became aware of her mediumship ability at age 29 during a psychic development class during which she became possessed. She shared her experience with the instructor and the other students; was able to establish boundaries to control the occupation of her body; participated in validation programs, including the Windbridge research program; has felt comfortable with her experiences; and has gone on to become a professional medium (Everist, 2018).

So, what are we left with? In this chapter, I have tried to distill the nature of mediumship. There are physically and mentally difficult aspects to mediumship, but, through a process of understanding and self-development, these can be worked through to enable a person to be in a psychological state that allows them to access correct information apparently provided by entities that are invisible to most people. And some of the features of those interactions, along with the manner in which they occur, strongly suggest that these really are interactions with discarnate beings. But I will let the reader decide just where the needle stops on the materialism–LAP–survival dial.

5 INSTRUMENTAL TRANSCOMMUNICATION

The dead, it seems, have been very fast to seize whatever we invent as a way to talk to us.

—George Noory and Rosemary Ellen Guiley (2011, p. 75)

Instrumental transcommunication (ITC) refers to apparent communication with discarnate entities through the use of electronic devices or other technologies (cf. Beischel, 2019). Several themes emerge as we explore our materialism–LAP [living agent psi]–survival explanations for these phenomena. The first is the human tendency to attribute meaning to ambiguous stimuli, a process called *pareidolia* (cf. Merriam-Webster, n.d.), so that questions arise about how much of ITC is constructed in this manner. Second, once we make it out of the murky pareidolia terrain and find instances of anomalies, we need to contend with LAP. However, whereas in the case of mediumship we were concerned with anomalous information acquisition, this time, we are faced with *anomalous influencing*, the direct mental influence over physical events—in this case, electronic devices. Unlike research concerning mediumship, for which there has been some effort to move the needle from

https://doi.org/10.1037/0000361-005
Death as an Altered State of Consciousness: A Scientific Approach, by I. Baruss
Copyright © 2023 by the American Psychological Association. All rights reserved.

LAP to survival, such argumentation does not exist in the context of ITC. Third, trying to assess our materialism–LAP–survival explanations becomes more difficult to do than previously because of the complexities of the technological aspects of these phenomena. These phenomena are no longer just psychological, but technological and, in addition, necessitate an examination of the relationship between the psychological and technological. In particular, it might be necessary to develop some sort of contact field between an investigator and discarnate entities for ITC to work. But let us start with a previously published example of ITC provided by one of my students, whom I will call Angela (Barušs, 2013).

Angela's mother was at her desk, working at the computer on a paper for a class that she was taking, when she glanced up at the screen to see that the word "perfect" had appeared in the document. She had not typed that, so she deleted it and continued working on the references for her paper. It happened again: The word "perfect" appeared. She called out to Angela and asked her if she knew how that could have happened. At that point, Angela's dog got up from underneath the desk with the computer, startling the mother so that she banged her knee on the desk as she jumped up. Angela screamed. The words "screaming" and "ouch" appeared on the screen. The letters of the words were not typed one at a time but, rather, appeared simultaneously. Afraid that someone was trying to gain access to the computer through the internet, Angela pulled out the connecting cables and unplugged the webcam (Barušs, 2013).

As she had been talking to her boyfriend on the phone when this occurred, Angela asked him if he knew what could be happening. He did not. Angela's father and brother were upstairs, so she ran up to ask them if they were responsible. They were not. Angela, her father, and her brother came downstairs. The words "get the Ouija board, or else" appeared on the screen. The Ouija board was kept in a cupboard in the laundry room. As Angela opened the door to the laundry room, her mother said that the word "boo" had appeared. Angela screamed again. And the word "screaming" appeared in the document next to "boo." At that point, the family members decided that they had had enough. As they were preparing to leave, the word "nite" appeared on the screen (Barušs, 2013).

In the morning, Angela's mother addressed Angela's deceased grandmother and told her that if she knew what was happening to "tell these spirits to go away; that they were not wanted" (Barušs, 2013, p. 89). No one was willing to go downstairs, but because they needed to retrieve things, Angela's brother and mother went down together. Her mother found a document open on the computer with the words "sorry loves" on it. Several weeks later, Angela's mother found out that she had received a perfect grade for her paper (Baruss, 2013).

This is an example of afterdeath communication (ADC) that entails an electronic device—in this case, a computer. Let me give another example of ADC: one with a dysfunctional radio.

Michael Shermer (2014) was getting married at his home in California to Jennifer Graf from Germany, who missed having her deceased grandfather present. Graf asked Shermer to speak to him alone, so they went to the back of their house, where they could hear music playing. They unsuccessfully searched for the source of music until Graf opened a desk drawer in their bedroom and "pulled out her grandfather's transistor radio, out of which a romantic love song wafted" (Shermer, 2014, p. 97). This was an old radio that had belonged to Graf's grandfather, which Shermer had been unable to activate previously. Graf was emotionally affected and felt that having the radio play music was a sign from her grandfather. Shermer said of the experience that "it rocked me back on my heels and shook my skepticism to its core as well" and that "the emotional interpretations of such anomalous events grant them significance regardless of their causal account" (Shermer, 2014, p. 97).

ITC occurs in the context of ADC, but the real thrust of ITC lies in efforts to establish deliberate communication with deceased beings. The idea is to get rid of the mediums and replace them with machines so that anyone can talk to dead people (Fontana, 2005/2010; Cardoso, 2017; Masí, 2004; Locher & Harsch-Fischbach, 1997; Wauters & König, 2016/2017). Alas, that has been easier to conceptualize than to carry out in practice, as we shall see as we proceed. In this chapter, we consider both spontaneous and deliberate ITC.

CONTEXT

Once I had laid out the topics for this book, I knew that this would be the most difficult chapter to write. For the subject matter of all the other chapters, academics have weighed in and provided empirical and theoretical input. Much of that material is patchy in that some aspects of these topics are better covered by academics than others, so I feel a bit as though I were walking from one ice floe to another with really thin ice beneath my feet much of the time as I move from floe to floe. For the subject matter of this chapter, almost nothing is to be found in the academic literature. Here, thin ice is a bonus, and much of the time I am trying to walk on open water. I will let the reader judge just how well that has worked out. Even materialists have been almost completely silent about ITC (but see Banks, 2012). They apparently see no need to critique something that has not been addressed in the first place (cf. Augustine, 2015a).

It is clear to the investigators who have been involved with this research that they have been deserted by the academic research community. For instance, as Anabela Cardoso has said,

> I firmly believe scientists should have taken this basic step [of investigating these phenomena] long ago. However, they did not. Instead, they have avoided the subject by ignoring it, thus trying—and in most cases succeeding—to discredit it and make it fall into oblivion. (Cardoso, 2017, p. x)

I agree with Cardoso. As a consequence of scientists' neglect, ITC research has been carried out by investigators with a broad spectrum of professional credentials. Cardoso herself was a Portuguese diplomat (Cardoso, 2010). Friedrich Jürgenson was a Swedish film producer and painter (Bender, 1972). Amerigo Festa was a lawyer. Paolo Presi was an aeronautical engineer with a shortwave listening license (Cardoso et al., 2007). William O'Neil was trained in electronics by the U.S. Navy and went on to have a series of electronics jobs; he also appeared to have had some mediumship skills (Fuller, 1985). By its nature, ITC has perhaps disproportionately attracted investigators with some background in electronics and technology. The problem is that the amateur investigators have not necessarily been good at scientific research design or the critical evaluation of the results of their studies (Heinzerling, 1997; MacRae, 1984). Having said that, outside the context of ITC, academic investigators have also not necessarily been good at research design or the critical evaluation of the results of their studies (Baruš & Mossbridge, 2017). In fact, disconnection from the academic research community gives one advantage to the amateurs: They are free to think as they wish and are not required to conform to the suffocating materialist ideology that pervades much of the academy.

At any rate, ITC is an important topic, as I think we will discover as we move through this material. And perhaps by writing about it, I will have encouraged more academics to take an interest and join in the research initiative. In the meantime, what we do have available to us will need to suffice.

Given the almost complete absence of academic publication about ITC, how trustworthy is the documentation that I am using? Well, the first example opening this chapter depends on the veracity of the testimony of one of my students. The second example has been taken from Michael Shermer's (2014) skeptic's column in *Scientific American*. So far, so good. What I have done is weigh the parameters about source material that I identified in Chapter 1 and have made the best decisions that I could.

As usual, we need some definitions. *Electronic voice phenomenon* (EVP) refers to ITC in which communication consists of voices usually heard only on playback from an acoustic recording (Baruš, 2001). However, the "electronic" aspect of EVP is somewhat misleading because the medium of communication can also be a stream of water or other natural noise source that is not electronic (Fontana, 2005/2010; Cardoso, 2010). *Direct radio voice* (DRV) refers to voices that are heard coming from the speakers of a radio rather than on playback from an audio recording (Cardoso, 2017, p. 2). Again, though, that is misleading—as we shall see—given that voices can also appear to originate from a point in space and may have nothing to do with a radio (Bogoras, 1901). In those cases, the expression *direct voice* is more appropriate (cf. S. Alexander, 2010/2020). *Anomalous telephone contacts* (ATCs), also known as *phone calls from the dead*, are instances of ITC with telephones, including cell phones (Cooper, 2011).

Let us start with a history of ITC phenomena. Because sound technology was invented before visual image technology, much of this is a history of EVP. Then, we consider EVP in more detail to see how much residue is left when conventional explanations, such as pareidolia, have been exhausted. Next, we look at other types of ITC and the promise they might hold for testing the survival hypothesis. But we already have devices designed for communication, namely, telephones, so we examine ATCs specifically. We end the chapter by bringing in some research using random event generators (REGs) to study direct mental influence on physical manifestation and look at the interface between ITC and REG research.

A SELECTIVE BRIEF HISTORY OF ITC

There is a myth surrounding ITC that the early inventors of electronics and communications technologies, namely, Samuel F. B. Morse, Guglielmo Marconi, Nikola Tesla, Thomas Edison, and Alexander Graham Bell, were trying to invent devices with which to communicate with the dead (see Noory & Guiley, 2011; Fuller, 1985; Watson, 1926; Sumption et al., 2018; Streiff, 2009; Locher & Harsch-Fischbach, 1997). I am already walking on open water here, so I will leave it to the historians to sort that out. The only thing to which I want to draw attention is an article in *Modern Mechanix and Inventions* magazine from October 1933 describing an experiment conducted by Edison in which he sent a beam of light from a lamp onto a photoelectric cell ("Edison's Own Secret Spirit Experiments," 1933). Then the "spiritualists in the group of witnesses were called upon to summon from eternity the etherial [ethereal] form of one or two of its inhabitants, and command the spirit to walk across the beam" ("Edison's Own Secret Spirit Experiments," 1933, p. 35). Any obstruction of the beam of light would have been registered by the photoelectric cell, producing a deviation of a meter to which it was attached. However, despite hours of watching, the meter's needle did not move ("Edison's Own Secret Spirit Experiments," 1933). This type of experiment recurs again more recently, as we shall see later in this chapter.

The usual starting point is with some recordings made by Waldemar Bogoras, an anthropologist who studied the Chukchi people of Siberia in the late 19th century and turn of the 20th century. Bogoras described a performance by a shaman, saying that "the spirits talk on all sides; they quarrel among themselves and attack the shaman and the assistants" (Bogoras, 1901, p. 100). At one point, Bogoras asked to have the spirits speak close to his ear, which, to his astonishment, resulted in an illusion so convincing that he "involuntarily held up [his] hand to catch the voice" (Bogoras, 1901, p. 100). In another instance, Bogoras convinced a shaman, Scratching-Woman, to come to his house, where he made a phonographic record of the shaman's performance. The shaman sat in the dark at a distance of 20 feet from Bogoras and beat his drum as the ostensible spirits entered the room and talked:

> The records show a very marked difference between the voice of the shaman himself, which sounds from afar, and the voices of the "spirits," who seemed to be talking directly into the funnel. . . . All the while, Scratching-Woman was beating the drum incessantly to show that he was in his usual place, and occupied with his usual function, that of beating the drum without interruption. (Bogoras, 1907, p. 436)

For Bogoras, this was an example of ventriloquism (Bogoras, 1901, 1907). We can also regard this as an example of ADC among Indigenous people. In the context of ITC, this has been frequently cited as the first known example of EVP (Kubis & Macy, 1995; Noory & Guiley, 2011).

On September 15, 1952, the magnetophone tape recorder of two Catholic priests, Pellegrino Ernetti and Agostino Gemelli, kept breaking as they were recording a Gregorian chant. On Gemelli's asking for help from his deceased father, his father's voice answered, as recorded on the tape: "Of course I shall help you. I'm always with you" (Kubis & Macy, 1995, p. 102). The priests wondered if this were the work of the devil. However, they tried again. This time, they got the message "But Zucchini, it is clear, don't you know it is I?" (Kubis & Macy, 1995, p. 102). At that point, Gemelli became convinced that this was indeed his father speaking given that "Zucchini" had been the nickname by which his father had called Gemelli. The two priests consulted with Pope Pius XII, who reassured them that the recorder was an acceptable objective device and that such experiments could help to "strengthen people's faith in a hereafter" (Kubis & Macy, 1995, p. 102).

Also in the 1950s, in an effort to capture anomalous voices (Winsper, 2020), Attila von Szalay and Raymond Bayless suspended from the ceiling of a soundproof closet an aluminum trumpet containing a microphone in the large end, which was connected to a tape recorder in the room outside the closet. "In addition, at times there was a loudspeaker in the room that allowed anyone in the room to hear what was happening in the closet" (Barušs, 2001, p. 356). On December 5, 1956, von Szalay sat in the closet for 15 minutes with Bayless sitting in the room outside of it. On playing back the tape for that time period, the two men heard a voice say, "This is G," even though it had seemed as though nothing had happened, and Bayless had heard nothing from the loudspeaker. "There were numerous other examples of recorded voices coming from the closet, in some cases, when there was no one in it" (Barušs, 2001, p. 356; Bayless, 1959).

In the summer of 1959, Friedrich Jürgenson, a "Swedish painter and filmproducer," was recording birdsong in the countryside when, on playback, he noticed a "male voice discussing 'nocturnal bird voices' in Norwegian, followed by a series of 'cackling, whistling and splashing sounds' among which he thought he recognized the voice of a bitterne" (Bender, 1972, p. 65). On further listening to his tapes, Jürgenson thought that he also heard the voice of his mother (Kubis & Macy, 1995). He became convinced that these were the voices of the deceased (Bayless, 1976; Raudive, 1971). He shared his findings with Pope Paul VI, whom he knew from "having done a documentary film about him" (Kubis & Macy, 1995, p. 103), who apparently initiated his own research program into EVP. In particular, for instance, a Swiss theologian, Leo Schmid, has ostensibly collected more than 10,000 voices. And in 1970, EVP was on the agenda of the International Society for Catholic Parapsychologists in Austria (Kubis & Macy, 1995).

Konstantīns Raudive was a Latvian writer who became interested in Jürgenson's voices, met with Jürgenson in 1965, and then began his own recording. His iconic setup was to tune a radio between stations and record the output, a procedure that he called the "radio-microphone recording" (Raudive, 1971, p. 29) method. By 1971, Raudive had obtained 72,000 "voice-texts" (Raudive, 1971, p. 29) and had "analysed roughly 25,000 voices according to speech content, language and rhythm" (Raudive, 1971, p. 22). His work has been so influential in the history of EVP that EVP voices are sometimes called "Raudive voices" (Barušs, 2001, p. 357). But there was a problem.

For both Jürgenson and Raudive, it was difficult to determine what the voices were saying. In Raudive's case, he frequently used multiple languages to interpret a single phrase. For instance, Raudive had translated a single passage, which he considered to be one of his clearest examples, using five languages. However, subsequently eight native German speakers identified it as a German sentence of about 37 words, which was likely from an Easter Sunday radio broadcast (Keil, 1980). Clearly, there is a problem with Raudive's analysis. One has to question how much of his interpretation was due to pareidolia.

In 1973, George Meek, an American industrialist, began collaborating with William O'Neil, who was then living in a small Pennsylvania town where he had an electronics and repair service, for the purpose of studying anomalous "partial or full body materialization" (Fuller, 1985, p. 83). In July 1977, O'Neil felt a hand on his shoulder and turned around. Standing there was a man in a business suit whom he had never seen before. O'Neil had experienced materializations previously and identified this as yet another materialization. He was upset and demanded that the man identify himself. The apparition responded. O'Neil's wife, hearing a conversation, came to the doorway of the room from which she could see but could not hear the apparition. The apparition gave details about himself, which O'Neil repeated out loud into a tape recorder. His name was George Mueller, he provided his Social Security number, said that he had received a PhD in experimental physics from Cornell University in 1933, had invented electronic medical equipment, and so on. Most of the details, such as the Social Security number, checked out (Fuller, 1985; Fontana, 2005/2010).

During further apparitional encounters, the deceased Mueller apparently provided instructions for building a device for communication with the dead, which they called Spiricom. It consisted of an "audio signal from a total of 13 oscillators set to different frequencies from 131 Hz to 701 Hz" (Heinzerling, 1997, p. 29). That signal was fed into a transmitter, which sent it to a radio that was tuned to receive its 29.57 MHz signal (Heinzerling, 1997). Starting in September 22, 1980, O'Neil ostensibly had 30 hours of conversations with Mueller using this device. These were not just ambiguous sounds but appeared to be actual two-way conversations. Meek analyzed the tapes of these sessions and consulted with EVP researchers. For instance, the tapes were examined at the University of Tokyo, where it was determined that Mueller's voice was not that of O'Neil or Meek (Fontana, 2005/2010). Meek became convinced that the voices were anomalous and that communication with the deceased had been established. He held a press conference in Washington on April 6, 1982, to announce his conclusions (Fuller, 1985).

But Spiricom went silent; no other communicator other than Mueller appeared to be able to speak through the device, and no one has been able to replicate the Spiricom results (Fontana, 2005/2010).

In 1997, Anabela Cardoso was Consul General to Spain when she tried to help a grieving couple who had lost their son in a sailing accident. Cardoso took them to visit a Jesuit priest, who recommended that they try to establish contact with their son through ITC. To that end, with the assistance of an electronics technician, Cardoso set up a continuous loop with a video camera and computer so that the camera was trained on the computer screen where the image from the camera was displayed. Cardoso tried this and got results. The images were not "extremely sharp" (Cardoso, 2010, p. 53) but of sufficient resolution to allow Cardoso to identify some of them as images of her deceased Great Dane dog. She found additional depictions of dogs as well as people, but not satisfied with the quality of the images, Cardoso switched to EVP.

Cardoso started with two radios tuned between stations, then added a third, and recorded the output on two tape recorders. She met with the bereaved couple and electronics technician once a week. And they asked questions out loud about whatever they wished. Not much happened for 2½ months. There were some "odd sounds . . . like sighs or muffled breathing" (Cardoso, 2010, p. 56) and some knocking sounds, which could sometimes only be heard on one of the tapes on playback, but not the other. Then, one day, while using a German radio transmission as part of the background noise, on playback of the tape, they "clearly heard a pretty loud 'Sim' in Portuguese, uttered by a completely different voice from that of the radio announcer during a pause in the German words" (Cardoso, 2010, p. 57). And then "the EVP replies to our questions became quite frequent and often of very good acoustic quality" (Cardoso, 2010, p. 57).

A few months later, to her surprise and shock, Cardoso heard a masculine voice coming directly from the loudspeaker of her old vacuum tube radio tuned to 14 MHz of the shortwave band that had been emitting a "soft buzz" (Cardoso, 2010, p. 62) to which it returned after several sentences. Cardoso could only make out three words at the time, but identified this as an instance of DRV. This, too, developed over time in terms of clarity and detail. At one point, the British psychologist David Fontana was present with Cardoso during an experiment; he asked that the voices repeat "Hello, David" and "How are you?" which they did (Fontana, 2005/2010, p. 378).

Ghosthunters, those who investigate potentially anomalous locations for unusual phenomena, frequently look for EVP as part of their operating procedure. Their technique is somewhat different from that of laboratory

EVP investigators in that they use devices that are set up to sweep through radio frequencies, hence the moniker *radio sweep EVP* (Winsper, 2020). The devices themselves are frequently referred to as *ghost boxes* (Noory & Guiley, 2011), with a "Frank's Box"—named for its inventor, Frank Sumption—being an iconic example of a ghost box (Sumption et al., 2018; Moon & Moon, 2017). The idea with the laboratory EVP is that the noise sources, such as radios tuned between stations, create a background noise that acts as a carrier wave for the voices that ride on top of it, so to speak. With radio sweep, the idea is that already existent voices are being chosen from the different bandwidths to convey a message (Winsper, 2020).

Initially, Cardoso used a feedback technique with a video camera and computer for obtaining possibly anomalous images. The occurrence of images, particularly images of faces of the deceased, is another extensive aspect of ITC. Cardoso also had an anomalous photograph of a face superimposed on the body of a woman seated on a chair. Advanced computer-based technologies were used by someone proficient with their application to examine the photograph. Color spectrum analysis revealed that the image in the photograph was cooler than expected for an actual person sitting in a chair. In addition, water macromolecules, associated particularly with the face, were detected in the photograph but would not have been expected were this a photograph of a living person. Furthermore, using physiognomic biometric recognition software, it is possible to compare ITC faces with photographs of those people's faces taken when they were alive. When the face in the photograph was compared to that of a deceased woman known to the seated woman's family, there was a positive match, enabling the confident conclusion that the anomalous image was that of the deceased woman (Gullà, 2007).

Sonia Rinaldi, a Brazilian investigator, has used various techniques for deliberately obtaining images, including the images of faces. One of them involves projecting the beams from four microprojectors toward a transparent plastic egg. On doing so, she found images of faces in the egg that matched the faces of the deceased as judged from photographs taken when they were alive. She modified the technique to try to produce three-dimensional images. This time, she used a humidifier to send water vapor vertically into two nested plastic eggs cut open at the ends. The vapor then came out of the openings at the top and fell along the outside of the eggs. A microprojector was trained on the eggs and falling vapor, and Rinaldi used her cell phone to photograph the eggs and falling vapor. Recognizable images of the deceased that could be matched to photographs from when they were alive appeared both in the eggs and the falling vapor (Champlain, 2021).

Well, this brief smattering from the history of ITC illustrates how messy, yet intriguing, these phenomena are. I have refrained from evaluating these historical examples, but I have, for the most part, laid them out flat for the reader to contemplate. Some of them, such as William O'Neil's account of a materialization, probably stretch many readers' boggle thresholds even though the information that he received ended up being accurate. This is also a cautionary tale, given that it is easy to get lost in some technical rabbit hole and not make it back out. Do we need to record on a magnetic tape, or will a digital audio recorder work just as well? Or, which electronic parts would it be beneficial to switch out in a Frank's Box or Spiricom? Or, what are the characteristics of someone who can get any of this to produce something anomalous? So, what to do? How about tuning a couple of radios between stations, recording the output, and listening to what there is to hear?

ELECTRONIC VOICE PHENOMENA

I ran an EVP study in 1997 and 1998 using the radio-microphone method with two radios tuned between stations and recording onto a cassette recorder. I devised a protocol and had two research assistants take turns coming into the room with the setup to execute the protocol. What they did essentially was to imagine that they were addressing deceased people and asking them whatever questions they wished. The tape was then played back afterward to listen for EVP. There were 81 sessions for a total of a little more than 60 hours of recording. We heard some interesting sounds, such as fluctuations in background noise, a low- to high-pitched whistle, and the sound of a kiss. The closest that we came to typical Raudive voices occurred on October 17, 1997, when one of the research assistants identified the phrase "Tell Peter" that was "apparently spoken by a woman's voice at a regular speed juxtaposed at one point on a cacophony of voices that had faded in and that subsequently faded out again" (Barušs, 2001, p. 363). The research assistant thought that it sounded like a friend's voice who was deceased and whose husband's name was Peter. However, I concluded that the experiment had resulted in a null result. Ever since, I have received considerable criticism for this study both from ITC enthusiasts as well as true believers in materialism, from opposite directions (e.g., Leary & Butler, 2015).

So, why the conclusion? What happened to the voices? EVP is sometimes identified as belonging to one of three categories. In *Group A*, the voices are clear, with agreement among all who are present as to the meaning of the voices. *Group B* consists of voices that are not as clear but "can be heard easily by trained listeners" (Winsper, 2020, p. 17; see also Leary & Butler, 2015). *Group C* voices are difficult to figure out. In our case, along with one of my research assistants, I also heard "Tell Peter," but the other research assistant did not hear that phrase. So, we have no Group A voices. Given that I am also a native Latvian speaker, I would have been impressed had Raudive left a message in Latvian for me on the tape. He had not. The problem is that much of what is identified as EVP is the result of pareidolia (Barušs, 2001; Banks, 2001). That is now well known among many EVP researchers, who make a point of taking pareidolia into account when interpreting their results (Cardoso, 2012; Butler, 2020).

Let us consider this problem of pareidolia a bit. EVPMaker is a software program created by Stephan Bion that takes a sound file, chops it into bits, randomly reassembles them, and then plays them back in reassembled form (Barušs, 2007a). In addition, there is a digitally generated audio clip of short speech segments that EVPMaker operators sometimes use (Boccuzzi & Beischel, 2011). The purpose of EVPMaker is to create a noise source for the production of EVP. In one study, an operator, who was experienced with using this configuration and capable of distinguishing genuine EVP from pareidolia, was given an opportunity to create 10 sessions that contained EVP without any constraints on how that was to be done. In particular, the operator had no limit on the number of sessions they could carry out to obtain 10 that did contain EVP. These were regarded as the active sessions. In addition, the experimenter created 10 control sessions of the same length as the active sessions.

The result? There were no differences between the active and control sessions for any of the measures used by the experimenters. For instance, if there were an effort to communicate through EVP, one would expect an increase in the 10 most common sounds in English in the active session versus the control session. There was not. A blinded listening panel was created of 98 online participants who were given the 20 audio clips and asked whether they could "hear any recognizable words in this audio sample" (Boccuzzi & Beischel, 2011, p. 226). The answer was "yes" for an average of 73% for the active sessions and 63% for the control sessions. That difference was not statistically significant, somewhat surprising given that the active sessions had already been prescreened by an EVP researcher to contain recognizable words. For eight of the 10 active session samples, none of the members of the listening panel heard what the operator had heard. The conclusion: EVP was not objectively detectable (Boccuzzi & Beischel, 2011, p. 226). And pareidolia becomes a likely explanation.

We would also expect an effect of priming. In one study in which 28 participants from undergraduate psychology courses had to respond "yes" or "no" if they heard a voice in a sound stimulus, those who were told that they were going to be listening to "electronic voice phenomena–purported voices of ghosts in recordings from paranormal research" (Nees & Phillips, 2015, p. 131) were more likely to report the presence of voices than those who were told that it was a "study of the identification of voices in noisy environments" (Nees & Phillips, 2015, p. 131). In a separate study with 46 participants who listened to sound files with and without a voice present, those who had been told that this was an auditory task were more likely to hear a voice than those who had been told that this was an EVP task. However, all of the participants in this study either believed in the paranormal or actually used EVP techniques during ghosthunting, so it appears that "participants are significantly more likely to show a more sceptical bias when the possibility of EVP is introduced" (Winsper, 2020, p. 114). In other words, those with greater belief in the paranormal or involvement with EVP are less likely to demonstrate pareidolia in a signal detection task. This is consistent with my previous comment: that EVP researchers have now been sensitized to the presence of pareidolia and are adopting a more cautious interpretive approach.

I want to consider one more example of EVP, that of Marcello Bacci from Grosseto, Italy. Bacci was familiar with the work of Jürgenson when he began his own experimentation early in the 1970s. Over the following 30 years, the quality of the voices improved as he experimented with different techniques, eventually through the use of an old Nordmende Fidelio vacuum tube radio (Presi, 2004; Cardoso et al., 2007). At one point, he opened up his laboratory to grieving parents, who found comfort from the voices they heard coming through his radio (Presi, 2004). Bacci took no money for this work (Cardoso et al., 2007). He would turn on his radio and tune it to the shortwave band between stations so that static could be heard coming from the radio. After about 10 to 20 minutes, the static would be replaced by the sound of an air vortex, which might be repeated a number of times. And then voices would begin to speak, engaging in a dialogue with Bacci and those present in the room with him. These voices would last from 10 seconds to 3 or 4 minutes. And when they would cease, the radio static would return. The entire event would last about 40 minutes (Presi, 2004). The radio has only worked in this manner when Bacci himself has been present. When others have tried to get the EVP to work, they could not. We can also note that this is DRV in that the voices are heard coming from the speakers rather than just on playback of a recording (Presi, 2004).

Bacci encouraged scientific investigation, and, on the evening of December 5, 2004, a group of investigators, along with bereaved parents—for a total of 37 people—attended one of his EVP sessions. The investigators were free to scrutinize the radio at their leisure before the session. Four of the investigators sat within touching distance of Bacci. The radio was turned on, and the procedure began as already described. After about 15 to 20 minutes of scanning radio transmissions, Bacci said, in Italian, that he could feel that "they will come" (Cardoso et al., 2007, p. 77). The background noise changed to a vortexlike sound, after which voices could be heard with the vortexlike sound frequently occurring simultaneously with the voices. There appeared to be five or six individual voices speaking in Italian, English, and Spanish, addressing investigators by name and replying to questions posed by the investigators. Not all of the questions were answered. About 70% of the voices were clear to those who were listening.

About 1 hour after the voices had started, one of the investigators leaned over the workbench supporting the radio, pulled out all five of the vacuum tubes, and laid them on the workbench in full view. "The voices continued with the same volume and clarity as before" (Cardoso et al., 2007, p. 78). During a pause in the voices, Bacci, without warning, turned off the radio:

> After 11 seconds of silence (the timings reported have been taken from the tape recorded during the experiment) the observers could hear modulated whistles (sounds similar to those of whip lashes) and the usual acoustic signal that precedes Bacci's reception of paranormal voices which is similar to a vortex of air. The voice of the invisible communicator, interspersed with whistles, recommenced 21 seconds after Bacci had turned the radio off and continued for 23 seconds (as timed from the audio tape) with the same acoustic quality previously heard, perhaps a little slower but as clear as before. When the speech ended the whistles remained for another 6 seconds while the vortex which was heard at the end of the vocal utterance became weaker and finally disappeared after 12 seconds. (Cardoso et al., 2007, pp. 78–79)

The lawyer, Amerigo Festa, had recorded what happened on video, made a written account of the events that had occurred, and had all of the investigators sign the account as being correct. The investigators who were present were convinced of the anomalous nature of the Bacci voices (Cardoso et al., 2007).

What we need is not just to report what people are hearing, but we need a proper analysis of the psychoacoustic properties of these voices using appropriate technology and software. Human speech can be deconstructed into sine waves, with the lowest frequency known as the *fundamental* and the higher frequencies as *harmonics*. In addition, sound is shaped by the structures of the throat and mouth, known as *formants*. It is these variables that are responsible for the differences in vocal sound production. So, for instance, it is easy to distinguish between a person's name being spoken by a human and a bird, even though they might sound quite similar to a person who is listening. And analysis of some EVP voices, including those obtained by Cardoso, have been shown to have anomalous structure, such as the absence of a fundamental frequency and missing vibration of vocal cords (Gullà, 2004). This could perhaps rule out breakthrough radio transmissions as the source of some of the voices.

The same technology can be used for voice recognition. So, for instance, there are two 3-second EVP fragments recorded from Bacci's radio: Both were interpreted as "UNBACIONE/A/TE/CHIARA [*Un bacione a te Chiara*: A big kiss to you, Chiara]." Giuseppe Lenzi, on hearing the EVP, claimed to recognize it as the voice of his deceased daughter, Chiara. A comparison of the word "Chiara" from the EVP and a recording of Chiara's voice spoken by her when she was alive matched sufficiently to meet the level of evidence required in an Italian court to say that the two voices "belong to the same person" (Gullà, 2004, p. 66). In this case, rather than having anomalous features, the EVP voice appears to match that of a person while alive. Indeed, there was a closer match between the EVP voice and the voice from the living Chiara than the two EVP samples of "Chiara" (Gullà, 2004). From the documentation that is available to us, it would appear that the Bacci voices are anomalous and require an adequate explanation.

INSTRUMENTAL TRANSCOMMUNICATION PHENOMENA

I realized at the conclusion of my EVP study how difficult it is to try to establish the anomalous nature of any EVP voices. We were neither able to record any Group A voices nor to rule out pareidolia. I received some funding for a second study, so I decided to get away from perceptually ambiguous stimuli and use computer text as the primary mode of communication. To that end, in 2003, I wrote three computer programs. The first of them generated random strings of letters, digits, and spaces. The second was a word generator that created strings of words randomly chosen from a library of 176 words. And the third was a yes/no generator that randomly typed either the word "yes" or "no" into a word processing document. All of the selections were determined by the computer's pseudorandom number generator. I set it up so that each of the three generators could be easily triggered by a single keystroke of a computer keyboard. In addition, because apparently successful cases of EVP, such as those of William O'Neil and Marcello Bacci, appear to depend on the presence of the right sort of person, whatever that might be, I recruited a medium to join me for the experiment. If nothing else, the idea was that the medium could talk to the dead people to ask them what we needed to do to get the experiment to work. I also recorded EVP both without noise sources and while using EVPMaker. The medium and I carried out 26 sessions in several rooms of the psychology laboratory at my university college when no one else was there. We asked questions, turned on the different random output generators, tried to determine from dead people what we should be doing, and so on, for a total of about 45 hours (Baruss, 2007a).

For our efforts, the medium and I ended up with 19,500 characters from the random character string generator, 3,732 words from the word generator, 49 yes/no responses, and 36 hours and 19 minutes of EVP recording. When we analyzed the data, we found . . . nothing—or almost nothing. Of the 11 yes/no questions to which we could verify the answers, nine were correct, which was marginally statistically significant even after correcting for the possibility that the random yes/no generator was biased. This could just have been a statistically rare event or perhaps the medium's or my ability to anomalously affect the yes/no generator. In other words, that result could have been due to nonconscious remote viewing and precognitive abilities combined with remote influencing of the computer's activity (Baruss, 2007a). At any rate, my reputation as the "failure to replicate guy" was becoming firmly established.

I think we need to think about a number of things. The first of those is the idea that for ITC to work, there needs to be a *contact field* established between the living and the dead that involves creating "a special synergy between operator/s, equipment, location and communicators" (Cardoso, 2012, p. 493). It is possible that creating such a contact field takes time and dedication. That does not explain spontaneous instances of ITC, such as Angela's or Shermer's experiences described at the opening to this chapter. And the clearest EVP candidate, "Tell Peter," that we obtained during my EVP experiment occurred during the 23rd of 81 sessions and not toward the end. Nonetheless, we do not even know whether there is a single mechanism or multiple mechanisms through which ITC could be possible.

The suggestion that a contact field is necessary is tied to the question of whether or not a person with the right qualities needs to be present for ITC to occur. In other words, there needs to be the right blend of psyche and equipment to create the contact field. But what exactly is that? I have heard that the person needs to be "spiritual" or a "medium" or someone who is "psychic" (Baruss, 2001). But those are separable constructs, so which is it? It seems to me that if anything, a *poltergeist* could be an asset, that is to say, someone around whom anomalous physical phenomena occur (Colvin, 2015), such as William O'Neil. After all, anomalous electronic activity is a type of poltergeist activity (Baruss, 2007a), something that we examine in greater detail in Chapter 6. How about a shaman? Or a Catholic priest? But then, again, what of spontaneous cases, such as those of Angela and Shermer? Do they have the right stuff without knowing it, or is the right stuff unnecessary? And then if we do find what the right stuff is, how do we know that we are not just getting LAP? How do we know that what we are experiencing is not just anomalous "ventriloquism?"

What about the electronic equipment that is required to manifest ITC? Everything from what was likely a portable Edison phonograph to a beam of light and photoelectric cell, to an old vacuum tube radio, to cassette tapes, to specialized equipment with 13 oscillators, to video cameras, to computers, to ghost boxes, and to falling water vapor has been used to produce ITC. Furthermore, the devices do not always even need to work properly, as evidenced by the dead radios of Shermer and Bacci coming to life in meaningful ways. In the next chapter, we discuss an experiment in which the deceased ostensibly instructed investigators to build a device with a germanium plate placed under slight pressure from the metallic tip of a screw (Transcommunication Switzerland, 2022). What is the common feature of all of these devices? There does not seem to be one. It would seem that, to talk to us, the dead just use whatever technologies we have created (Noory & Guiley, 2011; Cooper, 2011). The effort to identify the relevant technological and psychological parameters is almost nonexistent at this point.

One other aspect of this research is important to acknowledge: the deliberate effort to obtain information from the deceased as to what would be required to facilitate communication. We saw that with William O'Neil, who ostensibly received instructions from an occasionally materializing deceased engineer. Sonia Rinaldi has apparently obtained images and EVP from Nikola Tesla whom she feels is guiding ITC research (Champlain, 2021). And a medium and I tried to obtain information from the deceased for ways to improve communication in our ITC study. We see this again in the next chapter. In other words, if the survival hypothesis were true and conscious entities were somewhere out there, can we avail ourselves of their expertise for building communication devices for talking to them? That is, of course, circular, in that the communication needs to be present to receive information about building communication devices. But if we can get to a threshold level of communication, perhaps that is possible.

Not only has Gary Schwartz at the University of Arizona, Tucson, used information provided by mediums to design some of his studies, he has also tried to engage discarnate entities in specific tasks. Here is one of his studies that is reminiscent of Edison's experiment. Schwartz set up an automated system to take photographs in the middle of the night with a light-sensitive camera in a light-tight chamber. There was a 30-minute prebaseline period and 30-minute postbaseline period bracketing a 30-minute experimental session. One of two entities, either the deceased human Suzy Smith or the ostensible angel Sophia, was invited to enter the chamber during the time of the experimental session and asked to "please fill the chamber with your light" (Schwartz, 2021b, p. 207). There were also control sessions in which the protocol was executed without the invitations. The results showed that average pixel brightness was greater for the experimental periods than control periods. The experiment was run again, and the results were replicated. Further analyses revealed that pixel brightness was substantially greater for Sophia than for Smith (Schwartz, 2021b).

As a further evolution of this line of research, Schwartz designed an experiment with several entity tasks, one of which was a binary form of the "I'm Not a Robot" (INR) task. In such a task, there are, for instance, 12 images of parts of vehicles and 12 of parts of animals. Such images are presented to a participant one at a time, with each presentation called a trial, with the instruction to place their hands on the sides of the box in front of them if an image is that of a vehicle, for instance. The box is a light-tight enclosure containing a 5-inch plasma globe and webcam. *Plasma globes*, first invented by Nikola Tesla, are glass spheres filled with noble gases that are excited by sending an alternating current through the globe. Bringing one's hands close to a plasma globe changes the stream of current in a globe. Any changes to the current in the globe can be photographed and analyzed. With the participation of a skilled research medium, Schwartz claimed to have found that the effects of "hypothesized spirit participants" (Schwartz, 2021a, p. 351) on the globe were the same, although with a lesser magnitude, as physical human participants. So, participants were asked to place their "hands" on the sides of the box containing the globe if the answer to a question was yes and to keep their "hands" in their "laps" if the answer was no. The difference between the photographs of the plasma globe between answering a question with hands on the box and answering a question with hands in lap for specific regions of interest for the globe were noted. The data collection and analyses processes were fully automated, removing the need for a human researcher to run the study.

What happened? Four hypothesized spirit participants were invited by a medium to engage in an INR task with 24 trials. There were statistically significant differences for the regions of interest for the hypothesized spirit participants but not for the control trials. The experiment was repeated twice, each time with 20 sessions for each of four different hypothesized spirit participants but using a nonmedium research assistant rather than a medium.

Again, effects were found for the hypothesized spirit participants but not for the control sessions. Of course, despite the language around "spirit participants," Schwartz has acknowledged that the results of an INR task could be due to LAP (Schwartz, 2021a).

ANOMALOUS TELEPHONE CONTACTS

Research projects, such as those of Gary Schwartz, are designed to try to provide evidence for the survival hypothesis. But as we have seen already in this book, direct proof of life after death is difficult to obtain. But is that the most effective strategy for proving survival? What if we were to try an indirect approach? What if we were to figure out how people can communicate with the deceased using their cell phones in the same way that they communicate with the living? What if it were to become normal for everyone to talk, text, and share images with the deceased? And that is just the way life and death are in our everyday lives? In such a scenario, proof of the survival hypothesis could become an afterthought, which some compulsive scientists somewhere can clean up. Given the bizarre range of equipment that has been implicated in ITC, why not just stick with the most straightforward devices, namely, telephones, which are already designed for the purpose of communication, and figure out how to get them to work reliably on demand (cf. Noory & Guiley, 2011)? In fact, the compression algorithms used in cell phones create artifacts during a phone call or recording that could possibly be exploited by discarnate entities as a mechanism for creating anomalous output (S. Rizzo, personal communication, May 20, 2021). So, let us look at ATCs for a bit.

I want to start with a somewhat unusual example dating back to sometime before the mid-1960s, which illustrates several aspects of anomalous phenomena. For the purposes of entertainment, as part of a show, a telephone was brought out on stage, and the audience was told that this was a spirit-phone. This fake spirit-phone was handed around to the audience members with instructions for using it to talk to the dead. A performer, by the name of Marvell, was on the stage with a concealed transmitter that allowed offstage assistants to provide fake messages from the dead for the audience members. One night, an audience member, George Meyers, became so convinced that he was speaking with his deceased wife, Martha, that he asked to have a private session. This was granted for a small fee with Marvell's wife, Rhoda, surreptitiously impersonating Meyers's wife (Cooper, 2011).

Several days later, Meyers showed up at the stage door and requested to speak to Martha on the spirit-phone about an urgent matter. Marvell agreed.

However, he was not certain whether Rhoda was backstage or not to provide the voice of the deceased, so he picked up the phone himself to see if anyone were backstage.

> A female voice answered with, "Hello." He assumed, therefore, that voice was that of Rhoda and went on: "George Meyers is here and wishes to talk to his wife Martha", "Go ahead" replied the voice. (Cooper, 2011, p. 38)

Harry Walters, who worked for the show and has provided the account, said that he knew that all of the stage assistants were gone, so he went back to the dressing room to see what was happening. There was no one there. He put on the headphones himself to listen in. He heard "Hello Martha, this is George" (Cooper, 2011, p. 39). Then:

> At first there was a brief silence and then suddenly a female voice replied. Walters was shocked, as this was just simply not possible. The conversation which took place was very personal and contained specific information, but also addressed domestic problems regarding George and Martha's family. (Cooper, 2011, p. 39)

When the conversation was over and Meyers was gone, Marvell called out to Rhoda, but found Walters instead. They could not believe that what had just happened had happened. They ended up selling the phone to Meyers, who subsequently reported that it only worked when there was a crisis and not when he just wished to visit (Cooper, 2011).

There is a sporadic history over more than a century of deliberate ATCs using "psycho-phones" of various sorts (Cooper, 2011, p. 24; Noory & Guiley, 2011; Cardoso, 2017). In the late 1960s, Scott Rogo and Raymond Bayless started collecting accounts of telephone calls from the dead, analyzed about 50 cases for common features, and published the iconic *Phone Calls From the Dead* (Rogo & Bayless, 1979; see also Cooper, 2011). Callum Cooper was able to retrieve an additional 20 cases that Rogo had collected after publication of the book to add to Cooper's own collection of cases, which he used as material for *Telephone Calls From the Dead* (Cooper, 2011).

What did Cooper find? Most telephone calls from the dead fall into the category of *simple calls*: The phone rings, and

> the dead caller says only a few words and is unresponsive to any questions asked. At this point the caller may say nothing at all and the line will go dead without any sound of the caller hanging up the phone or being cut off. (Cooper, 2011, p. 47)

Prolonged calls, such as the calls in the spirit-phone hoax with Meyers, are longer with an apparently normal conversation between two parties. Common features of ATCs are the sound of static or wind and the caller's voice being distant or faint. A number of investigators have noted the similarity of such qualities of ATCs with those of EVP (Cooper, 2011; Cardoso, 2017). These phone calls can occur at any time after a person's death but include significant anniversaries and what is sometimes referred to as the *crisis period*, the 24-hour period following a person's death. A common conventional explanation for these ATCs is that these are calls to wrong numbers coupled with various degrees of delusional attribution and hallucination (Cooper, 2011).

A student, Durra Kadiragha, approached me after class one day and asked if she could be involved in my research. "How about talking to dead people on cell phones?" I asked. So, we developed an online survey of people who had had anomalous experiences with their cell phones that were suggestive of ADC. The goal of the study was to try to identify some of the psychological parameters that could give rise to such reports. We did not gather detailed information about the devices that participants were using. For the survey, we developed an After-Death Communication Questionnaire consisting of 41 Likert-type items regarding the nature of participants' experiences with their cell phones, their perception of the sender, and the impact that these events had had on the individuals. In addition, we used Carol Ryff's (1989, 2014) 42-item Scales of Psychological Well-Being Questionnaire to see if we could pick up any psychological covariates of participants' experiences. Participants were recruited from the ITC Collective private Facebook group and through researchers' connections, so that there were 21 participants at the time of data analysis with an additional participant who submitted their data afterward (Kadiragha & Baruš, 2021).

When we checked the measure of psychological well-being, we found that, even with a Bonferroni correction, participants scored statistically significantly higher than the norm on the Personal Growth scale of the inventory, indicating that they have a greater interest in self-development and openness to new experiences. Otherwise, there were no differences on any of the scales from the norms, which is consistent with the directive that anomalous experiences be addressed on their own terms rather than through a pathological lens (cf. Evrard, 2017). The most frequent ADC mechanisms were telephone calls, text messages, photos or videos on cell phones, nonvocal sounds during a telephone call, and voice during a telephone call, in that order (Kadiragha & Baruš, 2021). Here are some examples of what participants wrote, reproduced exactly:

> My daughter Angela passed, I was working, phone rang, it was Angela, she said mom it's me, don't hang up!
> —Participant Number 11

It was my friend. It happened twice. Her mother had died. She was texting with her siblings in a three-way text conversation. When she came back to her phone, it said I love you. as if she had texted it herself outgoing but not sent. Many months later, it happened exactly the same while she was texting her siblings. It happened both times while she had set the phone down between texts.

—Participant Number 8

Brother in law was killed in a road traffic accident and 3 days after he was killed his voice was recorded on my home telephone digital answering machine timed and dated. It imprinted on a voice mail left by another caller and she obviously heard the voice coming in live during the call.

—Participant Number 22

My mother, a few days after passing over. But it was not a cell phone; it was a 'phone call' during dream state.

—Participant Number 4

A few weeks after my Son's transcendence i was sitting at the edge of my bed crying, it was about 3 am, lights off, my Sons cell phone starts flashing light and making sounds and when i picked it up there was a video and a song, the video was about an artist who makes figures with sand on a glass surface and the drawings tell a story, the story was about a woman who is sad, sitting and crying until a cross appears and she looks up and she sees Jesus and Jesus consoles [her] and holds her in his hands . . . something like that, immediately i knew it was my Son sending the message, the phone was on top of the night table and no one had touched it, it was not a message from any one, it just started playing

—Participant Number 10

3½ years of weekly computer communication with my deceased wife and spirits surrounding her

—Participant Number 6

Here, we have a range of examples of voice, text, answering machine, dream, spontaneous ADC, and deliberate computer ITC. We cluster-analyzed the items from our After-Death Communication Questionnaire and turned the clusters into scales. For one of the scales, which had good reliability and which we called Spiritual Impact, high scores were associated with not previously having known about these types of experiences, having felt the presence of the deceased, and claiming that "these interactions have changed my life." Participants 10 and 11 had above-average scores on Spiritual Impact (Kadiragha & Baruš, 2021). In other words, ATCs can have a transformative effect on a person's life. The next step in this research would be for someone to follow up on these types of accounts and then bring participants with their cell phones into a lab to see if the relevant physical and psychological parameters could be identified. In any case, we see that telephones, including cell phones, appear in accounts of ADC and ITC.

REFLECTIONS

Can we move the needle on our explanatory dial from LAP to survival? To illustrate the difficulty of doing so, I want to consider another line of research, namely, the investigation of direct mental influence on electronic devices. At the heart of one version of this research is the use of an electronic device, a REG, that creates a binary string of pulses caused by the reverse current across a diode, which is a quantum process and hence truly random. The output from the electronic device is fed into a computer that collects together the pulses, analyzes them, and displays the result as a cumulative deviation graph on the computer screen. The task for a participant is to try to make the graph go high or low. The criterion measure is the difference between equal numbers of high-intention runs and low-intention runs. The expected value is zero (Williams, 2021a). Several decades of this sort of research was done at the Princeton Engineering Anomalies Research (PEAR) laboratory at Princeton University (Dobyns, 2015). To keep this simple, let me just discuss the work of some of my students.

One of my students decided to replicate the PEAR research protocol with a sample of 30 participants in our psychology laboratory. She found no effect and no psychological predictors of the criterion measure. A second student came along. We wondered what would happen if we were to lead participants through a guided imagery exercise, including the evocation of feelings of love, before their engagement with the REG. This time, there was an effect in the intended direction with a sample of 30 participants in the psychology laboratory (Collesso et al., 2021). A third student came along. If positive feelings are correlated with the REG moving in the intended direction, would negative feelings be associated with the REG moving opposite to intention, as suggested by the literature? In collaboration with colleagues at our medical school, this time, we had 30 clinically depressed outpatients as participants who interacted with the REG in the hospital, and the REG moved opposite to intention (Kadler et al., 2022). There are further intricacies to these data, but, overall. there is support for the existence of direct mental influence and correlations of the direction of influence with the emotional states of participants. More generally, the empirical evidence for direct mental influence is robust (Barušs & Mossbridge, 2017).

At one point, in one of the studies, a participant got frustrated because the REG was not behaving, so the participant asked spiritual beings to move the REG. That worked. In a separate study by other researchers investigating mediumship who used a REG running passively, there was a statistically significant deviation of the REG when one particular entity, "being 7," was being channeled but not when any of the other entities were being channeled (Wahbeh et al., 2018, p. 141). So, my question is, At what point does a REG experiment become an ITC experiment? And, indeed, REGs have been used alongside ITC experiments (García, 2017). Or, perhaps more to the point for this chapter, At what point does an ITC experiment become an REG experiment? Is there a difference? Is it just a matter of conceptualizing the causal source of anomalous deviation as a living person versus a dead entity? LAP versus *dead agent psi* [DAP]? In either case, we have direct mental influence, but whose mind is doing the influencing? The one that is alive, or the one that is dead?

In the first REG study of the series by my students, we found a correlation of −.4 between a measure of rationality and the REG running passively in the background without high or low intention. In other words, the more rational you were while the REG was running in the background, the more likely it was to deviate downward. There were no statistically significant correlations with any of the other 20 dimensions of consciousness that were being measured. We had a field of 21 variables, so one of them should have popped out as being statistically significant just by chance. And that is what we reported. However, in the second REG experiment, the same thing happened. We got a −.4 correlation between rationality and the REG running passively in the background and nothing with anything else. Getting the same dimension to pop out of the field of 21 variables in the same direction was statistically significant (Collesso et al., 2021). My lab manager and I stared at the result. What were we supposed to do with that? How was this to be interpreted? Was this a signal in the noise for us from some intelligence somewhere that has the ability to manipulate the REG? Was this our version of being 7?

There is something else that we need to address in the context of LAP. ITC researchers have found that sometimes text and images coming through transcommunication are similar to already existing material among the living. For instance, one of the Bacci voices in Grosseto, Italy, ostensibly said the following in German on November 15, 1986. All three sentences are attributed to the entity:

> What happens at the border of life?–The storeroom is last.–During his later attempts reporting to the other people about his experiences he encounters great difficulties. (Senkowski, 2013, p. 23)

The following passage was delivered as part of a lecture in October 1977 in Recanati, Italy:

> During his later attempts at reporting to other people about his experience he encounters great difficulties—The storeroom of thinking where we had locked

in death now opens up.—What happens at the border of life? (Senkowski, 2013, pp. 23–24)

The first sentence in this second quotation is itself a quotation from a German book (Senkowski, 2013). We have also already seen an example of this duplication in that the acoustic qualities of the EVP word "Chiara" matched the recorded word "Chiara" also in Grosseto. We would not expect the acoustic qualities of someone's voice when they are deceased to match those of their voice while alive unless there were some process by which that effect could be produced. Conscious manipulation on the part of ITC experimenters has been regarded as "too simple an explanation" (Senkowski, 2013, p. 22, italics removed). Querying discarnate communicators themselves about such parallel phenomena has led to contradictory statements (Senkowski, 2013). No one seems to have an adequate explanation. However, these could be examples of magic wand LAP, whereby ITC procedures somehow mine existing information. These also do not rule out survival—for instance, if the disembodied find it easier to use already existing embodied material than creating something new (cf. Senkowski, 2013).

In Chapter 4, we noted that it was not enough to find that good mediums could produce correct information for us to move our explanatory needle from LAP to survival, and we looked at additional parameters, such as motivation on the part of the deceased, the display of skills and mannerisms associated with the deceased, and the nature of the interactions between mediums and discarnates, to discriminate between the two theories. How well do those parameters carry over to ITC? An additional problem here is that the electronic devices act as buffers between the living and the dead so that the dead are another step removed from the living. For instance, when Jennifer Graf's grandfather's dead radio starts to play, all we have is a radio that is playing. Is this just a coincidence? Is this motivation on the part of Jennifer Graf's grandfather to console his granddaughter? Or is it motivation on Graf's part to have some contact with her grandfather that sets off the radio? To my knowledge, no one has tried to systematically analyze the evidence from ITC along these parameters to pull the phenomena cleanly away from LAP.

So, overall, what can we conclude? I think part of our evaluation depends on the credibility that attaches to the different stories and studies. Some readers might find nothing more than interesting anecdotes that prove nothing. One of the criticisms of the ATCs collected by Rogo and Bayless (1979) was that their work was never subjected to peer review and published in academic journals or books (Cooper, 2011). Can we have more thorough documentation and critical scrutiny of the anomalous phenomena? Others might be struck by the ambiguity. For the messier ITC output, just because we cannot rule out pareidolia does not mean that pareidolia is the correct explanation or that pareidolia is not the way that stimuli are meaningfully shaped. However, there are also investigators, such as Bacci, who emerge from the pareidolia fog to apparently produce clearly anomalous phenomena. The needle does move to LAP. I think that most ITC researchers think that establishing the anomalous nature of these phenomena means that they are finished and have proven the existence of life after death, such as George Meek, who called a press conference to announce that life after death had been proven. Can the needle move to survival? I think so, but it means going through the ITC data to extract the features that suggest that there is discarnate agency behind the electronic signal—and to use ingenuity to follow up on Gary Schwartz's (2021a) INR tasks to design studies to see if survival can be peeled away from LAP—and to understand how the REG versus ITC overlap can be resolved, which could entail a more complicated solution than simply teasing them apart. As usual, I leave it to the reader to draw their own conclusions.

6 ANOMALOUS PHYSICAL PHENOMENA

Authors of . . . spiritualist narratives discerned messages in countless everyday phenomena, for example, car license plates, small animals in the yard, songs on the radio, and flickering electrical lights. Thus the dead are attributed the power to manipulate traffic, nature, radio programming, and electricity.
—Susan Kwilecki (2011, p. 233)

At this point in the book, the subject matter gets really messy. I know, I know. It was already messy. I suspect some readers have been tempted on occasion to hurl the book into the fire. But, no, we were just flirting. What is the nature of this augmented messiness? Perhaps the first thing to note is just the difficulty in believing that what ostensibly happened really did happen. Some of these phenomena are probably well past most readers' boggle thresholds. So, the credibility of our discussion critically depends on the documentation for these anomalous phenomena. Alas, we are not just up against sketchy documentation but, in some cases, the perpetration of outright fraud. That fraud apparently includes proof of fraud that is itself fraudulent—in other words, fraudulent proof of fraud where there was no fraud in the first place

---

https://doi.org/10.1037/0000361-006
Death as an Altered State of Consciousness: A Scientific Approach, by I. Baruss
Copyright © 2023 by the American Psychological Association. All rights reserved.

(Fraser, 2020; see also Wehrstein & McLuhan, 2018). The deceased themselves sometimes apparently tell us not to trust them: "The thing that I utter is truth. Take the stuff of the weavin' of these [others] and smite it. If its metal ringeth true, then is it truth. Or if it crumbles into naught by the quirt of thy wit, then 'tis folly" (Patience Worth ostensibly channeled by Pearl Curran, as quoted in Prince, 1927, p. 299). As much as possible, we use material with good documentation to try to verify some of the mind-boggling events.

The second way in which this material gets messier is the disturbing feeling of losing our bearings. The solidity of the ground beneath our feet has a comforting banality to it that can be immediately lost during an earthquake. Suddenly, the unstable ground undermines any sense of security that we may have had. In our case, as the physical world acts up and disregards Newton's staid laws of motion, there goes our sense of comfort.

Third, who we thought we were as psychological beings is challenged. This is perhaps the most disorienting aspect of these phenomena. Who are we? What are we?

And, fourth, any investigation of anomalous phenomena introduces that suspect material into the narrative through a mixture of experiencers, investigators, believers, and skeptics, so that the descriptions and analyses of these phenomena resemble a Jackson Pollock painting, which, to some connoisseurs, might look like paint haphazardly smeared and splattered on a canvas.

So, why am I talking about this? The hope is that if we shake up this material and then allow the bits and pieces to settle, we might be able to see something that could be useful for our purpose of understanding death. As usual, the reader can judge just how well we have succeeded in doing that. Let me start with an example of the sort of material that we are considering. On November 9, 1996, during the Scole experiment, which we discuss in more detail in a bit, a self-illuminated crystal, about 4 inches in length, sat in a Pyrex bowl on a table in an otherwise dark room in a cellar in Scole, England. Arthur Ellison, one of three investigators who was present, was asked, ostensibly by a spirit presence speaking through a medium, to pick up the crystal. This he did, satisfying himself of the crystal's presence. He put it back down. He was then asked to pick it up again. According to Montague Keen, another of the three investigators,

> He picked it up, or he tried to, and his fingers closed right over it. In other words, he could see, and we could see, the essence of it, but not the reality of it. It had . . . dematerialized. Then he was asked to pick it up again and it rematerialized in his hand. Now, this dumbfounded him. This is what Arthur Ellison, after years and years of investigation, finally convinced him that this was real, because it couldn't have been faked in any way. And he had . . . his head right over the top of the bowl in order to ensure that no hand or no

instrument could interfere with it. (Montague Keen, as quoted in *The Afterlife Investigations* [Coleman, 2011], Disc 2, minute 110)

Then the experiment was repeated for Keen and also for David Fontana, to whom we were introduced in the previous chapter and who was the third of the investigators. We have apparent dematerialization in the sense that the crystal can be seen but, for a while, it cannot be touched and picked up. There is a discrepancy in documentation about the order of events with Robin Foy, who, together with Sandra Foy, was managing the session, writing that all of the investigators first picked up the crystal, then tried to pick up the dematerialized version, then the rematerialized crystal (Foy, 2008). See? We already have a problem with documentation. I have argued elsewhere for the reason to trust the first account over the second (Barušs, 2021), although neither order vitiates the striking nature of the experience.

So, what is the ground that we are covering here? In Chapter 4 about mediumship, we restricted ourselves almost entirely to mental mediumship, whereby, typically, a medium purportedly converses with a discarnate entity in their imagination. In the case of physical mediumship, an entity ostensibly takes over a medium's body during a séance and, using the body, interacts with those who are present. Not only is that not just a mental conversation, but with physical mediumship, anomalous physical phenomena can occur. For instance, voices can appear to originate from an unoccupied point in space, known as direct voice, carrying on meaningful conversations with those who are present (S. Alexander, 2010/2020). Lights of various sorts can appear, move around, and disappear. Furniture can move without anyone touching it. Knocking, whispers, and singing can be heard. Those who are present can feel breezes or touching (Haraldsson, 2018). *Apports*, objects that apparently arrive out of nowhere, such as a 4-inch-tall pink, plastic pig, can appear and disappear. Or, there can be materializations of hands that can be touched and sometimes seen in red light (S. Alexander, 2010/2020).

Unusual physical events need not be confined to a séance room but can occur more generally in different situations. In that case, we call this *poltergeist activity*. The word *poltergeist* literally means "noisy ghost" (Colvin, 2015, para. 1), although "ghosts" may or may not be the likely source of the unusual events. If mediums embody entities during a séance, then we need to consider what happens if those entities appear to have their own agendas that interfere with human well-being. In other words, what about unwanted intrusions? But I also want to flip the discussion and consider cases in which physical mediumship appears to be instrumental in physical healing. At the end, let us see if anything has settled down after our shakedown.

Where do the phenomena considered in this chapter lie on our explanatory materialism–LAP [living agent psi]–survival dial? For some readers, perhaps, we will not make it past the materialist setting. For instance, we might try to replace explanations of being possessed by entities with dissociative identity disorder (DID), whereby different alternate personalities take turns manifesting through a person's body (American Psychiatric Association, 2013). Thus, physical mediumship, poltergeist activity, and possession would be explained as the presence of an alternate personality entirely made from the fabric of a person's own psyche (Braude, 2003; Fraser, 2020). We saw at the end of the previous chapter that there is evidence for the direct influence of the mind on physical manifestation. So, we could explain any unusual physical events, if we acknowledge that there are any, as *recurrent spontaneous psychokinesis* (RSPK), the direct influence of physical manifestation by a living agent. In other words, we get to LAP. However, in a study with 236 participants with DID (mentioned in Chapter 4), 29% had an alter that was "identified as a demon" and 21% had an alter that was a "dead relative" (Ross et al., 1989, p. 415). So, which is it? Are the demon and dead relative alters—just aspects of a person's own psyche—or are they demons and dead relatives that have displaced a person's psyche (Pederzoli et al., 2022; Maraldi et al., 2021; Gallagher, 2020; see also Crooks, 2018)? Or, is there some other explanation? Can RSPK account for all of the unusual physical events, such as the dematerialization in the Scole experiment? Can we reject LAP and accept survival? Let us consider the details to see what happens to our explanatory dial.

PHYSICAL MEDIUMSHIP

In Chapter 4, we saw the inception of Spiritualism as a movement focused on ostensible communication with the deceased. In the late 1960s, Stewart Alexander became interested in Spiritualism and, together with his brother, visited several Spiritualist churches, which left them feeling disappointed. "The generally disenchanting proceedings could best be summed up as semi-religious services with a demonstration of mental mediumship tagged on and a cup of tea to follow" (S. Alexander, 2010/2020, p. 4). One evening, at the church, they were invited to a *home circle*, whereby physical mediumship is practiced privately in a person's home. They went, but that did not go well either, and the brothers left. Subsequently, while intoxicated during a Christmas party, the medium from that circle entertained the partygoers with his impressions of the same deceased Hollywood actors who had ostensibly been speaking through him during his séances. This led to the collapse of the home circle (S. Alexander, 2010/2020, p. 4). Over the years in different circles, Alexander heard many discourses that were "an absolute insult to intelligence and to the Spirit world that they were supposed to represent" (S. Alexander, 2010/2020, p. 20). It would appear that considerable nonsense can go on during mediumship (see also Braude, 2016; Nahm, 2016).

Eventually, Stewart Alexander decided to start his own home circle, meeting once a week on Monday evenings. It took him 2 hours on those evenings to completely black out his front room. According to Alexander, complete blackness was a necessary condition for the manifestation of physical phenomena. His understanding was that the extrusion of ectoplasm from some of the orifices of living beings and, in particular, the medium, was necessary, and that could only occur safely in complete darkness (S. Alexander, 2010/2020). The notion of "ectoplasm" has been attributed to French physiologist Charles Richet, who thought that a medium could project a self-organizing force outside of their body in the same way that an amoeba could project pseudopods. He believed that it is this mechanical force that is responsible for producing the physical phenomena during a séance (Alvarado, 2015). The concern is that if any light were to be introduced into the room at all, with the possible exception of low levels of red light, then the ectoplasm would snap back into the body, harming the medium to the point of possibly killing them (Zammit & Zammit, 2013). Alexander also made a funnel about a half-meter in length, called a *trumpet*, which he placed on the carpet in the center of the circle. The idea is that the ectoplasm levitates the trumpet, which moves around the room and is ostensibly used by discarnate entities to communicate with individual sitters (S. Alexander, 2010/2020). Alexander sat for about an hour with his home circle once a week for "many months" (S. Alexander, 2010/2020, p. 9). Nothing happened.

One night, Stewart Alexander's brother invited Alexander to a sitting with him. In this case, a dim red light was used. For 58 minutes, nothing occurred. Then Alexander heard a voice say repeatedly in his left ear, "Turn out the light—continue to sit" (S. Alexander, 2010/2020, p. 9). When his brother asked whether they should end the sitting, Alexander told him to turn out the light and to sit for a while longer. Once it was dark, Alexander became aware of an external presence approaching him. We already referred to this experience in Chapter 4. Alexander said that

> as it forced itself to merge with my very being, every nerve and every muscle in my entire body began to react violently, and it set in motion uncontrollable spasms and tremors. At the same time my consciousness seemed quickly to locate itself outside, behind and to the left of my body and from that position I observed my mouth fall open and with a rush the following words issued forth: "I come speak, brother, sister", every word of which I heard very clearly. (S. Alexander, 2010/2020, p. 10)

This was to be the only time that Alexander experienced fear in a séance. As a result of subsequent sittings, Alexander was to identify the source of those words as a spirit guide named White Feather. As White Feather approached Alexander, Alexander's "left hand would immediately begin to curl in upon itself as if grossly deformed, and then the remainder of the entrancement process would quickly and forcefully follow" (S. Alexander, 2010/2020, p. 11). He felt that his "conscious self became submerged and dissociated from [his] body" (S. Alexander, 2010/2020, p. 11) and that he could not affect whatever occurred.

For a long time, Alexander questioned whether White Feather was an independent entity or just an aspect of his own psyche. Then, while at someone else's séance, he heard White Feather begin to speak. After a while, Alexander interrupted him and asked if he had had a physical deformity while alive. "Do you mean my left hand?" (S. Alexander, 2010/2020, p. 15) was the response. This answer had a profound impact on Alexander, who was now convinced that White Feather was an "autonomous individual" (S. Alexander, 2010/2020, p. 15) and not just a product of his own psyche. It was at that point that Alexander committed himself to the development of his mediumship skills. I want to note that having a communicator speak through different mediums at different times has been suggested as one of the criteria for determining the existence of objective entities (Pederzoli et al., 2022). Apparently, that is the heuristic that Alexander used to draw his conclusion.

Thirteen years after first sitting in a circle, Stewart Alexander had a breakthrough experience. On finishing a séance, and with just two of the circle members left after tea and biscuits, Alexander became aware of White Feather returning. Then, he remembers nothing until he awoke some moments later. He was told that, while in the unconscious state, White Feather had requested that the light be turned off, the trumpet had levitated, and White Feather's voice had emanated from the trumpet. In subsequent séances, the trumpet apparently sailed around the room, as evidenced by the luminous tape around its wide end, with spoken words coming from it. There were instances of other anomalous phenomena as well, such as the apparent levitation of a sitter along with their chair, as Alexander's mediumship continued to develop (S. Alexander, 2010/2020).

After some 40 years of sitting, Stewart Alexander was joined by Leslie Kean, an American journalist and author of *Surviving Death: A Journalist Investigates Evidence for an Afterlife* (Kean, 2017). It was clear to her from her investigation of research concerning mediumship that, at least in some cases, anomalous phenomena reported during physical mediumship were genuine. Her question was: "Were the communications really from deceased people?" (Kean, 2020, p. 319) or was there some other explanation for them? In other words, is this LAP or DAP (dead agent psi)?

During a séance in 2015, Kean was sitting to the right beside Alexander, with her left hand on top of Alexander's right hand. Alexander was tied to his chair to ensure that he was not the cause of any physical phenomena that occurred during a séance. With her right hand, Kean could feel the cable tie around Alexander's right wrist, holding his arm to the arm of his chair. Then, "with a quick snapping sound," Alexander's right arm "flew upward" (Kean, 2017, p. 329), taking her left arm with it. When she checked with her right hand, the cable tie was still intact, fastened to the arm of the chair.

During a separate occasion, on May 20, 2019, Stewart Alexander was sitting in his chair in the corner of the room, which was designated as a "cabinet" on account of the presence of curtains, parted in the middle, which could be pulled across the front of the medium (Kean, 2017). The curtains were closed briefly. When they opened, there was apparently a materialized form of a spirit entity, Dr. Barnett, who emerged from the cabinet. That Alexander, who was again strapped down with cable ties, was still in the cabinet was evident from his "luminous knee pads" (Kean, 2020, p. 330). Dr. Barnett ostensibly usually spoke through a "voice box he constructs out of ectoplasm" (Kean, 2020, p. 330). According to Kean (2020),

> The materialised Dr. Barnett walked out of the cabinet and came over to me, touched my hair, and then placed both his large hands on top of my head, bouncing them up and down repeatedly. . . . His soft but clear voice was inches away—Stewart was secured to his chair in the cabinet. I recognized the voice of the Dr. Barnett I had heard many times before from his independent voicebox. (p. 330)

Is such materialization proof for the existence of life after death? "Or does it mean something else?" (Kean, 2020, p. 331). Kean says that she does not know.

POLTERGEISTS

Anomalous phenomena are not always contained within the physical space in which they have been known to occur but can carry over to other contexts. When the phenomena follow a person, this has sometimes been known as the *hitchhiker effect* (Kelleher, 2022). For instance, one evening, during a session with Stewart Alexander, the participants sat in the dark talking to one another. Nothing happened. No trumpet movement. No voices coming from the trumpet. They ended the circle and turned on the light. There, on the floor in front of each of the participants was "a little plastic animal about two inches (5 cm) in height—dogs, cats, sheep etc.—a gift, no doubt, in recognition of each sitter's patience and dedication" (S. Alexander, 2010/2020, p. 29). Everyone had received a plastic animal except for the host, who had worked so hard to black out a room once a week for 2 years. However, when she awoke in the morning, there was a pink, plastic pig on top of a book beside her bed. At the next circle meeting, one of the sitters identified the pig as his; it had gone missing the previous week, but he graciously allowed the host to keep it. Then the pig disappeared and could not be found despite thorough searching.

Several weeks later, a carpet fitter was installing new carpet for the host when he noticed the trumpet, which led to a discussion about séances. The carpet fitter told her that several weeks previously, he had awakened to find a pink, plastic pig on his bedside table. The host explained her experience of losing a pink, plastic pig and said that her pig had had "a distinctive mark at its base" (S. Alexander, 2010/2020, p. 30). The carpet fitter brought the pig the following day, and it was the same pig. About 8 years later, the original owner of the pink, plastic pig called the host to ask if she had realized that she no longer had the pig. He had had new kitchen cupboards installed and, on opening one of them, found the pink, plastic pig.

The traveling pig is an example of what has sometimes been called *just one of those things* (JOTT), to which I also refer to as *anomalous object displacement*. Several categories of JOTT have been identified. First, the *Comeback JOTT*, whereby an object disappears, cannot be found despite considerable searching, and then is found in exactly the place where it was supposed to be. Second, a *Walkabout JOTT*, whereby an object starts in one place and ends up somewhere else. The traveling plastic pig is an example of a Walkabout JOTT. Third, a *Flyaway JOTT*, whereby an object permanently disappears. Raymond Bayless, whom we met in Chapter 5, was giving a painting lesson to a student when a large paintbrush clattered to the linoleum-covered floor and was never found again. Fourth, a *Windfall JOTT* is a JOTT that ends up benefiting the finder of the object. In one case, the spark plug of a motorbike was oiling up, and as the rider rolled onto a side road, wondering what to do next, he noticed a brand new one lying in the gutter. He was able to install it and continue his journey. A Windfall JOTT can also be regarded as an example of synchronicity. And it is the Windfall JOTT that ties these experiences to survival. A person who has had such an experience can feel as though there is someone "out there" looking out for them. And it is the Walkabout JOTT that is associated with the early stages of poltergeist activity (Fraser, 2020).

Poltergeist phenomena are characterized by "anomalous disturbances arising in connection with a particular place or person" (Colvin, 2015, para. 1). What kind of disturbances? In a study of 500 poltergeist cases, small objects moved in 64% of them; large objects, in 36%; rapping sounds could be heard in 48%; vocal sounds, in 26%; and humanlike apparitions appeared in 29% of the cases. Sometimes, this collection of events appears to be associated with a particular person, in which case the label "poltergeist" is used (Fraser, 2020) both to designate that person as well as to designate the alleged "ghost." Otherwise, the phenomena are conceptualized as RSPK (Kruth & Joines, 2016). If the events attach to a location, then the phenomena are called *hauntings* (Fraser, 2020, p. 3). The presence of apparitions suggests that these phenomena are not just RSPK, but what, exactly, are the apparitions?

The notion of *Haunted People Syndrome* has been proposed to designate a "condition" whereby a person makes paranormal attributions about a specific collection of subjective and objective events. Subjective events include "sensed presences, hearing voices, unusual somatic or emotional manifestations, and perceptions of human forms" (O'Keeffe et al., 2019, p. 911). Objective events consist of "apparent object movements, malfunctioning of electrical or mechanical equipment, and inexplicable percussive sounds like raps or knockings" (O'Keeffe et al., 2019, p. 911). The specific attributions can change depending on the sociocultural context in which the "entity encounter experiences" (O'Keeffe et al., 2019, p. 911) occur so that they can be interpreted, for instance, as encounters with angels or with extraterrestrial beings.

The Sauchie case is a famous example of poltergeist activity, which was investigated by George Owen. Eleven-year-old Virginia Campbell was separated from her family in Ireland and sent to live with an older brother in Sauchie, Scotland, a situation about which she was considerably upset. On November 22, 1960, what sounded like a bouncing ball could be "heard in Virginia's bedroom, on the stairs, and in the living-room" (Irwin, 1994, p. 191). The following evening, a heavy sideboard in the living room moved about 5 inches (13 centimeters) before returning to its original position, as witnessed by Campbell's brother and his wife. Later that evening, loud knocks came from Campbell's bedroom. A minister was called over, and he thought that the sound was coming from the headboard of Campbell's bed. As he was trying to determine the source of the sound, a linen chest weighing about 50 pounds (23 kilograms) rocked sideways and moved "jerkily along parallel to the bed and back again" (Irwin, 1994, p. 191). At the suggestion that Campbell's niece should sleep with her, "there was a burst of violent knocking" (Irwin, 1994, p. 191).

The following evening, the minister came again, bringing a physician with him. There were more raps, more rocking by the linen chest, Virginia Campbell's pillow rotated 60 degrees beneath her head, and the physician saw a "curious rippling movement pass across the pillow on which Virginia's head lay" (Irwin, 1994, p. 191). The following day at school, Campbell's teacher saw her trying to hold down the lid of her desk, which kept straining to rise, and an empty desk behind her, which rose about an inch (2½ centimeters) off the floor before settling back down. Several other anomalous incidents occurred both at home and at school before the phenomena subsided over the course of about 3 months (Irwin, 1994). Of note in this case, the phenomena appeared to be associated with Virginia Campbell, so this is an example of poltergeist or RSPK activity, and she was frustrated, which could be relevant to the production of these types of phenomena.

George Owen moved to Canada, where he founded the Toronto Society for Psychical Research in 1970 (Willin, 2021; Owen, 1976) and, in 1973, began an experiment, the Philip experiment, to see whether a group of people could produce a collective hallucination of an imaginary ghost as a way to better understand these types of anomalous phenomena. The participants, eventually eight in number, none of whom claimed to have any psychic abilities, were drawn from a range of vocations. They invented a story about an aristocratic Englishman named Philip who lived with his wife in Diddington Manor during the mid-1600s. However, he was enamored by another woman whom he moved into his gatehouse. This did not end well: The other woman was burned at the stake, and Philip hurled himself to his death from the battlements of his manor. The only nonfictional aspect of the story was Diddington Manor, which actually does exist in England. The group met once a week and "trained themselves to concentrate upon Philip's materializing" (Owen, 1976, p. 20). After a year of sitting, nothing interesting had happened.

On reading about research by Kenneth Batcheldor and others who had investigated séance phenomena, the members of the group changed their strategy to adopt the more lighthearted style of the British groups. They engaged in casual conversation, told jokes, sang songs, recited poetry, and thought about producing an apparition of Philip. On the third or fourth session with this new approach, the members of the group felt a vibration in the card table on which their hands were resting. This vibration became more pronounced until all of the members of the group could hear what sounded as though "someone had struck the table a light blow" (Owen, 1976, p. 26). No one sitting around the table had actually expected anything like this. "The next thing that happened, to their surprise, was that the table started to slide about the floor. It moved quite rapidly, in random fashion, and without any apparent purpose" (Owen, 1976, p. 27). One of the members asked out loud whether Philip was doing this. There was a loud rap from the table. They agreed that one rap would mean "yes" and two raps would mean "no." In this way, communication was established with the fictional Philip.

In the following weeks, the group found that for questions to which they had unanimous agreement regarding the answers, they got loud raps. For questions without unanimous agreement, there would be delays before the raps. In one case, for a question with an ambivalent answer, "there were quite violent scratching sounds, as if Philip himself was registering disapproval" (Owen, 1976, p. 34). Film footage from some of their sessions exists and shows anomalous rapping and table movements (Brims, 1974). I have viewed the film footage and have frequently shown it to my students. It can be seen that the table moves dramatically on its own, at one point tipping upward on two legs at a steep angle. It is clear that these events are anomalous.

With the Philip experiment, we see some of the canonical phenomena associated with poltergeists. In this case, we have more than just the attachment of attributions to ambiguous stimuli, so this is not just Haunted People Syndrome. We actually have definitive anomalous events. So, we can move our needle to LAP. But does the Philip experiment rule out survival? Well, no, for several reasons. Just because fictional ghosts can do what real ghosts are said to do does not mean that there are no real ghosts. Or, more precisely, just because communication with fictional ghosts is just psychokinetic activity produced by the living does not mean that all apparent communication is psychokinetic activity produced by the living. Furthermore, we can turn the Philip phenomena around from LAP to survival. In some Tibetan traditions, a person can ostensibly, through the concentration of thought, create a *tulpa*, a visually and somatically materialized thoughtform. Such a tulpa can apparently become progressively autonomous and difficult to control by its creator (David-Neel, 1929/1971). The participants in the Philip experiment wondered whether they had created a tulpa, a semi-autonomous entity with which they interacted, which was responsible for the anomalous effects that they witnessed. So, we are back to deciding between LAP and survival.

THE SCOLE EXPERIMENT

We opened this chapter with the experiences of three investigators of the Scole experiment. They apparently witnessed the dematerialization of a crystal during a séance in a cellar room in a house in Scole, England, which was attended also by Robin Foy and Sandra Foy, who managed the séances, as well as two mediums, Alan and Diana (M. Keen et al., 1999). I want to return to this example because of the complexity of the phenomena that occurred. However, the Scole experiment has evoked considerable controversy (M. Keen, 2001), so I want to make a few comments about its legitimacy. First, the documentation of the events that occurred in this experiment is good, with not only at least one of the three primary investigators having been present for 30 of 36 sessions from October 2, 1995, to August 16, 1997, but a number of other investigators as well having witnessed the events at different times (M. Keen et al., 1999). So, there is little middle ground between fraud and legitimacy (M. Keen et al., 1999). Second, many of the phenomena were repeated at a series of séances in someone else's converted garage in California, making it unlikely that elaborate technological equipment for creating the effects was concealed somewhere in the Scole cellar, equipment that has never been found despite extensive searching (M. Keen et al., 1999; Coleman, 2011). Third, the Scole phenomena are striking but are consistent with what we have already encountered in this book, so there is no reason, prima facie, to discount them just because they are strange.

What we have is another home circle, this time, meeting twice a week since early 1993 in a cellar in a house in Scole. Their purpose was to develop "a new type of spirit energy, one which neither affected the health and safety of mediums nor involved the creation and manipulation of ectoplasmic forms" (M. Keen et al., 1999, p. 166). After considerable negotiation, three members of the British-based Society for Psychical Research (West, 2015) were invited to a sitting on October 2, 1995. During that and ensuing séances, the participants, wearing luminous wristbands, sat in the dark around a circular table that had luminous table strips; the base of the table was sectioned into quadrants, with boards extending almost to the edge of the table and on which were placed a number of crystals. The proceedings began by turning out the light, invoking the assistance of the "spirit Team" (M. Keen et al., 1999, p. 180), and playing music to accompany a meditative effort to create a bridge with the other side. As this occurred, the two mediums ostensibly entered trance states. The first to speak was Diana, who gave voice to Manu, who appeared to act as an impresario for the spirit team, and then to the pseudonymous Mrs. Emily Bradshaw. The two channeled entities welcomed the participants, made remarks about those who were present, and provided an outline of the activities that were to follow. A conversation ensued between the sitters and the channeled entities. This was followed by the occurrence of various phenomena. Sessions lasted from 2 to 2½ hours and were audiotaped and transcribed. In addition, Montague Keen made shorthand notes, as best he could in the dark, during some of the sessions.

Even though the participants sat in the dark, the room was illuminated some of the time by lights that appeared to have several anomalous features. For instance, it was one of the lights that illuminated from within the previously mentioned dematerializing crystal in the Pyrex bowl. At other times, single lights darted at high velocity or formed perfect circles "inconsistent with manual manipulation" (M. Keen et al., 1999, p. 190), sometimes with parts of the circle switched off. Sometimes a light made sounds on striking surfaces as a pinpoint of light. The lights could appear to one investigator but not another. Sometimes they created a "diffused glow" (M. Keen et al., 1999, p. 191) that was sufficient to illuminate whatever was in their vicinity, such as Montague Keen's notebook. They could respond to requests by investigators, such as to alight on parts of their bodies, thereby illuminating them. They could enter an investigator's body through the chest and exit from some other part, with the investigator subsequently reporting having had interoceptive sensations. These were some of the light phenomena. There were others. A professional magician with 40 years of experience attended a number of Scole sessions and could find no apparatus necessary for creating the observed effects, nor did he know of any means by which he or other magicians he knew could reproduce even just the lighting effects, let alone the other phenomena that he witnessed (Coleman, 2011).

It was during the Scole experiment that the germanium device mentioned in the previous chapter was built and used in an effort to allow for communication between the living and the deceased without the need for mediums. During a séance on September 14, 1996, one of the ostensible spirits asked that a small germanium plate be brought to a séance, which led to further instructions in other séances for building the device. The instructions were accompanied by a wiring diagram that showed up on a strip of film on January 11, 1997. Over the course of the investigation, 15 rolls of film that had been left unopened nonetheless were found to have writing and images on them. Some of the content on the films is controversial because it was found to be similar to existing documents and previously published material (M. Keen et al., 1999). In the previous chapter, we already saw the occurrence of such parallel phenomena with instrumental transcommunication (ITC) for which there was no good explanation. However, here, we just need to refer to the wiring diagram, which appears not to have been copied from elsewhere. Arthur Ellison, who had been a professor of electrical engineering, was concerned that outdated technologies were being suggested and asked that the "germanium rectifier" be replaced with "a diode version containing silicon" (M. Keen et al., 1999, p. 265). He was corrected by an ostensible spirit who insisted that this was not to be regarded as a rectifier. Ellison did build the germanium device to the spirit team's specifications.

During the final session that the investigators were allowed to attend, before the commencement of the séance, the germanium device was plugged into a cassette recorder from which the microphone had been removed. That machine was controlled by David Fontana throughout the sitting with his blank cassette inserted. The start button on that machine was pressed simultaneously with the button on the machine that was being used to record the sitting. This was followed by a conversation between the ostensible entities and living participants about the effort to communicate through the new device. The channeled entity, Mrs. Emily Bradshaw, said that Montague would have a treat. At first, all that could be heard was white noise, but then the sound of piano music, ostensibly played by the composer, could be heard emanating from the cassette recorder with the germanium device attached. Montague Keen recognized it almost immediately as Rachmaninoff's *Second Piano Concerto*, a piece that held particular emotional significance for him, something that he had not ever shared with any of those present in the room. The music faded a bit, and the participants could hear a voice-over in English, although they could not make out what was being said. Then "the second movement of the concerto . . . returned to fuller power" (M. Keen et al., 1999, p. 299). When the tape of the microphoneless machine was played back after the séance, the investigators could hear the concerto, the voice-over, and a lot of white noise, but nothing of what had transpired in the séance room. The tape on the other cassette recorder had registered everything that had happened in the room, including the concerto, the voice-over, and white noise.

After this session, the Scole group closed itself to outside investigators, who nonetheless tried to negotiate continued observation of the séances with better controls in place to eliminate alternate hypotheses. For instance, although it was unlikely, skeptics argued that the sounds on the modified cassette recorder could have been the result of radio signals that had been beamed to the room, and the investigators wanted to repeat the experiment with proper screening in place to rule out that explanation. The investigators were also frustrated that they were not allowed to videotape anything and that they were not even allowed to use thermal imaging and infrared cameras in the dark (M. Keen et al., 1999). After closing the sittings to visitors, the Scole group tried themselves to develop video techniques that could be used for communication purposes, but they were ostensibly told by the spirit team not to share any of their recordings. In some cases, they have claimed to have received video images synchronized with sound from the cassette recorder with the germanium device attached. Their final sitting was on November 6, 1998 (Foy, 2008). Having discussed the Scole experiment in person with Montague Keen, I see no reason to doubt the genuineness of the phenomena despite the difficulty of explaining them.

POSSESSION

We have been largely considering the physical aspects of the phenomena discussed in this chapter and their unsettling nature. I want to turn now to the psychological dimension. We have Stewart Alexander's description of the manner in which he experienced what he perceived to be the approach of White Feather, a deceased spirit communicator who, at one time, had been alive as a human being. In the Scole experiment, we have Manu and Mrs. Emily Bradshaw ostensibly taking over the medium Diana, and other communicators occupying Alan (M. Keen et al., 1999). These are cases of deliberately cultivated Haunted People Syndrome. There is an apparent psychological takeover with the normally inhabiting consciousness being displaced, frequently in such a way that a person has no memory for the events that occurred during the time of possession. Let us suspend our pathomorphic tendency and consider that there could be psychologically healthy, if sometimes difficult, expressions of such possession (Delmonte et al., 2016; Ribáry et al., 2017; Maraldi et al., 2021; Pederzoli et al., 2022). If so, then, moving from LAP to DAP, who exactly are these possessing entities?

In cases of possession, we typically assume that whatever it is that has been encountered is a person who was once alive. In Chapter 4, I mentioned the medium Jamie Butler, who channels the deceased Erik Medhus. Butler has had the ability to encounter a spirit entity in the way that she would encounter someone who is alive. So, she sees Medhus the way that he used to look, and she translates word for word what he says. This caused some hesitation for her at first due to Medhus's frequent use of profanity, to which she had to become acclimated. Occasionally, Butler would engage in trance channeling, whereby she allowed Medhus to use her body. According to Medhus, as determined by what he has said through Butler, Butler's grandfather showed him "how to change her energy pattern to enter her body through the side of her neck" (Medhus, 2015, p. 157). That that's the easiest way in. One of Butler's rules has been that Medhus must leave her body in better shape than he has found it, so he has had to pay attention to her state of health on any given day. Medhus says that when Butler has left her body, it is "kind of like this cocoon of white light that moves out of her upper back, neck, and head" (Medhus, 2015, p. 157). He says that he does not know where she goes. Once he is inside her body, he tries to mimic her behavior.

He also has the visceral sensations of her heartbeat, sweaty palms, and emotions. When he looks out through her eyes, he can "still see everybody, but . . . also see their energy" (Medhus, 2015, p. 158), which is the way he assumes that Butler sees people. He does not like her small voice because he wants to sound like a real "dude" (Medhus, 2015, p. 158, italics removed).

Erik Medhus had been close to his mother, Elisa, before his death, and they appeared to reestablish their relationship through the mediumship of Jamie Butler. Medhus's first experience of being inside Butler was at an event about channeling him. Elisa was at the event, but in a back row. So, Medhus claims that he got up and ran to her:

> I wanted to hug my mom, so I moved Jamie's arms and threw them around her. The arms moved, but they didn't go through her. They stopped on the surface of her body, and I wasn't used to that. When I hugged her, she felt so little. I liked feeling her touch and smelling her hair like I did when I was alive. I just wanted to savor it. It had been a long time. (Medhus, 2015, p. 158)

According to the deceased Medhus, that was a significant moment for him and his mother. This ostensible interaction is reminiscent of the behavior of Carter, the transplant recipient, whom we met in Chapter 3, who claimed that it had been Jerry, the donor, who had been the one to run up to Jerry's father in church. In both cases, there was an apparent possessing entity using someone else's body to physically meet a parent who had been emotionally close to them.

In this chapter, we have also discussed a fictional ghost, Philip, who could have just been a cognitive device to enhance psychokinetic ability, or a tulpa, a semiautonomous thoughtform, which interacted with the members of the Toronto Society for Psychical Research. How similar is such an entity, if it exists, to a human being? How similar is such an entity, if it exists, to a deceased human being? In particular, how developed is its memory, self-identity, and volition? But this just brings us back to the question of what else is out there. Here is a slightly longer list than the one we considered in Chapter 4: deceased human beings; nonhuman beings of both low and high intelligence; angels; djinn; demons; interdimensional aliens (Barušs, 2014); "Men in Black (MIBs), shamanic spirit guides, and folklore-type beings" (O'Keeffe et al., 2019, pp. 911–912); divine beings of various sorts; "master teachers . . . spirit guides . . . tricksters . . . wraiths . . . what most people would call Satan" (Stavis, 2018, p. 63, capitalization removed); and so on. Much of possession, such as the cases that we have reviewed, appears to be benign (Delmonte et al., 2016; Maraldi et al., 2021). However, there are also more problematical instances. Sometimes the expression *astral goons* has been used to refer to bullying entities that have nothing useful to contribute but simply seek to take advantage of a person or torment them for the sake of their own pleasure (Barušs, 1996, p. 140). According to some theorists, all intrusions are necessarily demonic in nature and harmful to the person for whom they occur (Crooks, 2018). *Demonic possession*, as such, has been defined as "the supposed invasion of the body by an evil spirit or devil that gains control of the mind or soul, producing mental disorder, physical illness, or criminal behavior" and has traditionally been treated with "ritual exorcism" (American Psychological Association, n.d.-a). Let me give an example of demonic possession.

Richard Gallagher is a psychiatrist who has worked with priests to try to help people who appear to be possessed. He has claimed that what he has witnessed is clearly not just DID (Gallagher, 2020; see also Allison, 1980). Other scholars agree that there is a distinctive *possession syndrome* with its own constellation of symptoms (Ferracuti & Sacco, 1996; McNamara, 2011a, 2011b): For Gallagher, some of the classic signs of possession include the ability to speak foreign languages that the possessed person does not know, demonstrate "supernormal strength" (Gallagher, 2020, p. 45), or display knowledge of information that has not been acquired through ordinary sensory channels. According to Gallagher, human beings do not have such abilities; they would belong to a "foreign evil spirit" (Gallagher, 2020, p. 45). We could, of course, argue that anomalous information acquisition is a normal skill at which people can be better or worse and is not itself symptomatic of pathological possession.

Gallagher has described some of the events that occurred for one of his patients who was devoted to Satan and underwent several exorcisms to try to rid herself of the possession. At one point, while speaking on the telephone to a priest about an upcoming exorcism for his patient, a different voice came on the line, cursing and threatening the priest. Then, during an exorcism carried out by eight people, the patient entered a trance with a voice arrogantly telling those in attendance that they had no right to try to liberate the woman and bullying them with "complaints, blasphemies, and boasts" (Gallagher, 2020, p. 63). The exorcism proceeded "for at least two hours" (Gallagher, 2020, p. 63). The woman struggled against three people holding her back. Then she levitated about a foot out of her chair for about a half hour and had to be held down by all of those present to prevent her from going up even farther. The woman "writhed in pain upon any contact with holy water" (Gallagher, 2020, p. 65) and spoke in languages she did not know, including speaking articulately in Latin, which the priest did know well, and the room became frigidly cold, then stiflingly hot. However, after several exorcism attempts, the woman gave up trying to rid herself of the possession but did give Gallagher permission to talk about her case to warn others who may be vulnerable (Gallagher, 2020).

According to Gallagher (2020), possession, although genuine, is rare. On the other hand, according to Rachel Stavis, a nondenominational exorcist, 99% of the population has entities attached to them, most of whom are unaware of the attachment. How does she know? Because she claims that she can see the entities that have burrowed into people's bodies and are feeding on their negative emotions. For Stavis, a range of entities can affect people, from fairly innocuous ones to the truly terrifying. For instance, what she has called *tricksters* can show up as an archangel, a deceased person, an imaginary friend, or as a favorite creature, such as a unicorn. Tricksters make people feel safe and encourage their hosts to befriend them as they suck the life out of them. Stavis has given numerous examples of improved well-being following her exorcisms (Stavis, 2018).

There was considerable interest in exorcism as a therapeutic strategy in North America in the mid-1970s, even though conventional evidence for actual possession was slim (Cuneo, 2001). It could be tempting to blame a malevolent entity for one's addictions, or depression, or anxiety, or whatever, and have it cathartically removed through an exorcism rather than engage in difficult psychotherapeutic work (Baruss & Mossbridge, 2017). This is not to say that various degrees of attachment are not possible, just that it is unlikely that all cases of psychological distress are the result of attachments.

At a more sinister level, there appears to be a contagion effect, in that exposure to poltergeist activity can sometimes lead to the propagation of health issues and disturbing events. Health issues can include autoimmune diseases, which we have already found to be associated with mediumship. Disturbing events can include the sound of loud footsteps, the appearance of wolflike or other creatures, and being "attacked by blue and red orbs" (Kelleher, 2022, p. 19). Such hitchhiker effects have been authenticated by investigators working for the U.S. Defense Intelligence Agency and appear to have been underreported (Kelleher, 2022; Lacatski et al., 2021).

There can also apparently be an effect opposite to malevolent influence, whereby physical mediumship and possession appear to have beneficial effects, such as healing. For instance, in the Scole experiment, a participant at one of the California sittings claimed that she had had a fast-moving cancer, which completely disappeared 2 or 3 weeks after the sitting, as documented by biopsies (Coleman, 2011). Similarly, Robin Hodson has claimed that he sat with Stewart Alexander on June 27, 2011. In the course of the séance, Hodson was told that a renowned deceased spiritual healer wanted to work with him. He was asked to move his chair up to the cabinet and then to turn his hands so that they were flat and extended forward. When he did so, he could feel Alexander's hands. At that point, he "experienced a strong sensation similar to an electric shock which travelled up both arms and into [his] chest" (S. Alexander, 2010/2020, p. 206). That sensation lasted for a few minutes after which time Hodson returned to his place within the circle and was told that he would "find out the result in three months" (Alexander, 2010/2020, p. 206). At the time, Hodson suffered from a heart condition. When he went for a routine appointment on September 27, exactly 3 months later, his heart specialist asked to know what he had done because his heart was now normal. It was only later that Hodson connected his spontaneous remission to the events during the séance (S. Alexander, 2010/2020).

In some cases of trance channeling, a medium appears to embody a deceased physician who uses whatever skills they have to treat a person. Such was the case with the medium George Chapman (1921–2006) in England, who appeared to be a conduit for William Lang (1851–1937), a deceased surgeon who had worked in several London hospitals. The mediumship lasted for 60 years. Chapman would go into trance for up to 6 hours and, subsequently, be unable to remember anything that had happened during that time. Chapman was an ordinary person who worked as a firefighter, whereas the Lang persona had an extensive vocabulary and knowledge of the time period for which he had been alive. William Lang's daughter, Lyndon Lang, heard about the healing sessions with her father and showed up to see for herself what was happening. When she heard the William Lang persona talk about things that only William Lang could have known, she accepted the manifesting personality as her father and supported Chapman in his mediumship efforts. The following is an example of the type of effects that appeared to occur. When S. G. Miron's wife had an upper molar extracted, a piece of the roof of her mouth went with it. Miron, who was a dental surgeon, tried to fix the hole but could not. After treatment by the ostensible deceased Lang, over the following few days, "the hole just slowly mended of its own accord" and "she was totally cured" (Mishlove, 2021a). There were so many cases of spontaneous remission after sessions with Chapman that the healing outcomes were taken seriously by those who had witnessed them. For instance, for a while, William Lang's son, Basil Lang, also a surgeon, along with a group of his colleagues, held weekly private sessions with Chapman in London (Mishlove, 2021a).

There is something obvious about trance mediumship that needs to be explicitly acknowledged. George Chapman would go into a trance state for up to 6 hours and remember nothing afterward of what happened. Is this an appropriate behavior in which to engage? I have defined *authenticity* as "the effort to act on the basis of one's own understanding" (Barušs, 1996, p. 28). So, living an authentic life means making deliberate, mindful decisions as one negotiates the challenges presented by being alive. Of course, we usually cede control while asleep, and there are situations over which we have little control for which surrender is appropriate (Ferrucci, 1982), but is adding large chunks of our waking time to that total a wise choice? One can, of course, make a decision, based on one's own understanding, that being unconscious while a deceased surgeon—or, perhaps, a deep part of oneself—tries to heal people is the best use of one's life. We can become enamored by the idea of channeling, but is it necessarily our best course of action? I think that sometimes there has been a rush to open oneself to weird experiences without considering the wisdom of doing so.

REFLECTIONS

We have given this subject matter a good shake. What are we left with as the ground settles? I think one of the most salient things to notice is the degree to which some of these phenomena violate Newton's laws of motion. We have a crystal that appears to dematerialize and then rematerialize. An arm that passes through a cable tie. A plastic pig that appears to travel around from place to place by itself. We have three cases in which levitation appears to have occurred. We have ostensible anomalous healing as a result of physical mediumship. In previous chapters, we had mist forming itself into images of faces; computers that printed words by themselves; dead radios that played music; voices coming from radios without vacuum tubes; flowers that smashed to the floor by themselves; and a random event generator that exhibited nonrandom behavior when a medium channeled "being 7." For many of us, this is not the way that the physical world is supposed to work.

An explanation that has been offered for some of these phenomena has been that there were tremors moving the buildings in which these events occurred, causing objects inside those buildings to move around. An experiment was conducted to test that hypothesis. An investigator borrowed some houses in England that were to be demolished. He attached "a robust vibrating device on the outer wall, and [placed] test objects inside to see if they would move" (Fraser, 2020, p. 29) in the presence of volunteer witnesses. The houses were "clearly shaking as if in an earthquake and plaster falling from the ceiling" (Fraser, 2020, p. 29), all of which was more terrifying than investigating actual poltergeist cases, yet that was not enough to create the anomalous object movements. So, unsurprisingly perhaps, poltergeist activity is not just the result of seismic tremors.

Another reaction is to deny the list on the grounds that these sorts of events violate the known laws of physics. Such a contention is problematic for two reasons. The first is that it is not clear that these events do violate the known laws of physics with physicist Wolfgang Pauli, for instance, seeing "a link between quantum mechanics and 'poltergeist'-style mind-matter interactions" (Sommer, 2014, p. 40). Second, in science, theory is supposed to give way to empirical observation. The physicist Richard Feynman has clearly articulated this idea:

> There is this possibility: after I tell you something, you just can't believe it. You can't accept it. You don't like it. A little screen comes down and you don't listen anymore. I'm going to describe to you how Nature is—and if you don't like it, that's going to get in the way of your understanding it. It's a problem that physicists have learned to deal with: They've learned to realize that whether they like a theory or they don't like a theory is *not* the essential question. Rather, it is whether or not the theory gives predictions that agree with experiment. It is not a question of whether a theory is philosophically delightful, or easy to understand, or perfectly reasonable from the point of view of common sense. The theory of quantum electrodynamics describes Nature as absurd from the point of view of common sense. And it agrees fully with experiment. So I hope you can accept Nature as She is—absurd. (Feynman, 1985/2006, p. 10; emphasis in original)

So, can we adopt the attitude of physicists and let the observations lead and the explanations follow? If the phenomena in this list violate the known laws of physics, then we need as yet unknown laws of physics to explain them (Baruš & Mossbridge, 2017).

In addition to the apparent physical phenomena, we have psychological phenomena that are equally difficult to accept. First, we appear to have instances in which a person's psyche gives way to some other intelligence. We saw this with Stewart Alexander, the Scole mediums, Jamie Butler, Richard Gallagher's possession case, and George Chapman. Perhaps the simplest explanation would be an *exosomatic theory*, which is to say an out-of-body theory, whereby we explain what is happening as what it looks like what is happening. It looks as though the mediums are leaving their physical bodies, which are then occupied by some other psychological entity. Just because that is the most obvious explanation does not mean that it is the wrong one. As with any other theory, it needs to be evaluated on the basis of the evidence. Second, we need to account for the apparent interaction between a living person or deceased entity and the anomalous physical phenomena on our list. What is the relationship? Did Virginia Campbell cause the poltergeist phenomena associated with her, or did she have assistance in the form of a deceased entity or demon? In either case, what is the mechanism of action? These are not easy questions to answer.

Whereas apparently exosomatic psychological events are relevant to the question of survival, it is not clear to what extent the physical phenomena are useful. Some of them, such as the levitated school desk, appear to be irrelevant. A fully materialized form of a deceased person patting Leslie Kean on the top of her head, on the face of it, seems to be more germane. "I just wanted to let you know that I am a solid human being," said the materialized form (Kean, 2020, p. 330). But ectoplasm, of which the apparition was ostensibly constructed, if it exists and whatever it might be, is not the whole of what a human being is made so that the materialized form is not "just" a "solid human being." It is also not clear why solidity, in itself, should count as evidence for being a human being. That seems to be going in precisely the wrong philosophical direction. Do we really want people to be identified with solidity? If so, then death, at which time the solid form becomes inactive, really is the end. Furthermore, given the variety of entities available for material expression, how are we to even know what that materialized form actually was?

These are obvious questions, but the focus of much of the academic literature is not on them. The focus is on the psychosocial and environmental variables that are responsible for creating an impression that something unusual has happened. How is it that ambiguous stimuli give rise to interpretations of paranormal activity (Lange & Houran, 2015)? We are back to pareidolia. For a wide swath of cases, such analyses could be helpful. For instance, in one study, one-third of participants in a mock séance claimed table levitation when the table did not levitate. So, why did they say that it did (Drinkwater et al., 2019)? For this chapter, though, I have deliberately chosen examples for which the documentation is good that something unusual actually did occur. Trying to force a pareidolia interpretation on such events constitutes gaslighting of the witnesses by questioning their sanity and deliberately challenging their ability to faithfully report their experiences in the absence of any actual evidence for pathology or distortion (Drinkwater et al., 2019). So, much of the academic literature is not helpful for answering our questions.

The phenomena discussed in this chapter typically do not manifest suddenly without preparation. It took Stewart Alexander weekly sitting for 13 years to manifest typical séance phenomena. Similarly, it took time for phenomena to occur for the Scole group. We saw the same protracted time period for development that was present for successful ITC cases. In these situations, when something did start to happen, it did not happen consistently. Furthermore, in the Scole experiment, the spirit team explicitly articulated a trial-and-error strategy in which specific beings tried to create phenomena, such as the dancing lights, text and images on film, and ITC using the germanium device (Foy, 2008). We saw with several lines of ITC research an effort to coordinate research among the living with that of the apparently deceased. The idea is that perhaps considerable time and effort is required by the right entities to establish a functional interface between the living and the dead. Then, one day, something works. And on another day, for whatever reason, the phenomena just cease, and all that is left is dead air, so to speak.

Given all of these considerations, how far did our dial move in this chapter? There is sufficient documentation by credible witnesses to get us, at least in some cases, from materialism to LAP. And we tried on the survival hypothesis. Can we make it stick? I think that the justification for such clockwise rotation lies in the details. We noted in Chapter 4 that some mediums have the experience of interacting with ostensible entities in the same way that they interact with living entities. It is this that convinces them that they are not simply encountering a projection of their own mind but a person who was at one time among the living. So, we are back to the quality of perceptual presence, if not solidity, analogous to the dematerialized crystal, perhaps. We can carry this over to physical manifestation of a person who is deceased. So, for instance, Lyndon Lang, the daughter of the deceased surgeon, William Lang, was convinced that she had been having a conversation with her father because of the specific information that the entranced George Chapman had provided during her conversation with him. Similarly, Elisa Medhus, as a result of her experiences, primarily with mediums channeling her son, Erik, including his physical possession of Jamie Butler, has said that she has made an "arduous journey from a skeptical physician who was raised by two atheists to a believer without so much as a shred of doubt" (Medhus, 2015).

What I take from these two examples is that, in both of these cases, the interactions with the deceased father, William Lang, and the deceased son, Erik Medhus, respectively, are so similar to the interactions with the living father and with the living son as to be functionally identical. What is recognized in these cases is not a "solid human being" who is the surrogate corpus of the father or the son, but their psyches as evidenced by the mediums' behavior. We are back to considering the grounds on which we make judgments about a person's identity. But could these merely be astral goons or demons able to mimic the behavior of the deceased? Perhaps, but if the experience is functionally identical to what it had been when alive, then the argument can be flipped so that the living father and the living son could already have been demons and astral goons before their demises. Are those attributes that we would have made? This does raise a deep question about pre- versus postmortem identity, which we are answering pragmatically here.

In Chapter 4, in addition to the quality of interaction with an entity, we looked at the source of motivation and specialized knowledge or skills attributed to the communicators as a way of trying to move from LAP to survival. Motivation for any particular anomalous event is difficult to judge. The communicator is buffered by the physical phenomena, which, one could argue, the living are motivated to experience in any case. In the Philip experiment, only known information was played back to the participants in the form of table knocks. The argument for specialized knowledge is stronger. For instance, at one point in the Scole experiment, there was a conversation about celestial mechanics that required specialized knowledge between a former professor of astronomy who was physically present and the apparent spirit communicators. There was also, of course, technical information for building a germanium device, which appeared to work when attached to a cassette recorder. Most significant, perhaps, was the dematerializing crystal because we do not have any technology that can create such an experience. So, there is some support for specialized knowledge on the part of communicators. Is it enough to move our needle to survival?

Thus far in this book, we have considered deathbed visions and coincidences; afterdeath communication; mediumship; ITC; and physical phenomena, such as poltergeist activity. We can think of these as interfaces between the living and the dead, whereby the dead intrude, to some degree, into the lives of the living. We can think of the material in the next chapter the other way around as the living intruding into the world of the dead; in other words, near-death experiences, possibly giving a glimpse of what is to come after death. In the chapter after that, about past-life experiences, we examine the possibility of having been here before. Then, after having done so, in Chapter 9, we position ourselves in the afterlife itself, as it appears, by drawing together the material from all of these chapters to see what we can see from there.

7 NEAR-DEATH EXPERIENCES

An Efé man brought a goat and other gifts back from the spirit-world, a Mbundu doctor brought a bracelet, and a twentieth-century Bakongo NDEr returned with fertility medicine.
—Gregory Shushan (2018, p. 229; NDEr, near-death experiencer)

Near-death experiences (NDEs) have already come up in our discussion several times in this book. They are frequently powerful experiences that change a person who has had them. However, despite their profound effects, how helpful are they for moving our dial from materialism to living agent psi (LAP) and survival? That depends, I think, on how carefully we pay attention to the details. In the first chapter, we considered the case of Lloyd Rudy's heart patient who had an NDE that included veridical perception with a temporal anchor. Such cases are strongly suggestive of survival.

Although we can make such a rational argument, I think that the real significance lies in the transformational power of the NDE phenomenology, which challenges us to reconsider the nature of reality itself. While we are busy nudging our needle toward survival, the NDE phenomenology calls into

https://doi.org/10.1037/0000361-007
Death as an Altered State of Consciousness: A Scientific Approach, by I. Baruss
Copyright © 2023 by the American Psychological Association. All rights reserved.

question whether that is even a meaningful pursuit. It is not that we somehow extend the physical world through NDEs but that physical manifestation itself comes apart. I mean, how does a goat get brought back from the spirit world? Okay. So, the goat might be a bit over the top for some readers. The point is that rather than trying to see how well NDE events match physical circumstances, the question gets raised of the extent to which physical occurrences are themselves projections of a deeper reality. It is not so much that survival follows death but that we are already part of an expanded consciousness that naturally resides in a timeless domain. That, I think, is the insight that NDEs have to offer.

Let us start our exploration with an example of an NDE that occurred for one of my former students, written in her own words:

> I was on my way to work one winter morning when I drove over a patch of black ice. I lost control of my car and it began to skid into oncoming traffic. Another vehicle sped toward me but swerved out of the way with mere seconds before impact. I was relieved, though only for a moment. When I looked up, I saw a speeding bus staring down at me as it moved closer and closer. I knew it had nowhere to go, it was going to hit me.
>
> I felt a force reach down into the Earth, into my car, and into my core to pull me out. I felt myself leave my body.
>
> I began to float.
>
> I was surrounded by a brilliant, beautiful, warm, white light. It was welcoming and accepting and unconditionally loving. Slowly I became aware of another presence. It was a presence that wasn't my own but one to which I knew I was connected. It was a presence that encompassed every single thing in existence.
>
> "Is this death?" I asked, "am I dying?"
>
> The answer came from a Silent Voice.
>
> "Yes. This is death. You are dying."
>
> It felt familiar to me, it felt like I belonged there.
>
> And to that the Voice said, "You've been here before, and you'll be here again."
>
> "Oh." I thought, "I guess this is okay." There was no pain, there was no worry, "this isn't so bad."
>
> Then I thought of my parents and my two siblings. I felt what it would be like for them if I died, I felt their sorrow. "Will they be okay?" I asked, "this will devastate them."
>
> I was shown an image of the four of them, they were smiling but there was something noticeably missing.
>
> "They will be okay. They will feel your absence. They will have an existence without you. And they will be okay."
>
> "I guess" I thought, "if I have no choice. . . ." I accepted that I was going to die but I didn't want to put my family through what I saw.
>
> Then I was shown another image, it was of me this time. I was on a mission. This image came with a question: "Did you do that?"

"Wait a minute, wait a minute" I thought "no, I haven't done that yet. Whatever that is, whatever I was supposed to do in my life, I haven't done it. I can't die yet! I'M NOT DONE!"

"Are you sure?" I was asked.

"YES!" I answered, "I CAN'T DIE YET!"

Then a silent and serene, "Okay." And with it, I felt an orb of white light thrown into me with the same force that pulled me out before, with such force that I began to fall backwards.

It was different on the way back down. I was in a dark, multi-dimensional tunnel with lights beaming back and forth all around me. I knew I was one of those beams, moving farther and farther away from the light above.

I saw two figures in the light on my way down. They were my grandparents* making sure to send me back, telling me it wasn't my time. (N. Wassie, personal communication, February 23, 2022)

---

*I didn't know my grandmother had died until days after my NDE.

In Chapter 1, we defined *NDEs* as experiences that occur when a person is close to death. Let us consider that definition a bit more carefully. First, what does it mean to be dead? If someone lived to talk about what happened to them, then they could not have been "dead," given that we think of death as a state from which one does not recover. Indeed, as the process of dying is increasingly researched with corresponding understanding of the resilience of brain cells and improvements in resuscitation technology, people are brought back to life from deeper and deeper stages of the dying process, stretching the gray zone of when a person is to be regarded as being dead (Parnia, 2014; Parnia et al., 2022). In fact, there is a medical procedure, *hypothermic cardiac arrest*, whereby a person's body temperature is lowered and their heart stopped for surgical purposes (Sabom, 1998), deliberately sending a person deep into the dying process before bringing them back out again. We need to keep the progressive nature of death in mind when we talk about experiencers being regarded as being dead, such as in the Lloyd Rudy case from Chapter 1 with the wife of Lloyd Rudy's patient being told that her husband had died. The point here is to pay attention to the relevant physiology rather than the attachment of the label of being dead.

Second, NDEs can occur outside the context of actually dying. So, someone who expects to die but remains unharmed could have an experience with the same features as someone who is physically harmed. An important class of such experiences are falls from mountains in which climbers land unharmed (Noyes & Kletti, 1977). But there are also NDE-like experiences which have the same features as NDEs except that they do not occur in the context of death, for instance, during syncope, epilepsy, anxiety, meditation, or while falling asleep (Martial et al., 2020; Charland-Verville et al., 2018).

It has been argued that experiences without physiological death should not be regarded as NDEs (Parnia et al., 2022).

Third, we are not talking about an experience as such but the report of a memory of an experience, given that there is no ordinary real-time communication during an NDE. In other words, we need to consider not just the occurrence of an experience but, concurrently, the consolidation of that experience into long-term memory. As we will see, this becomes an important consideration.

Fourth, we are not interested in just any experiences that occur around the time of death, such as those that we discussed in Chapter 2, but experiences with specific features. So let us start by characterizing the nature of the experiences of interest.

In the process of describing the characteristics of NDEs, we consider several additional examples. Then I mount the best materialist argument for explaining NDEs as hallucinations. There are numerous problems with such an argument, but perhaps the key challenge lies with veridical temporal anchors to points in time at which an experiencer's brain was not functioning in the manner that is necessary to produce phenomenal consciousness. After that, we consider the aftereffects of NDEs, which can mirror the profound change of worldview experienced by the released prisoner in Plato's cave allegory (Plato, ca. 360 B.C.E./1968). To move to a deeper examination of what NDEs can teach us, I want to go back to the nature of perception during an NDE and support for the notion of *mindsight*, seeing directly with the mind. We have also noted that NDEs can occur outside the context of death with similar aftereffects, so we look at the simulation of NDEs. Finally, we reflect on what we have learned, see how far we can move our explanatory materialism–LAP–survival needle clockwise, and suggest a reorientation of reality in which consciousness plays a greater role.

CHARACTERISTICS OF NEAR-DEATH EXPERIENCES

Let us approach the characteristics of NDEs through the updated version of the most commonly used instrument for measuring them. In 1983, Bruce Greyson invented a 16-item self-report NDE scale used for determining the presence of an NDE based on sufficiently high scores on the scale (Greyson, 1983). Rasch analyses of the NDE scale have confirmed that the total score represents an incremental unitary construct rather than a multidimensional one. In other words, the analyses have supported the notion that the scale items can be ordered linearly with regard to the degree to which a respondent has had an NDE, with higher numbers indicating a more profound experience. The scale was updated by removing one redundant item and adding five new ones to better reflect what experiencers were reporting; it was then renamed the Near-Death Experience Content (NDE-C) scale (Martial et al., 2020). In testing, it has demonstrated good discriminant validity, with the ability to differentiate NDEs from recreational drug, meditation, and cognitive trance states. *Cognitive trance* means a "volitional and self-induced modified state of consciousness characterized by lucid but narrowed awareness of external surroundings with hyper-focused immersive experience of flow, and expanded inner imagery" (Martial et al., 2020, p. 9); in other words, what could be regarded as a state of self-hypnosis (cf. Barušs, 2020). However, the new scale cannot discriminate between NDEs and NDE-like experiences, hence the use of the word "content" in the name of the scale. The scale can be used for determining content but not context.

Despite being unitary, the scale can be conceptualized as consisting of five factors resulting from a factor analysis, namely, Beyond the Usual, Harmony, Insight, Border, and Gateway. Eight items make up the Beyond the Usual factor and include altered temporality, unusual sensations, extrasensory perception, out-of-body experiences, and ineffability. The two items of the Harmony factor are concerned with peace and harmony. Five items make up the Insight factor with content about hearing a voice, self-understanding, precognition, life review, and encountering entities. Five items make up the Border factor: impressions of transitioning to another dimension, feelings of nonexistence or fear, reaching a border, making a decision to return to life, and the sense that one is dying or dead. Two items make up the Gateway factor: the perception of a bright light and the presence of a gateway, such as a "tunnel or a door" (Martial et al., 2020, p. 5, italics removed). The items are scored on a Likert scale from 0 (*not at all; none*) to 4 (*extremely; more than any other*), with higher scores more strongly indicating the presence of the characteristic, for a possible total score between 0 and 80 and a suggested cutoff score of 27 or above for stating that a person has had an NDE. We have seen some of these elements in the examples that we have introduced already, such as the out-of-body component, the feeling of peace, hearing a voice, and the presence of deceased relatives.

Not all NDEs are pleasant; some are distressing. The 15th item on the NDE-C scale reads, "You had a feeling of non-existence, of being in a total void, and/or of fear" (Martial et al., 2020, p. 5, italics removed). Different studies have found 0% to 23% of NDE accounts to be distressing, although these figures are likely underestimates, given that people having had distressing NDEs are unlikely to report them (Bush, 2009).

Distressing NDEs can be distressing in three different ways. First, there can be an NDE that proceeds with the same content as a pleasant NDE but is experienced as distressing. The emotional tone can flip from distressing to pleasurable, or vice versa, with positive emotional tone sometimes being associated with the ability to surrender to whatever is happening. Second, there can be a sense of meaninglessness and the conviction that the experiencer has never existed and that everything was just all made up. Third, an *inverted NDE* is one in which heavenly scenarios are replaced with hellish ones (Barušs, 2020; Bush, 2009; Greyson & Bush, 1992). For instance, Samuel Bercholz, a Buddhist practitioner, has given the following description:

> My senses were overwhelmed by the unbearable odor of burning flesh and extremes of heat and cold beyond imagination. . . . Amid these intense sensations, a second display arose in shimmering waves of agonizing pain—the images of contorted faces, writhing bodies and ghastly body parts, festering entrails, disembodied thumbs and noses, tormented animals of every kind, some of them ripped into pieces, and even ants and other insects whose extreme suffering was palpable to me. All of them—all of *it*—was a mass of unspeakable pain. With the constant mirage-like wavering of images, I could not discern anything as either real or unreal. (Bercholz, 2016, pp. 29–30)

People can react to having experienced a distressing NDE in at least three different ways. First, they can see these are warnings that prompt conversion experiences to change their lifestyles. Second, they can rationalize the experiences as some sort of brain malfunction. Third, they can fear death and continue to struggle with the existential meaning of their experiences (Bush, 2009). Consistent with our consideration of distressing deathbed phenomena, we could conceptualize distressing NDEs as shadow experiences. They could be an eruption of frightening psychological content or incursion into an objectively existent manifestation, or some combination of the two (cf. Krohn & Kripal, 2018).

One of the predominant features of an NDE and an item of the NDE-C scale is the alteration of temporality, so I want to comment on that and on some of the issues that are raised in that context. Time can be altered both through a mismatch between time taken in the ordinary world and time during the NDE as well as the loss of a sense of time altogether, leaving an experiencer with the impression that they are in a timeless domain. Let me give an example.

On September 2, 1988, Elizabeth Krohn had been walking through the rain, with her 2-year-old son at her right side, from her car to a synagogue when she was hit by lightning. Moments previous to being hit, she had told her 4-year-old son to run to the building. He had run back out and grabbed his younger brother's hand to drag him into the building with him. Krohn had followed. Or so she thought. A man coming from the bathroom back to the services encountered the boys. Krohn could not understand why they were ignoring her. She looked out the window of the door and there, over to the right, was her body lying in a greasy puddle. The soles of her shoes had been blown off so that her feet were sticking out. But when she looked down, she could see that her shoes were perfect. She also saw that she was floating and not touching the ground. This was confusing.

The man ran into the synagogue services and called for a doctor. About 40 hurried toward the back to help, one of whom, by coincidence, was the regional expert on electrocution. Krohn realized that her sons would be okay, so she floated out of the building over to her body. She noticed that she was ruining her new black-and-white suit, which was now gray, and willed herself to get up. That did not work, but she did have the metacognitive insight that nothing is black-and-white, that everything is nuanced. Krohn had learned to dissociate when she had been sexually abused as a child, so now she decided to use that ability to leave. She could see a glow over to the right and up a bit which wanted her to follow it, so she did (Mishlove, 2019; Krohn & Kripal, 2018).

The glow led Krohn to a garden, but it was not like any garden on earth. The colors were unlike any colors on earth. The scent in the air was heavenly. There was otherworldly music that was not played on any musical instruments that we have on earth. A voice told her to sit on a garden bench that conformed to her body. It was the voice of her maternal grandfather with its French accent, although she attributed the voice to God rather than her grandfather. She understood that this environment had been created to put her at ease. She and her companion had a lengthy conversation ranging across many topics. She was told that she could stay if she wished. If she returned, she would have a third child, a daughter, who had chosen her and her husband as her parents. Krohn felt that she instantly understood the nature of reincarnation. She was also told that her marriage would not withstand the transformations that this experience would create and that she and her husband would get divorced. This made her realize that she needed to be the person to raise her children. She had to return. The grandfather entity squeezed her tightly to get her newly expanded self back into her body, and she woke up on the pavement in the rain where people had come running to help her. She had had a clear understanding of the nature of time during her spell in the garden. In one sense, that time had appeared timeless. Yet she was convinced that the experience had taken 2 weeks of linear time even though only minutes had passed while her body lay on the pavement of the parking lot (Mishlove, 2019; Krohn & Kripal, 2018).

Krohn's experience of having to be crushed back into a physical body which had become too small for who she had become is an analog of the need to account for 2 weeks' worth of conversation into the few minutes that her body was lying unconscious on the pavement. This feature of NDE temporality is aggravated by some life reviews that can occur during NDEs. For instance, some life reviews have been multisensory experiences that have been indistinguishable from living physically. Whereas some life reviews are made up of highlights only, others apparently include every event that a person has experienced, sometimes from the perspective of those who have been affected by one's actions. Sometimes from one's own and others' perspectives simultaneously. Sometimes these life reviews have extended into the future. For example, one experiencer said,

> When I recovered, I could tell everyone about every part of my life, in great detail, because of what I had been through. It's quite an experience, but it's difficult to put into words, because it happens so rapidly, yet it's so clear. (Moody, 1975, p. 70)

But how are these detailed events created and encoded into long-term memory during the brief time interval during which an NDE takes place (Barušs & Mossbridge, 2017)? So, we have two issues with temporality. One has to do with the experience of time as altered or suspended entirely, such as the 2 weeks of conversation that was also timeless. The other has to do with the mismatch of the time course of subjective events that is too complex to fit into the consensual temporality of the body. Both of these, and particularly the second, erode a conventional interpretation of reality and open the possibility of the existence of an expanded consciousness that is not constrained by the limitations of the brain.

A MATERIALIST ARGUMENT

Before getting too deeply into the puzzling features of NDEs, I want to lay out a materialist explanation for them. In doing so, I think it will become apparent how woefully inadequate such an explanation is and help us to realize that we need some fresh thinking about NDEs. Ostensibly, the strongest materialist argument against survival is the correspondence between brain activity and subjective experiences. As the underlying neural substrate is damaged, such as occurs in dementia, cognitive abilities that are subsumed by the damaged neural networks disappear. We are reminded to adhere to some version of the *supervenience thesis*: that consciousness is a by-product of neural activity (Barušs & Mossbridge, 2017)—not just any neural activity but neural activity in specific regions and networks that corresponds to different cognitive, emotional, and behavioral events (Piccinini & Bahar, 2015). When the neural activity stops, then so does consciousness (Weisman, 2015; Lake, 2017; Fischer & Mitchell-Yellin, 2016; Augustine, 2015a). So, on the basis of such neuroscientific reasoning, given that brain activity of the right sort has ceased, there can be no phenomenal consciousness, and, in particular, NDEs cannot occur.

However, NDEs do occur. So now, in a reversal of the correspondence argument against survival, we have the *dying brain hypothesis*, whereby the damaged brain creates rich NDE phenomenology. In positing some such mechanisms, at least in some cases, the idea is not necessarily to seek evidence to support them but simply to speculate:

> We are not attempting to *prove* that the sorts of alternative scenarios described . . . actually took place. Rather, our point is that, given these possibilities, it does *not* seem extremely likely that the only or best explanation of these experiences implies supernaturalism. (Fischer & Mitchell-Yellin, 2016, pp. 20–21, emphasis in original)

In other words, materialist explanations without evidence are better explanations than any "supernatural" explanations irrespective of the evidence for them. Let me go through the steps to show what is required of a materialist explanation of NDEs. Other materialist mechanisms have been proposed in addition to the ones I consider, such as blood gases, anoxia, psychological comfort, and so on, but the ones I present, weak as they are, appear to be the strongest.

First of all, even though they are psychometrically indistinguishable, we need to split off NDE-like experiences from NDE experiences in which the brain is actually dying (Parnia et al., 2022) to advance a dying-brain hypothesis. If the brain is not dying, such as in the case of a fall from a mountain in which a climber lands unhurt, then, from a materialist perspective, that mechanism must be different from the mechanism for a case with an actual dying brain. Furthermore, despite being psychometrically a unitary construct, although multifactorial, we need to fragment the NDE into independent components, each of which can have its own neural substrate, thereby making it easier to explain it (Craffert, 2019; Lake, 2017).

Now, here is the problem. Within 20 seconds of cardiac arrest, blood flow to the brain stops along with any meaningful cortical activity (van Lommel, 2013). This means that the brain has, at most, 20 seconds to produce the rich experience of an NDE. This seems like a tall order. Experiencers have frequently asserted that their cognitive abilities were enhanced rather than degraded during their experience. In one study, 29% agreed that their "thinking was more logical than usual," and 45%, that their thinking was "clearer than usual" (Baruss, 2020, p. 205; E. W. Kelly et al., 2007/2010; see also Charland-Verville et al., 2018). As we have seen already from our examples, there can be complex envisaged activities that take place during an NDE that appear to last for 2 weeks or an entire lifetime, in the case of some life reviews:

> Verified cases of NDEs that take place almost instantaneously do not support simple or linear correlations between the relative depth, complexity, and apparent duration of phenomenal content, and the actual duration of a period of loss of consciousness or alteration in the level of consciousness during which they are reported to take place. (Lake, 2017, p. 130)

So, we have a problem. Suggesting that this is an artifact of encoding or recall (Lake, 2017) does not somehow provide additional computational capacity for those few seconds during which the phenomenal content is supposed to occur. Given that there is no additional capacity, we have to posit an encoding or decoding process that operates at some other time to create more phenomenal content than what is available during the time of the NDE.

However, there is an actual encoding issue. In general, no one remembers the moment of falling asleep. And when someone is awakened from sleep, interacts with a person, and falls asleep again within a few minutes, they might remember none of that on awakening in the morning. Why not? Because neither of those events might have been consolidated into long-term memory. In one study, participants were played pairs of words at 1-minute intervals as they were falling asleep. They were awakened either after 30 seconds or 10 minutes of having been asleep and asked to name the word pairs. The researchers found impaired performance for word pairs presented within 3 minutes of falling asleep at the 10-minute mark but not the 30 second mark. The explanation was that sleep interferes with the process of long-term memory consolidation (Wyatt et al., 1992). Even if it does not, this experiment reveals that people are unlikely to remember what happened within 3 minutes of falling asleep. Logically, it would be even more difficult to remember something that happened 3 minutes before dying, given that dying is obviously going to disrupt the memory consolidation process even more than sleep. So, how does any phenomenal content within the available few seconds ever get encoded into long-term memory to be later recalled as an NDE?

One way around the problem of running out of time is to claim that the brain is actually doing more than we think it is as it is dying. There has been considerable enthusiasm the past several years about finding some transient neural activity using an electroencephalogram (EEG) around the time of cardiac arrest in both rats (van Rijn et al., 2011; Borjigin et al., 2013; D. E. Lee et al., 2017) and humans (Norton et al., 2017; Chawla et al., 2017; Vicente et al., 2022). Let us just think about this for a minute. According to a neuroscientific thesis, if I imagine in my mind a conversation with my grandfather while imagining sitting on a park bench, that is going to involve specific patterns of neural activation throughout my brain over the length of time that it takes me to have that imagined conversation (cf. Piccinini & Bahar, 2015). The presence of the phenomenal consciousness that underlies such imagined events itself has been associated with coherent EEG activity in the gamma range (Meador et al., 2002). In other words, the right parts of the brain need to be working properly and accompanied by coherent gamma on measurement with an EEG for there to be meaningful subjective experiences.

The problem with the residual neural activity findings in these experiments is that there is simply too little, too soon. By too little, I mean that, in some cases, the EEG signal does not rise above the level of delta, let alone display gamma (Norton et al., 2017). By too soon, I mean that any surges that reach gamma occur within minutes after cardiac arrest (Vicente et al., 2022) and cannot account for the phenomenology of protracted NDEs. In cases with longer temporal periods, authors have acknowledged that formal EEG analyses were not carried out (Chawla et al., 2017), making it difficult to interpret their results. It is also not clear why these EEG surges around the time of cardiac arrest are not just more of whatever was happening immediately before cardiac arrest as the brain loses its capacity to sustain consciousness. How is this transient perimortem neural activity a marker of an NDE which has a distinctive phenomenology? In other words, before the loss of oxygen to the brain, there is no dying brain, so the NDE starts at some point as the brain starts dying. However, explaining the complex NDE phenomenology, which requires high levels of activation and synergistic functioning in the correct parts of the brain, cannot begin to be explained by occasional sporadic firing of nerve cells for a few minutes following cardiac arrest.

One strategy for keeping the dying brain hypothesis alive has been to note the similarity between the effects of some psychedelic drugs and NDE content. The idea is that an endogenous chemical creates a surge of neural activity at the time of death that is experienced as an NDE. Two drugs have separately been proposed, namely, dimethyltryptamine (DMT; Timmermann et al., 2018; Fischer & Mitchell-Yellin, 2016) and ketamine (Greyson et al., 2009). However, it turns out that the body cannot produce the amounts of DMT that would be required to create a psychedelic experience (Nichols, 2018), let alone be able to do so within 20 seconds. Similarly, there is no ketamine in the brain, but perhaps there are ketaminelike substances that act on N-methyl-D-aspartate, or NMDA, receptors at subanesthetic doses to produce out-of-body, tunnel, light, feelings of dying, and communicating with divinity experiences. However, the match with NDE experiences is not good in that ketamine experiences are generally unpleasant and are usually recognized by experiencers as illusory in nature, unlike most NDEs (Greyson et al., 2009). There have also been cases of NDEs during hypothermic cardiac arrest when the brain is monitored throughout the procedure. Pam Reynolds, for instance, had a rich NDE but no brain surges (Rivas et al., 2016). So, the brain surge theories, including those caused by endogenous psychedelic drugs, have limited explanatory scope.

Another strategy for saving a materialist explanation is to suggest that maybe we are looking for an NDE at the wrong time. The NDE does not occur when the brain is dying but afterward, when the person has recovered from the neurological insult (Fischer & Mitchell-Yellin, 2016). In other words, the argument is that all NDE experiences are actually NDE-like experiences that occur when the brain is functioning adequately. So, we are no longer proposing a dying brain hypothesis. The obvious problem with such temporal displacement is the difficulty of accounting for veridical perceptions that occur during the course of actually dying, such as Lloyd Rudy's patient seeing him standing with arms folded in a doorway or Elizabeth Krohn seeing her body lying in a greasy puddle in a parking lot with shoes blown off. These temporal anchors tie the NDE experience to the time when the brain was compromised. There are two ways of dealing with such data. The first is to deny that veridical perception has ever occurred. That statements of such events are false memories formed by the person who learned afterward about the events through ordinary means and then inserted them into their NDE narrative as a false memory. The second is to assert that a person acquired sensory information about their environment, not through sight but through their other senses while their brain was not working and then later formed those sensations into perceptual experiences (Fischer & Mitchell-Yellin, 2016). To think that Lloyd Rudy's patient could sense Rudy standing in the doorway with his arms folded seems like asking for too much from a body without a heartbeat. We also have the case of Bettina Peyton, who was without a heartbeat for 8 minutes and who told hospital staff what had happened in the operating room before anyone had said anything to her. In other words, there are cases to which such speculation does not apply (Woollacott & Peyton, 2021).

There is some independent verification for veridical temporal anchors, for instance, examples in which people with whom an experiencer interacted during an NDE recall that interaction. Bettina Peyton is herself a physician. While apparently outside her body during her NDE, she saw that the anesthesiologist could not insert a catheter into her right wrist because of the collapsed artery, and she could feel pain from his efforts to do so. According to Peyton,

> I suggest to the anesthesiologist that he try the larger, more proximal artery at the elbow. I sense his negative response as concretely as if he shakes his head in refusal. I know that he is concerned about injuring the nerve that runs alongside the larger artery. I urge him again and again, more forcefully, but he continues to poke at the collapsed artery. Finally, with a surge of will, Consciousness bursts forth in a blast of silent power, *Just go for it!* With a start, the anesthesiologist straightens up, turns to the larger artery in the crook of my arm and inserts the catheter, gaining access on the first try. (Woollacott & Peyton, 2021, p. 216, emphasis in original)

According to Peyton, before her caregivers had informed her of what had happened, she told them about the events that she had witnessed,

> including the anesthesiologist's efforts to catheterize the artery in my wrist, and how I told him to go for the brachial artery, and how he refused. I recounted how I'd inwardly shouted to him, "Just go for it!" He went pale, saying he'd heard the actual words inside, "Just go for it," which compelled him to abandon the wrist and go for the artery in the elbow. (Woollacott & Peyton, 2021, p. 217)

Examples such as this undermine the reconstruction argument because of the apparent interaction between the patient and a living witness during the time of the NDE.

In another case of corroboration, in 1989, a woman in California was receiving a heart transplant, when complications arose at 2:15 a.m. but were successfully overcome. When her family went in to talk to her in the morning, she told them that she had "left her body and watched the doctors work on her for a few minutes" (Moody, 2010, p. 61, italics removed) and then gone to the waiting room, where her family was gathered. However, she became frustrated when they could not communicate with her, so she had gone to her daughter's home, where she "had stood at the foot of her son-in-law's bed and told him that everything was going to be all right" (Moody, 2010, p. 61, italics removed). Her son-in-law "had awakened at 2:15 AM to see his mother-in-law standing at the foot of his bed" (Moody, 2010, p. 61, italics removed). He said that she had said that she would be all right, that there was nothing to worry about, and had then disappeared. He got out of bed and wrote down the time and what she had said. On investigating the family members, the investigators of this case could find no discrepancies in their accounts (Moody, 2010). Considered in isolation, this case might seem strange. However, we have seen this sort of thing before.

This is just a deathbed coincidence, except that the person who is visiting is just having a near-death rather than death experience.

What I have done in this section is to present a materialist argument that the NDE phenomenology is caused by the dying brain. As I did that, I ran into insurmountable problems. According to neuroscientific data about the functioning of the brain, particular brain circuits need to be engaged for phenomenal consciousness to occur, something that cannot happen as the brain dies, even if there were to be occasional sporadic brain activity for several minutes after cardiac arrest. Furthermore, whatever is experienced, needs to be encoded into long-term memory, something for which there is simply insufficient time. Speculation about the existence of chemically induced brain surges of sufficient activation to create the NDE phenomenology has, until now, failed; and it is not likely to succeed, given that there are cases of profound NDEs for people whose brains were monitored and no surges found. Relinquishing the dying brain hypothesis and displacing the NDE to some point during recovery runs into the problem of being unable to account for veridical temporal anchors that occur during the time when the brain is incapable of phenomenal consciousness. In mounting this argument, it becomes clear that it is not just that there are a few remaining details to be cleaned up but that the argument is so grossly faulty as to be no argument at all. It is difficult not to reach the conclusion that the brain is not the source of the NDE. Consciousness can function without the brain.

AFTEREFFECTS

One of the most striking aspects of NDEs is the impact they have on a person's life. Perhaps the most obvious aftereffect is the frequent loss of the fear of death. For instance, in a study of four dying patients who had previously had an NDE, anxiety about dying was low, with one patient saying that they "couldn't wait to die" (Lawrence & Repede, 2013, p. 632). In another study, "48% of 350 experiencers reported having become convinced of the survival of life after death" (Barušs, 2020, p. 198; Fenwick & Fenwick, 1995). Some experiencers feel as though they have gone to where you go when you die, and they are not afraid of going back there (Fenwick & Fenwick, 1995).

But it is more than just a loss of the fear of death. NDEs are frequently deeply transformative experiences (Kason, 2019). In Chapter 1, we considered Raymond Moody's (1988) use of Plato's allegory of the cave as a way of characterizing just how powerfully these experiences can impact a person. According to Phyllis Atwater, experiencers frequently refer to an NDE not as an experience but as a "power punch" (Atwater, 2007, p. 328), which has the effect of forcing them open and turning on a wide range of anomalous abilities (Atwater, 2007). The following is a continuation of my former student's account of her NDE and its aftermath:

> I returned from my NDE a different person. I felt myself become a conduit of energy, intuition, and precognition. It changed my worldview, my perception of reality, of life, and of death. I experienced aftereffects which were challenging and frightening at times but ultimately served my understanding of NDEs.
>
> Technologies began to malfunction in my presence and on many occasions, function would be restored to them while in my hands. Sometimes I was able to do this remotely. I also started to have future memories. I'd suddenly and clairvoyantly receive information about future events or conversations before they happened. They felt as real as any other memory except I had no sense of forming them myself. Similarly, I started having precognitive dreams. Initially they were mostly about death and trauma but eventually these dreams expanded to include pregnancies, births, engagements, and weddings. Most of my precognitions involved people who were in the peripheries of my circle—new acquaintances, friends of friends, or distant family members—people with whom I had little to no connection in the physical world. I had no way of knowing any of the information except through a new frequency to which I was becoming attuned. (N. Wassie, personal communication, February 23, 2022)

I want to consider two of the aftereffects that the experiencer has mentioned, namely, precognitive abilities and the effect on electronic equipment, usually called the *Pauli effect* (Baruss & Mossbridge, 2017).

My former student says that she started to get precognitive dreams about significant events in people's lives, such as deaths, births, and marriages. Elizabeth Krohn also had precognitive abilities switched on. Three months after her NDE, she had a dream that a woman she knew, but not well, was dead. In the morning, she deliberately drove out to see an acquaintance, who offered the information that the woman "had died early that morning" (Krohn & Kripal, 2018, p. 37). This confused and frightened Krohn. About 8 years after her NDE, she had the first of many nightmares in which airplanes crashed. In her dream, she could see "the letters 'WA' on the wreckage," (Krohn & Kripal, 2018, p. 38), knew that 230 people had been on board and died, that it had crashed in water, and that it was flight 800. She told her mother about the dream on July 17, 1996. On July 18, 1996, "TWA Flight 800 had crashed in the Atlantic Ocean with 230 people on board. No survivors" (Krohn & Kripal, 2018, p. 38). Distraught, Krohn told her husband what had happened, but it was "more than he could handle" (Krohn & Kripal, 2018, p. 39), and within 10 days, he had moved out (Krohn & Kripal, 2018). The divorce rate for couples, when one of them has had an NDE, is 65% (Greyson, 2021a).

The precognitive dreams have not been Krohn's ordinary dreams. Usually, she has been aware that she has been dreaming in her dreams and can alter their course, and she remembers nothing on awakening. The precognitive dreams have an energy of their own: Krohn knows that they are not dreams, she cannot change the course of events, she cannot force herself to awaken until she has reached the end of the dream; and she recalls "every detail of what [she] was shown" (Krohn & Kripal, 2018, p. 84). Some of the precognitive dreams have been off with their timing, and some never occurred. She started emailing descriptions of her airplane crash dreams to herself as a way of creating a record of them. She does not know what to do with them and would like these dreams to stop but does not know how to get them to do that.

For Krohn, precognition usually occurred during dreams but sometimes also during the waking state. She has given an example of grabbing her husband's arm as they were driving and saying to him that there was an earthquake in western China. Indeed, it turned out that there had been a "severe earthquake" (Krohn & Kripal, 2018, p. 40) around that time in western China. Other experiencers appear to have *future memories* during the waking state, whereby there is an overlay of a series of events from the future onto present events, which is "so thorough, there is no way to distinguish it from everyday reality while the phenomenon is in progress" (Atwater, 1999/2013, p. 24). We could regard these as instances of precognition. Phyllis Atwater has given several examples of future memories. During one of them, she was at her desk at work when everything froze, "sparkles descended from the ceiling" (Atwater, 1999/2013, p. 33), she found herself back in the state of consciousness in which she had been during one of her NDEs, and

> found herself preliving almost the entire following year of her life in which she left Idaho and travelled across the United States to end up in Virginia, near Washington, DC, a trip that she had had no intention of taking. (Barušs & Mossbridge, 2017, p. 76)

When the future memory ended, she found herself sitting at her desk. About 10 minutes had elapsed. No one around her had noticed anything. She was upset. Then the future memory replayed itself, extending even further into the future, including meeting "someone during a walk in the countryside in the southern part of Virginia whom she ended up marrying" (Barušs & Mossbridge, 2017, p. 77). According to Atwater, actual events sometimes followed the future memory scenario, whereas other times, they did not. She did end up "encountering and marrying a man matching the description of the one in her future memory scenario while on a walk in the countryside in the southern part of Virginia" (Barušs & Mossbridge, 2017, p. 77).

The failure of electronic equipment, and sometimes other devices as well, called the Pauli effect, is so common among experiencers that the first question I usually ask someone who tells me that they have had an NDE is whether they can wear a wristwatch. I do not remember anyone having said that they can. My former student alludes to this, as well as the opposite effect, which I have dubbed the *reverse Pauli effect*, whereby broken equipment, such as dysfunctional cell phones, spontaneously start to work again. Elizabeth Krohn has said that her husband gave her a beautiful wristwatch that sits in a safe-deposit box because she cannot wear watches. She also went through four fitness trackers, each of which "fritzed out shortly after [she] put it on" (Krohn & Kripal, 2018, p. 98). Light bulbs pop as she goes near them. Frequently, when she changes a bulb for a new one, the new one pops as she screws it in. Phyllis Atwater, who has interviewed more than 3,000 adults and 277 children who have had NDEs, has said that 73% fit the profile of electrical sensitivity, psychic phenomena, healing abilities, and emotional intensity or instability, and cannot wear watches without having problems with them (Atwater, 2007). In other words, these are common aftereffects, even though they are frequently omitted from academic writing about NDEs.

As a further example of anomalies, Elizabeth Krohn received a telephone call from her deceased grandfather. One and a half years after being struck by lightning, at the beginning of her third pregnancy, the telephone, which was on her side of the bed, rang around 3:30 a.m. Her husband shook her awake. She picked up the phone. It was her deceased grandfather with the French accent. She asked where he was. He said that she knew, that she had been there. He said that he was calling because he needed to tell her mother something. He said that he had tried to contact her mother, but she could not hear him. He also told her that he knew that she was pregnant and that she would have a girl. He told her to remember the unconditional love that she had experienced in the garden. With that, the connection faded. The bedroom filled with a dense vapor, creating a fog. There was a bright red light shining through the fog that triggered "the same palpable sense of unconditional love [she] had experienced in the Garden" (Krohn & Kripal, 2018, p. 43). Her husband insisted on knowing with whom she had been speaking. She asked if he had seen anything. His reply, "What smoke?" (Krohn & Kripal, 2018, p. 43), convinced his wife that he had also seen the fog because she had not said anything about it to him. This is consistent with the experiences we described in Chapters 3 and 5.

I have focused on just three aftereffects of NDEs to illustrate the profound effect that they can have on those who have had them. Something has fundamentally changed in such a way that an experiencer has been thrust into an interactive world that no longer follows the rules that a person assumed to be true before having had an NDE. There is typically a shift from materialism toward transcendent beliefs about consciousness and reality. Thus, NDEs contribute to turning our explanatory dial from materialism to survival for those who have had them.

MINDSIGHT

Another aspect of NDEs provides helpful information about the nature of consciousness and reality, and that is the quality of perception that occurs during an NDE. Kenneth Ring and Sharon Cooper found 21 people who were blind and who had had NDEs. What is notable is that their NDEs did not differ from those of people who are sighted, including the visual elements of NDEs. Fifteen of the 21 participants in the study "claimed to have had some kind of sight" (Ring & Cooper, 1997, p. 115), including five who had been blind from birth. It is possible that some of the five others who had been blind from birth also experienced some form of sight but could not identify it as such. Notably, there is a critical period of development that is required for the brain to learn to process visual sensations as meaningful visual perceptions (e.g., Hirsch & Spinelli, 1971). In fact, those who are blind from birth or lose their sight before age 5 years do not experience visual images (N. H. Kerr, 2000), whereas those "who lose their sight after age 7 do retain visual imagery, although its clarity tends to fade with time" (Ring & Cooper, 1999/2008, p. 84). Indeed, some of the participants claimed that they knew that they were not just dreaming because they do not have visual impressions during their dreams. Ophthalmologists who were consulted about the details of this study did not know how to account for them (Ring & Cooper, 1999/2008). So, if those who are blind from birth can see during their NDEs, then it cannot be the brain that is doing the seeing, at least not in the way that we understand the brain to work.

One of the criticisms of Ring and Cooper's (1999/2008) study of NDEs of blind individuals has been that the NDEs themselves occurred many years previous to the investigators' queries about them and that the details of such memories would not survive the passage of time. The problem is that most critics of NDE research themselves have not engaged in such research and are unfamiliar with the details of the phenomena (Ring, 2007). The memories of NDEs are unlike other memories in that they do remain clear and stable over time and, in fact, contribute to an experiencer's self-identity

(Cassol et al., 2019). There was no difference in recollection of their experiences on administration of the NDE scale to experiencers at the beginning and end of a 2-decade interval (Ring, 2007). Furthermore, in a study of 21 coma survivors, eight of whom had had NDEs as measured by Greyson's (1983) NDE scale and "18 age-matched healthy volunteers" (Thonnard et al., 2013, p. 1), the memories of NDEs had "more characteristics than memories of imagined and real events" and contained "more self-referential and emotional information and [had] better clarity than memories of coma" (Thonnard et al., 2013, p. 1). In a separate study of 122 people who survived a close encounter with death, the memories of their NDEs were recalled as being more real than real or imagined events that occurred around the same time as their NDEs (Moore & Greyson, 2017). An NDE appears to remain fresh in an experiencer's memory as they work to integrate its effects into their lives over time (Atwater, 2007).

One of the participants in Ring and Cooper's (1999/2008) study, Vicki, had been born prematurely and placed in an incubator with an overly high concentration of oxygen, which caused optic nerve damage, leaving her completely blind. She had an NDE at age 12 and another at age 22. The second one occurred after a car crash in which she was seriously injured. She had a "very brief glimpse" (Ring & Cooper, 1999/2008, p. 15) of the crumpled vehicle but then nothing until she was looking down at a body at a hospital. She recognized it as hers because she could see her long hair and the wedding ring on her finger. She could feel the concern of the medical personnel whom she saw working on her body. Then she went up through the ceiling until she was above the roof, which she could see below her as well as see lights, other buildings, and streets. Then she went up through a tube to a place of light with trees, flowers, and people. She interacted with deceased friends and relatives as well as a being whom she identified as Jesus. She then watched a "panoramic review of her life" (Ring & Cooper, 1999/2008, p. 17) from birth to the time of the NDE before finding herself, heavy and painful, back in her body.

Vicki said that the life review was both a matter of seeing her life as well as reliving it. She said, "It was like seeing a movie, but yet being in it at the same time—and yet I was separate from it" (Ring & Cooper, 1999/2008, p. 31). What is noteworthy is the juxtaposition of the way in which she initially experienced her life events and how they were perceived with the addition of sight. In Vicki's words:

> When I was going into the dining room or into the dormitory generally, of course, I would perceive the things by bumping into them, or by touching them, or whatever. This time I could see them from a distance. It was not like

> I had to be right on top of them, touching them, or sitting on them or whatever, before I was aware of them. I don't imagine things very well in my mind until I get there. I have a lot of trouble dealing with images of things when I'm not directly there. This time, it was like I didn't have to be right there to be aware of the chairs. I saw the metal chairs that we sat on as children and the round tables in the dining room, and they had plastic table cloths on them. I didn't have to touch the plastic table cloths to be aware of them. (Ring & Cooper, 1999/2008, p. 32)

This description suggests that another mode of perception became functional during Vicki's NDE. But is it sight or something else?

Another of the participants in Ring and Cooper's (1999/2008) study, who had been born with cataracts and then lost her sight after the age of 19 years, could not decide whether the perception of her body during her NDE had been visual. She finally settled on "semi-visual" (Ring & Cooper, 1999/2008, p. 96) as a descriptor of her experience. In this case, the participant had a basis for comparison because she had been sighted during her childhood and adolescence. In describing the nature of her perception, another participant said that

> I didn't suddenly see. I didn't see at all. But I was aware of things in a way that was kind of tactile . . . even though from where I was I couldn't have had any tactile experience of it and that's the difference. (Ring & Cooper, 1999/2008, p. 98)

In another case, Harold lost his sight at 16 years of age as a result of an automobile accident. During the ensuing effort to save his life, he had an NDE during which he could perceive his body as well as the medical team working on him. In Harold's words:

> I think what it was that was happening here was a bunch of synesthesia, where all these perceptions were being blended into some image in my mind, you know, the visual, the tactile, all the input that I had. I can't literally say I really saw anything, but yet I was aware of what was going on, and perceiving all that in my mind. (Ring & Cooper, 1999/2008, p. 99).

What became clear to the investigators was that the sight during NDEs had as much to do with some sort of direct knowing as it did with sight. When Vicki was asked whether her perceptions were seeing or knowing, she responded by saying that "it's both seeing and knowing" (Ring & Cooper, 1999/2008, p. 101).

The notion of synesthesia could be helpful in understanding perception during NDEs. *Synesthesia* is "a condition in which stimulation of one sense generates a simultaneous sensation in another" (American Psychological Association, n.d.-c). Synesthesia is a frequent consequence of having had an NDE, with one study finding that 64% of participants experienced "sensory confusion or synesthesia" (Bonenfant, 2004, p. 169). While lying in bed, trying to heal her electrocuted feet, Elizabeth Krohn noticed that whenever someone mentioned a day of the week, there would automatically be a color associated with it. So, Monday was red, Tuesday was blue, Wednesday was yellow, and so on. Then she realized that this applied to numbers as well, with zero being white, one being orange, two being blue, and so on. This affected the outfits she wore and the food she ate as she tried to synchronize their colors with the times at which those events occurred (Krohn & Kripal, 2018).

Synesthesia can also be conceptualized as the blending of multiple modalities into a single perception, which is the meaning that Harold appears to have been using in the description of his experience during his NDE. So, perception during an NDE is a synthesis of knowledge from different sensory modalities, itself none of them. For many of us, materialist ideology is so ingrained in our interpretation of reality that we assume that whatever happens during an NDE must be a pathological composite of ordinary physical processes. But what if we flip our thinking upside down? What if we think that the intrinsic nature of perception occurs during expanded states of consciousness, such as those that occur during an NDE, and the perceptual products of our sensory modalities are limited projections of that perception pushed through the channels of the physical body? In the case in which some of those channels are blocked, such as sight in the case of participants in the Ring and Cooper study, we have only partial physical realization of whatever the expanded perception is (cf. Barušs & Mossbridge, 2017; Ring & Cooper, 1999/2008; Hilton, 2021). But it is the expanded perception that is primary.

Ring and Cooper came up with the expression *transcendental awareness* to refer to this expanded mode of knowing and seeing. "The *mind itself* sees, but more in the sense of 'understanding' or 'taking in' than of visual perception *per se*" (Ring & Cooper, 1999/2008, p. 107, emphases in original), or, perhaps, we could say that the psyche itself has the capacity for direct perception. They have also used the expression *mindsight* (Ring & Cooper, 1999/2008, p. 108). Vision on the part of the blind is only a limiting case. It is mindsight that is operative whenever a person sees something during an NDE. We can go back to our first example in this book of Bruce Greyson's patient Holly, who described the red stain that she had seen on his tie, or the perception by Lloyd Rudy's patient of the surgeons standing in the doorway, and so on. The scope of mindsight includes the apparent ability to count the number of mosquitoes in the frozen frame of a life review (Ring & Valarino, 1998) and to have 360-degree vision, which allows an experiencer to know exactly how many hairs are on a nurse's head and how many sparkles on her "glittery white nylons" (Ring & Cooper, 1999/2008, p. 107). Similar *exosomatic vision* has been found in descriptions of out-of-body experiences as well as other altered states of consciousness, such as those induced by meditation (Ring & Cooper, 1999/2008, p. 107). In other words, mindsight naturally becomes available during NDEs but does not necessarily require a compromised brain for its occurrence.

Mindsight fits into the broader discussion of the ability to know what is happening at a place and time to which a person does not have sensory access (Barušs & Mossbridge, 2017). This includes remote perception, with the word "remote" usually designating that a target is out of the range of the physical senses, and *veridical immediate seeing*, whereby the target is within range of a person's physical senses but unavailable to them either because it is blocked or the person's senses are impaired, such as in the case of being blind. Veridical immediate seeing is sometimes called *seeing blindfolded* because of the use of blindfolds for practicing the skill of seeing without physical sensations. A person ostensibly learns this skill by "attending to things placed in front of them, like colored cards, printed symbols, or their own hands" (Hilton, 2021, p. 9) and works up to reading a newspaper or webpage. With sufficient skill, presumably, a practitioner can engage in veridical immediate seeing with the eyes open and be able to switch between an image that has been accessed through physical sight and an image that has been produced through veridical immediate seeing (Hilton, 2021). In other words, mindsight could be continuously available if a person were just to know how to access that aspect of their psyche. I think that the occurrence of mindsight reveals latent qualities of the psyche that become exposed during an NDE.

SELF-TRANSFORMATION

It is not just experiencers who are affected by the gut punch of their NDEs, but those with whom they come in contact and those who learn about NDEs secondhand more generally. A number of studies have shown beneficial effects from education about NDEs. For instance, "nursing students who completed a course on NDEs had less fear of death, a more spiritual orientation, and a greater sense of purpose in life" (Greyson, 2021a, p. 213). In addition, other studies have found increased self-worth, "appreciation of life, more self-acceptance, and more compassionate concern for other people" (Greyson, 2021a, p. 213), and "less anxiety about material possessions and achievement" (Greyson, 2021a, p. 214). In my experience of teaching undergraduate students about NDEs and altered states of consciousness associated with death for the past 35 years, students have frequently told me how profoundly their lives have been impacted by learning such material.

Can we go one step further? Can we amplify the beneficial effects of NDEs by somehow giving those who have not had an NDE the experience of having had an NDE without actually bringing them close to death? The answer is yes. In a German study, 21 psychology students were led through a guided imagery exercise that mimicked the stages of an NDE. It started by having the participants relax; then imagine having an out-of-body experience; then undergo a life review; then move through a tunnel with a light at the end; have experiences with a golden light, such as ecstatic feelings; encounter an obstacle; and return to their usual state of consciousness. The imagery with the light was accompanied by actual changes in light intensity of a lamp to match the guided imagery text. The investigators were surprised by the extent to which the simulation matched an actual NDE:

> We were able to establish that some of the subjects in our sample (more than we had expected) reported having impressive, novel experiences during the simulation. Such experiences included a vivid memory of long-forgotten childhood scenes, strong ecstatic feelings, some spiritual visions, and, in some cases, even anger or sadness when asked to re-enter the still-living body! (van Quekelberghe et al., 1995, p. 163)

Without gathering any formal data, I have run simulations with my students, without the lighting effects, and experienced them myself, with the lighting effects. I, too, have been surprised by the impact that such simple simulations can have on participants.

But NDEs can be difficult experiences for a person to accommodate into their lives. In one study of individuals who had had NDEs who were seeking help, the main reason for seeking help was because of their difficulty dealing with the aftereffects. The second reason had to do with problematic elements of their NDEs themselves. The third most common reason was their difficulty in their relationships with others that had been triggered by their NDEs. Three quarters of those seeking help were able to find help that was positive. However, one quarter were unable to find help. What experiencers need is to be guided to an understanding of their NDE that is the most useful to them. They need an appreciation of the power of the NDE to change their lives. They need assistance with their goals going forward in life (Greyson, 2021a).

REFLECTIONS

Now that we have learned something about NDEs, I want to use that information to reflect on the question of epistemology, first in the context of NDEs and then more generally. So, what is the nature of knowledge during an NDE? Experiencers frequently report direct knowledge. For instance, Elizabeth Krohn has claimed she knew how reincarnation worked, she knew that she had been in the garden for 2 weeks, and so on. This is reminiscent of the noetic quality of mystical experiences, whereby experiencers think that they have direct insight into the nature of reality along with the conviction that such knowledge is not delusional (Barušs, 2020). This is one of the similarities between NDEs and mystical experiences. Indeed, Kenneth Ring has argued that

> in their essence, *NDEs have nothing inherently to do with death at all*, much less with life after death. Instead they reflect the shining core of the Self—the hallmark of what many have called "cosmic consciousness." (Ring, 1987, p. 174, emphasis in original)

Well, clearly NDEs do have to do with death, particularly if we restrict ourselves to NDEs in which progressive deterioration associated with death occurs. But this quotation emphasizes the notion that an NDE could be a transcendent experience with associated noetic features. Of course, that does not solve the epistemological problem.

In psychology, we usually just study the content of experiences and ignore the phenomenological framework within which that content takes place. That framework is known as *fringe consciousness* (American Psychological Association, n.d.-b) and includes *feelings of knowing*, the metacognitive sense that one knows something (Barušs, 2020), such as we have in NDEs. But we also have *feelings of reality* (FORs), a sense of everything going on being real. FORs can be diminished, as occurs in derealization disorder (American Psychiatric Association, 2013); they can be normal, during the ordinary waking state; or they can be enhanced, such as in lucid dreaming and NDEs (Barušs, 2020). In a study of 15 participants made up of students and near-death experiencers, one of my students found that judgments about what is real were based on the "objective nature of sensory objects" in the ordinary waking state, "whereas feelings of reality played a greater role in . . . altered states" (Barušs, 2007b, p. 121). In other words, we are so used to deciding that what is happening in the ordinary waking state is real on the basis of our interactions with sensorially objective manifestation that we do not notice other facets of our experiential stream. However, such a heuristic does not work in nonordinary states of consciousness because we are not interacting in the ordinary physical world. We become more dependent on FORs as a basis for making judgments about what is real and, hence, what is true.

Here is the point: FORs are enhanced during NDEs, so that what we appear to learn during an NDE can feel more true than what we experience during our ordinary waking state. If FORs fail us during derealization, they could fail us during an NDE as well. However, before concluding that the contents of NDEs are fictional, we can note that FORs can also fail us during the ordinary waking state. If NDEs and the ordinary waking state have comparable FORs, and we are using FORs to make judgments about reality, then, if NDEs are fictional, so is the ordinary waking state. There is considerable evidence that the ordinary waking state is fictional (Hoffman, 2019; Hoffman & Prakash, 2014). The point is that trying to undermine the veracity of NDEs can undermine what we think we know about our everyday experiences.

However, there are some objective ways of establishing the truthfulness of NDEs. A *Peak in Darien experience* is an experience during an NDE in which an experiencer interacts with a deceased person not known to the experiencer to be deceased at the time (Greyson, 2010). We saw that in my former student's account of encountering her grandmother, whom she learned only later had been deceased at the time of her NDE. In some cases, the person who is seen in the NDE is unknown to the experiencer and only identified later. A famous such case is that of Eben Alexander, who rode on a butterfly wing during his NDE with a woman he later recognized from a photograph to have been his birth sister, Betsy (E. Alexander, 2012). The second case involves an anomalous process of information transfer, so it moves the needle of our explanatory dial toward LAP. The first case is interesting but not necessarily anomalous because the living as well as the deceased can show up in NDEs, a fact that has been regarded as undermining the survival hypothesis (Augustine, 2015b). In Bruce Greyson's database of more than 1,000 NDEs, in 7% of them, an experiencer encountered someone "in the realm of the NDE" (Greyson, 2021a, p. 136) who was still living. But in none of those cases was the living person mistaken as being deceased (Greyson, 2021a).

However, there is something else. Elizabeth Krohn said that she loves gardens, and so her NDE conformed to her expectations of what heaven would be like to put her at ease (Mishlove, 2019). There are also frequently greeters as one enters the transcendental phase of an NDE. These can be familiar relatives, friends, animals, religious figures, or deities. Or, in the case of children, living people such as "a playmate or a favorite teacher" (Atwater, 2007, p. 58). Once the NDE is fully underway, the greeter might disappear. In other words, the NDE is not the apperception of an objective afterlife but, rather, an admixture of fact and fiction tailored to an experiencer's psyche (Krohn & Kripal, 2018).

In Chapter 5, we considered the results of random event generator experiments showing that physical reality can be bent in the direction of our intentions. Thus, it is not just the phenomenology of NDEs that can conform to personal dispositions, but physical manifestation itself. So, we cannot establish veridicality just by reference to the apparent stability of objects of physical sensation. At most, that provides a relative framework. What we need is a more comprehensive way of making judgments about truth, both during NDEs and the ordinary waking state, that takes into account the plasticity of reality. That is going to require some work (Mandoki, 2021).

We started this chapter by describing some NDEs and the features that define them. We tried to account for them as hallucinations created by a dying brain. That did not go well. So, our explanatory needle moves clockwise. The discussion kicked into another gear as we considered the anomalous aftereffects of the gut punch that NDEs bring with them. Then we considered mindsight, the nature of the knowledge and perception that occur during NDEs. So, we are definitely in LAP territory. Then we considered how to optimize the opportunities that NDEs provide, both for those who hear about them as well as those who have experienced them. Can we move the needle to survival?

I think that there are several keys in this material that could allow us to move the needle to survival. The first is the acknowledgment that NDEs are not by-products of brain activity but consciousness functioning somehow on its own. The second is the hybrid knowledge and perception quality of mindsight, whereby the psyche appears to have perceptual abilities without the need for physical sensations, which appears to be a property of consciousness independent of a brain. The third is the impact that NDEs frequently have on experiencers' lives in such a way that physical manifestation itself becomes both more predictable and more unstable, thereby suggesting a greater role for the psyche in physical manifestation. What becomes revealed is that there are expanded modes of consciousness that are usually concealed from the ordinary functioning of the psyche. And it is these expanded modes that could survive death. So, I think we can get to survival. We will get a better feeling for what consciousness without a brain could be like in Chapter 9, when we consider the nature of the afterlife.

8 PAST-LIFE EXPERIENCES

I had always been puzzled that others seemed unable to remember any of their other lives, and at times I found it hard to believe that they could not.
—Jenny Cockell (1993, p. vi)

Maha Ram Singh was near a tea shop close to his home in the village of Kuinya Kera in northern India on the evening of September 28, 1954, when "someone emerged in the dark and discharged a shotgun at him from within a few meters" (Stevenson, 1997a, p. 458), killing him almost immediately. The assailant fled and was never found. Inhabitants from the village came to look at the body, including Gainda Wati Sexena. About 3 weeks after the shooting, Sexena had a dream in which Singh "appeared and said: 'I am coming to you,' and lay down on a cot" (Stevenson, 1997a, p. 460). Around August 1955, Sexena gave birth to a son, Hanumant, who was born with a prominent birthmark consisting of areas of "diminished pigmentation of the skin" (Stevenson, 1997a, p. 466) near the midline of his lower chest. Subsequent examination of the pattern of entry wounds of the shotgun pellets into Singh's chest from the autopsy report credibly corresponded to

---

https://doi.org/10.1037/0000361-008
Death as an Altered State of Consciousness: A Scientific Approach, by I. Baruss
Copyright © 2023 by the American Psychological Association. All rights reserved.

the pattern of lighter skin on Hanumant's chest, but the match was not exact. Around the age of 3, Hanumant began talking and behaving as though he remembered the life of Singh:

> He said he was Maha Ram and, pointing to the birthmark on his chest, said that he had been shot there. He made a few other statements that were correct for Maha Ram, and he recognized some people and objects connected with him. He liked to visit Maha Ram's house and also to be with Maha Ram's mother, who lived there. (Stevenson, 1997a, p. 456)

When Hanumant Sexena first saw Singh's mother, he cried. When asked by her the reason for his tears, he replied, "You are my mother" (Stevenson, 1997a, p. 463), at which point she cried as well. Hanumant did not seem to be as involved with such apparent previous life memories as other children who have them and appeared to have stopped talking about the previous life between the ages of 5 and 6, although "he continued to visit Maha Ram's house up to the age of 10" (Stevenson, 1997a, p. 456). This is an example of a child's past-life experience, whereby a child identifies with someone who has lived previously.

Let us start by establishing the context for this material. Then, we examine children's spontaneous past-life experiences, which take up much of the academic landscape. We follow that by considering specifically cases with the presence of birthmarks and congenital deformities, such as those we saw with Hanumant Sexena. We then turn to adult cases, past-life regression, and the possible benefits of such regression. It is not just past lives that are recalled, but sometimes also the *interregnum*, the period of time between lives, so we have a look at that. We also consider materialist explanations for these phenomena and reflect critically on this subject matter to see what happens to our materialism–LAP [living agent psi]–survival dial.

CONTEXT

So far in this book, we have been looking at death, the possible transition of consciousness across death, and a possible afterlife from which the deceased continue to communicate with the living. But what about the other end of life? What happened before we were born? Did we really just appear out of nowhere as a product of biological processes? Or, did we come from somewhere? Staring forward, into death—at first, perhaps it just looks like a wall. The end. Oblivion. Nothing there. But as we listen to the experiences of the dying and the bereaved, the wall starts to fracture and break apart. Not oblivion, but an altered state of consciousness perhaps. Whether the wall still holds up at all depends on the reader. As we stare in the other direction, backward, into our earthly origins, shrouded in infantile amnesia, there is nothing to remember. Nothing to draw our attention. Or is there? Also an altered state of consciousness?

Sarah Hinze has claimed that she could sense the children who were to be born to her before their being born. With her fifth pregnancy, she has said that she could feel a "gentle female presence" (Hinze, 1994/1997, p. 4) before her daughter, Sarah, was conceived. She miscarried at 3 months. But then, within the next few months, in a dream, she saw that the same child with her long, brown hair and brown eyes would be born to her. And, in Hinze's estimation, she was. Then, while attending to her infant daughter, she had the impression of a male entity hovering over her daughter's crib, a future son. Before he was born, one of her other daughters ostensibly gave a correct description of her future brother so that it was not just Hinze who had premonitions of the children who were to be born to her, but others as well (Hinze, 1994/1997). Premonitions of unborn children can also occur during NDEs. For instance, a girl ostensibly saw a brother during an NDE. When her mother, who had been told that she could no longer conceive, gave birth to another child, it was "the same one her daughter had seen during her near-death episode" (Atwater, 2007, p. 59).

Here is another case with a connection to NDEs, which brings in several additional features. David Moquin had an NDE while hospitalized at age 48. As he drifted in and out of a coma, he had visions of himself crashing an airplane, hitting his head, being engulfed in flames, being unable to breathe, and dying as he tried to crawl to a field beyond a line of trees. Years later, a psychic told him that he had died in his most recent previous lifetime while "landing a fighter plane on an odd single digit day in November 1944" (Greyson, 2021b, p. 8). Through an internet search, his daughter found only one pilot who fit those dates, namely, Captain Fryer, who had "died trying to land his burning P-51 Mustang" (Greyson, 2021b, p. 8). Moquin's favorite plane had been the P-51; he had a model of it sitting on his desk. When asked by his daughter, he correctly knew the names of Captain Fryer's "wing commander, squadron commander, mother, and father" (Greyson, 2021b, p. 8).

Let us introduce some definitions. Perhaps the first thing to note is that there are parallels between the afterlife and prebirth. From the point of view of the living, sensing those who are to be born is analogous to afterdeath communication (ADC), so we could call it *before-birth communication*. From the point of view of an experiencer, remembering a time before birth is analogous to deathbed phenomena, which function as projections into the afterlife. This can include "birth memories, . . . womb memories, . . . [and]

prelife memories" (Ohkado, 2015, p. 3). Ostensible memories of a lifetime lived as someone else is a *past-life experience* (Baruss, 2020). The person identified as that someone else is called the *previous personality*. If there is sufficient information to identify a previous personality and that personality is found, then the case is called a *solved case*. If a previous personality cannot be found, for whatever reason, then the case is described as *unsolved* (Stevenson, 1997b). *Past-life regression* refers to psychological regression using guided imagery or hypnosis ostensibly to access information about a previous lifetime. *Reincarnation* can be defined as the transmigration of a psychological being from one embodiment to another (cf. White, 2016). With these definitions, we are not making any ontological claims at this point, just designating the domain of discourse.

There have been three main approaches to reincarnation research: the study of children who remember previous lives; the use of guided imagery or hypnosis to retrieve past-life memories; and the acquisition of information about someone's past lives by mediums, psychics, or others who claim to have anomalous access to information (Olesen, 2020). In addition, apparent past-life memories can occur during altered states of consciousness, such as NDEs or dreams (Cockell, 1996). The case of Hanumant Sexena is an example of the first of those approaches, and Moquin's case, which includes a consultation with a psychic as well as visions during an NDE, is an example of the last two. We consider instances of past-life regression later. Of these four methods, the first is usually regarded as producing the best evidence for reincarnation because of the greater likelihood of distortions that are introduced by the others.

We do not consider the cultural variations of reincarnation beliefs, for instance, which might include an interregnum between lives, or belief in animal incarnations occurring in alteration with human incarnations, or a belief that incarnation is voluntary, or might occur on other planets. Some traditions deny the occurrence of reincarnation altogether, while others maintain the belief that a process of transmigration is actually leading to some perfected state of being, and so on (Wauters & König, 2016/2017; Mills, 1994; Matlock, 2019). However, I do want to provide some incidence numbers of reincarnation beliefs in specific populations. In the initial survey of 334 academics who could be interested in consciousness, in 1986, Robert Moore and I found that 13% agreed that "reincarnation actually does occur" (Baruss, 1990, p. 174). Ten years later, with a sample of 212 attendees at the Toward a Science of Consciousness Conference 1996, that number was 23% (Baruss & Moore, 1998). In a 1999–2002 World Values Survey, belief in reincarnation peaked at 91% in India, was 57% for Brazil, and was 50% for

Japan. In the 2008–2010 European Values Survey with 62,816 participants from 44 European countries, 44% indicated that they believed in life after death and 21%, that they believed in reincarnation. In the European Values Survey, of those who believed in life after death, 38% believed in reincarnation (Haraldsson & Matlock, 2016). What these frequencies reveal is considerable acceptance of the notion of reincarnation both among academics and people around the world.

We have now established a context by considering some examples, some definitions, research agendas, and incidence figures for belief in reincarnation. Let us turn to children's past-life experiences.

CHILDREN'S PAST-LIFE EXPERIENCES

One figure towers over the academic research of children's past-life experiences: Ian Stevenson (Mills & Tucker, 2015). Stevenson was born in Canada and graduated with a medical degree from McGill University in 1943. He moved to the United States, completed psychoanalytic training, and in 1957, joined the medical faculty at the University of Virginia, where he spent the remainder of his career. Having become interested in children's accounts of past-life experiences, in 1961, he traveled to India and Ceylon to study such cases for himself. In 1965, Chester Carlson, who invented the Xerox machine, endowed a research chair for Stevenson, which gave the opportunity for Stevenson to fully engage in his studies. In 1966, Stevenson published his first book, *Twenty Cases Suggestive of Reincarnation* (Stevenson, 1966/1974). In studying these cases, he was surprised to find behaviors and physical characteristics of children that corresponded to the previous personality's features. Pursuing such correspondences, in 1997, he published a massive two-volume book, *Reincarnation and Biology* (Stevenson, 1997a), in which he collected "225 cases with birthmarks, birth defects and other congenital abnormalities that linked a case subject to a deceased person" (Matlock, 2020, para. 18). The case of Hanumant Sexena, described earlier, was taken from that collection. Stevenson retired in 2002, giving up the endowed Carlson Chair to Bruce Greyson. At this point, the research unit at the University of Virginia associated with that Chair has more than 2,500 cases (Mills & Tucker, 2015) and a searchable database of more than 2,242 cases (Haraldsson & Matlock, 2016) scored along 200 dimensions (Mills & Tucker, 2015).

Sometimes children's cases of past-life experiences begin when someone has an announcing dream. An *announcing dream* is a dream in which a person appears in someone's dream to announce that they are the person who is to be born to a particular individual. Frequently, it is the mother who has an announcing dream of a child who is to be born to her. We saw this with Gainda Wati Sexena, who dreamed that Maha Ram Singh was coming to her, and with Sarah Hinze, who dreamed that her daughter, Sarah, would be born to her. Frequently, in these dreams, the person who is to be born is already a deceased family member (Mills & Tucker, 2015). Of course, there need not necessarily be anything anomalous about these dreams. In Sexena's case, she had seen Singh's corpse, so she knew that he was deceased, and her dream could have just been a posttraumatic dream about him. Then, on the basis of the dream and the birthmark on her newborn son's chest, she could have encouraged him to imagine that he had been Singh. Indeed, parental coaching is a skeptical explanation for children's past-life experiences (Ransom, 2015; Augustine, 2015a), although we also need evidence in each case that that is the best explanation for the past-life experience.

In a typical case of this type, when children first begin to speak, they identify as someone who lived in the past. It is not that they talk about someone from the past, but they speak as though they were that person from the past in the present. For instance, Hanumant Sexena said to Singh's mother, "You are my mother." In a separate case in Turkey, when the boy Süleyman Çapar saw the killer of his previous personality in the street, he pointed toward him and said, "He killed me" (Stevenson, 1997a, p. 1438). Sometimes children only make a few statements about a previous life. In other cases, there can be 60 to 70 separate items of information. Such talking can increase up to the age of 5 or 6, at which time it falls off to about age 8, when children might no longer spontaneously speak about experiences from a previous life (Mills & Tucker, 2015).

In addition to just talking, children can exhibit behaviors that are consistent with those of the previous personality. So, for instance, Christian Haupt not only talked about baseball from the time that he could talk but carried a small baseball bat with him everywhere, wore a baseball uniform and cleats all the time, played with balls and bats at every opportunity, and would even waggle his head to shake off a sign when he was pitching. At 2 years of age, on his way to a baseball game at Fenway Park, he and his mother passed a large photograph of Babe Ruth. "I do not like him," he said, "He was mean to me!" (Byrd, 2017, p. 24). When shown a photograph of the 1927 Yankees baseball team, he pointed out Babe Ruth. When asked to point out anyone who did not like Babe Ruth, he pointed to one of the players. When asked if he knew that player, he answered, "That's me" (Byrd, 2017, p. 47). It was Lou Gehrig. Haupt identified with Lou Gehrig, not just through what he said, but also his obsessive baseball behavior.

So far, this discussion has been rather loose. A child talks and behaves in a way that baffles the parents who are trying to figure out what is happening. And then, perhaps, academic researchers show up and recast the situation as a scientific project. Or, perhaps the parents themselves do that. So, statements made by the child need to be uninfluenced by the parents or others around the child, and they need to be recorded properly with a clear time line established of what the child said and did at what time. The researchers need to investigate the case before the previous personality has been identified so that they can establish a list of verifiable statements. They might also want to assess the degree to which the child is prone to fantasize, given that fantasy proneness could be an alternative explanation for some cases, although, of course, a child could be both fantasy prone and have a past-life experience. Researchers also need to document the extent to which the child's family was familiar with the previous personality. Then, the researchers need to take the child to the place where the previous personality lived and observe the actions of the child to see if the child recognizes significant people, objects, and places that were associated with the previous personality. A scoring protocol needs to be in place to determine the correspondence of the child's behavior with that of the previous personality's situation (cf. Mills & Tucker, 2015).

These are the idealized elements of an appropriate research agenda. However, given that cases of past-life experiences were never prospective scientific experiments, the degree to which they can be reconceptualized as scientific projects in the course of their occurrence is variable. So, we are left with imperfect methodology trying to determine what these experiences can tell us about the nature of the psyche and life after death.

BIRTHMARKS AND CONGENITAL DEFORMITIES

Sometimes something physically tangible carries more persuasive weight than just statements and behaviors. So, let us consider birthmarks and other congenital abnormalities that correspond to physical aberrations associated with the previous personality and, in particular, that correspond to the manner of death of a previous personality. Are these just coincidences? Was the correspondence of the spray of pellets entering Singh's chest with the pattern of discoloration on Hanumant Sexena's chest just a coincidence? Or, was there a meaningful connection? Let us consider yet another case.

Kathy had a child, James, born in March 1978. Unfortunately, around 16 months of age, James fell over as he tried to walk. He had fractured his left leg. It turned out that there was also a nodule above his right ear that turned out to be cancerous. The boy's health deteriorated to the point at which an incision was made in James's neck for an intravenous attachment. But the situation did not get better. James bled from tumors in his mouth and went blind in his left eye from a large tumor that disfigured his face. He died in April 1980 (Bowman, 2001).

In December 1992, Kathy gave birth to a boy whom she named Chad. The doctors were solemn as they told her that her son was blind in his left eye, although they could find no medical reason for the blindness. The nurses brought in the newborn and handed him to her. She noticed immediately "a dark, slanting birthmark on the right side of his neck exactly where the IV incision had been on James! . . . It was a straight line, like a surgical scar" (Bowman, 2001, p. 25). The pediatrician told her that it was "just a birthmark" (Bowman, 2001, p. 25). When she checked her newborn more thoroughly, she saw that there was a "cyst on the right side of his head one inch behind his ear—the very place where doctors had removed tissue for a biopsy of James's tumor" (Bowman, 2001, p. 26). There had been three signs by which everyone could tell that James had been ill: "The opaque eye from his blindness, the scar on his neck, and the tumor above his right ear" (Bowman, 2001, p. 26). And then Kathy had the insight that Chad was James, returned to her. Of course, such an insight could influence the way that she interacted with her child during the course of his development.

As Chad grew, his physical features resembled those of James. Then, one day, Chad asked her if she remembered the other house in which they had lived. He described the colors of the house and the furniture, and asked for specific toys. Kathy asked why he wanted to go back to that house, for the toys? His answer was *"Because I left you there"* (Bowman, 2001, p. 29, emphasis in original). Kathy found and contacted Carol Bowman, a psychotherapist who helps mothers to come to terms with their children's past-life experiences. With Bowman's guidance, Kathy was able to communicate more effectively with Chad and work through their residual emotional difficulties from their apparent previous lifetime. Eventually, she acknowledged to her son that he had been with her previously, had gone away, and come back again to her. His response was, "I know" (Bowman, 2001, p. 44). A couple of days later, Chad told her that he could see out of his left eye. And, indeed, the vision in his left eye had improved incrementally, although not as much as Kathy had thought. By age 6, Chad rarely spoke of his life as James and seemed to be fully embodied as Chad (Bowman, 2001).

Let me consider another case, this one with congenital deformities. In late 1971, U Nga Than, who worked at a rustic roadside restaurant in Burma, disappeared. About a year later, his body was exhumed from a dry well and pulled from a gunny sack along with some ropes. The body had been folded and presumably tied with the ropes. Ma Oh Tin happened on the crowd watching the police remove the body from the sack. The following night, Ma Oh Tin had a dream about a man "with stumps" who followed her into her house. This dream was repeated a second time after awakening and falling asleep again. At the time, she was about 2½ months pregnant with a daughter, Ma Htwe Win (Stevenson, 1997a).

When Ma Htwe Win was born, parts of her head, thighs, and hands were swollen with some of them bleeding. The fifth finger on her left hand was missing. She had a congenital abnormality of her left thigh that appeared, at about 11 years of age, as a "deep groove around the middle of the left thigh . . . almost 1.5 centimeters [about 0.6 inches] wide and about 3–4 centimeters [about 1.2–1.6 inches] deeper than the surface of the surrounding skin" (Stevenson, 1997a, p. 1562). There was a smaller groove above the right ankle and possibly another, even less prominent one, above the left ankle. One day, around when she was 2 years of age, Ma Htwe Win showed her legs to her grandfather and said, "Look at what they did to me. How cruel they were" (Stevenson, 1997a, p. 1557). She said that she had been named Nga Than and named three men who she said had killed her, two of whom had actually been convicted and incarcerated for the murder of U Nga Than, with the third having been implicated. She described the events that had occurred, the fight against the three assailants, having had Nga Than's hands cut off, having been struck on the head, and then having Nga Than's legs tied with rope so as to be able to fit the body into the gunny sack before dropping it into a dried-up well. She described having been able to hear the voices of the murderers drinking and talking afterward (Stevenson, 1997a).

A weakness of this case from an evidential point of view is that everyone who lived in that region would have known about the murder. They would not have known the details of the murder which Ma Htwe Win provided, but those details remain unverified. However, what is interesting in this case are the congenital deformities that correspond to the manner of death of the previous personality. In particular, binding with rope appears to have carried over as malformation in the form of grooves, although there is no direct evidence of any actual binding of the previous personality corresponding to the abnormalities (Stevenson, 1997a).

If birthmarks and congenital deformities, particularly those associated with a person's death, appear to have carried over from the lifetime of a previous personality, could it be possible to mark the body of the deceased with the intention of creating a birthmark that would allow family members to identify a future incarnation of that person? The answer for some regions of Asia with such a practice appears to be yes. In the context of past-life research, those are sometimes called *experimental birthmarks*. The materials for marking the body vary, with soot being the most commonly used. The mark is usually made on a part of the body that would usually be clothed (Stevenson, 1997a).

Consider this example. A girl, A. W., was born in Thailand with a "flat, hyperpigmented nevus on her right leg" (Tucker & Keil, 2013, p. 272). Within several hours after the death of her maternal grandfather 5 years before her birth, A. W.'s aunt, who knew of the practice of marking the body, had made a "mental wish that her father would take the mark with him whenever and wherever he was reborn" (Tucker & Keil, 2013, p. 272). Then, she had scraped some soot with her index finger from the bottom of a rice pot and made a mark above the ankle on her father's right leg in a location that "seems to be in good agreement" (Tucker & Keil, 2013, p. 272) with the location of A. W.'s birthmark. A number of people, including A. W.'s mother, saw the body marked in this way. About 7 days after the grandfather's death, A. W.'s mother had a dream in which her father appeared and "told her that he wanted to live with her again" (Tucker & Keil, 2013, p. 272). At the time of investigation of this case, A. W. was only 2 years of age and had not made any statements about being her maternal grandfather. The only two possibly relevant behaviors were her objection to her mother's gambling, something that her grandfather had also expressed, and, about half of the time, standing while urinating, a behavior that has been found in other girls who have claimed to remember having been male in previous lifetimes (Tucker & Keil, 2013).

What are we to make of these birthmarks and congenital deformities? Perhaps the first thing to note is just the usual problem of paucity of documentation. So, for instance, in the case of Ma Htwe Win, we do not know whether the murdered U Nga Than had been bound with rope in a manner that corresponded to Ma Htwe Win's congenital deformities.

Second, in cases in which the mother was aware of the injuries or markings of the deceased, as in the cases of Hanumant Sexena, Chad, Ma Htwe Win, and A. W., the question arises of whether the birthmarks and birth defects resulted from "maternal impression on the fetus during gestation" (Stevenson, 1997a, p. 877), although it is not at all clear what the mechanism for such impression would be.

Third is the difficult issue of trying to determine the baseline probabilities of different birthmarks and congenital deformities. That works a bit for same-family experimental birthmarks in which one can rule out the presence of birthmarks similar to the experimental birthmark in the same place on other family members. But how many of these cases are simply coincidental (Stevenson, 1997a)?

Fourth is the coincident behavior of a child with birthmarks and congenital deformities that corresponds to a previous personality, which somewhat mitigates the problem of coincidence. Not only does a child have birthmarks and congenital deformities, but the child behaves in a manner that is consistent with the previous personality.

Fifth, how? What is the mechanism for the correspondence? If the correspondences really are meaningfully related, then what is the mechanism for their occurrence? How does the physical state of a previous personality become imprinted in modified form on a later body? In some cases, such as that of Ma Htwe Win, there is oozing and bleeding of the birthmarks and congenital deformities; in others, such as that of Hanumant Sexena, there is not (Stevenson, 1997a). And how does soot, placed on a corpse 2 hours after death, show up as a birthmark on a girl's leg 5 years later? Is the previous personality still aware of what is happening to the corpse after death, understands the meaning of the marking, and somehow impresses a facsimile of that marking on a fetus 5 years later? Stevenson introduced the neologism *psychophore* to designate the "vehicle for memories between lives" (Stevenson, 1997a, p. 2083), between the previous personality and their apparent reincarnation.

Does the psychophore have the ability to manipulate matter? Sixth, why? Why would Chad carry James's burden of vision loss into a future incarnation? Is there no choice? If so, then how frequently are congenital aberrations residue from a person's past lives, of which they remain unaware? Or, is the point of the physical correspondences precisely to alert family members and others to the transmigration of the personality? These are some of the issues that are raised by the occurrence of birthmarks and congenital deformities.

ADULT CASES

We already saw one adult case, that of David Moquin, who had memories of crashing a P-51 airplane as Captain Fryer, during an NDE that he had at age 48. We do not have any information, from before his NDE, beyond his affinity for the P-51 airplane, about any sense that he may have had of having been Captain Fryer. The most convincing adult cases appear to also be children's cases in that the identification of a previous personality has been present from childhood. Such is the situation with perhaps the most famous adult case: that of Jenny Cockell.

Cockell, a British woman born in July 1953, has said that, as a child, she had recurring dreams of dying as a woman named Mary in a hospital room by herself. Mary was being wrenched away from her children whom she did not want to leave, and she fought to stay alive. But over and over again in Cockell's dreams, death did come, leaving her saddled with fear and guilt on awakening. During her waking state, Cockell has said that she could remember more pleasant memories. She had difficulty seeing the physical Mary, although she knew the clothing that Mary wore. Most salient were Mary's children, of whom there were seven or eight. She had memories of the cottage in which Mary had lived with her children, of walking along the lane that ran beside it, and the layout of walls and gates. The cottage was small, and she could see herself cooking and making dough for a "round flat loaf of bread" (Cockell, 1993, p. 4). There was never enough money to buy the food that they needed. Cockell says that she mimicked Mary's housekeeping in her child's play by "mixing grass seeds with water" (Cockell, 1993, p. 4) and sweeping the floor of the garden shed. She remembered details of the nearby village, where she went to church with her children and a husband, who seemed to be peripheral to her life. She drew maps of the village, locating her cottage in relation to the roads. She somehow knew that 1898 to the 1930s was the time of Mary's life span. And she knew that Mary had lived in Ireland. One day, she had the feeling that if she looked at a map of Ireland, she would be able to tell where Mary had lived. She turned to a one-page map of Ireland in her school atlas and closed her eyes to evoke her memories. And when she opened them, she was drawn to Malahide, a village north of Dublin (Cockell, 1993).

Although she kept trying to piece together the apparent memories from her life as Mary, it was not until 1988 that Cockell obtained an Ordnance Survey map that allowed her to compare the maps that she had drawn as a girl with the actual roadways of Malahide. Eventually, she was able to visit Malahide herself to try to match the Malahide of 1989 with that of her memories from the 1930s but was unable to find the cottage itself. Then, through placing an ad in a magazine, she was led to someone living in Mary's neighborhood who remembered a family living in the cottage that she had identified. On corresponding with him, she found that Mary's surname had been Sutton. Mary's children had been placed in orphanages on her death. After considerable investigation, Cockell was able to obtain the baptismal records of six of Mary's children, then Mary's death certificate of October 1932, and the birth certificates of two of Mary's children. She placed a letter in a Dublin newspaper. At that point, she reached out to Ian Stevenson as well as Peter Fenwick for advice. She wondered whether it was ethically permissible to contact the children (Cockell, 1993).

Cockell's search for Mary's children broke when she received an anonymous note with an address. She wrote to the address and subsequently received a telephone call. It was the daughter of the second of Mary's sons. Cockell felt awkward trying to explain how she knew the family, but was able to establish her credibility by correctly describing the personality characteristics of some of the children. Now she had the names and addresses of the boys. At the time of Mary's death, the girls had been sent to a convent school and had lost contact with the boys. She called Mary's eldest son, who was 71 years of age at this point. He was able to verify some of the details that she felt she had known about Mary but had been unable to confirm otherwise. She learned that the eldest daughter had died at age 24. And then, in September 1990, she visited with Mary's eldest son in person. She was not certain how Mary's children would receive her because she regarded them as her children from the past when she was Mary. But they seemed to accept her without disapproval. Again, Mary's son confirmed many of the details that Cockell had compiled from her memories. In particular, Mary's husband had been a drunkard who had beaten both her and the children. There was never any money because it had been spent drinking. This helped to clarify for Cockell the absence of spousal support that she appeared to have remembered. Knowledge of Mary's husband's irresponsible behavior also helped Cockell to understand why, as Mary, she had felt a sense of responsibility toward the children at the time that Mary had died (Cockell, 1993).

Cockell returned to Malahide in February 1993. This time she found the ruins of the cottage at the edge of a housing development:

> For a moment or two I stood, aware of both the past and the present simultaneously. The ruins of that tiny cottage sharpened the focus of my memory and I could picture the internal walls, the fire for cooking on, and other parts that were now gone. Memories flooded back and the physical remains added an extra dimension, making it so very easy to recall. I knew that all I needed was to have the chance to be there, to remember that place in a special way, and then to say goodbye. (Cockell, 1993, p. 144)

Cockell's dreams and apparent memories had been confirmed.

The following is a case of someone who was told about a previous incarnation. Kenneth Doka is a Lutheran minister with a Christian understanding of the afterlife. Nonetheless, in the course of writing a book about end-of-life experiences, he "somewhat reluctantly and very skeptically" (Doka, 2020, p. 171) decided to have a past-life reading from someone who said that she would tell him what issues he needed to work on in his current life. The reader told him that he had been a prosperous farmer in a previous life who had lost everything as a result of a natural disaster, leaving him embittered and alienated both from his faith and his family. In this life, she said, he needed to correct his relationship with God and, because he had not loved his biological children, would need to love a child who was not biologically his. He is a member of the clergy with an adopted son and a "number of loving godchildren" (Doka, 2020, p. 171). He had not shared any of that information with the reader.

We have reviewed several adult cases in which details about past-life experiences to some degree match the facts of the previous personalities' lives. This is consistent with the children's cases. Are such correspondences just LAP on the part of a person recalling a past life or a medium talking about it? Or, is survival a better explanation?

PAST-LIFE REGRESSION

Having read about past-life experiences, it would be natural for the reader to wonder whether they have had past lives and, if so, who they had been and what they had done. This is where past-life regression comes in, psychologically going back to earlier ostensible lifetimes. There are two ways this is usually done: through hypnosis or guided imagery.

Hypnosis refers to a technique for inducing a *hypnotic trance*, which is a state in which a person loses their sense of agency such that they feel as though they are not in control of their actions. Such a hypnotic trance is typically possible only for the few people, called *hypnotic virtuosos*, who are fantasy prone or who have highly dissociative tendencies (Barušs, 2020). In practice, hypnosis is just a guided imagery technique that has been labeled as hypnosis, so let us just focus on regression as a guided imagery technique, whether or not it is labeled as hypnosis, without concerning ourselves with the virtuoso outliers.

Regression consists of leading a person through a series of symbolic images in which they disidentify with their body and seek to identify with a personality in a previous lifetime. For instance, I have used the so-called *christos technique* (Glaskin, 1976) a number of times, usually in a group setting. In my modified version, I have participants lie on the floor and then imagine stretching progressively greater distances through the tops of their heads and the bottoms of their feet until I tell them to just continue to expand lengthwise and sideways, getting bigger and bigger. The idea here is to disidentify with their bodies. Then, I tell them to imagine seeing the front doors of the places where they live and describing their doors to themselves in as much detail as possible. The idea here is to activate the imagination. Then, I suggest that they float above the buildings in which they live and look at the details of what there is to see below them. I ask them to turn through the four cardinal points of the compass and repeat their observations. Then to do that at progressively greater distances from the ground. Next, I suggest that they turn day into night and night into day to show to themselves that they have control over their experiences. I ask them to rise even further into the sky to the point where the earth is no longer visible and they are simply in an undifferentiated environment.

Once in the undifferentiated environment, I tell participants to come down in a time and a place that is meaningful to them. I consolidate that new location by immediately asking them to look at their feet and to describe to themselves what they see. Then, I ask them to describe more of themselves and the environment in which they find themselves. Then to move backward in time to find how they got to where they are. Then to move forward in time to the next significant event in their lifetimes. I repeat that several times. Finally, I ask them to move forward to their deaths, to go through their deaths, and then to reflect on that lifetime from the afterdeath state (cf. Woods & Barušs, 2004).

In my experience using this regression technique, it has not been difficult to evoke spontaneous images that can be identified as the lifetime of a previous personality. In some cases, participants land in the future. I have also noticed the realism with which these lifetimes are frequently experienced. Even though someone can be answering questions and speaking to the group and me as they are going through these imagined experiences, they are simultaneously immersed in the events that appear to be occurring and are frequently deeply emotionally affected by them afterward. In other words, such lifetimes can feel quite real.

However, that is not a universal experience (Barham, 2016). Here is someone else's description of what happened when they had a hypnotist regress them:

> I found the process to be relaxing, soothing, and oddly narcissistic, but completely devoid of any sense that forgotten past lives were opening to memory. Instead, I had the clear perception that I was attempting to supply the hypnotist with what she wanted, scenes from a time before I was born. I waited for an image to pop into my mind, and then attempted to embellish it into an appropriate life situation—exactly what I did when I was trying to write a piece of fiction or drifting off to sleep. When I became even more relaxed, more deeply "into" a slightly altered state of consciousness, the images began to come without any conscious effort. But even then, they never carried with them any more weight of authenticity than a garden-variety daydream. (Shroder, 1999, p. 21)

This is the usual dynamic of guided imagery, whereby deliberate thinking, following the guide's instructions, creates a framework within which spontaneous thinking can emerge. That spontaneous thinking can be purely fictional or can meaningfully correspond to events in physical manifestation (Baruš, 2020). In this case, the results sound like fiction without even rising to the status of false memories. Are any of such spontaneous productions veridical, in the sense that they refer to a life that was actually lived by someone?

At one point, Jenny Cockell tried hypnotic regression in an effort to acquire additional information in her quest to find Mary's family. While she felt deeply immersed in the scenes from Mary's life that she experienced, she also produced incorrect information. When asked for the name of her husband, Cockell said, "Bryan" (Cockell, 1993, p. 37), and when asked to look at the marriage register, she saw that the last name was "O'Neil" (Cockell, 1993, p. 38). Both were wrong. Mary's husband's name had been John Sutton, as she eventually learned. Trying to match details from a past-life regression with actual details about a previous personality is usually impossible both because of the unreliability of the information obtained through regression as well as the lack of documentation and access to records about a previous personality. The cases of children's past-life experiences that have been solved have involved previous personalities that had lived close in time and geographical proximity to the child's circumstances so that such information has been more readily available. That is not usually the situation in adult cases.

Another striking attribute of the past lives found by my participants has been their relevance to whatever issues they were facing in this lifetime. This led me to think that past life induction can function as a projective technique, which displays a person's inner psychological dynamics using the context of a previous lifetime. In other words, a previous life scenario gives a person an opportunity to examine and work with psychological issues that need attention. Whether or not an actual previous lifetime has been recovered becomes irrelevant. What is important is the therapeutic benefit that could be gained (cf. Matlock, 2019). In this way, past life regression can become *past-life therapy*.

Perhaps the most obvious use of past-life therapy has been for the treatment of phobias. Stevenson found that the manner of death of a previous personality was reflected in the phobias that a child had. "In a series of 240 cases in India phobias occurred in 53 (39%) of the 135 cases with violent death, but in only 3 (3%) of the 105 cases having a natural death" (Stevenson, 1990, p. 247). Following a traumatic event, a person would express fear of the specific elements of that event and also generalize the fear to other similar situations. So, for instance, a Turkish boy who claimed to have been killed in a car accident had a fear of the bridge into which the vehicle had crashed as well as a fear of cars in general (Stevenson, 1990). So, there is a connection, but can finding a traumatic event in a previous life help to resolve a phobia? There is little formal research about past-life therapy (Matlock, 2019), although, in one study, it was found that the phobias of 20 of 25 patients remitted with the use of past-life therapy (Moody, 1991).

Carol Bowman has given examples of therapeutic benefit from past-life analyses. In her case, she has said that she had chronic lung problems. Simultaneously with the lung problems, she was getting waking visions of another lifetime. So, she tried past-life therapy and found two relevant lifetimes: one in the 19th century in which she died of consumption and another emotional recollection in which she had died in the gas chambers of World War II (Thanatos TV EN, 2020). She could see that she had carried over her fear and anguish and sadness from that lifetime. She had had hints of this previously, but the regression allowed for the pieces of the puzzle to pop into place. And then her lungs cleared up.

Bowman has also described her 5-year-old son's fear of loud sounds, such as fireworks going off or the sound of a diving board. While he sat on Bowman's lap, a hypnotist asked him what he saw when he heard loud sounds. He said that he was a soldier with a long gun that had a sword at the end. He was on a battlefield, confused, and unsure who he was shooting any more. A bullet hit him in the wrist. He was bandaged and sent back to the front. He was behind a cannon and had to pull a rope. Then, he found himself floating above the battlefield. Subsequently, his fear of loud noises disappeared, as did the chronic eczema on his wrist at the location at which he believed that he had been shot in a previous lifetime. Over the following 1½ years, her son provided additional details of having been a Black soldier in the American Civil War. Civil War historians found that his description of the artillery that was used was accurate and were even able to locate the field in which he had apparently died, even though they could not find the previous personality (Thanatos TV EN, 2020).

Whereas some past-life regression appears to be clearly fictional, although potentially useful as a projective technique, other cases could be both veridical and therapeutic. However, given the difficulty of checking the details of past-life experiences, their accuracy is difficult to establish. On the other hand, it would be straightforward to conduct studies to determine the potential therapeutic benefits of past-life regression, irrespective of their ontological status.

INTERREGNUM

We considered the example of Sarah Hinze, who claimed to have had communication with her children before they were born. If that sort of thing happens, then where are these children at the time of the communication? What does the interlude between lives look like? And just as there are past-life memories, children can have prebirth memories. These are sometimes also called *intermission memories*. In parallel with NDEs, there can be both terrestrial and transcendent aspects of prelife memories. From the University of Virginia database of 2,242 children who remember previous lives, 9% (199) remembered their funeral or "handling of bodily remains" (Haraldsson & Matlock, 2016, p. 128), 11% (247) remembered other terrestrial events following their death, 11% (253) had "memories of being in another realm" (Haraldsson & Matlock, 2016, p. 128), and 5% (116) "report[ed] memories of conception or being born" (Haraldsson & Matlock, 2016, p. 128).

Jenny Cockell has said that her death as Mary was the strongest memory that she has had of that previous lifetime. She remembered lying alone in a hospital bed and dying alone. At the point of death, she said that she was "suddenly thrust out" (Cockell, 1996, p. 66) from her body and found herself "some 10 feet above the body and slightly to one side of it" (Cockell, 1996, p. 66). She was above the level of the ceiling, but her view was not obscured. She saw her husband come to the bedside. Then, she says she was drawn backward in a "loose foetal [fetal] position" into a "long, narrow tube" that drew her into "another dimension" (Cockell, 1996, p. 66). Intense "beams of light" (Cockell, 1996, p. 66) emerged on either side of her. And then she found herself somewhere else, floating peacefully in "something like a soap bubble" with other bubbles that she "knew to be people" (Cockell, 1996, p. 67). "Here the existence I had left behind, physical life as we know it, seemed no more than a vague memory" (Cockell, 1996, p. 67). It is notable that Cockell appeared to have severed connections with terrestrial events and did not engage in ADC.

Most of the apparent memories of the interregnum cannot be verified. Nonetheless, let me just list some of them. The previous personality of a Sri Lankan girl, Purnima, had been hit by a bus as she was bicycling to the market. She said that she "floated in the air in semi-darkness for a few days" (Haraldsson & Matlock, 2016, p. 125). She saw her funeral and people mourning her and crying. In another case in Sri Lanka, a boy who had remembered the life of a monk, said that he had been among the devas, spiritual beings of a particular type. In a case in Lebanon, the previous personality had been shot during the civil war and felt helpless because he could not warn his comrades about enemy action that he could see. In a case in Finland, a boy recalled being in a place with a lot of coffins, which was correct for the previous personality. Another man who died while driving after drinking "correctly recalled having been carried over a bridge after the accident" (Haraldsson & Matlock, 2016, p. 126). A woman from Thailand recalled the previous personality's ashes having been scattered rather than buried. A Thai man had witnessed his own murder and stayed near the murder site until he had followed home a man who became his father. A Sri Lankan woman recalled that the body of her previous personality had been buried by an anthill, that site having been decided only after the death of the previous personality. An Indian man claimed that he had remained near the house of the previous personality after his death. A Thai monk remembered that after dying in his previous life, he had gone to the funeral and thought that he was in charge of the ceremony, even though no one could see him. In some cases, informants "claimed to have engaged in poltergeist activity after they died," in one case, throwing a stone and, in another, breaking a "plank on a swing on which some people were playing" (Haraldsson & Matlock, 2016, p. 127). We consider the transcendent features of the interregnum in more detail in the next chapter.

In a Japanese study in 2014, 10,000 randomly selected women in their twenties to fifties were asked questions about children's birth, womb, prelife, and past-life memories. The first question asked women whether they knew in general that there were such memories. The rates for each of the four were 65%, 73%, 30%, and 26% respectively. For the women who had a child aged 3 years to 12 years, the actual incidence numbers for each of the types of memories was 16%, 28%, 13%, and 4%, respectively. In response to more detailed questions, the investigators found that "the majority of the children started to talk about the relevant memories between two and five" (Ohkado, 2015, p. 7). Elements of birth, womb, and prelife memories were verified in 87%, 71%, and 42% of cases, respectively. For past-life memories, the question that was asked was whether the previous personality had been solved. Of the 32 mothers in this category, three said yes. When verified elements were present, the parents were more likely to regard the memories as real. The following are some of the reasons why parents thought that the memories were verified:

> Some children correctly pointed out the people present when they were born. Some children delivered by Caesarean section said they had been surprised by the sudden exposure to bright light. Some children started to sing the songs their mother often listened to while they were in the womb. Some children claiming to have chosen their mother before conception correctly described the wedding ceremony or other specific situations. One of the mothers having

a child with past-life memories believed that the child was her mother reborn because the child talked about something only her mother knew. Another believed that the child had been a baker she knew because the child explicitly said so. (Ohkado, 2015, p. 11)

The investigators did not seek to confirm these verifications beyond the claims made by the mothers. But, as Carol Bowman (2001) pointed out, in some cases, it becomes obvious to a mother that her child is someone she has already known irrespective of what the scientists and skeptics think. Some mothers make judgments about their children's memories on the basis of the experiences that the mothers have with their children.

REFLECTIONS

So, can we move the needle to survival? Do we have transmigration of psychophores? Perhaps, but the matter is, as usual, not so simple. Sometimes there are different children who recall the same lifetime. In other cases, a child can remember being two different people who lived at the same time. Sometimes the previous personality did not die before a child was born (Greyson, 2021b). So, let us consider some skeptical arguments for a minute.

One materialist approach to the subject matter of this chapter is to offer an explanation for it from the cognitive science of religion. The idea is that the reason why people believe survival narratives is because they conform to people's implicit expectations about what survival would be like if it were to occur. So, in particular, people are "folk-dualists," whereby they think that some things belong to a physical domain, such as eating and drinking, whereas others belong to a mental domain, such as personal identity and memories. At death, the activities of the physical domain cease, whereas those of the mental domain continue, so that people can imagine being at their own funerals, for instance. Because we are alive, and can only imagine from the standpoint of being alive, we suffer from *simulation constraint* (White et al., 2018, p. 286) so that we imagine ourselves and others to still have those mental properties. In particular, these ideas can help to explain belief in reincarnation. *Episodic memory*, memory for specific events in a person's life, is one of the most important criteria that we use for establishing personal identity. We also use physical features for establishing identity, particularly those that are distinctive, such as a tattoo. In one study, autobiographical memories and physical marks were judged to be equally reliable means of establishing past-life identity (White, 2016).

Such cognitive science analyses have been carried out in the context of a materialist ideology to discount the evidence for reincarnation. But we need not make such an association. We know from studies using the Beliefs About Consciousness and Reality Questionnaire (BACARQ; Barušs, 1990; Barušs & Moore, 1989, 1992) that lots of people are dualists; whether they are labeled as "folk-dualists" or just "dualists" is inconsequential. We also know from surveys using the BACARQ that there are people who are mental monists so that the folk-dualism of the cognitive science of religion is not the only nonmaterialist option. But it seems to me that these analyses are helpful without being assigned to an ideological position. As we have discussed several times in this book, we do use criteria for establishing personal identity, and it is helpful to know the details of the ways in which we do that. That does not mean that materialism is the correct ontological position and that dualism and mental monism are incorrect. But knowledge of these reasoning strategies can help us with specific questions, such as, Why should birthmarks count as evidence of reincarnation (Sudduth, 2021)? The answer is that they are distinctive physical features of a person's body that help us to identify that person. When Kathy saw the birthmark on Chad's neck that looked like a surgical scar, it helped her to identify her son as James. Physical features are a judgmental heuristic that we use to identify people. It does not mean that they are always wrong. They could be right when we identify the currently living and they could be right when we identify the previously living. It is helpful to understand that we can use a person's physical or psychological features to establish what we think is their identity.

One of the criticisms of reincarnation research is that evidence is based on correspondences between a person with memories of a past life and the facts associated with the previous personality, and that it has not been established that those correspondences actually rise above chance. One way that has been suggested to check for that is to create "X" pairs and "Y" pairs. An X pair comprises two people, A and B, who are alive at the same time. Memory statements for Person A are simply statements about Person A's life. They are matched to the details of Person B's life. A Y pair comprises Person C who remembers facts about the life of Person D who died before Person C's birth. The memory statements of Person C are matched with the actual facts of Person D's life, as we have seen in the cases in this chapter. Now, blinded participants are asked to differentiate the X cases from the Y cases without knowing which is which. If the judges cannot discriminate the X cases from the Y cases by the number of correspondences, then the experiment proceeds to the second stage.

In the second stage, the X cases and Y cases are mixed up, and given to blinded judges to determine which of the cases need special explanations. If the proportions of X cases and Y cases requiring special explanations are statistically indistinguishable, then we cannot reject the null hypothesis, and nothing needs to be explained (Angel, 2015). In other words, the argument is, first, that the correspondences need to rise above the level of chance and, second, if not, then there needs to be some reason, other than just correlation, to make a judgment that there is something anomalous about the correspondences between pairs of people.

Conventional explanations have been offered for past-life experiences. The first is fraud. Such possibilities have been investigated at length and appear to be rare. They can be recognized by characteristics that are specific to the fraud cases. The second is self-deception creating *paramnesia*, distortions of memory. Such cases are possible, but they become evident when the data do not fit a person's statements. Furthermore, one can ask whether there is anything to be gained psychologically by the self-deception. And, in many cases, there is not. Third, an explanation to which we have already alluded is that of fantasy. Some children exhibit a "reversal of generations" (Rawat & Rivas, 2021, p. 122) so that they might talk as though they were big and their parents were small. However, for any of the conventional explanations, correct information about a previous personality means that they cannot just be self-deception or fantasy. Fourth is *cryptomnesia*, having learned information that is later repeated without the awareness of how such information was obtained. This is an easy supposition to make, but there also needs to be some evidence that there were ordinary channels through which a child could have acquired the information and that that is a likely source for it. Frequently, that is not the case. Fifth is paramnesia in others, typically parents, who misinterpret a child's language as being suggestive of reincarnation. Sixth, for within-family past-life experiences, there could be genetic memory, which is to say that somehow a person's experiences are encoded genetically and thereby transmitted. That seems illogical given that only parental memories up to the time of conception of a child in a previous incarnation could be encoded and that many of the past-life memories are of a previous personality's death (Rawat & Rivas, 2021). I will let readers decide how adequately the conventional explanations account for the data.

If we move from the materialist position on our explanatory dial to LAP, then we can consider these data to result from suggestibility combined with anomalous information transfer of some sort, so that a child is induced to imagine having been someone from the past and then gathers that information through a process of remote viewing (Rawat & Rivas, 2021). In fact, Jenny Cockell also experienced precognitive dreams and *psychometric skill*, which is the ability to produce correct information about a person from an object belonging to that person, so such abilities are certainly possible. Something that we have not yet considered in this chapter are cases in which children demonstrate learned behaviors, such as dances and songs, that they have not acquired in their current lifetime. For such behavior, there needs to be more than just access to information; there needs to be an opportunity to practice the skills. But we can keep stretching LAP to fit those cases as well. What becomes more difficult to do is to stretch LAP to situations in which there are birthmarks and congenital deformities (Rawat & Rivas, 2021). It is not clear how such synchronous connections occur, but trying to fit them to LAP seems overwrought.

Does the survival hypothesis fit? Yes (Gibbs, 2017; Pandarakalam, 2018), although we need to account for the idiosyncrasies of some cases, such as having been born while a previous personality was still living. However, survival does not automatically imply the transmigration of a psychophore from one body to another. In Chapter 6, we saw instances of apparent possession. Discarnate entities could displace the personality occupying a body at times. For instance, the James and Chad personas of Kathy's son appeared to take turns until the James persona eventually gave way to Chad. But, in a way, this just sharpens the question of what, and who, exactly, it is who we are. Perhaps the processes of reincarnation and possession are the same. Is reincarnation just a permanent form of possession? But by whom or what? With our conventional and LAP explanations, we are not required to confront fundamental questions about what we are. But the survival hypothesis forces us to challenge our ideas about personal identity.

One way to think about what we are is to consider the possibility of the existence of a timeless domain of consciousness from which personalities are projected into linear time (Baruš & Mossbridge, 2017). I have proposed the existence of meaning fields as patterns directing the occurrence of events on the basis of meaning (Baruš, 2018, 2019, 2021). For instance, we can think of an aspect of consciousness projecting itself as an imperfect temporal sequence of individual human lives structured by a meaning field that includes physical markings and deformities belonging to that sequence. In such a theory, consciousness is primary, and physical manifestation with its attendant phenomenology is a secondary by-product of the projected consciousness structured by meaning fields (Baruš, 2021). This is a mental monist or idealist theory that fits the data. What does the reader think?

9 THE NATURE OF THE AFTERLIFE

For the average good citizen, death is a continuance of the living process in his consciousness and a carrying forward of the interests and tendencies of the life. His consciousness and his sense of awareness are the same and unaltered.
—Alice A. Bailey (1985, p. 37)

Death is an altered state of consciousness in that it is clearly not the ordinary waking state. For a materialist, that altered state is just oblivion. There is nothing there. Consciousness for a given individual who is dead has simply ceased to exist. But, perhaps, on thinking about the material in the previous eight chapters, the reader wants to entertain other possibilities. Not, perhaps, because they have become prepared to accept survival outright, but just to see what the alternatives might look like. In other words, we want to see what happens when the explanatory needle is turned all the way clockwise to survival. If death were to be a nontrivial altered state of consciousness, then what would be its characteristics? The purpose of this chapter is to explore what it could be like to be dead.

---

https://doi.org/10.1037/0000361-009
Death as an Altered State of Consciousness: A Scientific Approach, by I. Baruss
Copyright © 2023 by the American Psychological Association. All rights reserved.

Our data are going to come from using the phenomena from the previous chapters as potential sources of information about the afterlife: deathbed visions, afterdeath communication (ADC), mediumship, instrumental transcommunication (ITC), poltergeist activity, near-death experiences (NDEs), and past-life experiences. Previously, we considered this material from the point of the view of the living; this time, we are doing so from the point of view of the deceased. If we felt queasy about accepting information from these sources in the first place, then the situation does not improve now. Except, perhaps, by noticing that an exosomatic rationale is consistent with all of them, namely, that phenomenal consciousness could exist as a disembodied reality that temporarily expresses itself in embodied form. So, in this chapter, we use the best information from these sources to put together some ideas about the nature of the afterlife.

I opened Chapter 3 with Karen McCarthy's conviction that her deceased fiancé, Johann, was still alive when a monarch butterfly landed on her foot. The following is a similar example. Suzanne Giesemann is a medium who channeled a woman's deceased son, who had told his mom that he was sending her owls. "No, Suzanne," the mom said, "I haven't sensed any owls." Within a week, Giesemann said that she received an email from the woman saying that as she had opened the front door of her house, an owl had flown in past her and up the stairs to her son's bedroom, where it had stayed for an hour before being shooed out. The woman said that she had given credit to her son "for guiding that owl like remote control" so as to confirm the medium's message (Giesemann, 2022). Are the deceased really guiding animal movement? How are such synchronicities possible?

In Chapters 4 and 6 we encountered the deceased Erik Medhus, who ostensibly speaks through "gifted spirit translator" (Medhus, 2015, p. xv) Jamie Butler. Medhus had been 20 years old at the time of his death and apparently had liked engaging in pranks. Through Butler, Medhus has explained how, as someone who is deceased, he is able to affect physical reality to pull off his pranks, including those involving insects. He has claimed that he can "steer anything that can fly" (Medhus, 2015, p. 177) but prefers different colored dragonflies because he finds them "pretty easy to steer" (Medhus, 2015, p. 177). He says that he does this by using his "energy to manipulate the energy around the dragonfly" (Medhus, 2015, p. 177), which then enters the insect and allows him to direct it. He says that he got a dragonfly to fly in circles around his mother before landing and sitting on a chair beside her. He has said that he gets together with his deceased grandmother and aunt to steer insects. His grandmother likes to "steer monarch butterflies because she thinks they're pretty" (Medhus, 2015, p. 177), and his aunt likes tattered moths, although Medhus does not know why. He says that the point of doing this is to chip away at people's "skepticism bit by bit" (Medhus, 2015, p. 177). Throughout this chapter, we consider some of his other posthumous experiences. I draw heavily on the material channeled from Medhus because of the apparent quality of the mediumship, the explicit detail with which the afterlife is discussed, and its consistency with other sources.

Usually, we interject theory into a chapter as we go along, or leave it to the end, but this time, I want to work backward by considering some theoretical ideas about the afterlife first to create a framework. In particular, I want to start with the way we project knowledge about what it is like to be alive into our ideas about what the afterlife might be like. Then, we consider an influential essay about the nature of the afterlife. Afterward, we turn to the empirical information. In doing so, I want to start with people's accounts of what happened to them when they died. We already did this in the previous chapter with some of the interregnum cases, but I want to consider additional examples. Then, I have a list of eight questions about features of the afterlife that I want to answer. After that, we turn to the main question: What exactly is the psychological nature of that which survives? Then, I say a bit about communicating with the living from the point of view of the deceased. At the end, I use the information in this chapter to explicitly analyze death as an altered state of consciousness.

In considering the empirical information, the problem is not that of insufficiency, but, rather, excess. So much has been written about the purported experiences of discarnates that it is difficult to do a systematic analysis of that material. Several syntheses do exist (e.g., Fontana, 2005/2010, Holzer, 1994), but they are necessarily based on partial compilations. Little of this material has been produced by academics or published in the academic literature, leaving it almost entirely outside the academy. I cannot rectify those deficiencies here. All I can do is to cut a swath through the material that is available to me and try to draw out the more meaningful ideas.

CONCEPTUALIZATIONS OF THE AFTERLIFE

Some writing in the academic literature has analyzed the carryover of the ways we experience life to speculations about what the afterlife must be like (White et al., 2018). As a simple example of that, there was a series of studies in which participants were exposed to photographs or written descriptions of people's deaths in which the dying were portrayed as being in a more vivid or less vivid condition, such as having eyes open or eyes closed. Exposure to targets in the more vivid conditions increased participants' attributing a "richer postmortem mind" (Doyle & Gray, 2020, p. 1) to the deceased individuals.

Although this is contrary to the usual materialist ideology, it has been argued that, in modern culture, traditional religious preparation for an afterlife has been replaced with secular emphasis on living here and now to optimize one's personal growth while one is alive. For such self-development, there is a self that is undergoing the development that gets projected into a nebulous terrain beyond death. In other words, a disembodied self survives the demise of the physical body. Furthermore, that self has the capacity for "world construction" (R. L. M. Lee, 2013, p. 113) in the sense that one's outer reality is a production of the self's mind on which it remains dependent. These "inner realms" (R. L. M. Lee, 2013, p. 113) are accessible after death as well as while alive. Indeed, without interference by the body, these realms can "become experientially intense" (R. L. M. Lee, 2013, p. 113). It is not just that these other worlds of the mind are available during waking and death but also while asleep, with sleep providing an opportunity to investigate the afterlife landscape and to encounter those who are deceased. This would be particularly the case with lucid dreaming—dreaming while one knows that one is dreaming (R. L. M. Lee, 2013, p. 113). In other words, we assume that there is a self that will continue to construct a world after death.

In a similar manner, the afterlife has been conceptualized as "a continuation of lifespan development involving acceptance, adjustment, and spiritual growth" (Heath, 2017, p. 7). The idea is that death does not introduce any substantive changes in "an individual's basic personality, beliefs, attitudes, and moods" (Heath, 2017, p. 8). The following speculations are based on channeled material and other sources, such as the ones discussed in this book. On finding oneself dead, there may be a need to emotionally release from what remains of one's physical body. Beings may be present to help the newly deceased. However, if such assistance is rejected, and a person has "false expectations, psychological baggage, or addictions" (Heath, 2017, p. 8), the newly deceased can remain in dimensions of reality that are close to the earth plane. Otherwise, they appear to end up in the "middle level" (Heath, 2017, p. 8) of the afterlife, where there could be greeters—in addition to ones they may already have encountered—but also family members and friends.

Some time after death may be spent in recovery that can include periods of sleep, although it is not clear exactly what such sleep entails, given that the physiological mechanisms of sleep would be absent. Some discarnates may try to connect with the living to reassure them of their continued existence. There can be multiple life reviews to learn everything possible from the recently lived lifetime. On completion, the deceased may freely choose to engage in some type of spiritual work, such as "working as spirit guides to the living or the dead, acting as spirit greeters, transmitting messages to the living, or spending time in quiet contemplation" (Heath, 2017, p. 9). The focal idea is that of self-development, which can include reincarnating a number of times so as to "eventually unfold to our greatest potential" (Heath, 2017, p. 9).

Perhaps the most frequently cited philosophical examination of the nature of the afterlife is from an essay by Henry Price published in 1953. Price began by pointing out that there is actually considerable empirical evidence for the survival hypothesis. The problem is that some people find it difficult to conceptualize what survival could be like because they cannot imagine how experiences could be possible without the inflow of sensory impressions. One has experiences because one has access to a world that provides those impressions. This sort of reasoning leads to the idea of there being "'another world' or a 'next world'" (Price, 1953, p. 3) if survival were to occur. So, what is the nature of such a next world?

Price argued from an analogy to sleep, during which sensory impressions are cut off, yet experiences continue to occur in the form of dreams. We have the psychological ability to produce images in the absence of sensory input. So, for Price, the next world is a "world of mental images" (Price, 1953, p. 4). These images can be in any of the sensory modalities, and the appearances thus produced can fit together seamlessly to create the impression that one is interacting with an objective world. According to Price, some memories are less detailed than others, so some of the images of the next world would be generic images, with the result that the next world would not be an exact replica of the physical world.

In such a conceptualization, there is no reason to suppose that the qualia of experiences of the next world would be any different from those that occur while alive. Thus, there is no reason to suppose that one would feel any less alive in such a world than one feels in the physical world. We can imagine the organic sensations that are necessary to produce the feelings of being alive, and we can imagine looking down and seeing our own bodies so that our experience would be indistinguishable from that of being alive.

However, not everything would be the same. One substantive difference would be that, in the image world, whatever desires one would have would be immediately fulfilled. For instance, a wish to go to Oxford could result in "the occurrence of a vivid and detailed set of Oxford-like images"

(Price, 1953, p. 8) that are incongruent with one's initial location. As a result of such experiences, one could empirically find that the world in which one finds oneself has different rules than the physical world to which one has been accustomed. If one were not an empiricist but a more "dogmatic philosopher" (Price, 1953, p. 8) who mistrusts their experiences, then they might never discover that they are dead.

It is not just the experiential stream that would continue after death, but one's personal identity as well, which need not be destroyed by the disembodiment of death. Of course, it is not at all clear what such personal identity entails. However, even if it were to include the manner in which a person is perceived by others, this could be possible in the disembodied state through interaction with "telepathic apparitions" (Price, 1953, p. 10, italics removed) of people other than oneself, which are perceived as having the same features as those people had while alive. Indeed, if such apparitions are mutual and there is some telepathic interaction between two people, then we have reestablished "social intercourse" (Price, 1953, p. 10). In other words, our experiences in the afterlife could be quite similar to those while alive.

Price asked where this image world would be found. He answered it with reference to dream images by saying that it is nowhere relative to the physical world. It is its own space. In that sense, death is a transition from the physical world with its sensorily perceptual consciousness to an image world in which sensory perception has been replaced by imagining. Such a world would be experienced as being real and would only be regarded as unreal by comparison with the physical world so that the distinction between real and unreal would be irrelevant.

Given that these image worlds are subjective, there would be as many image worlds as there are people in the afterlife. However, because of the telepathic rapport between people, those with similar dispositions would mutually create "'semi-public' next worlds" (Price, 1953, p. 16). Because these worlds are based on people's desires, they would be experienced as being materialistic in character. Furthermore, it is possible that the boundary between the subconscious and conscious becomes loosened so that unpleasant tendencies could be more easily expressed as terrifying images than those tendencies could be while alive. A person could also have conflicting desires, so that the afterdeath state resembles that of a purgatory in which the conflict between beneficial and harmful wishes is played out. There could also be "'second-order' desires" (Price, 1953, p. 23), whereby a person seeks to resolve conflicting wishes to improve the quality of their afterlife environment. In other words, here, we have again a developmental perspective of continued personal growth in the afterlife. Eventually, a person could get tired of the imagined expression of desires. And then what? Die to the world of desires with a further awakening into another kind of world, perhaps (Price, 1953).

Price's model does not sit in a vacuum. He did acknowledge his influences, including his understanding of the notion of *kāmaloka*, which has sometimes been identified as "domains of desire and attachment" in Buddhism (Bowker, 1997, p. 585). Price's student, John Hick, noted further correspondences with Price's ideas, such as their agreement with channeled material from Western mediums, and modified Price's theory by proposing a single-image world created by the reinforcement and canceling of everyone's desires rather than multiple semipublic worlds (Shushan, 2018).

Perhaps an immediate objection to Price's theory is to note that the analogy with sleep fails for the obvious reason that sleep occurs when there is a properly functioning brain. During sleep, the brain has the ability to present images to itself without sensory input so as to create a stream of consciousness similar to one that would be created while processing sensory stimuli during the waking state. Without a brain, there is no substrate for phenomenal consciousness. This is, of course, a materialist argument: that there needs to be some substance on which phenomenal consciousness can supervene. One way to fix that problem is to suggest that a human being has a *double*, some sort of subtle body that coexists with the physical body while awake but has the ability to function independently of the physical body while asleep or dead. The introduction of a double is unlikely to please a materialist but allows our insistence on supervenience to be satisfied by introducing some sort of ethereal substrate for phenomenal consciousness (Baruss & Mossbridge, 2017). However, we could also argue that the double is not made of anything and that a substrate is not necessary. The idea that anything needs to be "held up" is a reductionist notion that belongs to materialism. We could argue that all that exists is the surface, without anything holding it up. For ease of expression, I use the word "double" functionally without any ontological implications. Whether or not the analogy with sleep holds, it does provide an approach to thinking about how an afterdeath state could be possible.

DYING

What does dying look like from the point of view of those who are dead? We had some brief examples of this in Chapter 8 in the context of an interregnum between incarnations. In particular, we considered the experiences of Jenny Cockell, who claimed to have had dreams of coming out of her body at death and watching her husband at her bedside before being drawn into another dimension of reality. Let us consider some examples that are based on communications by mediums.

Karl Novotny died in 1965 and, subsequently, described his experience of death through a medium who could apparently mimic Novotny's handwriting style. Novotny said that he had not been feeling well but had agreed to go for a walk with friends:

> As we started out, I felt very tired and thought perhaps I ought not to accompany them. However, I forced myself to go. Then I felt completely free and well. I went ahead and drew deep breaths of the fresh evening air, and was happier than I had been for a long time. How was it, I wondered, that I suddenly had no more difficulties, and was neither tired nor out of breath. (Lorimer, 1984/2017, p. 272)

On turning back toward his companions, he found himself looking at his body lying on the ground, with his friends in despair. He says that he bent down and checked the heart of the prone body. No heartbeat. Clearly dead. He spoke to his friends, but they neither noticed him nor responded. He said that his dog was whining, "unable to decide to which of me he should go, for he saw me in two places at once, standing up and lying on the ground" (Lorimer, 1984/2017, p. 272). He saw his body placed in a coffin but refused to acknowledge that he had died. He tried to interact with others of his friends, but they were unresponsive as well. His deceased mother came to greet him, telling him that he had passed to the next world, but he did not believe her, thinking that he must be dreaming. It was a long time before he acknowledged that he was dead (Lorimer, 1984/2017).

Here is another case in which the deceased has difficulty accepting that he is deceased. Alf Pritchett was the name of the communicator that was given through the medium. The communicator also mentioned Billy Smart. Both names were subsequently found in military records. Pritchett was killed in 1918 near Ypres, Belgium. Pritchett said that he had been running forward with German soldiers coming toward him. However, to his astonishment, the soldiers ran right past him without noticing him. So, he just kept on running until he found a crater in which to hide. He fell asleep and, on awakening, saw a bright light. His friend Smart emerged from the light. He got up and noticed that he did not feel stiff. Smart took his hand and reassured him that he was all right. Pritchett realized that his friend had been killed several months previously, so this made no sense to him, except to think that perhaps he was dreaming. They started to float upward with the battle below them, receding farther and farther into the distance. Smart told him that he, Pritchett, was dead. No, Pritchett had said, "You got a packet [got shot]"

(Lorimer, 1984/2017, p. 284) but claimed that he himself was dreaming. It took a while for Pritchett to accept that he, too, had "got a 'packet' in a charge" (Lorimer, 1984/2017, p. 284). Given the use of sleep as an analogy for death in the previous theories, it is noteworthy that the default explanation that the deceased themselves appear to use for their condition is that of dreaming.

Let us consider another example: that of Roger Greaves, who was hit on the head by a cable and apparently never recovered consciousness. He ostensibly said through his wife, the medium Helen Greaves, that he could see his body lying on the bed but could neither get away from it nor "get back into it" (Lorimer, 1984/2017, p. 286). This sort of thing had happened previously for him in his dreams, but this time, he was unable to wake up. He "could still hear and see, though not, somehow with [his] eyes" (Lorimer, 1984/2017, p. 287). Roger Greaves described a conversation between an intern and his son that was later confirmed to have occurred, and ostensibly gave the correct number for a combination lock known only to himself (Lorimer, 1984/2017).

Whitley Strieber's wife, Anne, died. Through his grieving process, Strieber was able to apparently develop the ability to communicate telepathically with his wife. At one point, he asked her what it was like to die. Her answer:

> You feel a shock down your spine. Something unlocking. Then you're loose. I flew out of the front of my body, not the top of my head. I shot out. Then I looked around and there you were with your hand on my chest. O my soul, I felt such strong feelings! I reconnected in an instant with everyone I have ever been and everything I have ever known. You looked so little all packed into your body. You're enclosed light. We're free light. (Strieber & Strieber, 2020, p. 108)

Whitley Strieber asked for further details:

> The second I was out, I felt an explosion of joy. I was out and there really was an afterlife! There was love all around me. I put my hand on you but you didn't notice. I showed you I could walk to make you feel better, and you saw that. Like I said, I was me. I still felt physical. I was still in the bedroom. (Strieber & Strieber, 2020, p. 108)

Unlike the previous examples in which the communicators had not noticed the process of extraction, in Anne Strieber's case, perhaps because her health had been deteriorating due to a brain tumor (Strieber & Strieber, 2020, p. 108), she was more aware of the process of death itself.

One of the obvious questions to ask is, How similar are these experiences of dying to NDEs? The resemblance to an NDE has been noted, in particular, for the Roger Greaves case. However, in some of our examples, dying has been confused with dreaming, something that NDE experiencers have been careful to separate, such as in the cases of NDEs by those who are blind, insisting that their experiences were not dreams. Using another approach to that question, in one study, 44 experiences of death obtained from 36 participants through hypnotically induced past-life regression were scored by two of the investigators using the Italian language Near-Death Experience Scale (Pistoia et al., 2018). On the basis of the total score, 18% of the reports were in the range of true NDEs. In addition, the frequencies of types of experiences during the regressed death experiences matched the frequencies for actual NDEs; for instance, the most common category for each type of NDE is the affective one, followed by the transcendental category, and then the "parapsychological and cognitive ones" (Pederzoli et al., 2021, p. 325). This is an example of the convergence of information that I noted at the beginning of the chapter.

QUESTIONS ABOUT THE AFTERLIFE

As we think about the possibility of an afterlife and wonder what it could be like, we are bound to have questions. These were the ones that occurred to me from reading the literature, being involved in research, and talking to experiencers. There is no particular order to these questions except that we need answers to some of the earlier ones to ask the later ones.

Does Survival Apply to Everyone or Just to Some People?

This is a difficult question to answer. Obviously, we would not hear from those whose consciousness is extinguished and who disappear, so we have no way of knowing. There are two relevant comments to make. The first has to do with what it is exactly that survives. In the preceding examples, the deceased appear to retain the identity of who they were when alive. However, it is possible that, in some cases, all that survives is some sort of psychological residue that is left over from a person's life that could respond in conditioned ways to efforts to communicate (cf. Sudduth, 2015). This is one of the explanations for hauntings, which we considered in Chapter 6. It is also the reason why Gary Schwartz has used an "I'm Not a Robot" (INR) task when attempting to communicate with discarnate entities (Schwartz, 2021a; see Chapter 5). We will consider just what it is that survives in a bit. The second comment is that we assume that all humans who are alive are human beings. There is the possibility that some people who look like humans are not human beings but are simply using a human body for a while. In those cases, whether or not they have dimensions of themselves that would survive the death of the physical body is unknown and would need to be investigated on a type-by-type or even case-by-case basis (e.g., Jacobs, 2015). Of course, we have the same problem with humans. Do all human beings survive?

To What Extent Does One's Thinking Shape the Environment?

The idea that one's environment in the afterlife responds to one's thoughts is a central tenet of the theories that we have considered and has arisen as a consistent theme throughout the history of survival research. For instance, the late 19th-century scholar Frederic Myers has ostensibly said through the medium Geraldine Cummins:

> On higher planes of being your intellectual power is so greatly increased that you can control form; you learn how to draw life to it. As a sculptor takes up the formless clay and shapes it, so does your mind draw life and light to it and shape your own surroundings according to your vision. (Cummins, 1932/2012, p. 12)

So, what a person encounters apparently objectively is a product of what is in their mind.

Erik Medhus has ostensibly described how he built a house for himself. He said that the process is like that of daydreaming, except that it requires effort. He said that other beings helped him to create his house in a remote landscape reminiscent of Norway. He manifested a hammer and nails because he likes to do things manually. But he need not have brought them into manifestation. Here is his description of the inside of his house:

> It's a two-story house with pale wooden floors. On the first floor, I have a fireplace, some musical instruments, and a bar stocked to the hilt with liquor, so it's decked out like a party pad where I can entertain if I wanted to. On the second story, I have my couch and a TV with kickass speakers. No bed, though, because I don't sleep. Spirits don't need to. On both floors I have a bunch of big windows because I like a lot of light. Oh, and it's not dirty. That's the one thing about my environment I didn't bring over from Earth, where I was a slob. I'm kind of a neat freak as a spirit! I also made sure to include some more material possessions to make my place feel more earthlike, like some video games, a skateboard, and a motorcycle, of course. (Medhus, 2015, p. 94)

He has said that he found that the moment that he no longer needed something, "it stopped existing," so "all these things just disappeared" (Medhus, 2015, p. 95).

We could argue that such manifestation is, in principle, not dissimilar to the ability of the mind to shape reality while alive on earth. We have already considered such a possibility throughout this book, for instance, in Chapter 5 with the random event generator studies and in Chapter 6 with recurrent spontaneous psychokinesis. In other words, the afterlife may not be essentially different from life; it is just that it manifests differently because of the speed at which mental images are realized as features of one's experience in the afterlife (cf. Fontana, 2005/2010).

It is not just that humans shape the landscape in which they find themselves to their liking, but they gravitate toward those who are similar to themselves (Holzer, 1994; Mishlove, 2015; Wauters & König, 2016/2017). We tend to create communities of like-minded individuals while alive. This tendency could be exaggerated in the afterlife as we move more easily toward what we desire. This could lead to differences in ideology between different groups in the afterlife, so that we could get different accounts of the nature of reality, depending on which groups we have encountered. For instance, one communicator speaking through a medium could allege that we choose our time of death, whereas another communicator, speaking through electronic voice phenomenon (EVP), could state that a person's time of death is predetermined (Cardoso, 2017). So, which is it? Is there any choice regarding the time of death or not? Yet we have communicators giving contradictory answers. But, then, why would we even expect the deceased to know the answer? Both communicators could be confabulating. To complicate matters, this need not, of course, be a difference among communicators from the afterlife, but distortion in one or both of the communication channels (Baruss & Mossbridge, 2017).

Is There a Body?

We have already considered the notion of a double as a substrate on which phenomenal consciousness could supervene. We have seen examples in which the deceased cannot tell that they have died, implying that they seem to themselves to have bodies. In contrast, Jenny Cockell, whose experiences we considered in Chapter 8, on finding herself floating inside a bubble, has said that "I was bodiless, and this didn't matter at all; there was no need for a body" (Cockell, 1996, p. 67). When bodies are reported, a common message is that those bodies look the way that the person did in the prime of their life, so that someone who was older appears to be younger (Fontana, 2005/2010). Children who die appear to have aged in the afterlife (S. Alexander, 2010/2020; Fontana, 2005/2010). There seems to be a period of adjustment, however, to learn to create the proper appearance. For instance, Rachel Stavis, introduced in Chapter 6, has said,

> My grandma was what I now call "freshly dead," and she wasn't yet ready to be seen. She hadn't learned how to compose herself in death, so she still looked

sick. She was malformed, with the lower half of her body missing. People always expect that the dead are going to glow with an otherworldly beauty the moment they die, but that's not the case. It takes time for them to figure out how they're supposed to appear. My grandma hadn't had that time yet, but that didn't stop her from trying to help me. (Stavis, 2018, p. 223)

Given the plasticity of appearance after death, it should probably not be surprising to learn that there might be nothing underneath the surface appearance. The same may be true of materialized hands and other body parts during physical mediumship (S. Alexander, 2010/2020; Fontana, 2005/2010; Foy, 2008). In fact, it might be easier to materialize clothing than body parts, as acknowledged by one materialized being who agreed that "it was indeed easier to materialize robes than the whole body, and drew back the hem of her robe to show that she had no feet" (Fontana, 2005/2010, p. 450). This is not to say that physical materialization necessarily follows the same rules as materialization in the afterlife, but it is interesting to note the similarities. The answer to our question appears to be that bodies are optional in the afterlife.

Are There Levels or Dimensions of the Afterlife?

We have already seen this in some of the examples that we have considered. The plane of desire as characterized by Price is sometimes called the *astral plane*, which has lower, middle, and higher levels. The idea is that people gravitate after death to the level with which they resonate. The resonance arises from shared degrees of spiritual development, although it is not clear what exactly is subsumed by that (Barušs, 1996; Heath, 2017). We can also conceptualize the presence of an etheric plane between the physical and astral and the mental and spiritual planes above the astral. This leads to the idea that we could die on the astral plane in a second death and find ourselves on the mental plane (Barušs, 1996; Wauters & König, 2016/2017). In general, the idea is that, over time, people move from whatever plane they land on toward the higher planes (Heath & Klimo, 2010).

David Fontana, one of the three investigators of the Scole phenomena (see Chapter 6), has said that the participants had been told that beings who are beyond the astral plane have their messages relayed by those who are on the astral plane (Fontana, 2005/2010). There could also be difficulty producing physical phenomena if such phenomena depend on a discarnate being's ability to function on the lower astral levels that are closer to the physical plane. In our ITC experiment, discussed in Chapter 5, the medium and I had the impression that such functioning could be the equivalent for discarnates of having to go into a dangerous neighborhood with the attendant risk of personal injury (Barušs, 2007a). This leads us to the question of hells.

Are There Hells? If So, What Are They Like?

We already have hells of various sorts during life that we create for one another as a result of nasty aspects of our psyches (Mishlove, 2021b). So, if people have the ability to manifest their minds' contents, then it makes sense that there would be hells of various sorts also on lower astral planes that reflect dysphoric states of mind (Fontana, 2005/2010; Holzer, 1994). We also have the notion of *hungry ghosts*, entities close to the earth plane who to seek to satisfy their continued cravings by preying on the living. Although, if the essential theme of *kāmaloka* is the satisfaction of desire, which is possible simply through the imagination, then it is not clear why hungry ghosts would need the living (Barušs & Mossbridge, 2017).

I find that the question of hells brings out the greatest divergence of opinion about the nature of the afterlife. Older, channeled material is consistent with religious ideas about inescapable suffering (Heath & Klimo, 2010). Sometimes such torment is considered to be the outcome for someone who has committed suicide (Heath & Klimo, 2010; Wauters & König, 2016/2017), although other commentators explicitly disagree (Medhus, 2015). Then, there is the other end of the spectrum, whereby hells are considered to be inconceivable (Hogan, 2021). So, for instance, we have a bifurcation with the statement that there are "no sulphuric caverns" (Holzer, 1994, p. 142), although there could be self-created hells, versus "a complete cosmos made of sulfurous gases," in which one is "overwhelmed by the unbearable odor of burning flesh" (Bercholz, 2016, p. 29). These are directly contradictory statements. I think that if people can materialize and gravitate toward landscapes compatible with their psychological states, then anything is possible, including different types of hells.

What Kinds of Beings Are There?

Who do we have so far? We have deceased human beings and, from channeled sources through mediums and ITC, in particular, we have lots of famous human beings, such as Nikola Tesla (Champlain, 2021, 1:04:31) and Richard Feynman (Barušs & Mossbridge, 2017). There could be other advanced minds on higher levels of reality who are trying to help humans (Wauters & König, 2016/2017; Locher & Harsch-Fischbach, 1997). We have possible psychological residue (cf. Barušs, 1996). From Chapter 6, we have demons and poltergeists of various sorts (Parker, 2014; Kelleher, 2022). Indeed, there appears to be a menagerie of entities that attach to living people and drain them of their energy. We have mentioned hungry ghosts. But there are also others, including *tricksters*, who fool people into thinking that they are archangels or spirit guides trying to help them but whose purpose is to actually undermine them (Stavis, 2018). There are lots of non-human entities, some of which we considered in Chapter 4, such as angels and djinn; and "sliders," who apparently materialized peculiar hands in the Scole basement, which was discussed in Chapter 6 (Foy, 2008, p. 504, italics removed; Medhus, 2015). There are animals, some of which are not present on earth (Medhus, 2015).

What might surprise some readers is the frequency with which extraterrestrials show up. At the core of the syncretic Brazilian religious tradition Umbanda is the incorporation of different types of entities, including tricksters and extraterrestrials (Schmidt, 2014). For Whitley Strieber, the "dead often appeared with the supposed aliens, especially [the] short, dark blue figures" (Strieber & Strieber, 2020, p. 97). Sometimes the grey aliens purportedly have come through ghost boxes, producing "scratchy, popping sounds as well as high-pitched reverberations" (Moon & Moon, 2017, p. 99). One theory that has been proposed is that extraterrestrials are not interstellar but interdimensional travelers, so that their physical appearance is not the result of space travel, but dropping down into physical manifestation from higher planes of reality (Barušs, 2020).

What Is the Nature of Time?

The discussions about time in the afterlife appear to be contradictory in that the statement is frequently made that time does not exist in the afterlife (Holzer, 1994; Medhus, 2015; Parker, 2014), yet we are told about sequences of events that occur over time. For instance, we just considered Rachel Stavis's "freshly dead" grandmother who had not yet had sufficient time to figure out how to compose herself so as to properly appear to the living.

So, which is it: no time or time? Perhaps it depends on what we mean when we use the word "time." The linear ordering of events as we usually experience it during the ordinary waking state could be an artefact of the expression of consciousness through a nervous system. Without strict temporal progression, there could still be the sequential ordering of events so that a person sips wine before swallowing it, but time is no longer an overarching structure for experience (Barušs & Mossbridge, 2017). Instead, all events are somehow simultaneously available (Hamilton-Parker, 2001; Medhus, 2015). This is consistent with the ideas about time that we introduced in Chapter 8 but does not really explain anything. Much as in the case of Elizabeth Krohn, described in Chapter 7, perhaps such a juxtaposition of temporal features needs to be experienced for time to be understood (Krohn & Kripal, 2018).

What Is the Afterdeath Environment Like?

To a large extent, we have already answered this question by noting that the mind shapes the environment in which a person finds themselves. We have also considered levels and hells. But perhaps there are a few observations to add.

The first is the absence of alteration between day and night. Sometimes there is just a glow (Holzer, 1994) or a "background light" that "seemed to be reflected a little like the reflection of headlights in fog" (Cockell, 1996, p. 67). The second is the idea that if something has been created physically, then it has an astral counterpart, with those counterparts being more perfectly formed without the limitations of physical expression (Baruss, 1996; Holzer, 1994). In other words, anything that exists physically can have a counterpart somewhere in the afterlife. Third, there are aspects of one's landscape whose purpose is simply to help a deceased person to feel more at home. For instance, there can be "well-worn dirt paths" (Medhus, 2015, p. 90), even though one's feet do not touch the ground. Fourth, as part of one's landscape, there are people who can change in appearance depending on how they are being perceived and how they choose to present themselves. But one need not engage with them (Medhus, 2015). Of course, we have an entire panoply of other sorts of beings that could be part of an environment.

SURVIVAL OF THE PSYCHE

What survives? Perhaps the most straightforward answer is to say that the psyche survives, both its conscious and nonconscious aspects, and that the only thing that disappears is the physical body along with compulsions that are specific to the physical body, although it is not clear exactly what those are (Hamilton-Parker, 2001; Moon & Moon, 2017). The idea is that an ongoing stream of phenomenal consciousness continues after physical death, including the "knowledge, specific memories, beliefs, intentions, desires, and other mental states that are constituents of a first-person perspective"

(Sudduth, 2015; cf. Roberts, 1978). Such a robust continuation of personal survival has been intimated from the theories and examples that we have considered. It is apparently such a rich personality, channeled by George Chapman in the case described in Chapter 6, that appears to have been encountered by Lyndon Lang, which convinced her that she really was speaking to her deceased father (Mishlove, 2021a).

For there to be continuity of personality, there needs to be continuity of memory. For that to occur, memories cannot just be stored in the brain, but must also be accessible by the double. In Chapter 2, we considered the phenomenon of terminal lucidity, whereby a person functions in a cognitively meaningful way even though their brain has suffered organic deterioration that is so severe as to prohibit such behavior. What this suggests is that a person's autobiographical memories are not stored in the brain, or solely in the brain, but, rather, in some incorporeal aspect of reality. In the double, perhaps. In the case of terminal lucidity, a person has a brief period of access to such memories as well as the ability to use a secondary psychokinetic mechanism that enables the expression of relevant behavior. In other words, memory is already not just in the brain, but in some aspect of reality that survives the termination of the physical body (Baruš & Mossbridge, 2017; Fontana, 2005/2010).

One of the implications of the carryover of memory to the afterlife is that a person's experience of a physical condition can carry over. The physical condition itself ceases with the death of the physical body, but the person has memories of the experiences of that condition that can persist. If we combine such memories with the ability of the mind to manipulate reality and that such manipulation extends from the astral to the physical, then a person could shape a fetus to conform to the physical conditions of a previous personality (cf. Holzer, 1994). For instance, from Chapter 8, James's incision on his neck becomes an incisionlike birthmark on Chad's neck. The actual incision was left behind, but the memory carried over. Experimental birthmarks that were not part of a person's experience while alive could be carried over as memories to a future body if a person observes the deliberate marking of their corpse and takes up the intention behind it. It is also possible that some nonconscious aspect of a person's psyche picks up on the experimental marking and carries it over to a future life.

We need to be careful if we say that the "self" survives. The notion of a self is already problematic while alive, and we are not going to resolve that in the context of death. However, one way to think about the self is to differentiate a trait self from a core self. A *trait self* is just a collection of personal attributes that persist over time, whereas a *core self* is an essential core of a person's subjective experience (Nichols et al., 2018; Ferrucci, 2015), which is to say that the psychological structure and qualia that underlie the occurrence of phenomenal consciousness (Baruš & Mossbridge, 2017).

In a study with 1,585 participants representing a range of religious and nonreligious views, in which concepts of self and fear of death were surveyed, it was found that Monastic Tibetans were more likely to fear self-annihilation than any of the other groups. This surprised the investigators, given that Monastic Tibetans believe that there is no persistent trait self and no core self, so there is no self to annihilate and hence no reason to fear self-annihilation. However, there is a distinction in Buddhism "between *innate* self-grasping and *philosophical* self-grasping" (Nichols et al., 2018, p. 330; emphasis in original). *Philosophical self-grasping* refers to intellectual acceptance of the existence of self, which could be more easily relinquished, whereas *innate self-grasping* is an implicit understanding of the presence of self, which may take considerable meditation practice to dislodge. Although the Monastic Tibetans may have intellectually grasped the transience of a core self, they may have been psychologically unable to release an innate attachment to the notion of a core self (Nichols et al., 2018). Or perhaps philosophical self-grasping is correct, and there really is a core self. For our purposes, it is possible that both the core self and the trait self, to the extent that they are present during life, survive death.

The capacity for emotional experiences is also carried over into the afterlife. Perhaps most ubiquitous are expressions of love, including idyllic forms of love (Fontana, 2005/2010). In the cases of Karen McCarthy (2020) and Whitley Strieber (Strieber & Strieber, 2020), we have seen romantic relationships continue after one member of the couple has died. Erik Medhus ostensibly claims that his relationship with his mother has deepened after his death and that he has come to love himself in a way that he did not while alive. Furthermore, he claims that he cannot hold on to negative emotions for very long (Medhus, 2015).

However, clearly dysphoric emotional states could also occur in the afterlife, as evidenced by our discussion about hells. There is a famous Icelandic case from 1937 whereby an irascible drop-in communicator, who eventually gave his name as Runólfur Runólfsson, showed up during a séance demanding that his leg be given back to him. It turned out that a Runólfur Runólfsson, a tall man, had been washed ashore in a dismembered state, although there was no documentation of a missing femur. However, the Runólfur communicator said that his leg was at the house of one of the sitters and, indeed, when the sitter tore down one of the walls of his house, the femur of a tall man was found. That femur was ceremoniously buried, after which event the communicator mellowed out (Braude, 2003). According to Erik Medhus, "emotions create the thoughts, and thoughts create experiences" (Medhus, 2015, p. 81). Whether or not we agree with Medhus, if *kāmaloka* is the plane of desire, then it is possible that emotional expression is an essential aspect of this layer of the afterlife (Baruss, 1996).

Let us consider perceptual experiences. In Henry Price's conception of the afterlife, perception is replaced by imaging, so that instead of receiving sensory impressions, we create them. But could there be a dual process, the creation of images through the use of the imagination that are then perceived by the double? If so, what is that perceptual process? Here is Erik Medhus's description of sensory impressions:

> I don't get just one sensation on my fingertips, on my skin, through my eyes, ears, or nose, if I had those. Every sensation is all over and in me. What's also really cool is that all these senses overlap and get jumbled together. When I see something, it comes with a taste, a smell, and a sound. Kind of like how synesthesia works for people who have it. When I hear, taste, feel, see, or smell something, I get a symphony of other sensory input as well, and when I clap my hands together, I can actually see the sound waves coming out. (Medhus, 2015, pp. 69–70)

This sounds like mindsight, which we discussed in Chapter 7. In other words, there is a mode of perception that belongs to the mind. While we are in a physical body during the ordinary waking state, that mode of perception usually remains unnoticed. When the physical body is compromised or absent, then that is the perceptual mode with which we are left. It is mindsight that is going to be an ability of the surviving self, alongside that self's memories and emotions.

COMMUNICATING WITH THE LIVING

Communication among the deceased appears to be telepathic (Hamilton-Parker, 2001; Wauters & König, 2016/2017). That is consistent with Henry Price's speculation that interaction between discarnate entities is telepathic. Also, apparently some sort of telepathy carries over to communication with the living, even though the deceased are in their dimensions of reality and the living in theirs (Cardoso, 2017). We have also seen examples of communication through psychokinetically guiding insects and animals in physical manifestation. But let us start with perhaps the more common experience of the deceased's inability to communicate with the living.

Among the cases that we have previously considered, such as that of Karl Novotny, were those in which the recently deceased have tried to communicate with the living but have been unable to get through to them, even though they think that their presence is obvious. Such was the case also with Anne Strieber:

> I had been going around trying to talk to people and nobody was noticing me. It was just plain odd and really annoying. You feel like yourself and you talk and nothing whatsoever happens. You yell. You completely forget about being dead, at least I did. . . . I was with Trish MacGregor, who was sitting there writing about me. I said hello. No response. I touched her head. Nothing. Finally I just blew up. Then she sits up and yells and they both start running around their house. (Strieber & Strieber, 2020, p. 118)

Apparently Anne Strieber's emotional outburst had manifested as a physical "flash of light and an explosion" (Strieber & Strieber, 2020, p. 118) to her friend and friend's partner. On inquiry by her husband, Whitley, Anne Strieber said that she "was frustrated that everybody's so blind and deaf and—just plain thick" (Strieber & Strieber, 2020, p. 118).

So, the living usually cannot perceive the deceased. But sometimes, there is a breakthrough, as in the case when Anne Strieber became frustrated and "just blew up." Erik Medhus has claimed that he was hopping at the foot of his mother's bed when, to his surprise, she saw him (Medhus, 2015). Whitley Strieber had heard his wife's laughter, then the words "I can talk to you" (Strieber & Strieber, 2020, p. 149). He was shocked. He has said that "that voice had not been part of me, it had come as if somebody else was speaking in my mind, somebody besides me" (Strieber & Strieber, 2020, p. 149). On establishing communication, they had talked and talked. For Karen McCarthy, it had been the butterfly landing on her foot that had convinced her that the deceased Johann was communicating with her. Similarly, we have Medhus's description at the beginning of this chapter of guiding insects as a way of communicating with the living, thereby eroding their skepticism.

Karen McCarthy and Whitley Strieber claimed to have developed telepathic communication with their deceased partners. Anabela Cardoso claimed that her ITC research led to the development of telepathic abilities so that she could telepathically receive spontaneous messages or responses to questions (Cardoso, 2017). Those who have these abilities could become mental mediums and, in McCarthy's case, she did become a medium (McCarthy, 2020). Such mediumship can ostensibly become highly accurate. According to Erik Medhus, Jamie Butler, the "spirit translator" who channels him, can translate word for word and at the same time see and feel him (Medhus, 2015).

Medhus has also explained how he learned to create voiceprints for EVP. He said that he went to an EVP center in Italy, where lots of discarnates go to learn how to create EVP from other discarnates who are good at producing it. He claimed to have learned to interact with electrical energy in such a way as to leave an imprint of his voice. He said that it is easier to leave the voice imprint on the recorder than to have himself heard audibly because then he does not have to lower his "frequency to make it louder for the human ear" (Medhus, 2015, p. 165); the recorder does that for him. When a person plays back the recording, they hear his voice.

The reader may have noticed that we have come full circle and that we are just cycling through the material that we have already covered in earlier chapters—ADC, mediumship, and ITC. The first time around, we were looking at it from the side of the living. This time, we are taking the perspective of the deceased. But these are the same phenomena.

There has been some discussion about what the deceased are and are not able or allowed to do when they interact with the living. So, for instance, it is not always possible to talk to the deceased person of choice (Cardoso, 2017), although Erik Medhus has described how he can be in 100 different places at once. But it is Medhus who has also said that there are limits to what he is allowed to do when helping people—that too much interference removes a person's ability to learn for themselves (Medhus, 2015). The Scole group shut down due to interference by beings from the distant future (Foy, 2008). Others have given lists of what the deceased are not allowed to do, such as providing information about the future, fixing things, intervening medically, and so on (McKay, 2021). That seems like an odd list given that we have already seen examples of such interference. For instance, in Chapter 6, we saw the apparent healing of Robin Hodson's heart condition when he sat in one of Stewart Alexander's séances. As a separate example, McCarthy's fiancé directed her to the perfect apartment for her to live in (McCarthy, 2020). Furthermore, if there are rules, then these are being broken by nasty entities that interfere with the lives of human beings, as we discussed in Chapter 6. If there are rules, what are they, what is the extent of possible interference, and how are the rules enforced?

Using the theory of meaning fields, rules are just specific meaning fields. As long as someone is under the influence of a particular meaning field, those are the rules that will apply. Or, a person can switch to a different meaning field with different rules. For instance, if a person is convinced that the deceased cannot heal the living, then that could well limit such possibilities. Healing by the deceased could become possible by switching to a meaning field in which it occurs. We can also notice that this theory of meaning fields includes the idea that a person's thinking can shape their environment, which was a property of the afterlife that we noted previously.

But this does leave us with the question of the extent to which the deceased and other entities in the afterlife provide assistance of various sorts to the living. Is there more that is possible to do to help the living to resolve global crises? By failing to adequately investigate the afterlife, are we shutting ourselves off from a resource that could be critical to our survival on this planet? One way of conceptualizing global crises is to see them as an opportunity for radical self-transformation toward expansions of consciousness that include encompassing the afterlife as part of lived experience (cf. Baruš, 2021; Strieber & Strieber, 2020; Kowalewski, 2019). The point is that we could use all the help we can get, including from beings in other planes of reality that are able to help (Baruš, 2021; Baruš & Mossbridge, 2017).

DEATH AS AN ALTERED STATE OF CONSCIOUSNESS

What we have done thus far in this chapter is to consider the nature of the afterlife. As part of doing that, we have noted the apparent characteristics of the afterdeath psyche. I want to use what we have learned to compare the state of consciousness of a person while alive with their state when deceased. To remind ourselves, an altered state of consciousness is a stable state of consciousness that is different from the ordinary waking state along some dimensions of interest (Baruš, 2020; Walsh, 1995; Pekala, 1991; Farthing, 1992). What does that altered state of consciousness look like?

Let us start with some obvious dimensions and then move toward more subtle ones; otherwise, there is no strict ordering. In the list that follows, the dimensions for which there appears to be a substantial change between the ordinary waking state to death are marked with an asterisk. I am not committed to these dimensions or the judgment of which ones are associated with changes. On the contrary, I encourage readers to do this exercise for themselves and come up with their own analyses:

- **Physiology***: The physical body ceases to be functionally able to sustain life and enters a state of decomposition.

- **Behavior***: Accompanying the physiological shift, there is no meaningful physical behavior. This is similar to sleep insofar as the physical body usually does not engage in meaningful behavior while asleep. Exceptions for sleep would be eye movements, fist clenches, sleeptalking, sleepwalking, and so on (Baruš, 2020) which do not apply to death.

- **Phenomenal consciousness:** There appears to be an experiential stream suffused with qualia. This was Henry Price's assumption, which appears to be supported from our reports. Given that time is not the same, it is possible that the stream is not a stream as we ordinarily encounter it.

- **Behavioral consciousness*:** With behavior gone, behavioral consciousness is gone, at least insofar as the corpse is concerned. Patterns of synchronous physical events, such as successfully responding to an INR task or the presence of a butterfly, could be interpreted as markers of an experiential stream.

- **Time sense*:** Sequences of events occur, yet all events appear to be simultaneously present.

- **Cognition:** Not much different. Cognition is possibly clearer and more rational than during the ordinary waking state, as judged from descriptions of NDEs.

- **Memory:** Memory appears to be intact and include events from the life previously lived, although those events can begin to seem dreamlike. This can apply to episodic memory for events in one's life as well as semantic memory, such as Géza Maróczy's ability to play chess (described in Chapter 4).

- **Metacognition:** Despite some problems figuring out that one is dead, there seems to be awareness of one's own mental states.

- **Attention:** Attention appears to function the same as during life, but it is possible that there can be variations if there is an ability to be in 100 places at once.

- **Affect:** Emotional experiences occur, although there could be, in particular, augmented feelings of love.

- **Motivation:** There appears to be motivation present, for instance, meeting one's desires, engaging in self-improvement, or interacting with the living.

- **Perception*:** The presence of mindsight, which is a form of perception somewhat altered relative to the ordinary waking state, in that perception is more holistic rather than broken into a montage of inputs from individual sensory modalities.

- **Communication*:** Communication with other discarnates appears to be in the form of telepathy, which, for most people, is only partially realized during physical life.

- **Self-talk:** The presence and nature of self-talk are unknown, made more difficult to judge because one's mode of communication is through telepathy.

- **Decision making:** Decision making appears to be the same as in the ordinary waking state.

- **Meaningfulness:** Meaningfulness is preserved to the extent that it is part of the occurrence of phenomenal consciousness. It is also possible for there to be psychological residue that does not experience meaningfulness.

Using the preceding dimensions, death is an altered state of consciousness, altered along six of 16 dimensions. The most salient dimension is that of behavior of the body, which has ceased to be meaningfully expressive. Time sense, perception, and communication have changed, but not as radically as behavior. The remaining dimensions appear to be pretty much the same after death as before. So, we have an altered state of consciousness, but not that altered. The experience of death might not be that different from the experience of being alive. Indeed, we have seen examples of the recently deceased who cannot tell the difference.

If we were to use the same dimensions to compare death, not to the ordinary waking state but to sleep, then there would be an even closer match. The physiological and behavioral dimensions would remain the same. Just time sense, perception, and communication would differ, although those are sometimes distorted during dreams in the same direction as death. Indeed, the deceased themselves apparently easily mistake their state for sleep. There is the philosophical parallel between sleep and death as noted by Price. There has also been speculation that the domain of dreams is the astral plane in which the deceased find themselves (Baruš, 1996).

So, where does this leave us? For a materialist, this entire chapter is fictional speculation resulting from the use of reasoning heuristics that we use for making sense of living experience. Agreement among sources of communication demonstrates nothing except to show how robust such reasoning heuristics are for any given culture at any given time. All this telepathic communication is just made-up stuff. If we think that the synchronicities point toward something meaningful, then we might be inclined toward living agent psi. McCarthy was led to find a good apartment not by her fiancé, Johann, but by her own anomalous abilities, which framed her intuitions in the context of communication with Johann.

But the point of this chapter was to let the survival hypothesis loose. If survival were to occur, what would that look like based on information from the sorts of phenomena that we have considered in this book? Despite some points of friction, a fairly consistent picture does emerge, particularly if we acknowledge that the features of the afterlife could be shaped by a person's disposition. That picture includes the ability of phenomenal consciousness to survive the demise of the physical body. We can conceptualize the psychophore as a double that was always there but that is released by death from its association with the physical body. The double has perceptual abilities in the form of mindsight with which to see physical events as well as transcendent ones. The double typically lands at some level of the astral planes that is consistent with a person's spiritual development; anything from hells to more idyllic domains. One's activities can include anything that was part of a person's life before death, given that one can mentally bring about whatever circumstances are necessary for the realization of one's fears and desires. The deceased can interact with one another as well as with other discarnate beings, communicating through the use of telepathy. There can be communication with the living as well as some manipulation of physical reality. And when one gets tired of the plane of desire, one dies and moves on to the next plane of expression. Is that what happens?

EPILOGUE

The mystical may elude us, but death will not. . . . Death and what follows—communication through the veil—may be the ordinary person's most transparent entrée into mystical experience. . . . We need not close this book and blink our way out into the light, as we do from a movie matinee, emerging back into the real world. After-death communication is of the real world. It is magnificent. And it is within reach.

—Annie Mattingley (2017, p. 202, emphasis in original)

This has been a book about death. In particular, a book about death considered as an altered state of consciousness. In conclusion, I want to gather together what I think are nine key points that arise from this material and see what they tell us.

NINE KEY POINTS

Changing Boggle Thresholds

Perhaps the first thing to notice is that there are individual differences in beliefs about consciousness and reality of a person who is thinking about death, whether that person is a researcher, experiencer, or someone just interested in the subject matter. Our underlying beliefs about consciousness and reality, from materialism to extraordinary transcendence, affect how we think about this material. In particular, each person has a boggle threshold that sets a limit on what they believe is possible. For one person, the idea that telepathy could occur is outrageous, whereas someone else has no difficulty accepting that a pink, plastic pig can travel from place to place by itself.

However, boggle thresholds can change. They can change through adherence to an authentic scientific attitude that allows for expansions of one's understanding. What we have seen in this book, however, are instances of more dramatic shifts caused by the occurrence of anomalous experiences, such as Elizabeth Krohn's near-death experience (NDE) when she was hit by lightning. Such a transformational process can be symbolized by Plato's cave allegory. The prisoner is dragged into the light and, on coming back to the cave, sounds like a lunatic to the remaining prisoners. Self-transformation that changes boggle thresholds has been a key theme throughout this book. And the direction of change is typically away from materialism toward extraordinarily transcendent beliefs about consciousness and reality.

Neutralizing Materialism

Perhaps the second thing to note is the prominence of philosophical materialism in the academy and in science more generally. In fact, materialism is not just prominent but frequently dogmatic and forcibly imposed on academic and scientific discourse. In some cases, those presenting evidence or theories contrary to materialism are sanctioned and silenced. Materialists sometimes insist that all possible materialist explanations be completely exhausted before any nonmaterialist theories are entertained. Such rules have nothing to do with science. Authentic science is an open exploration in which the theories with the best goodness of fit are used until such time as they themselves no longer fit the facts. Then we move on. When confronted with evidence against materialism, some materialists twist and turn to try to force materialist ideology onto the anomalous data, even though it might be time to relinquish their beliefs. My strategy in this book has been to acknowledge and present to the reader the most substantive materialist arguments when appropriate but to otherwise not allow materialist agendas to take over the content.

Neutralizing Pathomorphism

There is a third element—linked to the prominence of materialism—that surfaces with each of the phenomena that we have discussed, namely, pathomorphism, the tendency to label as pathological any psychological states that do not conform to a narrow band of acceptable behavior. This would include deathbed phenomena, afterdeath communication, mediumship, possession, NDEs, and past-life experiences. What we have found is that we can usually separate out anomalous phenomena from pathological states.

Two nuances are notable, however. One is that physical and psychological pathology can produce conditions that are conducive to the expression of anomalous phenomena. In other words, we have the occurrence of mixed states involving pathology and genuinely anomalous experiences. The second nuance is that anomalous phenomena, while not pathological of themselves, can create psychological duress that can lead to impaired social functioning or psychopathology. In fact, gaslighting by mental health professionals can contribute to experiencers' distress, as we have noted several times. It is important to provide properly informed care for those who have had anomalous experiences and need help with them.

Pivotal Role of Near-Death Experiences With Temporal Anchors

I think that the fourth key in this material is the collection of cases of NDEs with temporal anchors. In expanding human knowledge, a scientist can deliberately direct themselves toward anomalies that drive a wedge into the chinks of a prevailing theory. Famously, in the late 19th century, investigation of blackbody radiation and the photoelectric effect led to quantum theory, which obliterated earlier ways of conceptualizing matter and replaced them with absurdities, in the words of Richard Feynman, as we noted toward the end of Chapter 6. I think that NDEs with temporal anchors are the late 20th-century version of blackbody radiation. They are the wedge driven into a chink in materialism that could lead to a radical reconceptualization of reality. Someone without the right kind of brain activity that is supposed to be required for phenomenal consciousness to arise nonetheless, afterward, correctly describes physical events that occurred at the time when the necessary brain activity for such perceptions was absent. I think this wedge is also a fulcrum that enables other anomalous phenomena to be more readily accepted. Consciousness appears to be able to function without a brain, which is congruent with the idea that disembodied beings could be communicating through butterflies, or mediums, or electronic voice phenomenon, or that we ourselves were disembodied beings before birth. NDEs with temporal anchors lend credibility to drawing the remaining phenomena into a meaningful network of exosomatic ideas.

Living Agent Psi Versus Dead Agent Psi

The fifth significant element is the explanatory power of living agent psi (LAP). An NDE with a temporal anchor could be the result of an experiencer's retrocognitively remote viewing what happened while their brain was unable to produce phenomenal consciousness and then erroneously interpreting those perceptions as real-time events. More generally, the phenomena we ascribe to discarnate beings could be the nonconscious production by the living through the use of remote viewing and remote influencing. But this is where it gets tricky. How exactly would discarnate beings produce anomalous effects except through remote viewing and remote influencing? So, the problem narrows to determining the source of the anomalous phenomena. Is it LAP or dead agent psi (DAP)? Or what is sometimes likely a combination of LAP and DAP, as in some cases of poltergeist activity or ITC, whereby the right kind of person needs to be present before anything happens?

I think that LAP alone is an inadequate explanation for all cases. It seems to me that, with LAP, we are demanding too much nonconscious anomalous activity on the part of living individuals and that anomalous activity on the part of discarnate individuals is required to make up the difference to actually produce the phenomena that occur. Just as materialist explanations need evidence to support them, so too do LAP explanations need evidence that LAP is a better explanation than survival. Indeed, in Chapter 4, we presented reasons to prefer DAP to LAP. So, for some cases, we have good arguments to favor survival over LAP.

Implications of Mindsight

My sixth key observation is that the occurrence of mindsight is significant. The psyche, without appropriate physical sensory pathways or a brain that can process visual information, can "see" in the sense of some combination of perception and knowledge. Again, this is a pivotal point. We can add qualities of disembodied memory, cognition, emotions, desires, and other psychological attributes to an exosomatic double. This does not always result in beatific experiences. Shadow elements also carry over to form distressing experiences. Appropriate self-transformation becomes critical for integrating dysphoric events into a meaningful psychological synthesis. The net result is that, by the time we are finished noting the features of an expanded psychological state, we see that survival does not just connote some minimal postmortem residue, but a fully functioning human being. Furthermore, as implied by the nature of mindsight, such functioning can constitute an expanded state of consciousness in which we have transcended the materialism–LAP–survival explanatory arc.

Implications of the Plasticity of Physical Manifestation

The seventh key observation is the plasticity of the physical world. We have the occurrence of apparent anomalous deviations of a random event generator, the Pauli effect, anomalous object displacement, levitation, dematerialization, and phone calls from the dead. Sometimes physical manifestation appears to follow the imagination rather than Newton's mechanics. Does the ability of the mind to shape the landscape in the afterlife apply to physical existence among the living? Is physical manifestation simply one expression of the multiple levels of reality that have been noted in the afterlife? Is life just a temporal blip in an eternal afterlife? Is consciousness primary? Is physical manifestation an expression of consciousness guided perhaps by meaning fields that allow for unconventional variations to occur? It could be that it is matter that is a by-product of consciousness. That is, of course, one of the characteristics of the extraordinarily transcendent position about beliefs about consciousness and reality. Is that where we all end up?

Death as an Altered State of Consciousness

The eighth key point is the thesis of this book. If we have a fully functioning human being in the afterlife minus just the physical meat jacket that is visible to the physically living, then is death not just an alteration of consciousness? When, in Chapter 9, we analyzed death as an altered state of consciousness along 16 dimensions, we found that there were only six of them along which consciousness was demonstrably altered. Although this could be an artifact of biased projections on our part, this analysis does suggest the possibility that being dead is not much different than being alive. Phenomenal consciousness appears to continue in much the same way as it did during life. If that is the case, then we have an answer to the question of survival.

Reflections

Is there anything that we can take away from this list of key points? I think so. In Chapter 6, Erik Medhus's incarnate mother felt "little" to the discarnate Erik. In Chapter 9, the discarnate Anne Strieber used the same word "little" to describe the incarnate Whitley. While alive, we appear to be in a diminished corporeal form. Reflecting on death allows us to see that we are not the little creatures that we appear to be, but that we are already expanded beings who express themselves for a while within physical manifestation. So, my ninth point is that the story is not about the materialism–LAP–survival dial. The story is about the realization of our true nature.

References

Alexander, E. (2012). *Proof of heaven: A neurosurgeon's journey into the afterlife.* Simon & Schuster.

Alexander, E., & Newell, K. (2017). *Living in a mindful universe: A neurosurgeon's journey into the heart of consciousness.* Rodale.

Alexander, S. (2020). *An extraordinary journey: The memoirs of a physical medium.* White Crow Books. (Original work published 2010)

Ali, D. (2018). *An empirical examination of contemporary American spiritualist mediumship at Lily Dale, New York* [Unpublished master's major research project]. Western University, London, Ontario, Canada. https://ir.lib.uwo.ca/wrf/2019/poster/37/

Allison, R. (with Schwarz, I.). (1980). *Mind in many pieces.* Rawson, Wade.

Alvarado, C. S. (2015). Charles Richet. In *Psi encyclopedia.* The Society for Psychical Research. https://psi-encyclopedia.spr.ac.uk/articles/charles-richet

American Psychiatric Association. (2013). *Diagnostic and statistical manual of mental disorders* (5th ed.). https://doi.org/10.1176/appi.books.9780890425596

American Psychological Association. (n.d.-a). Demonic possession. In *APA dictionary of psychology.* https://dictionary.apa.org/demonic-possession

American Psychological Association. (n.d.-b). Fringe consciousness. In *APA dictionary of psychology.* https://dictionary.apa.org/fringe-consciousness

American Psychological Association. (n.d.-c). Synesthesia. In *APA dictionary of psychology.* https://dictionary.apa.org/synesthesia

Anastasia, J., Wahbeh, H., Delorme, A., & Okonsky, J. (2020). A qualitative exploratory analysis of channeled content. *EXPLORE: The Journal of Science and Healing, 16*(4), 231–236. https://doi.org/10.1016/j.explore.2020.02.008

Angel, L. (2015). Is there adequate empirical evidence for reincarnation? An analysis of Ian Stevenson's work. In M. Martin & K. Augustine (Eds.), *The myth of an afterlife: The case against life after death* (pp. 575–583). Rowman & Littlefield.

Anthony, M. (2021). *The afterlife frequency: The scientific proof of spiritual contact and how that awareness will change your life*. New World Library.

Assagioli, R. (1965). *Psychosynthesis: A manual of principles and techniques*. Penguin Books.

Atwater, P. M. H. (2007). *The big book of near-death experiences: The ultimate guide to what happens when we die*. Hampton Roads Publishing.

Atwater, P. M. H. (2011). *Near-death experiences, the rest of the story: What they teach us about living, dying, and our true purpose*. Hampton Roads Publishing.

Atwater, P. M. H. (2013). *Future memory*. Hampton Roads Publishing. (Original work published 1999)

Augustine, K. (2015a). Introduction. In M. Martin & K. Augustine (Eds.), *The myth of an afterlife: The case against life after death* (pp. 1–47). Rowman & Littlefield.

Augustine, K. (2015b). Near-death experiences are hallucinations. In M. Martin & K. Augustine (Eds.), *The myth of an afterlife: The case against life after death* (pp. 529–569). Rowman & Littlefield.

Bailey, A. A. (1985). *Death: The great adventure*. Lucis Publishing Company.

Banks, J. (2001). Rorschach audio: Ghost voices and perceptual creativity. *Leonardo Music Journal, 11*, 77–83. https://doi.org/10.1162/09611210152780728

Banks, J. (2012, August 9). Rorschach audio and the electronic séances of Prof Imants Baruss. *Rorschach Audio*+Disinformation. https://rorschachaudio.com/2012/08/09/itc/

Barbato, M., Blunden, C., Reid, K., Irwin, H., & Rodriguez, P. (1999). Parapsychological phenomena near the time of death. *Journal of Palliative Care, 15*(2), 30–37. https://doi.org/10.1177/082585979901500206

Barbell, S. (1993). Play and the paranormal. A conversation with Dr. Raymond Moody [Interview]. https://web.archive.org/web/20110707055203/http://magazine.14850.com/9311/interview.html

Barber, K. (Ed.). (2004). Twaddle. *Canadian Oxford dictionary* (2nd ed.). Oxford University Press.

Barham, A. C. (2016). *The past life perspective: Discovering your true nature across multiple lifetimes*. Simon & Schuster. (Original work published 2014)

Barnosky, A. D. (2014). *Dodging extinction: Power, food, money, and the future of life on earth*. University of California Press. https://doi.org/10.1525/9780520959095

Baruss, I. (1987). Metanalysis of definitions of consciousness. *Imagination, Cognition and Personality, 6*(4), 321–329. https://doi.org/10.2190/39X2-HMUL-WB7B-B1A1

Baruss, I. (1990). *The personal nature of notions of consciousness: A theoretical and empirical examination of the role of the personal in the understanding of consciousness*. University Press of America.

Baruss, I. (1996). *Authentic knowing: The convergence of science and spiritual aspiration*. Purdue University Press.

Barušs, I. (2000). Psychopathology of altered states of consciousness. *Baltic Journal of Psychology, 1*(1), 12–26.

Barušs, I. (2001). Failure to replicate electronic voice phenomenon. *Journal of Scientific Exploration, 15*(3), 355–367. https://www.scientificexploration.org/docs/15/jse_15_3_baruss.pdf

Barušs, I. (2007a). An experimental test of instrumental transcommunication. *Journal of Scientific Exploration, 21*(1), 89–98. https://www.scientificexploration.org/docs/21/jse_21_1_baruss.pdf

Barušs, I. (2007b). *Science as a spiritual practice*. Imprint Academic.

Barušs, I. (2008). Beliefs about consciousness and reality: Clarification of the confusion concerning consciousness. *Journal of Consciousness Studies, 15*(10–11), 277–292. https://www.ingentaconnect.com/content/imp/jcs/2008/00000015/f0020010/art00013

Barušs, I. (2013). *The impossible happens: A scientist's personal discovery of the extraordinary nature of reality*. John Hunt Publishing.

Barušs, I. (2014). Questions about interacting with invisible intelligences. *EdgeScience, 18*, 18–19.

Barušs, I. (2018). Meaning fields: Meaning beyond the human as a resolution of boundary problems introduced by nonlocality. *EdgeScience, 35*, 8–11.

Barušs, I. (2019). Categorical modelling of conscious states. *Consciousness: Ideas and Research for the Twenty-First Century, 7*(7), 1–10.

Barušs, I. (2020). *Alterations of consciousness: An empirical analysis for social scientists* (2nd ed.). American Psychological Association. https://doi.org/10.2307/j.ctv1chs19d

Barušs, I. (2021). *Radical transformation: The unexpected interplay of consciousness and reality*. Imprint Academic.

Barušs, I., & Moore, R. J. (1989). Notions of consciousness and reality. In J. E. Shorr, P. Robin, J. A. Connella, & M. Wolpin (Eds.), *Imagery: Current perspectives* (pp. 87–92). Springer. https://doi.org/10.1007/978-1-4899-0876-6_8

Barušs, I., & Moore, R. J. (1992). Measurement of beliefs about consciousness and reality. *Psychological Reports, 71*(1), 59–64. https://doi.org/10.2466/pr0.1992.71.1.59

Barušs, I., & Moore, R. J. (1998). Beliefs about consciousness and reality of participants at "Tucson II." *Journal of Consciousness Studies, 5*(4), 483–496.

Barušs, I., & Mossbridge, J. (2017). *Transcendent mind: Rethinking the science of consciousness*. American Psychological Association. https://doi.org/10.1037/15957-000

Bastos, M. A. V., Jr., Bastos, P. R. H. O., dos Santos, M. L., Iandoli, D., Jr., Boschi Portella, R., & Lucchetti, G. (2018). Comparing the detection of endogenous psychedelics in individuals with and without alleged mediumistic experiences. *EXPLORE: The Journal of Science and Healing, 14*(6), 448–452. https://doi.org/10.1016/j.explore.2018.04.013

Bastos, M. A. V., Bastos, P. R. H. O., Filho, G. B. F., Conde, R. B., Ozaki, J. G. O., Portella, R. B., Iandoli, D., & Lucchetti, G. (2022). Corpus callosum size, hypnotic susceptibility and empathy in women with alleged mediumship: A controlled study. *EXPLORE: The Journal of Science and Healing, 18*(2), 217–225. https://doi.org/10.1016/j.explore.2021.01.001

Bastos, M. A. V., Jr., Bastos, P. R. H. O., Osório, I. H. S., Muass, K. A. R. C., Iandoli, D., Jr., & Lucchetti, G. (2016). Frontal electroencephalographic (EEG) activity and mediumship: Between spiritist mediums and controls. *Archives of Clinical Psychiatry, 43*(2), 20–26. https://doi.org/10.1590/0101-60830000000076

Batthyány, A., & Greyson, B. (2021). Spontaneous remission of dementia before death: Results from a study on paradoxical lucidity. *Psychology of Consciousness, 8*(1), 1–8. https://doi.org/10.1037/cns0000259

Battista, C., Gauvrit, N., & LeBel, E. (2015). Madness in the method: Fatal flaws in recent mediumship experiments. In M. Martin & K. Augustine (Eds.), *The myth of an afterlife: The case against life after death* (pp. 615–630). Rowman & Littlefield.

Bayless, R. (1959). Correspondence. *Journal of the American Society for Psychical Research, 53*(1), 35–38.

Bayless, R. (1976). *Voices from beyond*. University Books.

Beischel, J. (2007). Contemporary methods used in laboratory-based mediumship research. *The Journal of Parapsychology, 71*, 37–68.

Beischel, J. (Ed.). (2014). *From the mouths of mediums: Conversations with Windbridge Certified Research Mediums: Vol. 1. Experiencing communication*. Windbridge Institute.

Beischel, J. (2019). Spontaneous, facilitated, assisted, and requested after-death communication experiences and their impact on grief. *Threshold: Journal of Interdisciplinary Consciousness Studies, 3*(1), 1–32. https://tjics.org/index.php/TJICS/article/view/31

Beischel, J., Boccuzzi, M., Biuso, M., & Rock, A. J. (2015). Anomalous information reception by research mediums under blinded conditions II: Replication and extension. *EXPLORE: The Journal of Science and Healing, 11*(2), 136–142. https://doi.org/10.1016/j.explore.2015.01.001

Beischel, J., Mosher, C., & Boccuzzi, M. (2017). The potential therapeutic efficacy of assisted after-death communication. In D. Klass & E. M. Steffen (Eds.), *Continuing bonds in bereavement: New directions for research and practice* (pp. 176–187). Routledge. https://doi.org/10.4324/9781315202396-17

Beischel, J., Tassone, S., & Boccuzzi, M. (2019). Hematological and psychophysiological correlates of anomalous information reception in mediums: A preliminary exploration. *EXPLORE: The Journal of Science and Healing, 15*(2), 126–133. https://doi.org/10.1016/j.explore.2018.04.009

Beischel, J., & Zingrone, N. L. (2015). Mental mediumship. In E. Cardeña, J. Palmer, & D. Marcusson-Clavertz (Eds.), *Parapsychology: A handbook for the 21st century* (pp. 301–313). McFarland & Company.

Bender, H. (1972). The phenomena of Friedrich Jurgenson. *Journal of Paraphysics, 6*(2), 65–75.

Bercholz, S. (2016). *A guided tour of hell: A graphic memoir* (P. N. Thaye, Illus.). Shambhala Publications.

Blastland, M., Freeman, A. L. J., van der Linden, S., Marteau, T. M., & Spiegelhalter, D. (2020). Five rules for evidence communication. *Nature, 587*(7834), 362–364. https://doi.org/10.1038/d41586-020-03189-1

Blundon, E. G., Gallagher, R. E., & Ward, L. M. (2022). Resting state network activation and functional connectivity in the dying brain. *Clinical Neurophysiology, 135*, 166–178. https://doi.org/10.1016/j.clinph.2021.10.018

Boccuzzi, M., & Beischel, J. (2011). Objective analyses of reported real-time audio instrumental transcommunication and matched control sessions: A pilot study. *Journal of Scientific Exploration, 25*(2), 215–235.

Bogoras, W. (1901). The Chukchi of Northeastern Asia. *American Anthropologist, 3*(1), 80–108. https://doi.org/10.1525/aa.1901.3.1.02a00060

Bogoras, W. (1907). Part II.—The Chukchee—Religion. *Memoirs of the American Museum of Natural History* (Vol. 11). E. J. Brill.

Bolsheva, A. (2014). *After-death communication phenomenon: A depth perspective on the lived experience* [Unpublished doctoral dissertation]. Pacifica Graduate Institute.

Bonenfant, R. J. (2004). A comparative study of near-death experience and non-near-death experience outcomes in 56 survivors of clinical death. *Journal of Near-Death Studies, 22*(3), 155–178.

Borjigin, J., Lee, U., Liu, T., Pal, D., Huff, S., Klarr, D., Sloboda, J., Hernandez, J., Wang, M. M., & Mashour, G. A. (2013). Surge of neurophysiological coherence and connectivity in the dying brain. *PNAS, 110*(35), 14432–14437. https://doi.org/10.1073/pnas.1308285110

Botkin, A. L. (with Hogan, R. C.). (2014). *Induced after death communication: A miraculous therapy for grief and loss*. Hampton Roads Publishing Company. (Original work published 2005)

Bowker, J. (Ed.). (1997). *The Oxford dictionary of world religions*. Oxford University Press.

Bowman, C. (2001). *Return from heaven: Beloved relatives reincarnated within your family*. HarperCollins.

Braude, S. E. (2003). *Immortal remains: The evidence for life after death*. Rowman & Littlefield.

Braude, S. E. (2016). Follow-up investigation of the Felix Circle. *Journal of Scientific Exploration, 30*(1), 27–55. https://www.scientificexploration.org/docs/30/jse_30_1_Braude.pdf

Braude, S. E. (2017). Transplant cases considered as evidence for postmortem survival. In *Psi encyclopedia*. The Society for Psychical Research. https://psi-encyclopedia.spr.ac.uk/articles/transplant-cases-considered-evidence-postmortem-survival

Breier, J. M., Meier, S. T., Kerr, C. W., Wright, S. T., Grant, P. C., & Depner, R. M. (2018). Screening for delirium: Development and validation of the Buffalo

Delirium Scale for use in a home-based hospice setting. *The American Journal of Hospice & Palliative Care, 35*(5), 794–798. https://doi.org/10.1177/1049909117739386

Brims, I. (Director). (1974). *Philip: The imaginary ghost* [DVD]. Bruce Raymond Limited; Toronto Society for Psychical Research.

Broadhurst, K., & Harrington, A. (2016). A thematic literature review: The importance of providing spiritual care for end-of-life patients who have experienced transcendence phenomena. *The American Journal of Hospice & Palliative Care, 33*(9), 881–893. https://doi.org/10.1177/1049909115595217

Bush, N. E. (2009). Distressing Western near-death experiences: Finding a way through the abyss. In J. M. Holden, B. Greyson, & D. James (Eds.), *The handbook of near-death experiences: Thirty years of investigation* (pp. 63–86). Praeger.

Butler, T. (2020). *Transcommunication white paper: With emphasis on electronic voice phenomena*. AA-EVP Publishing.

Byrd, C. (2017). *The boy who knew too much: An astounding true story of a young boy's past-life memories*. Hay House.

Callanan, M., & Kelley, P. (1997). *Final gifts: Understanding the special awareness, needs, and communications of the dying*. Bantam Books. (Original work published 1992)

Cardeña, E. (2014). A call for an open, informed study of all aspects of consciousness. *Frontiers in Human Neuroscience, 8*, Article 17. https://doi.org/10.3389/fnhum.2014.00017

Cardeña, E. (2018). The experimental evidence for parapsychological phenomena: A review. *American Psychologist, 73*(5), 663–677. https://doi.org/10.1037/amp0000236

Cardeña, E., Krippner, S., & Lynn, S. J. (2014). Anomalous experiences: An integrative summary. In E. Cardeña, S. J. Lynn, & S. Krippner (Eds.), *Varieties of anomalous experience: Examining the scientific evidence* (2nd ed., pp. 409–426). American Psychological Association. https://doi.org/10.1037/14258-014

Cardoso, A. (2010). *Electronic voices: Contact with another dimension*. O-Books.

Cardoso, A. (2012). A two-year investigation of the allegedly anomalous electronic voices or EVP. *NeuroQuantology: An Interdisciplinary Journal of Neuroscience and Quantum Physics, 10*(3), 492–514. https://doi.org/10.14704/nq.2012.10.3.571

Cardoso, A. (2017). *Electronic contact with the dead: What do the voices tell us?* White Crow Books.

Cardoso, A., Festa, M. S., Fontana, D., & Presi, P. (2007). The reality of instrumental transcommunication (ITC) voices scientifically demonstrated on 5th December 2004 during experiments with Marcello Bacci at Grosseto, Italy, Europe. In A. Cardoso & D. Fontana (Eds.), *The Second International Conference on Current Research Into Survival of Physical Death With Special Reference to Instrumental Transcommunication* (pp. 75–80). Saturday Night Press Publications.

Cassol, H., D'Argembeau, A., Charland-Verville, V., Laureys, S., & Martial, C. (2019). Memories of near-death experiences: Are they self-defining? *Neuroscience of Consciousness*. Advance online publication. https://doi.org/10.1093/nc/niz002

Castelnovo, A., Cavallotti, S., Gambini, O., & D'Agostino, A. (2015). Post-bereavement hallucinatory experiences: A critical overview of population and clinical studies. *Journal of Affective Disorders, 186*, 266–274. https://doi.org/10.1016/j.jad.2015.07.032

Champlain, S. [We Don't Die Radio]. (2021, March 3). *Sonia Rinaldi presents "Images from the afterlife" 7 June 2020 on wedontdie.com* [Video]. YouTube. https://www.youtube.com/watch?v=5y5ep9-dLqQ

Chang, S. O., Ahn, S. Y., Cho, M.-O., Choi, K. S., Kong, E. S., Kim, C.-G., Kim, H. K., Lee, Y. W., Song, M., & Kim, N. C. (2017). Identifying perceptions of health professionals regarding deathbed visions and spiritual care in end-of-life care: A Delphi consensus study. *Journal of Hospice & Palliative Nursing, 19*(2), 177–184. https://doi.org/10.1097/NJH.0000000000000328

Charbonier, J. J. (2012). *7 reasons to believe in the afterlife: A doctor reviews the case for consciousness after death*. Inner Traditions.

Charland-Verville, V., Martial, C., Cassol, H., & Laureys, S. (2018). Near-death experiences: Actual considerations. In C. Schnakers & S. Laureys (Eds.), *Coma and disorders of consciousness* (pp. 235–263). Springer International Publishing. https://doi.org/10.1007/978-3-319-55964-3_14

Chawla, L. S., Terek, M., Junker, C., Akst, S., Yoon, B., Brasha-Mitchell, E., & Seneff, M. G. (2017). Characterization of end-of-life electroencephalographic surges in critically ill patients. *Death Studies, 41*(6), 385–392. https://doi.org/10.1080/07481187.2017.1287138

Claridge, G. (1997). Final remarks and future directions. In G. Claridge (Ed.), *Schizotypy: Implications for illness and health* (pp. 301–314). Oxford University Press. https://doi.org/10.1093/med:psych/9780198523536.003.0014

Claxton-Oldfield, S., Gallant, M., & Claxton-Oldfield, J. (2020). The impact of unusual end-of-life phenomena on hospice palliative care volunteers and their perceived needs for training to respond to them. *Omega—Journal of Death and Dying, 81*(4), 577–591. https://doi.org/10.1177/0030222818788238

Cockell, J. (1993). *Across time and death: A mother's search for her past life children*. Fireside.

Cockell, J. (1996). *Past lives, future lives*. Fireside.

Coleman, T. (Director). (2011). *The afterlife investigations* [Documentary; DVD]. UFO TV.

Collesso, T., Forrester, M., & Baruss, I. (2021). The effects of meditation and visualization on the direct mental influence of random event generators. *Journal of Scientific Exploration, 35*(2), 311–344. https://doi.org/10.31275/20211891

Colman, A. M. (Ed.). (2015). Availability heuristic. In *Oxford dictionary of psychology* (4th ed.). Oxford University Press.

Colvin, B. (2015). Poltergeists (overview). In *Psi encyclopedia*. The Society for Psychical Research. https://psi-encyclopedia.spr.ac.uk/articles/poltergeists-overview

Combs, A. (2009). *Consciousness explained better: Towards an integral understanding of the multifaceted nature of consciousness*. Paragon House.

Cooper, C. (2011). *Telephone calls from the dead: A revised look at the phenomenon thirty years on*. Tricorn Books.

Cooper, C. E. (2017). Considering anomalous events during bereavement as evidence for survival. In D. Klass & E. M. Steffen (Eds.), *Continuing bonds in bereavement: New directions for research and practice* (pp. 201–213). Routledge. https://doi.org/10.4324/9781315202396-20

Craffert, P. F. (2019). Making sense of near-death experience research: Circumstance specific alterations of consciousness. *Anthropology of Consciousness*, *30*(1), 64–89. https://doi.org/10.1111/anoc.12111

Crooks, M. (2018). On the psychology of demon possession: The occult personality. *The Journal of Mind and Behavior*, *39*(4), 257–344. https://www.jstor.org/stable/26614369

Cummins, G. (2012). *The road to immortality: Being a description of the afterlife purporting to be communicated by the late F. W. H. Myers*. White Crow Books. (Original work published 1932)

Cuneo, M. W. (2001). *American exorcism: Expelling demons in the land of plenty*. Broadway Books.

Dannenbaum, S. M., & Kinnier, R. T. (2009). Imaginal relationships with the dead: Applications for psychotherapy. *Journal of Humanistic Psychology*, *49*(1), 100–113. https://doi.org/10.1177/0022167808323577

David-Neel, A. (1971). *Magic and mystery in Tibet*. Dover Publications. (Original work published 1929)

DeGroot, J. M. (2018). A model of transcorporeal communication: Communication toward/with/to the deceased. *Omega—Journal of Death and Dying*, *78*(1), 43–66. https://doi.org/10.1177/0030222816683195

Delmonte, R., Lucchetti, G., Moreira-Almeida, A., & Farias, M. (2016). Can the *DSM-5* differentiate between nonpathological possession and dissociative identity disorder? A case study from an Afro-Brazilian religion. *Journal of Trauma & Dissociation*, *17*(3), 322–337. https://doi.org/10.1080/15299732.2015.1103351

Delorme, A., Beischel, J., Michel, L., Boccuzzi, M., Radin, D., & Mills, P. J. (2013). Electrocortical activity associated with subjective communication with the deceased. *Frontiers in Psychology*, *4*, Article 834. https://doi.org/10.3389/fpsyg.2013.00834

Depner, R. M., Grant, P. C., Byrwa, D. J., LaFever, S. M., Kerr, C. W., Tenzek, K. E., LaValley, S., Luczkiewicz, D. L., Wright, S. T., Levy, K., & AdvStat, M. (2020). Expanding the understanding of content of end-of-life dreams and visions: A consensual qualitative research analysis. *Palliative Medicine Reports*, *1*(1), 103–110. https://doi.org/10.1089/pmr.2020.0037

Diamond, D. (2019). *Diary of a death doula: 25 lessons the dying teach us about the afterlife*. John Hunt Publishing.

Dinicastro, M. (2007). Psi research and fraud. In A. Cardoso & D. Fontana (Eds.), *The Second International Conference on Current Research Into Survival of Physical Death With Special Reference to Instrumental Transcommunication* (pp. 91–106). Saturday Night Press Publications.

Dobyns, Y. (2015). The PEAR laboratory: Explorations and observations. In D. Broderick & B. Goertzel (Eds.), *Evidence for psi: Thirteen empirical research reports* (pp. 213–236). McFarland & Company.

Doka, K. J. (2020). *When we die: Extraordinary experiences at life's end*. Llewellyn Publications.

Dosa, D. M. (2007). A day in the life of Oscar the cat. *The New England Journal of Medicine, 357*(4), 328–329. https://doi.org/10.1056/NEJMp078108

dos Santos, C. S., Paiva, B. S. R., Lucchetti, A. L. G., Paiva, C. E., Fenwick, P., & Lucchetti, G. (2017). End-of-life experiences and deathbed phenomena as reported by Brazilian healthcare professionals in different healthcare settings. *Palliative & Supportive Care, 15*(4), 425–433. https://doi.org/10.1017/S1478951516000869

Doyle, C. M., & Gray, K. (2020). How people perceive the minds of the dead: The importance of consciousness at the moment of death. *Cognition, 202*, Article 104308. https://doi.org/10.1016/j.cognition.2020.104308

Drinkwater, K., Laythe, B., Houran, J., Dagnall, N., O'Keeffe, C., & Hill, S. A. (2019). Exploring gaslighting effects via the VAPUS model for ghost narratives. *Australian Journal of Parapsychology, 19*(2), 143–179.

Durek, S. (2019). *Spirit hacking: Shamanic keys to reclaim your personal power, transform yourself, and light up the world*. St. Martin's Essentials.

Edison's Own Secret Spirit Experiments. (1933). *Modern Mechanix and Inventions, 10*(6), 34–36.

Eisenbeiss, W., & Hassler, D. (2006). An assessment of ostensible communications with a deceased grandmaster as evidence for survival. *Journal of the Society for Psychical Research, 70*(2), 65–97.

Elsaesser, E., Roe, C. A., Cooper, C. E., & Lorimer, D. (2021). The phenomenology and impact of hallucinations concerning the deceased. *BJPsych Open, 7*(5), Article E148.

Everist, W. G. (2018). Spiritually transformative experience of mediums. *Threshold: Journal of Interdisciplinary Consciousness Studies, 2*(1), 5–49.

Evrard, R. (2017). Ghost in the machine: A clinical view of anomalous telecommunication experiences. *Journal of Exceptional Experiences and Psychology, 5*(2), 21–30.

Exline, J. J. (2021). Psychopathology, normal psychological processes, or supernatural encounters? Three ways to frame reports of after-death communication. *Spirituality in Clinical Practice, 8*(3), 164–176. https://doi.org/10.1037/scp0000245

Farthing, G. W. (1992). *The psychology of consciousness*. Prentice-Hall.

Fenwick, P., & Fenwick, E. (1995). *The truth in the light: An investigation of over 300 near-death experiences.* Berkeley Books.

Fenwick, P., & Fenwick, E. (2013). *The art of dying: A journey to elsewhere.* Bloomsbury Academic.

Fenwick, P., Lovelace, H., & Brayne, S. (2010). Comfort for the dying: Five year retrospective and one year prospective studies of end of life experiences. *Archives of Gerontology and Geriatrics, 51*(2), 173–179. https://doi.org/10.1016/j.archger.2009.10.004

Ferracuti, S., & Sacco, R. (1996). Dissociative trance disorder: Clinical and Rorschach findings in ten persons reporting demon possession and treated by exorcism. *Journal of Personality Assessment, 66*(3), 525–539. https://doi.org/10.1207/s15327752jpa6603_4

Ferrucci, P. (1982). *What we may be: Techniques for psychological and spiritual growth through psychosynthesis.* Jeremy P. Tarcher.

Ferrucci, P. (2015). *Your inner will: Finding personal strength in critical times.* Jeremy P. Tarcher/Penguin.

Feynman, R. P. (2006). *QED: The strange theory of light and matter.* Princeton University Press. (Original work published 1985)

Fields, C., Hoffman, D. D., Prakash, C., & Singh, M. (2018). Conscious agent networks: Formal analysis and application to cognition. *Cognitive Systems Research, 47,* 186–213. https://doi.org/10.1016/j.cogsys.2017.10.003

Fischer, J. M., & Mitchell-Yellin, B. (2016). *Near-death experiences: Understanding visions of the afterlife.* Oxford University Press.

Fontana, D. (2010). *Is there an afterlife? A comprehensive overview of the evidence.* O-Books. (Original work published 2005)

Foy, R. P. (2008). *Witnessing the impossible.* Torcal Publications.

Fraser, J. (2020). *Poltergeist! A new investigation into destructive hauntings, including "The Cage—Witches Prison," St Osyth.* John Hunt Publishing.

Freire, E. S., Rocha, A. C., Tasca, V. S., Marnet, M. M., & Moreira-Almeida, A. (2022). Testing alleged mediumistic writing: An experimental controlled study. *EXPLORE: The Journal of Science and Healing, 18*(1), 82–87. https://doi.org/10.1016/j.explore.2020.08.017

Fuller, J. G. (1985). *The ghost of 29 megacycles: A new breakthrough in life after death?* Souvenir Press.

Gallagher, R. (2020). *Demonic foes: My twenty-five years as a psychiatrist investigating possessions, diabolic attacks, and the paranormal.* HarperOne.

García, C. (2017). Letter received from Carol García on August 25, 2017. *ITC Journal, 54–55,* 112–115.

Gibbs, J. C. (2017). Tucker, Stevenson, Weiss, and Life: Renditions of the transcendent view from past-life memories. *Journal of Near-Death Studies, 35*(3), 123–165.

Giesemann, S. (2022, February 20). *The afterlife is real ... I guarantee it!* [Video]. YouTube. https://www.youtube.com/watch?v=_PBa_KGYiCM

Glaskin, G. M. (1976). *Worlds within: Probing the Christos experience*. Wildwood House.

Glazier, J. W., Beck, T., & Simmonds-Moore, C. (2015). A phenomenological analysis of the relationship between grief, emotional stress and anomalous experiences. *Mortality, 20*(3), 248–262. https://doi.org/10.1080/13576275.2015.1015116

Goertzel, T., & Goertzel, B. (2015). Skeptical responses to psi research. In D. Broderick & B. Goertzel (Eds.), *Evidence for psi: Thirteen empirical research reports* (pp. 291–301). McFarland & Company.

Goranson, A., Ritter, R. S., Waytz, A., Norton, M. I., & Gray, K. (2017). Dying is unexpectedly positive. *Psychological Science, 28*(7), 988–999. https://doi.org/10.1177/0956797617701186

Grant, P. C., Depner, R. M., Levy, K., LaFever, S. M., Tenzek, K. E., Wright, S. T., & Kerr, C. W. (2020). Family caregiver perspectives on end-of-life dreams and visions during bereavement: A mixed methods approach. *Journal of Palliative Medicine, 23*(1), 48–53. https://doi.org/10.1089/jpm.2019.0093

Greeley, A. (1987). The "impossible": It's happening. *Noetic Sciences Review, 2*, 7–9.

Greyson, B. (1983). The Near-Death Experience Scale: Construction, reliability, and validity. *The Journal of Nervous and Mental Disease, 171*(6), 369–375.

Greyson, B. (2010). Seeing dead people not known to have died: "Peak in Darien" experiences. *Anthropology and Humanism, 35*(2), 159–171. https://doi.org/10.1111/j.1548-1409.2010.01064.x

Greyson, B. (2021a). *After: A doctor explores what near-death experiences reveal about life and beyond*. St. Martin's Essentials.

Greyson, B. (2021b). Claims of past-life memories in near-death experiences. *EdgeScience, 46*, 5–9.

Greyson, B., & Bush, N. E. (1992). Distressing near-death experiences. *Psychiatry, 55*(1), 95–110. https://doi.org/10.1080/00332747.1992.11024583

Greyson, B., Kelly, E. W., & Kelly, E. F. (2009). Explanatory models for near-death experiences. In J. M. Holden, B. Greyson, & D. James (Eds.), *The handbook of near-death experiences: Thirty years of investigation* (pp. 213–234). Praeger.

Grosso, M. (2021). The new story: UFOs, psychical research, and religion. *EdgeScience, 46*, 1519.

Gullà, D. (2004). Computer-based analysis of supposed paranormal voices: The question of anomalies detected and speaker identification. In A. Cardoso & D. Fontana (Eds.), *Proceedings of the First International Conference on Current Research Into Survival of Physical Death With Special Reference to Instrumental Transcommunication* (pp. 49–68). Artes Gráficas Vicus, S. A. L.

Gullà, D. (2007). Applying biometrics in the analysis and identification of photographic images (I.P.S.). In A. Cardoso & D. Fontana (Eds.), *The Second International Conference on Current Research Into Survival of Physical Death With Special Reference to Instrumental Transcommunication* (pp. 159–173). Saturday Night Press Publications.

Hall, C. (2014). Bereavement theory: Recent developments in our understanding of grief and bereavement. *Bereavement Care, 33*(1), 7–12.

Halligan, P. W., & Oakley, D. A. (2021). Giving up on consciousness as the ghost in the machine. *Frontiers in Psychology, 12*, Article 571460. https://doi.org/10.3389/fpsyg.2021.571460

Hamilton-Parker, C. (2001). *What to do when you are dead: Living better in the afterlife*. Sterling Publishing Company.

Haraldsson, E. (2012). *The departed among the living: An investigative study of afterlife encounters*. White Crow Books.

Haraldsson, E. (2018). Extraordinary physical phenomena in Poland. *The Journal of Parapsychology, 82*(2), 208–209. https://doi.org/10.30891/jopar.2018.02.09

Haraldsson, E., & Matlock, J. G. (2016). *I saw a light and came here: Children's experiences of reincarnation*. White Crow Books.

Hastings, A. (2012). Effects on bereavement using a restricted sensory environment (psychomanteum). *Journal of Transpersonal Psychology, 44*(1), 1–25.

Heath, P. R. (2017). The afterlife as an extension of lifespan development. *Threshold: Journal of Interdisciplinary Consciousness Studies, 1*(1), 7–10.

Heath, P. R., & Klimo, J. (2010). *Handbook to the afterlife*. North Atlantic Books.

Heidegger, M. (1962). *Being and time* (J. Macquarrie & E. Robinson, Trans.). Harper & Row. (Original work published 1926)

Heinzerling, J. (1997, November). All about EVP. *Fortean Times: The Journal of Strange Phenomena, 104*, 26–30.

Hill, J. (2011). *Synchronicity and grief: The phenomenology of meaningful coincidence as it arises during bereavement* [Unpublished doctoral dissertation]. Institute of Transpersonal Psychology.

Hilton, A. (2021). Seeing without eyes. *EdgeScience, 47*, 9–14.

Hinze, S. (1997). *Coming from the light: Spiritual accounts of life before life*. Pocket Books. (Original work published 1994)

Hirsch, H. V. B., & Spinelli, D. N. (1971). Modification of the distribution of receptive field orientation in cats by selective visual exposure during development. *Experimental Brain Research, 12*(5), 509–527. https://doi.org/10.1007/BF00234246

Hockley, J. (2015). Intimations of dying: A visible and invisible process. *Journal of Palliative Care, 31*(3), 166–171. https://doi.org/10.1177/082585971503100306

Hoffman, D. (2019). *The case against reality: Why evolution hid the truth from our eyes*. W. W. Norton & Company.

Hoffman, D. D., & Prakash, C. (2014). Objects of consciousness. *Frontiers in Psychology, 5*, Article 577. https://doi.org/10.3389/fpsyg.2014.00577

Hogan, R. C. (2021). *Reasons for what happens to you in your life & your afterlife revealed by speakers in the afterlife*. Greater Reality Publications.

Holden, J. M. (2009). Veridical perception in near-death experiences. In J. M. Holden, B. Greyson, & D. James (Eds.), *The handbook of near-death experiences: Thirty years of investigation* (pp. 185–211). Praeger.

Holzer, H. (1994). *Life beyond: Compelling evidence for past lives and existence after death*. Contemporary Books.

Hood, R. W., Jr., Hill, P. C., & Spilka, B. (2018). *The psychology of religion: An empirical approach* (5th ed.). Guilford Press.

Irwin, H. J. (1994). *An introduction to parapsychology* (2nd ed.). McFarland & Co.

Jacobs, D. M. (2015). *Walking among us: The alien plan to control humanity*. Disinformation Books.

Jahn, D. R., & Spencer-Thomas, S. (2018). A qualitative examination of continuing bonds through spiritual experiences in individuals bereaved by suicide. *Religions, 9*(8), Article 248. https://doi.org/10.3390/rel9080248

Jahn, R. G. (1989). Anomalies: Analysis and aesthetics. *Journal of Scientific Exploration, 3*(1), 15–26.

Jahn, R. G. (2001). 20th and 21st century science: Reflections and projections. *Journal of Scientific Exploration, 15*(1), 21–31.

Janis, I. L. (1971, November). Groupthink. *Psychology Today, 5*, 43, 44, 46, 74–76.

Jewkes, S., & Barušs, I. (2000). Personality correlates of beliefs about consciousness and reality. *Advanced Development: A Journal on Adult Giftedness, 9*, 91–103.

Kadiragha, D., & Barušs, I. (2021, July 23–31). *After-death communication with cell phones* [Conference session]. SSE-PA Connections 2021: A Combined Online Convention of the Parapsychological Association & Society for Scientific Exploration.

Kadler, G., Vasudev, A., Ionson, E., & Barušs, I. (2022). Unintended deviations of a random event generator by patients with late life depression and anxiety during a direct mental influence task. *Journal of Nervous and Mental Disease, 210*(4), 282–289. https://doi.org/10.1097/NMD.0000000000001443

Kamp, K. S., Steffen, E. M., Alderson-Day, B., Allen, P., Austad, A., Hayes, J., Larøi, F., Ratcliffe, M., & Sabucedo, P. (2020). Sensory and quasi-sensory experiences of the deceased in bereavement: An interdisciplinary and integrative review. *Schizophrenia Bulletin, 46*(6), 1367–1381. https://doi.org/10.1093/schbul/sbaa113

Kaplan, W. (2017). *Why dissent matters: Because some people see things the rest of us miss*. McGill-Queen's University Press.

Kason, Y. (2019). *Touched by the light: Exploring spiritually transformative experiences*. Dundurn.

Kason, Y., & Degler, T. (1994). *A farther shore: How near-death and other extraordinary experiences can change ordinary lives*. HarperCollins Publishers.

Kastrup, B. (2014). *Why materialism is baloney: How true skeptics know there is no death and fathom answers to life, the universe and everything*. John Hunt Publishing.

Kean, L. (2017). *Surviving death: A journalist investigates evidence for an afterlife*. Three Rivers Press.

Kean, L. (2020). Epilogue. In S. Alexander (Author), *An extraordinary journey: The memoirs of a physical medium* (pp. 319–332). White Crow Books.

Keen, C., Murray, C. D., & Payne, S. (2013). A qualitative exploration of sensing the presence of the deceased following bereavement. *Mortality, 18*(4), 339–357. https://doi.org/10.1080/13576275.2013.819320

Keen, M. (2001). The Scole investigation: A study in critical analysis of paranormal physical phenomena. *Journal of Scientific Exploration, 15*(2), 167–182.

Keen, M., Ellison, A., & Fontana, D. (1999). The Scole report: An account of an investigation into the genuineness of a range of physical phenomena associated with a mediumistic group in Norfolk, England. *Proceedings of the Society for Psychical Research, 58*(Pt. 220), 149–392.

Keil, J. (1980). The voice on tape phenomena: Limitations and possibilities. *European Journal of Parapsychology, 3*(3), 287–296.

Kelleher, C. A. (2022). The pentagon's secret UFO program, the hitchhiker effect, and models of contagion. *EdgeScience, 50*, 19–24.

Kelly, E. F., Crabtree, A., & Marshall, P. (2015). *Beyond physicalism: Toward reconciliation of science and spirituality.* Rowman & Littlefield.

Kelly, E. F., Kelly, E. W., Crabtree, A., Gauld, A., Grosso, M., & Greyson, B. (2010). *Irreducible mind: Toward a psychology for the 21st century.* Rowman & Littlefield. (Original work published 2007)

Kelly, E. W. (2018). Mediums, apparitions, and deathbed experiences. In D. E. Presti (Ed.), *Mind beyond brain: Buddhism, science, and the paranormal* (pp. 69–90). Columbia University Press.

Kelly, E. W., Greyson, B., & Kelly, E. F. (2010). Unusual experiences near death and related phenomena. In E. F. Kelly, E. W. Kelly, A. Crabtree, A. Gauld, M. Gross, & B. Greyson (Eds.), *Irreducible mind: Toward a psychology for the 21st century* (pp. 367–421). Rowman & Littlefield. (Original work published 2007)

Kerr, C. W., Donnelly, J. P., Wright, S. T., Kuszczak, S. M., Banas, A., Grant, P. C., & Luczkiewicz, D. L. (2014). End-of-life dreams and visions: A longitudinal study of hospice patients' experiences. *Journal of Palliative Medicine, 17*(3), 296–303. https://doi.org/10.1089/jpm.2013.0371

Kerr, N. H. (2000). Dreaming, imagery, and perception. In M. H. Kryger, T. Roth, & W. C. Dement (Eds.), *Principles and practice of sleep medicine* (3rd ed., pp. 482–490). W. B. Saunders.

Klein, S. B. (2021). Thoughts on the scientific study of phenomenal consciousness. *Psychology of Consciousness, 8*(1), 74–80. https://doi.org/10.1037/cns0000231

Koedam, I. (2015). *In the light of death: Experiences on the threshold between life and death.* White Crow Books.

Koons, R. C., & Bealer, G. (2010). Introduction. In R. C. Koons & G. Bealer (Eds.), *The waning of materialism* (pp. ix–xxxii). Oxford University Press. https://doi.org/10.1093/acprof:oso/9780199556182.002.0005

Kowalewski, D. (2019). The shamanic renaissance: What is going on? *Journal of Humanistic Psychology, 59*(2), 170–184. https://doi.org/10.1177/0022167816634522

Kramvis, I., Mansvelder, H. D., & Meredith, R. M. (2018). Neuronal life after death: Electrophysiologic recordings from neurons in adult human brain tissue obtained through surgical resection or postmortem. In I. Huitinga & M. J. Webster (Eds.), *Handbook of clinical neurology* (Vol. 150, pp. 319–333). Elsevier. https://doi.org/10.1016/B978-0-444-63639-3.00022-0

Krippner, S. (2017). A unique partnership: Examining information in dreams about deceased veterans. *Journal of the Society for Psychical Research, 81*(3), 180–193.

Krippner, S., & Achterberg, J. (2014). Anomalous healing experiences. In E. Cardeña, S. J. Lynn, & S. Krippner (Eds.), *Varieties of anomalous experience: Examining the scientific evidence* (2nd ed., pp. 273–301). American Psychological Association. https://doi.org/10.1037/14258-010

Krohn, E. G., & Kripal, J. J. (2018). *Changed in a flash: One woman's near-death experience and why a scholar thinks it empowers us all*. North Atlantic Books.

Kruth, J. G., & Joines, W. T. (2016). Taming the ghost within: An approach toward addressing apparent electronic poltergeist activity. *The Journal of Parapsychology, 80*(1), 70–86.

Kubis, P., & Macy, M. (1995). *Conversations beyond the light: Communication with departed friends & colleagues by electronic means*. Griffin Publishing with Continuing Life Research.

Kwilecki, S. (2011). Ghosts, meaning, and faith: After-death communications in bereavement narratives. *Death Studies, 35*(3), 219–243. https://doi.org/10.1080/07481187.2010.511424

Lacatski, J. T., Kelleher, C. A., & Knapp, G. (2021). *Skinwalkers at the Pentagon: An insiders' account of the government's secret UFO program*. RTMA.

Lake, J. (2017). The near-death experience: A testable neural model. *Psychology of Consciousness, 4*(1), 115–134. https://doi.org/10.1037/cns0000099

Lange, R., & Houran, J. (2015). Giving up the ghost to psychology. In M. Martin & K. Augustine (Eds.), *The myth of an afterlife: The case against life after death* (pp. 503–518). Rowman & Littlefield.

Lange, R., Ross, R. M., Dagnall, N., Irwin, H. J., Houran, J., & Drinkwater, K. (2019). Anomalous experiences and paranormal attributions: Psychometric challenges in studying their measurement and relationship. *Psychology of Consciousness, 6*(4), 346–358. https://doi.org/10.1037/cns0000187

Larsen, C. F. (2015). Conjecturing up spirits in the improvisations of mediums. In M. Martin & K. Augustine (Eds.), *The myth of an afterlife: The case against life after death* (p. 585614). Rowman & Littlefield.

Law, R. (2009). "Bridging worlds": Meeting the emotional needs of dying patients. *Journal of Advanced Nursing, 65*(12), 2630–2641. https://doi.org/10.1111/j.1365-2648.2009.05126.x

Lawrence, M., & Repede, E. (2013). The incidence of deathbed communications and their impact on the dying process. *The American Journal of Hospice & Palliative Care, 30*(7), 632–639. https://doi.org/10.1177/1049909112467529

Leary, M. R., & Butler, T. (2015). Electronic voice phenomena. In E. Cardeña, J. Palmer, & D. Marcusson-Clavertz (Eds.), *Parapsychology: A handbook for the 21st century* (pp. 341–349). McFarland & Company.

Lee, D. E., Lee, L. G., Siu, D., Bazrafkan, A. K., Farahabadi, M. H., Dinh, T. J., Orellana, J., Xiong, W., Lopour, B. A., & Akbari, Y. (2017). Neural correlates of consciousness at near-electrocerebral silence in an asphyxia cardiac arrest model. *Brain Connectivity*, *7*(3), 172–181. https://doi.org/10.1089/brain.2016.0471

Lee, R. L. M. (2013). Facing the beyond: Experiences, metaphors, and spiritualities of the afterlife. *Journal of Contemporary Religion*, *28*(1), 109–123. https://doi.org/10.1080/13537903.2013.750847

Levy, K., Grant, P. C., Depner, R. M., Byrwa, D. J., Luczkiewicz, D. L., & Kerr, C. W. (2020). End-of-life dreams and visions and posttraumatic growth: A comparison study. *Journal of Palliative Medicine*, *23*(3), 319–324. https://doi.org/10.1089/jpm.2019.0269

Lilly, J. C. (1978). *The scientist: A novel autobiography*. J. B. Lippincott.

Lim, C.-Y., Park, J. Y., Kim, D. Y., Yoo, K. D., Kim, H. J., Kim, Y., & Shin, S. J. (2020). Terminal lucidity in the teaching hospital setting. *Death Studies*, *44*(5), 285–291. https://doi.org/10.1080/07481187.2018.1541943

Lindbergh, C. A. (1953). *The Spirit of St. Louis*. Charles Scribner's Sons.

Liu, T.-H., & Field, N. P. (2022). Continuing bonds and dreams following violent loss among Cambodian survivors of the Pol Pot era. *Death Studies*, *46*(2), 297–306. https://doi.org/10.1080/07481187.2019.1699202

Lo, C., Panday, T., Zeppieri, J., Rydall, A., Murphy-Kane, P., Zimmermann, C., & Rodin, G. (2017). Preliminary psychometrics of the Existential Distress Scale in patients with advanced cancer. *European Journal of Cancer Care*, *26*(6), Article e12597.

Locher, T., & Harsch-Fischbach, M. (1997). *Breakthroughs in technical spirit communication* (M. Macy & Heckmann, Eds. & Trans.). Continuing Life Research.

Long, J. (with Perry, P.). (2016). *God and the afterlife: The groundbreaking new evidence for God and near-death experience*. HarperOne.

Lorimer, D. (2017). *Survival? Death as a transition*. White Crow Books. (Original work published 1984)

Luhrmann, T. M., Weisman, K., Aulino, F., Brahinsky, J. D., Dulin, J. C., Dzokoto, V. A., Legare, C. H., Lifshitz, M., Ng, E., Ross-Zehnder, N., & Smith, R. E. (2021). Sensing the presence of gods and spirits across cultures and faiths. *PNAS*, *118*(5), Article e2016649118. https://doi.org/10.1073/pnas.2016649118

Luke, D., & Hunter, J. (2014). Talking with the spirits: Ethnographies from between the worlds. In J. Hunter & D. Luke (Eds.), *Talking with the spirits: Ethnographies from between the worlds* (pp. 9–16). Daily Grail Publishing.

Lukey, N., & Baruš, I. (2005). Intelligence correlates of transcendent beliefs: A preliminary study. *Imagination, Cognition and Personality*, *24*(3), 259–270. https://doi.org/10.2190/5H80-2PCY-02YB-F7HN

MacRae, A. (1984). Some findings relating to the electronic voice phenomenon. *Psi Research*, *3*(1), 36–46.

Mandoki, M. (2021). *Are near-death experiences veridical? A philosophical inquiry* [Unpublished doctoral dissertation]. Western University, London, Ontario, Canada. https://ir.lib.uwo.ca/etd/7895/

Maraldi, E. d. O., Costa, A., Cunha, A., Flores, D., Hamazaki, E., de Queiroz, G. P., Martinez, M., Siqueira, S., & Reichow, J. (2021). Cultural presentations of dissociation: The case of possession trance experiences. *Journal of Trauma & Dissociation*, 22(1), 11–16. https://doi.org/10.1080/15299732.2020.1821145

Maraldi, E. d. O., Ribeiro, R. N., & Krippner, S. (2019). Cultural and group differences in mediumship and dissociation: Exploring the varieties of mediumistic experiences. *International Journal of Latin American Religions*, 3(1), 170–192.

Maraldi, E. d. O., Zangari, W., Machado, F. R., & Krippner, S. (2014). Anomalous mental and physical phenomena of Brazilian mediums: A review of the scientific literature. In J. Hunter & D. Luke (Eds.), *Talking with the spirits: Ethnographies from between the worlds* (pp. 257–299). Daily Grail Publishing.

Martial, C., Simon, J., Puttaert, N., Gosseries, O., Charland-Verville, V., Nyssen, A. S., Greyson, B., Laureys, S., & Cassol, H. (2020). The Near-Death Experience Content (NDE-C) scale: Development and psychometric validation. *Consciousness and Cognition*, 86, Article 103049. https://doi.org/10.1016/j.concog.2020.103049

Martin, M., & Augustine, K. (2015). Preface. In M. Martin & K. Augustine (Eds.), *The myth of an afterlife: The case against life after death* (pp. xxvii–xxxi). Rowman & Littlefield.

Mashour, G. A., & Hudetz, A. G. (2018). Neural correlates of unconsciousness in large-scale brain networks. *Trends in Neurosciences*, 41(3), 150–160. https://doi.org/10.1016/j.tins.2018.01.003

Masí, F. (2004). Scientific research on life after death: Functional aspects and methods of ITC. In A. Cardoso & D. Fontana (Eds.), *Proceedings of the First International Conference on Current Research Into Survival of Physical Death With Special Reference to Instrumental Transcommunication* (pp. 69–82). Artes Gráficas Vicus, S. A. L.

Masman, A. D., van Dijk, M., van Rosmalen, J., Blussé van Oud-Alblas, H. J., Ista, E., Baar, F. P., & Tibboel, D. (2016). Bispectral index monitoring in terminally ill patients: A validation study. *Journal of Pain and Symptom Management*, 52(2), 212–220.e3. https://doi.org/10.1016/j.jpainsymman.2016.01.011

Massullo, B. (2017). *The ghost studies: New perspectives on the origins of paranormal experiences*. New Page Books.

Matlock, J. G. (2019). *Signs of reincarnation: Exploring beliefs, cases, and theory*. Rowman & Littlefield.

Matlock, J. G. (2020). Ian Stevenson. In *Psi encyclopedia*. The Society for Psychical Research. https://psi-encyclopedia.spr.ac.uk/articles/ian-stevenson

Mattingley, A. (2017). *The after death chronicles: True stories of comfort, guidance, and wisdom from beyond the veil*. Hampton Roads Publishing Company.

McCarthy, K. F. (2020). *Till death don't us part: A true story of awakening to love after life*. White Crow Books.

McKay, M. (2021). *The luminous landscape of the afterlife: Jordan's message to the living on what to expect after death*. Park Street Press.

McNamara, P. (2011a). *Spirit possession and exorcism: History, psychology, and neurobiology: Vol. 1: Mental states and the phenomenon of possession*. Praeger.

McNamara, P. (2011b). *Spirit possession and exorcism: History, psychology, and neurobiology: Vol. 2: Rites to become possessed, rites to exorcise "demons."* Praeger.

Meador, K. J., Ray, P. G., Echauz, J. R., Loring, D. W., & Vachtsevanos, G. J. (2002). Gamma coherence and conscious perception. *Neurology, 59*(6), 847–854. https://doi.org/10.1212/WNL.59.6.847

Medhus, E. (with Medhus, E.). (2015). *My life after death: A memoir from heaven*. Atria Paperback.

Menezes, A., Jr., & Moreira-Almeida, A. (2011). Mental health of mediums and differential diagnosis between mediumship and mental disorders. *Journal of Scientific Exploration, 25*(1), 103–116.

Merriam-Webster. (n.d.). Pareidolia. In *Merriam-Webster.com dictionary*. https://www.merriam-webster.com/dictionary/pareidolia

Metcalfe, J., & Shimamura, A. P. (Eds.). (1994). *Metacognition: Knowing about knowing*. MIT Press. https://doi.org/10.7551/mitpress/4561.001.0001

Mills, A. (1994). Making a scientific investigation of ethnographic cases suggestive of reincarnation. In D. Young & J.-G. Goulet (Eds.), *Being changed by cross-cultural encounters: The anthropology of extraordinary experience* (pp. 237–269). Broadview Press. https://doi.org/10.3138/9781442602366-010

Mills, A., & Tucker, J. B. (2015). Reincarnation: Field studies and theoretical issues today. In E. Cardeña, J. Palmer, & D. Marcusson-Clavertz (Eds.), *Parapsychology: A handbook for the 21st century* (pp. 314–326). McFarland & Company.

Mishlove, J. [New Thinking Allowed with Jeffrey Mishlove]. (2015, August 18). *The Spiritualist vision of the afterlife with Stafford Beatty* [Video]. YouTube. https://www.youtube.com/watch?v=Y8042-M4NPw

Mishlove, J. [New Thinking Allowed With Jeffrey Mishlove]. (2019, January 18). *The power of the near-death experience, part 1 with Elizabeth Krohn* [Video]. YouTube. https://www.youtube.com/watch?v=S_Yomwcod3E

Mishlove, J. [New Thinking Allowed With Jeffrey Mishlove]. (2021a, April 12). *Dr William Lang's return from the grave with Roy Stemman* [Video]. YouTube. https://youtu.be/jW0sEvN9oDQ

Mishlove, J. [New Thinking Allowed With Jeffrey Mishlove]. (2021b, June 21). *InPresence 0228: Living in the afterlife, part 1* [Video]. YouTube. https://www.youtube.com/watch?v=XlaBYrlGtK8

Moody, R., Jr. (with Perry, P.). (1993). *Reunions: Visionary encounters with departed loved ones*. Villard Books.

Moody, R., Jr. (with Perry, P.). (2010). *Glimpses of eternity: Sharing a loved one's passage from this life to the next*. Guideposts.

Moody, R. A., Jr. (1975). *Life after life: The investigation of a phenomenon–survival of bodily death*. Bantam/Mockingbird.

Moody, R. A., Jr. (1988). *The light beyond*. Bantam Books.

Moody, R. A., Jr. (with Perry, P.). (1991). *Coming back: A psychiatrist explores past-life journeys*. Bantam Books.

Moon, C., & Moon, P. (2017). *Ghost box: Voices from spirits, ETs, shadow people & other astral beings*. Llewellyn Publications.

Moore, L. E., & Greyson, B. (2017). Characteristics of memories for near-death experiences. *Consciousness and Cognition, 51*, 116–124. https://doi.org/10.1016/j.concog.2017.03.003

Moorjani, A. (2012). *Dying to be me: My journey from cancer, to near death, to true healing*. Hay House.

Moreira-Almeida, A. (2012). Research on mediumship and the mind–brain relationship. In A. Moreira-Almeida & F. S. Santos (Eds.), *Exploring frontiers of the mind-brain relationship, Mindfulness in behavioral health* (pp. 191–213). Springer. https://doi.org/10.1037/e639232012-001

Mossbridge, J. (2003, November). *Grief relief: Visiting the dead*. Induced After-Death Communication. http://www.induced-adc.com/experiences/

Murray, C. D., & Wooffitt, R. (2010). Anomalous experience and qualitative research: An introduction to the special issue. *Qualitative Research in Psychology, 7*(1), 1–4. https://doi.org/10.1080/14780880903304535

Nahm, M. (2016). Further comments about Kai Mügge's alleged mediumship and recent developments. *Journal of Scientific Exploration, 30*(1), 56–62.

Nahm, M., & Greyson, B. (2009). Terminal lucidity in patients with chronic schizophrenia and dementia: A survey of the literature. *Journal of Nervous and Mental Disease, 197*(12), 942–944. https://doi.org/10.1097/NMD.0b013e3181c22583

Nahm, M., Greyson, B., Kelly, E. W., & Haraldsson, E. (2012). Terminal lucidity: A review and a case collection. *Archives of Gerontology and Geriatrics, 55*(1), 138–142. https://doi.org/10.1016/j.archger.2011.06.031

Naiman, R. R. (2014). *Healing night: The science and spirit of sleeping, dreaming, and awakening* (2nd ed.). New Moon Media.

Nani, A., Manuello, J., Mancuso, L., Liloia, D., Costa, T., & Cauda, F. (2019). The neural correlates of consciousness and attention: Two sister processes of the brain. *Frontiers in Neuroscience, 13*, Article 1169. https://doi.org/10.3389/fnins.2019.01169

Nees, M. A., & Phillips, C. (2015). Auditory pareidolia: Effects of contextual priming on perceptions of purportedly paranormal and ambiguous auditory stimuli. *Applied Cognitive Psychology, 29*(1), 129–134. https://doi.org/10.1002/acp.3068

Neppe, V. M. (2007). A detailed analysis of an important chess game: Revisiting "Maróczy versus Korchnoi." *Journal of the Society for Psychical Research, 71*(3), 129–147.

Nichols, D. E. (2018). N, N-dimethyltryptamine and the pineal gland: Separating fact from myth. *Journal of Psychopharmacology, 32*(1), 30–36. https://doi.org/10.1177/0269881117736919

Nichols, S., Strohminger, N., Rai, A., & Garfield, J. (2018). Death and the self. *Cognitive Science, 42*(Suppl. 1), 314–332. https://doi.org/10.1111/cogs.12590

Noakes, R. (2019). *Physics and psychics: The occult and the sciences in modern Britain.* Cambridge University Press. https://doi.org/10.1017/9781316882436

Noory, G., & Guiley, R. E. (2011). *Talking to the dead.* Tom Doherty Associates.

Norton, L., Gibson, R. M., Gofton, T., Benson, C., Dhanani, S., Shemie, S. D., Hornby, L., Ward, R., & Young, G. B. (2017). Electroencephalographic recordings during withdrawal of life-sustaining therapy until 30 minutes after declaration of death. *The Canadian Journal of Neurological Sciences, 44*(2), 139–145. https://doi.org/10.1017/cjn.2016.309

Nosek, B. A., Spies, J. R., & Motyl, M. (2012). Scientific utopia: II. Restructuring incentives and practices to promote truth over publishability. *Perspectives on Psychological Science, 7*(6), 615–631. https://doi.org/10.1177/1745691612459058

Nosek, C. L., Kerr, C. W., Woodworth, J., Wright, S. T., Grant, P. C., Kuszczak, S. M., Banas, A., Luczkiewicz, D. L., & Depner, R. M. (2015). End-of-life dreams and visions: A qualitative perspective from hospice patients. *The American Journal of Hospice & Palliative Care, 32*(3), 269–274. https://doi.org/10.1177/1049909113517291

Noyes, R., & Kletti, R. (1977). Panoramic memory: A response to the threat of death. *OMEGA—Journal of Death and Dying, 8*(3), 181–194. https://doi.org/10.2190/0UD7-H3WR-1ENN-57CN

Ohkado, M. (2015). Children's birth, womb, prelife, and past-life memories: Results of an internet-based survey. *Journal of Prenatal & Perinatal Psychology & Health, 30*(1), 3–16.

Ohnsorge, K., Rehmann-Sutter, C., Streeck, N., & Gudat, H. (2019). Wishes to die at the end of life and subjective experience of four different typical dying trajectories. A qualitative interview study. *PLOS One, 14*(1), Article e0210784. https://doi.org/10.1371/journal.pone.0210784

O'Keeffe, C., Houran, J., Houran, D. J., Dagnall, N., Drinkwater, K., Sheridan, L., & Laythe, B. (2019). The Dr. John Hall story: A case study in putative 'haunted people syndrome.' *Mental Health, Religion & Culture, 22*(9), 910–929. https://doi.org/10.1080/13674676.2019.1674795

Olesen, T. (2020). Reincarnation research: I. An old idea re-examined with new methods in the 21st century. *Australian Journal of Parapsychology, 20*(2), 139–160.

Osis, K., & Haraldsson, E. (1997). *At the hour of death* (3rd ed.). Hastings House.

Owen, I. M. (with Sparrow, M.). (1976). *Conjuring up Philip: An adventure in psychokinesis.* Fitzhenry & Whiteside.

Pana, R., Hornby, L., Shemie, S. D., Dhanani, S., & Teitelbaum, J. (2016). Time to loss of brain function and activity during circulatory arrest. *Journal of Critical Care, 34,* 77–83. https://doi.org/10.1016/j.jcrc.2016.04.001

Pandarakalam, J. P. (2018). Do reincarnation-type cases involve consciousness transfer? *NeuroQuantology: An Interdisciplinary Journal of Neuroscience and Quantum Physics, 16*(11), 30–43. https://doi.org/10.14704/nq.2018.16.11.1882

Paraná, D., Rocha, A. C., Freire, E. S., Lotufo Neto, F., & Moreira-Almeida, A. (2019). An empirical investigation of alleged mediumistic writing: A case study of Chico Xavier's letters. *Journal of Nervous and Mental Disease, 207*(6), 497–504. https://doi.org/10.1097/NMD.0000000000000999

Parker, M. [Michael Parker Media]. (2014, September 22). *A course in demonology—John Zaffis on dark matter with Michael Parker* [Video]. YouTube. https://www.youtube.com/watch?v=M5fDBfojSDE

Parnia, S. (2014). Death and consciousness—An overview of the mental and cognitive experience of death. *Annals of the New York Academy of Sciences, 1330*(1), 75–93. https://doi.org/10.1111/nyas.12582

Parnia, S., Post, S. G., Lee, M. T., Lyubomirsky, S., Aufderheide, T. P., Deakin, C. D., Greyson, B., Long, J., Gonzales, A. M., Huppert, E. L., Dickinson, A., Mayer, S., Locicero, B., Levin, J., Bossis, A., Worthington, E., Fenwick, P., & Shirazi, T. K. (2022). Guidelines and standards for the study of death and recalled experiences of death—A multidisciplinary consensus statement and proposed future directions. *Annals of the New York Academy of Sciences, 1511*(1), 5–21. https://doi.org/10.1111/nyas.14740

Pearsall, P., Schwartz, G. E. R., & Russek, L. G. S. (2000). Changes in heart transplant recipients that parallel the personalities of their donors. *Integrative Medicine, 2*(2–3), 65–72. https://doi.org/10.1016/S1096-2190(00)00013-5

Pearson, P. (2014). *Opening heaven's door: What the dying may be trying to tell us about where they're going.* Random House Canada.

Pearson, P. (2021). Marginalizing the sacred: The clinical contextualization of sensed presence experiences. In T. G. Plante & G. E. Schwartz (Eds.), *Human interaction with the divine, the sacred, and the deceased: Psychological, scientific, and theological perspectives* (pp. 7–21). Routledge.

Pederzoli, L., De Stefano, E., & Tressoldi, P. (2021). Hypno-death-experiences: Death experiences during hypnotic life regressions. *Death Studies, 45*(4), 322–326. https://doi.org/10.1080/07481187.2019.1626949

Pederzoli, L., Tressoldi, P., & Wahbeh, H. (2022). Channeling: A non-pathological possession and dissociative identity experience or something else? *Culture, Medicine and Psychiatry, 46*(2), 161–169. https://doi.org/10.1007/s11013-021-09730-9

Pekala, R. J. (1991). *Quantifying consciousness: An empirical approach.* Plenum Press. https://doi.org/10.1007/978-1-4899-0629-8

Piccinini, G., & Bahar, S. (2015). No mental life after brain death. In M. Martin & K. Augustine (Eds.), *The myth of an afterlife: The case against life after death* (pp. 135–170). Rowman & Littlefield.

Pistoia, F., Mattiacci, G., Sarà, M., Padua, L., Macchi, C., & Sacco, S. (2018). Development of the Italian version of the Near-Death Experience Scale. *Frontiers in Human Neuroscience, 12*, Article 45. https://doi.org/10.3389/fnhum.2018.00045

Plato. (1968). *The Republic* (B. Jowett, Trans.). Airmont Publishing Company. (Original work published ca. 360 B.C.E.)

Presi, P. (2004). The ITC work of Marcello Bacci. In A. Cardoso & D. Fontana (Eds.), *Proceedings of the First International Conference on Current Research Into Survival of Physical Death With Special Reference to Instrumental Transcommunication* (pp. 41–48). Artes Gráficas Vicus, S. A. L.

Presti, D. E. (2018). An expanded conception of mind. In D. E. Presti (Ed.), *Mind beyond brain: Buddhism, science, and the paranormal* (pp. 121–146). Columbia University Press.

Price, H. H. (1953). Survival and the idea of "another world." *Proceedings of the Society for Psychical Research, 50*(182), 1–25.

Prince, W. F. (1927). *The case of Patience Worth: A critical study of certain unusual phenomena.* Boston Society for Psychic Research.

Pronin, E., & Schmidt, K. (2013). Claims and denials of bias and their implications for policy. In E. Shafir (Ed.), *The biological foundations of public policy* (pp. 195–216). Princeton University Press. https://doi.org/10.2307/j.ctv550cbm.17

Puhle, A., & Parker, A. (2017). An exploratory study of lucid dreams concerning deceased persons. *Journal of the Society for Psychical Research, 81*(3), 145–160.

Radin, D. I. (1997). *The conscious universe: The scientific truth of psychic phenomena.* HarperEdge.

Ransom, C. (2015). A critique of Ian Stevenson's rebirth research. In M. Martin & K. Augustine (Eds.), *The myth of an afterlife: The case against life after death* (pp. 571–574). Rowman & Littlefield.

Raudive, K. (1971). *Breakthrough: An amazing experiment in electronic communication with the dead* (N. Fowler, Trans.). Colin Smythe.

Rawat, K. S., & Rivas, T. (2021). *Reincarnation as a scientific concept: Scholarly evidence for past lives.* White Crow Books.

Renz, M., Reichmuth, O., Bueche, D., Traichel, B., Mao, M. S., Cerny, T., & Strasser, F. (2018). Fear, pain, denial, and spiritual experiences in dying processes. *The American Journal of Hospice & Palliative Care, 35*(3), 478–491. https://doi.org/10.1177/1049909117725271

Rhine, L. E. (1963). Spontaneous physical effects and the psi process. *The Journal of Parapsychology, 27*(2), 84–122.

Ribáry, G., Lajtai, L., Demetrovics, Z., & Maraz, A. (2017). Multiplicity: An explorative interview study on personal experiences of people with multiple selves. *Frontiers in Psychology, 8,* Article 938. https://doi.org/10.3389/fpsyg.2017.00938

Richards, W. A. (2016). *Sacred knowledge: Psychedelics and religious experiences.* Columbia University Press.

Ring, K. (1987). Near-death experiences: Intimations of immortality? In J. S. Spong (Ed.), *Consciousness and survival: An interdisciplinary inquiry into the possibility of life beyond biological death* (pp. 165–176). Institute of Noetic Sciences.

Ring, K. (2007). Letter to the editor: Response to Augustine's "Does paranormal perception occur in near-death experiences?" *Journal of Near-Death Studies, 26*(1), 70–76.

Ring, K., & Cooper, S. (1997). Near-death and out-of-body experiences in the blind: A study of apparent eyeless vision. *Journal of Near-Death Studies, 16*(2), 101–147. https://doi.org/10.1023/A:1025010015662

Ring, K., & Cooper, S. (2008). *Mindsight: Near-death and out-of-body experiences in the blind* (2nd ed.). iUniverse. (Original work published 1999)

Ring, K., & Valarino, E. E. (1998). *Lessons from the light: What we can learn from the near-death experience.* Moment Point.

Rivas, T., Dirven, A., & Smit, R. H. (2016). *The self does not die: Verified paranormal phenomena from near-death experiences* (J. M. Holden & W. J. Boeke, Eds. & Trans.). IANDS Publications.

Roberts, J. (1978). *The afterdeath journal of an American philosopher: The world view of William James.* Prentice-Hall.

Rock, A. J., Thorsteinsson, E. B., Tressoldi, P. E., & Loi, N. M. (2021). A meta-analysis of anomalous information reception by mediums: Assessing the forced-choice design in mediumship research, 2000–2020. In S. Krippner, A. J. Rock, H. L. Friedman, & N. L. Zingrone (Eds.), *Advances in parapsychological research 10* (pp. 49–69). McFarland & Company.

Roe, C. A. (2019, September 20–22). *A representative survey of paranormal beliefs and experiences* [Conference presentation]. The Society for Psychical Research, 43rd International Conference, Leicester, England.

Rogo, D. S., & Bayless, R. (1979). *Phone calls from the dead.* Prentice-Hall.

Ross, C. A., Norton, G. R., & Wozney, K. (1989). Multiple personality disorder: An analysis of 236 cases. *Canadian Journal of Psychiatry, 34*(5), 413–418. https://doi.org/10.1177/070674378903400509

Rousseau, D., & Billingham, J. (2021). *What would have to be true about the world? On evidence for the possibility of consciousness surviving death.* https://www.bigelowinstitute.org/wp-content/uploads/2022/10/rousseau-consciousness-surviving-death.pdf

Routledge, C., & Vess, M. (Eds.). (2019). *Handbook of terror management theory.* Academic Press.

Ryan, T. (2014). Cyber psychics: Psychic readings in online social spaces. In J. Hunter & D. Luke (Eds.), *Talking with the spirits: Ethnographies from between the worlds* (pp. 131–154). Daily Grail Publishing.

Ryff, C. D. (1989). Happiness is everything, or is it? Explorations on the meaning of psychological well-being. *Journal of Personality and Social Psychology, 57*(6), 1069–1081. https://doi.org/10.1037/0022-3514.57.6.1069

Ryff, C. D. (2014). Psychological well-being revisited: Advances in the science and practice of eudaimonia. *Psychotherapy and Psychosomatics, 83*, 10–28. https://doi.org/10.1159/000353263

Sabom, M. B. (1998). *Light & death: One doctor's fascinating account of near-death experiences*. Zondervan.

Sarraf, M., Woodley of Menie, M. A., & Tressoldi, P. (2021). Anomalous information reception by mediums: A meta-analysis of the scientific evidence. *EXPLORE: The Journal of Science and Healing, 17*(5), 396–402. https://doi.org/10.1016/j.explore.2020.04.002

Schmidt, B. E. (2014). Mediumship in Brazil: The holy war against spirits and African gods. In J. Hunter & D. Luke (Eds.), *Talking with the spirits: Ethnographies from between the worlds* (pp. 207–227). Daily Grail Publishing.

Schwartz, G. E. (2021a). A computer-automated, multi-center, multi-blinded, randomized control trial evaluating hypothesized spirit presence and communication. *EXPLORE: The Journal of Science and Healing, 17*(4), 351–359. https://doi.org/10.1016/j.explore.2019.11.007

Schwartz, G. E. (2021b). Contemporary evidence for communication with the departed and the sacred. In T. G. Plante & G. E. Schwartz (Eds.), *Human interaction with the divine, the sacred, and the deceased: Psychological, scientific, and theological perspectives* (pp. 194–210). Routledge. https://doi.org/10.4324/9781003105749-13

Senkowski, E. (2013). Parallel realities? Correspondences between transcommunication transmissions and existing terrestrial material. *ITC Journal, 46*, 22–37.

Shared Crossing Research Initiative. (2021). Shared death experiences: A little-known type of end-of-life phenomena reported by caregivers and loved ones. *The American Journal of Hospice & Palliative Care, 38*(12), 1479–1487. https://doi.org/10.1177/10499091211000045

Shermer, M. (2014, October). Infrequencies. *Scientific American, 311*(4), 97. https://doi.org/10.1038/scientificamerican1014-97

Shinar, Y. R., & Marks, A. D. (2015). Distressing visions at the end of life: Case report and review of the literature. *The Journal of Pastoral Care & Counseling, 69*(4), 251–253. https://doi.org/10.1177/1542305015616103

Shroder, T. (1999). *Old souls: The scientific evidence for past lives*. Simon & Schuster.

Shushan, G. (2018). *Near-death experience in indigenous religions*. Oxford University Press.

Sokal, A. D. (1996a). A physicist experiments with cultural studies. *Lingua Franca, 6*(4), 62–64.

Sokal, A. D. (1996b). Transgressing the boundaries: Toward a transformative hermeneutics of quantum gravity. *Social Text, 14*(46/47), 217–252. https://doi.org/10.2307/466856

Sommer, A. (2014). Psychical research in the history and philosophy of science. An introduction and review. *Studies in History and Philosophy of Biological and Biomedical Sciences, 48*(Pt. A), 38–45. https://doi.org/10.1016/j.shpsc.2014.08.004

Stavis, R. H. (with Durand, S.). (2018). *Sister of darkness: The chronicles of a modern exorcist.* HarperCollins.

Steffen, E., & Coyle, A. (2017). "I thought they should know . . . that daddy is not completely gone: A case study of sense-of-presence experiences in bereavement and family meaning-making." *Omega—Journal of Death and Dying, 74*(4), 363–385. https://doi.org/10.1177/0030222816686609

Stevenson, I. (1974). *Twenty cases suggestive of reincarnation.* University Press of Virginia. (Original work published as Volume 26 of the *Proceedings of the American Society for Psychical Research,* 1966)

Stevenson, I. (1990). Phobias in children who claim to remember previous lives. *Journal of Scientific Exploration, 4*(2), 243–254.

Stevenson, I. (1997a). *Reincarnation and biology: A contribution to the etiology of birthmarks and birth defects.* Praeger.

Stevenson, I. (1997b). *Where reincarnation and biology intersect.* Praeger.

Strada, E. A. (2018). *Palliative psychology: Clinical perspectives on an emerging specialty.* Oxford University Press. https://doi.org/10.1093/med/9780199798551.001.0001

Streiff, J. (2009). *Edison, psycho-phone and ITC technology.* https://www.sdparanormal.com/f/Edison_Psychophone_and_ITC_Technology.pdf

Strieber, W., & Strieber, A. (2020). *The afterlife revolution.* Beyond Words.

Sudduth, M. (2015, August 7). Personal reflections on life after death. *Cup of Nirvana.* https://michaelsudduth.com/personal-reflections-on-life-after-death/

Sudduth, M. (2016). *A philosophical critique of empirical arguments for postmortem survival.* Palgrave Macmillan. https://doi.org/10.1057/9781137440945

Sudduth, M. (2021). Signs of reincarnation: Exploring beliefs, cases, and theory by James Matlock. *Journal of Scientific Exploration, 35*(1), 183–208. https://doi.org/10.31275/20212089

Sumption, N., Clune, B., Pfister, J., & Davis, B. (2018). *Thinking outside the box: Frank Sumption: Creator of the ghost box.* Vertel Publishing.

Szarpa, K. L., Kerr, C. W., Wright, S. T., Luczkiewicz, D. L., Hang, P. C., & Ball, L. S. (2013). The prodrome to delirium: A grounded theory study. *Journal of Hospice & Palliative Nursing, 15*(6), 332–337. https://doi.org/10.1097/NJH.0b013e31828fdf56

Tart, C. T. (2009). *The end of materialism: How evidence of the paranormal is bringing science and spirit together.* New Harbinger Publications.

Taylor, S. F. (2005). Between the idea and the reality: A study of the counselling experiences of bereaved people who sense the presence of the deceased. *Counselling & Psychotherapy Research, 5*(1), 53–61. https://doi.org/10.1080/14733140512331343921

Thanatos TV EN. (2020, December 10). *Past life memories: An in-depth interview with Carol Bowman*. [Video]. YouTube. https://www.youtube.com/watch?v=vdMDsSR9crQ

Theosophical Classics. (2018, May 17). *Theosophical classic 2004: Evidence for life after death: Part 1 with Ian Stevenson* [Video]. YouTube. https://www.youtube.com/watch?v=xLUour3gb-o

Thonnard, M., Charland-Verville, V., Brédart, S., Dehon, H., Ledoux, D., Laureys, S., & Vanhaudenhuyse, A. (2013). Characteristics of near-death experiences memories as compared to real and imagined events memories. *PLOS ONE, 8*(3), Article e57620. https://doi.org/10.1371/journal.pone.0057620

Thorngate, W. (1990). The economy of attention and the development of psychology. *Canadian Psychology, 31*(3), 262–271. https://doi.org/10.1037/h0078910

Timmermann, C., Roseman, L., Williams, L., Erritzoe, D., Martial, C., Cassol, H., Laureys, S., Nutt, D., & Carhart-Harris, R. (2018). DMT models the near-death experience. *Frontiers in Psychology, 9*, Article 1424. https://doi.org/10.3389/fpsyg.2018.01424

Tomlinson, M. (2019). How to speak like a spirit medium: Voice and evidence in Australian Spiritualism. *American Ethnologist, 46*(4), 482–494. https://doi.org/10.1111/amet.12832

Transcommunication Switzerland. (2022, May 25). *The Germanium receptor V1.0 documentation (originally from the Scole Group)* [Video]. YouTube. https://www.youtube.com/watch?v=Vo5JVZ5pRyw

Tressoldi, P., Liberale, L., Sinesio, F., Bubba, V., Pederzoli, L., & Testoni, I. (2022). Mediumship accuracy: A quantitative and qualitative study with a triple-blind protocol. *EXPLORE: The Journal of Science and Healing, 18*(4), 411–415. https://doi.org/10.1016/j.explore.2021.05.009

Tucker, J. B., & Keil, H. H. J. (2013). Experimental birthmarks: New cases of an Asian practice. *Journal of Scientific Exploration, 27*(2), 269–282.

Tymn, M. (2016, July 11). *Life after death: Keith Parsons reaches the masses!* White Crow Books. http://whitecrowbooks.com/michaeltymn/entry/life_after_death_keith_parsons_reaches_the_masses/

van Lommel, P. (2013). Non-local consciousness: A concept based on scientific research on near-death experiences during cardiac arrest. *Journal of Consciousness Studies, 20*(1–2), 7–48.

van Quekelberghe, R., Göbel, P., & Hertweck, E. (1995). Simulation of near-death and out-of body experiences under hypnosis. *Imagination, Cognition and Personality, 14*(2), 151–164.

van Rijn, C. M., Krijnen, H., Menting-Hermeling, S., & Coenen, A. M. L. (2011). Decapitation in rats: Latency to unconsciousness and the "wave of death." *PLOS One, 6*(1), Article e16514. https://doi.org/10.1371/journal.pone.0016514

Vicente, R., Rizzuto, M., Sarica, C., Yamamoto, K., Sadr, M., Khajuria, T., Fatehi, M., Moien-Afshari, F., Haw, C. S., Llinas, R. R., Lozano, A. M., Neimat,

J. S., & Zemmar, A. (2022). Enhanced interplay of neuronal coherence and coupling in the dying human brain. *Frontiers in Aging Neuroscience, 14,* Article 813531. https://doi.org/10.3389/fnagi.2022.813531

Wahbeh, H., & Butzer, B. (2020). Characteristics of English-speaking trance channelers. *EXPLORE: The Journal of Science and Healing, 16*(5), 304–309. https://doi.org/10.1016/j.explore.2020.02.002

Wahbeh, H., Cannard, C., Okonsky, J., & Delorme, A. (2019). A physiological examination of perceived incorporation during trance. *F1000 Research, 8,* Article 67. https://doi.org/10.12688/f1000research.17157.2

Wahbeh, H., Carpenter, L., & Radin, D. (2018). A mixed methods phenomenological and exploratory study of channeling. *Journal of the Society for Psychical Research, 82*(3), 129–147.

Walsh, R. (1995). Phenomenological mapping: A method for describing and comparing states of consciousness. *Journal of Transpersonal Psychology, 27*(1), 25–56.

Ward, P. (2009). *The Medea hypothesis: Is life on earth ultimately self-destructive?* Princeton University Press. https://doi.org/10.1515/9781400829880

Watson, T. A. (1926). *Exploring life: The autobiography of Thomas A. Watson.* D. Appleton and Company. https://babel.hathitrust.org/cgi/pt?id=mdp.39015053577154&view=1up&seq=9

Wauters, A. M., & König, H. O. (2017). *Listen! New discoveries about the afterlife. Scientific research on contact with the invisible. Experiences of instrumental transcommunication (ITC)* (R. C. Hogan & E. Meuren, Eds. & Trans.). Greater Reality Publications. (Original work published 2016)

Wehrstein, K. M. (2017). Psychomanteum (mirror-gazing). In *Psi encyclopedia.* The Society for Psychical Research. https://psi-encyclopedia.spr.ac.uk/articles/psychomanteum-mirror-gazing

Wehrstein, K. M., & McLuhan, R. (2018). Fox sisters. In *Psi encyclopedia.* The Society for Psychical Research. https://psi-encyclopedia.spr.ac.uk/articles/fox-sisters

Weisman, D. (2015). Dissolution into death. In M. Martin & K. Augustine (Eds.), *The myth of an afterlife: The case against life after death* (pp. 83–104). Rowman & Littlefield.

West, D. (2015). Society for Psychical Research. In *Psi encyclopedia.* The Society for Psychical Research. https://psi-encyclopedia.spr.ac.uk/articles/society-psychical-research

White, C. (2016). The cognitive foundations of reincarnation. *Method & Theory in the Study of Religion, 28*(3), 264–286. https://doi.org/10.1163/15700682-12341381

White, C., Kinsella, M., & Bering, J. (2018). How to know you've survived death: A cognitive account of the popularity of contemporary post-mortem survival narratives. *Method & Theory in the Study of Religion, 30*(3), 279–299. https://doi.org/10.1163/15700682-12341431

Wilde, D. J., Murray, J., Doherty, P., & Murray, C. D. (2019). Mental health and mediumship: An interpretative phenomenological analysis. *Mental Health, Religion & Culture, 22*(3), 261–278. https://doi.org/10.1080/13674676.2019.1606186

Williams, B. J. (2021a). Minding the matter of psychokinesis: A review of proof- and process-oriented experimental findings related to mental influence on random number generators. *Journal of Scientific Exploration, 35*(4), 829–932. https://doi.org/10.31275/20212359

Williams, B. J. (2021b). Too strange to be true? On two recent efforts to empirically examine and critically assess claims of psychic phenomena. In S. Krippner, A. J. Rock, H. L. Friedman, & N. L. Zingrone (Eds.), *Advances in parapsychological research 10* (pp. 15–48). McFarland & Company.

Willin, M. (2021). ARG Owen. In *PSI Encyclopedia*. https://psi-encyclopedia.spr.ac.uk/articles/arg-owen

Winsper, A. R. (2020). *Interpreting electronic voice phenomena: The role of auditory perception, paranormal belief and individual differences* [Unpublished doctoral dissertation]. University of Central Lancashire.

Woods, K., & Baruš, I. (2004). Experimental test of possible psychological benefits of past-life regression. *Journal of Scientific Exploration, 18*(4), 597–608.

Woollacott, M., & Peyton, B. (2021). Verified account of near-death experience in a physician who survived cardiac arrest. *EXPLORE: The Journal of Science and Healing, 17*(3), 213–219. https://doi.org/10.1016/j.explore.2020.03.005

Woollacott, M., Roe, C. A., Cooper, C. E., Lorimer, D., & Elsaesser, E. (2022). Perceptual phenomena associated with spontaneous experiences of after-death communication: Analysis of visual, tactile, auditory and olfactory sensations. *EXPLORE: The Journal of Science and Healing, 18*(4), 423–431. https://doi.org/10.1016/j.explore.2021.02.006

Wright, S. T., Kerr, C. W., Doroszczuk, N. M., Kuszczak, S. M., Hang, P. C., & Luczkiewicz, D. L. (2014). The impact of dreams of the deceased on bereavement: A survey of hospice caregivers. *The American Journal of Hospice & Palliative Care, 31*(2), 132–138. https://doi.org/10.1177/1049909113479201

Wyatt, J. K., Bootzin, R. R., Anthony, J., & Stevenson, S. (1992). Does sleep onset produce retrograde amnesia? *Sleep Research, 21,* 113.

Zammit, V., & Zammit, W. (2013). *A lawyer presents the evidence for the afterlife.* White Crow Books.

Index

A

Academics. *See also* Studying death
  analysis of the afterlife by, 201–202
  bias toward materialism among, 12–13
  lack of ITC research by, 101–102
  materialism imposed on, 226
  mediums' warnings against, 92
  studying death avoided by, 7–9
ADCs. *See* Afterdeath communication
Affective states, 221. *See also* Grief
  affective NDEs, 208
  as alterations of consciousness, 6
  in altered states of consciousness, 221
  anger, 69
  anguish, 191
  anxiety, 29, 41, 63, 142, 151, 162, 170
  depression, 41, 63, 142
  in dying process, 29, 31, 38, 42, 202
  emotional bonds with deceased, 57, 71, 140
  emotional bonds facilitating communication, 77, 140
  emotional healing, 64
  emotions in the afterlife, 6, 216–218, 221, 228
  fear, 19, 41
  feelings of peace, 28, 42, 46, 52, 69, 96, 153, 192
  happiness, 40, 43, 66
  and haunting phenomena, 133, 138
  joy, 43–46, 52, 66–67
  loneliness, 63–64
  and mental influence, 121
  and NDEs, 154, 165, 167
  negative affect, 41–42, 142, 216
  and neural correlates, 157
  neutralized with EMDR, 65
  from past-life analysis, 182, 189, 191
  peaceful death, 34, 36–37, 41, 49
  and personal meaning, 101
  positive affect increased near death, 29
  in possession, 40, 142
  "raw feels," 5
  sadness, 31, 69, 191
  in simulations of NDEs, 171
After-Death Communication Questionnaire, 119
Afterdeath communication (ADC), 51–74. *See also entries for specific types of communication*
  and arguments against materialism, 52
  butterflies, 52, 54, 200
  characteristics of, 53–57
  and continuing bonds approach to grief counseling, 63–64
  critical features of, 72–73
  defined, 8, 53
  distinguishing explanations of, 73–74
  in dreams, 59–61
  examples of, 57–59
  induced communications, 53, 64–69
  in organ transplant cases, 70–71
  other terms used for, 53
  owls, 200
  as pathological, 61–63
  physicality of, 74
  prevalence of, 54–55
  reflections on, 71–74
  sensed presence, 55–56

259

spontaneous, 120
themes in, 57
through electronic devices or other technologies. *See* Instrumental transcommunication (ITC)
through mediums. *See* Mediumship
types of, 53–54
underreporting of, 55
Afterlife, 199–223
  body in the, 210–211
  communicating with the living from, 217–220
  conceptualizations of, 201–205
  and death as altered state of consciousness, 220–223
  dying from point of view of, 205–208
  effects of deathbed phenomena on belief in, 49
  environment in the, 6, 209–210, 214
  hells, 212
  levels or dimensions of, 211–212
  and nature of time, 213–214
  and nonhuman beings, 212–213
  parallels between prebirth and, 177
  questions about, 208–214
  for some or for all, 208–209
  and survival of the psyche, 214–217
  thoughts shaping the environment in, 209–210
Alexander, Betsy, 173
Alexander, Eben, 173
Alexander, Stewart, 79, 128–132, 142–143, 146
Aliens (extraterrestrial), 78, 133, 140, 213
  interdimensionality of, 78, 140
Alterations of consciousness, 6, 26
Altered state(s) of consciousness
  conducive to anomalous phenomena, 66
  death as, 4, 6, 199, 220–223, 229
  defined, 4, 6, 220
  dimensions of, 4–6, 220–222
  life impacts of learning about, 170
Amado-Cattaneo, Roberto, 15
Ambiguity, as aspect of inauthenticity, 20
Anastasia, Joyce, 75
Angels, 78, 133, 142, 213, 214
Animals. *See also* Insects
  attached to living people, 214
  channeling, 78
  communication through, 217
  as expressions of a disembodied reality, 200

Oscar the cat, 33, 46
  reactions to someone's dying in, 47–48
  symbolic, experiencing appearance of, 48
Announcing dreams, 179–180
Anomalous influencing, x, 99–100, 122.
  See also Remote influencing
Anomalous object displacement, 132
Anomalous phenomena. *See also individual phenomena*
  altered states of consciousness conducive to, 66
  and boggle threshold, 18–19
  controversy over, 17–18
  cumulative effect of, 22
  defined, 17
  evidence for, 17
  and living agent psi, x
  materialist stance on, x
  meaningfulness of, 71–72
  in near-death experiences with temporal anchors, 16
  and normative ideas, 19–21
  personal experience of, 18
  reflecting on questions about, 71–74
  separating pathological states and, 227
  and survival hypothesis, x–xi
Anomalous physical phenomena, 54, 125–148. *See also individual phenomena*
  clocks stopping at time of death, 47
  physical mediumship, 127–131
  poltergeists, 131–135
  possession, 139–144
  reflections on, 144–148
  Scole experiment, 135–139
Anomalous telephone contacts (ATCs), 103, 117–120
  in crisis period (after death), 119
  following near-death experiences, 165
  prolonged calls, 118
  simple calls, 118
Anthony, M., 77
Anticipating death, 29–30, 32–35
Apparent deathbed communications, 35–41
Apparition(s)
  afterdeath protection by, 58
  in the afterlife, telepathic interaction among, 204
  appearing to O'Neil, 106
  ectoplasm of, 146
  facilitated, 66–69

feeling of reality associated with, 68
observed by caregivers, 40
sensory component of, 56
shared afterdeath experiences of, 58–59
use of term, 53
and violent death, 72
Appearance of deceased. *See also* Deathbed phenomena; Shared death experiences
appearing younger, 210
clothing, 211
as communicated by mediums, 76
plasticity of, 211, 214
remaining same as just before death, 60, 73
unusual, 60, 67
without a body, 210–211
Apports, 127, 132, 144, 226. *See also* "Just One of Those Things" (JOTT)
Approaching death. *See also* Affective states
process of transformation when, 41–42
stages of, 30–31
Archangels, 142, 214
Aristone, Angie, 75–77, 84
Astral goons, 140–141, 147–148. *See also* Entities
Astral planes, 211, 214, 222–223
ATCs. *See* Anomalous telephone contacts
Attention
of the deceased, 139
deceased's efforts to attract, 90
impaired, 48
as needed on parts of psyche, 190
preserved in the afterlife, 221
Atwater, Phyllis M. H., 162–165, 177
Augustine, K., 24–25, 88
Authenticity, 22, 144. *See also* Inauthenticity; Self-transformation
authentic science, 5, 21, 226
Automatic writing, 80, 89–90
Availability heuristic, 19
Awakenings, sudden, 46–47

B

BACARQ (Beliefs About Consciousness and Reality Questionnaire), 10–12, 195
conservatively transcendent position, 11–12
extraordinarily transcendent position, 11–12

and intelligence, 12
and openness, 12
Bacci, Marcello, 111–113, 124
Bailey, Alice A., 199
Baruss, I., 4–6, 38–39, 164
authenticity and inauthenticity, 20–21, 144
beliefs about consciousness and reality questionnaire, 10–13, 18, 178–179, 195
boggle threshold, 18
on EVP, 103, 105, 110
EVP studies, 109, 113–114
on feelings of knowing, 172
ITC studies, 8, 119–120, 211–212
on meaning fields, 197, 219, 229
medium's visits to class, 75–77
on need for self-transformation, 22
past-life regressions with students, 188–189
on pathomorphism, 61
on postmaterialism, 25
problems with supervenience thesis, 156–158
room allegory, 23–24
on scientism, 14
on Scole experiment, 127
student's account of ITC, 100–101
Transcendent Mind (with Mossbridge), 17, 88
Batcheldor, Kenneth, 134
Batthyány, A., 39
Battista, C., 84
Bayesian statistics, 86–87
Bayless, Raymond, 105, 118, 123, 132
Before-birth communication, 177–178
Behavior, 35, 38–39, 157, 215, 220, 222, 227
in altered states of consciousness, 220
in animals, 33, 46, 48
of deceased, 81, 147
during sleep, 222
dysfunctional, 9–10, 66, 94–95, 141, 187
imitative, 81, 139–140, 179
in groups, 19
learned behaviors, past-life experiences and, 197
of mediums, 83, 93, 147
during mediumship, 144
and previous personality, 180–181, 184–185, 197

Behavioral consciousness, 5–6, 10, 16
  when approaching death, 31
  lost upon death, 221–222
Beings. *See* Entities
Beischel, Julie, 53, 64, 84–87, 90, 95, 110
Beliefs. *See also* BACARQ
  about consciousness and reality, 10–14, 195, 226
  and intelligence, 12
  and openness, 12
  about reincarnation, 178–179
  contradictory, 5
  that give meaning to life, 29
Bell, Alexander Graham, 103
Bender, H., 105
Bercholz, Samuel, 154
Bereavement
  continuing bonds grief counseling following, 54, 63–64
  crisis period in, 119
  deathbed experiences and outcomes of, 28
  psychomanteum booth in counseling for, 69
Bias
  bias blindness, 22
  recognizing and neutralizing, 22
  toward materialism, 12–13
Bion, Stephan, 110
Birthmarks
  as evidence of reincarnation, 195
  experimental, 184–185, 215
  and past-life experiences, 175, 181–185
Blastland, M., 7
Blind people, near-death experiences of, 166–168
Boccuzzi, M., 110
Body
  in the afterlife, 210–211
  afterlife memories of, 215
  emotional release from remains of, 202
  leaving, in near-death experiences, 14–16
  subtle and physical, 203–205
Boggle threshold, 18–19
  and anomalous physical phenomena, 68
  change in, 226
  defined, 18
  physical phenomena exceeding, 125
  with shared death experience, 45
Bogoras, Waldemar, 104
Botkin, Allan, 65–66
Bowman, Carol, 182, 191, 194
Brain surge theories, 160
"Bridging worlds," (in dying) 30, 33–35
Butler, Jamie, 90–91, 139–140, 147, 200, 218
Butterflies, 48. *See also* Afterdeath communication; Insects
  in afterdeath communication, 52, 228
  manipulated by deceased, 54, 200
Byrd, C., 180

C

Callanan, M., 34
Campbell, Virginia, 133–134
Çapar, Süleyman, 180
Cardoso, Anabela, 102, 107, 108, 112, 114
Caregivers to the dying
  messages to, 34
  pathologization by, 61
  self-transformation process in, 30
Carlson, Chester, 179
Castelnovo, A., 55, 56, 62–63
Cave allegory (Plato), 18–19, 22, 24, 226.
  See also Room allegory
Cellular memory theory, 71
Channeling, 78, 80, 143–144. *See also* Mediumship
Chapman, George, 143–144, 147
Cheyne-Stokes respiration, 31
Children
  birthmarks or congenital deformities in, 175–176, 181–185
  past-life experiences of, 175–176, 179–181
  who die, afterlife appearance of, 210
Christos technique (in regression), 188
Clocks stopping at time of death, 47
Cockell, Jenny, 175, 185–187, 190, 192, 196–197, 205–206, 210, 214
Cognition
  impaired, 48
  improved in afterlife, 221
  improved in NDEs, 39
  improved in terminal lucidity, 38–39
  mental clarity, 6, 38–39, 49–50
  present in mindsight, 228
Cognitive trance, 153
Coincidences
  afterdeath, butterflies as, 52, 54, 200
  deathbed. *See* Deathbed coincidences
Coincidence Scale (Fenwick & Fenwick), 47

Cold reading (in mediumship), 81–85
Coleman, T., 127
Colvin, B., 133
"Comeback JOTT", 132
Communication(s)
   from the afterlife, 217–220. *See also* Afterdeath communication (ADCs)
   in altered states of consciousness, 221
   before-birth, 177–178
   deathbed, apparent, 35–41
   with discarnates, using electronics or technology. *See* Instrumental transcommunication (ITC)
   messages given when one is dying, 34
   during sleep, 222
Concurrence-seeking (in groupthink), 19
Congenital deformities, past-life experiences and, 181–185
Conscious channeling, 80
Consciousness, ix, 228. *See also* Altered state(s) of consciousness
   alterations of, 6
   altered state of, 4
   behavioral, 5–6, 10, 31, 221
   beliefs about reality and, 10–14, 226
   at death, materialist argument for extinguishment of, 24–25
   death as altered state of, ix–x, 220–223, 229
   definitions of, 5–6
   fringe, 172
   materialist–LAP–survival dial for, x
   materialist view of, 199
   neural correlates of, 24
   pathologization of, 61
   phenomenal, 5–6, 10. *See also* Phenomenal consciousness
   post-death survival of, x, 4, 6
   states of, 6, 28
   survival of, 214–215
   timeless domain of, 197
   types of states of, 6
Contact field (in ITC), 114
Continuing bonds approach to grief, 54, 63–64. *See also* Grief; Grief counseling
   interactive connection with deceased, 64
   mental representation of deceased, 64
Control (in mediumship), 80
Controversial nature of anomalous phenomena, 7, 17, 136–137

Conversion experience, 22
Cooper, Callum, 117–118
Cooper, Sharon, 166–170
Credibility of research, 9, 123–125, 187, 228
Crisis period, 119. *See also* Afterdeath communication (ADC)
Cryptomnesia, 196
Cummins, Geraldine, 209
Curiosity, as aspect of inauthenticity, 20
Curran, Pearl, 126

D

DBCs. *See* Deathbed communications
Dead agent psi (DAP), 122, 131, 228
Death
   anticipating, 29–30, 33
   approaching, stages in, 30–31
   controlling/knowing time and circumstances of, 32–35
   conventional view of, 81–82
   deceased person's acceptance of, 206
   dying. *See* Dying
   facing inevitability of, 28
   fear of. *See* Fear of death
   label of, 151
   materialist argument for extinguishment of consciousness at, 24–25
   possibilities for consciousness following, 6
   shared death experiences, 43–45
   studying. *See* Studying death
Death, as altered state of consciousness, ix–x, 4, 6, 199, 229
   dimensions of alteration, 220–223
Deathbed coincidences, 46–48
   clocks stopping at time of death, 47
   Coincidence Scale, 47
   defined, 8, 46
   explanations for, 49, 50
   during near-death experiences, 162
   in shared death experiences, 44
   sudden awakenings, 46–47
Deathbed communications (DBCs)
   apparent, 35–41
   distressing, 40–41
   terminal lucidity with, 39–40
   of those dying with invisible persons, 46
Deathbed phenomena (DBP), ix–x, 27–50
   anomalous, x–xi
   anticipating death, 29–30

apparent deathbed communications, 35–41
approaching death, 30–31
beneficial effects of, on the living, 49
deathbed coincidences, 46–48
defined, 28
distressing, 40–42
explanations of, 48–50
health care professionals' perspective on, 48–49
invisible process of dying, 31–35
shared death experiences, 43–45
terminal lucidity, 38–40
visible processes of dying, 29–31
Death doulas, 32, 45
Death rattle, 31
Deceased persons
  acceptance of death by, 206
  in close-earth-plane dimensions of reality, 202
  determining presence of, 91
  end-of-life visions of, 28, 32, 34–35, 37–41, 43, 45
  interactive connection with, 64. *See also specific types of interactions*
  limits on interactions with the living by, 219–220
  mental representation of, 64
  motivation of, 73
  senses involved in sensed presence of, 56
  survival of. *See* Survival; Survival hypothesis
  telepathic communication among, 217
  telepathic communication between the living and, 217
Decision making, preserved after death, 222
Delirium, 48
Delorme, Arnaud, 75
Dematerialization, 126–127, 135–139, 148
Demonic possession, 141–142, 147–148
Demons, 78, 140, 213. *See also* Entities
Diamond, Debra, 32, 45
DID. *See* Dissociative identity disorder
Dimensions, in the afterlife, 211–212
Direct knowledge, 171–172
Direct mental influence, on electronic devices, 121–122
Direct radio voice (DRV), 103, 107
Direct voice, 127

Discarnates. *See also* Entities
  creation of voiceprints by, 218–219
  electronic/technological communication with. *See* Instrumental transcommunication (ITC)
  personality displacement by, 197
  phenomena ascribed to, 228. *See also* Anomalous phenomena
  telepathic interaction among, 217
  use of term, 78
Disease burden, for mediums, 95
Dissociation, 93–94
Dissociative identity disorder (DID), 71, 93, 97, 128, 141
  alternate personalities, 128
Distressing deathbed phenomena, 40–42
Distressing NDEs, 153–154
Divine beings, 140
Doka, Kenneth J., 33, 187–188
Dosa, D. M., 33
Dos Santos, C. S., 49
Double (subtle body), 205, 210, 215, 217, 223, 229
Dreaming
  confusion of dying and, 207–208
  precognitive, 22
Dreams, 222
  afterdeath communication in, 59–61
  announcing, 179–180
  at approaching death, 37–38
  distressing, 40
  end-of-life, 49
  following organ transplant, 70
  lucid, 59–60
  precognitive, 163–164
Drugs. *See also* Psychedelics
  and deathbed phenomena, 42, 48, 49
  in inducing afterdeath communication, 65
DRV (direct radio voice), 103, 107
Dualists, 195
Durek, Shaman, xi, 3, 19
Dying. *See also* Anticipating death; Approaching death; Deathbed phenomena
  being brought back to life from, 151
  imagining, 29
  imminent death, 31
  invisible processes of, 30–35, 45
  from point of view of the afterlife, 205–208
  peripheral shutdown, 31

recognizing, 30
similarity of near-death experiences and, 207–208
visible processes of, 29–31
Dying brain hypothesis, 157–160, 162, 174

E

Ectoplasm, 80, 129, 131, 146
Edison, Thomas, 103–104
Eisenbeiss, Wolfgang, 89–90
Electronic devices
  communication with discarnate entities via. *See* Instrumental transcommunication (ITC)
  direct mental influence on, 121–122
  malfunction of, following near-death experiences, 163, 165
Electronic voice phenomena (EVP), 109–113
  anomalous structure of, 113
  categories of, 109–110
  defined, 103
  discarnates' creation of voiceprints for, 218–219
  in history of ITC, 103–109
  psychoacoustic properties of, 112
  similarity to anomalous telephone contacts, 119
Ellison, Arthur, 126, 137
Elsaesser, Evelyn, 56, 64
EMDR (eye-movement desensitization and reprocessing), 65–66
Emotions. *See* Affective states
Energy (anomalous), 78, 136
  in anomalous influencing, 3, 200
  in deathbed phenomena, 44
  in dying process, 30, 45
  in ITC, 219
  in NDEs, 163
  in possession, 139–140, 200, 213
Entities. *See also* Aliens; Angels
  astral goons, 140–141, 147–148
  attached, prevalence of, 142
  demons, 78, 140, 213
  djinn, 78, 140, 214
  during first solo transatlantic flight, 54
  folklore-type beings, 140
  intelligent agents, 73–74
  master teachers, 140
  mediums' embodiment of, 127

mediums' interactions with, 79, 123
mythological beings, 78
nonhuman beings, 208–209, 213
phenomena suggesting interaction with, 89
in possession, 140–142
sliders, 213
tricksters, 140, 142, 213
tulpas, 140
types of, 140, 212–213
use of term, 78
wraiths, 140
Environment, in the afterlife, 6, 209–210, 214, 219
Episodic memory, 194, 221
Epistemology
  in context of near-death experiences, 171–172
  reflections of, 171–173
  science as, 13
  in studying death, 6, 10, 23–26
Ernetti, Pellegrino, 104–105
Etheric plane, 211
Ethical dilemmas, for mediums, 96
Everist, W. G., 97
EVP. *See* Electronic voice phenomena
EVPMaker, 110, 114
Existential distress/terror, 28–29
Existential qualia, 5
Exline, J. J., 53
Exorcisms, 141–142
Exosomatic theory, 145–146, 200, 228–229
Exosomatic vision, 170. *See also* Mindsight; Remote Perception
Experiencer (term), 45, 47, 53, 57, 68, 72–73, 226
  of NDEs, 149, 154, 156, 160, 163, 166, 169, 173
  of past lives, 177
Experimental birthmarks, 184–185, 215
Extraordinarily transcendent position, 11–12
  and beliefs about consciousness and reality, 12–13
  first-person data in, 22
  and marginalization of anomalous phenomena, 17–18
Extrasensory perception, 11
Extraterrestrials. *See* Aliens; Entities
Eye-movement desensitization and reprocessing (EMDR), 65–66

F

Fantasy, past-life experiences as, 196
Fear of death, 28–29
   attenuated, following NDEs, 30, 162
   beneficial effects of deathbed phenomena on, 49
   and distressing deathbed phenomena, 40–42
   effect of afterdeath communications on, 54
   and fear of living one's life, 30
   in Monastic Tibetans, 216
Feelings of knowing, 172
Feelings of reality (FORs), 68, 172–173
Fenwick, Elizabeth, 28, 32, 34–35, 40, 46–49
Fenwick, Peter, 28, 32, 34–35, 40, 46–49, 186
Festa, Amerigo, 102, 112
Fever, deathbed phenomena and, 38, 48–49
Feynman, Richard P., 145, 212, 227
Fischer, J. M., 157
"Flyaway JOTT", 132
Folk-dualists, 194–195
Fontana, David, 107, 127, 138, 211
Formants (in psychoacoustics), 112. *See also* Electronic Voice Phenomena (EVP)
Fox, Catherina, 82
Fox, Margaretta, 82
Foy, Robin, 127, 135
Foy, Sandra, 127, 135
"Frank's Box", 108. *See also* Ghost boxes
Fraser, J., 144–145
Fraud, 10, 81, 84, 90, 136, 196
   fraudulent proof of, 125
Freire, E. S., 87
Fringe consciousness, 172
Fuller, J. G., 106
Full trance mediumship, 80
Fundamental (in psychoacoustics), 112. *See also* Electronic Voice Phenomena (EVP)
Future memories, 164

G

Gallagher, Richard, 141–142
Gehrig, Lou, 180
Gemelli, Agostino, 104–105
Genetic memory, 196
Germanium device (in ITC), 115, 137–138, 147–148
Ghost boxes, 108, 115, 213
Ghosthunters, 107–108
Ghosts. *See also* Apparition(s); Poltergeists; RSPK
   fictional, 135, 140
   hungry, 212
Giesemann, Suzanne, 200
Glazier, J. W., 56–57
Global crises, 220
Global warming, 20
Goranson, A., 29
Graf, Jennifer, 10, 123
Greaves, Helen, 207
Greaves, Roger, 207
Greyson, Bruce, 3–4, 17, 38–39, 152, 169, 170, 173, 177, 179
Grief
   afterdeath communications for release of, 57
   beneficial effects of deathbed phenomena on, 49
   for mediums, 96
   messages through mediums during, 77
   phenomena experienced during, 51–52, 54
Grief counseling
   afterdeath experiences in, 72
   continuing bonds approach to, 54, 63–64
   differing views of, 63
Grosso, M., 25
Groupthink, 18–22
   in military invasion, 21
Guiley, Rosemary Ellen, 99
Gullà, D., 113

H

Hallucination(s), 73, 94
   as afterdeath communications, 53, 61–63
   collective, 134
   drug- or fever-induced, 33, 48–49
   and mediumship, 94–95
   and NDEs, 152, 174
   Moody on, 68
   prevalence of, 94
   veridicality of, 62
Happy schizotype, 95

Haraldsson, Erlendur, 40–41, 54, 55–59, 72–73, 192–193
Harmonics (in psychoacoustics), 112. *See also* Electronic Voice Phenomena (EVP)
Hassler, D., 89–90
Hastings, A., 69, 72
Haunted People Syndrome, 133, 135, 139
Hauntings, 73, 133, 208
Haupt, Christian, 180
Healing, 46, 64, 78
  as effect of mediumship, 127, 142–144, 219
  as effect of NDEs, 165
Heath, P. R., 202–203
Heidegger, Martin, 20–21
Hells, 212
Hick, John, 205
Hill, Jennifer, 51
Hilton, A., 170
Hinged dialogue, 83
Hinze, Sarah, 177, 180
Hitchhiker effect, 131, 142
Hockley, J., 31–33, 38
Hodson, Robin, 142–143, 219
Home circles (in mediumship), 128–130, 136
Hospital grapevine theory (in NDEs), 71
Hot reading (in mediumship), 82
Hover hypothesis, 71
Hungry ghosts, 212–213. *See also* Ghosts; Poltergeists
Hypnosis, 94, 178, 188–190. *See also* Past-life regression; Regression
  self-hypnosis, 153
Hypnotic trance, 188
Hypnotic virtuosos, 188
Hypothermic cardiac arrest, 151

I

Idealists, 11
Identity
  after death, 204, 208
  criteria for establishing, 195
  past-life, establishing, 194–195
  pre- and postmortem, 147–148
Idle talk, as aspect of inauthenticity, 20
Images
  in the afterlife, 217
  afterlife as world of, 203–205
  in instrumental transcommunication, 108

Imagining dying, 29
Imminent death, 31
"I'm Not a Robot" (INR) task, 116
Inauthenticity. *See also* Groupthink; Scientism
  consequences of, 21–22
  curiosity as element of, 20
  ambiguity as element of, 20
  idle talk as element of, 20
  in science, 21
Information
  afterdeath communication of, 57, 60–62, 73
  anomalous transfer of, 88
  conveyed by mediums, 76–77, 81–82
  cryptomnesia, 196
  transferred during near-death experiences, 173
Innate self-grasping, 216. *See also* Self
Insects. *See also* Butterflies
  afterdeath butterflies, 52
  communication through, 217
  manipulated from the afterlife, 200–201
Insights
  from birthmarks, 182
  following attempted contact with deceased, 69
  in period before death, 28
  in presence of those dying, 30, 44
  as result of self-transformation, xi, 30
  of transcendent quality, xi, 44, 172
Instrumental transcommunication (ITC), 54, 99–124
  and anomalous physical phenomena, 146–147
  anomalous telephone contacts, 117–120
  contact field for, 114
  context for examining, 101–103
  defined, 8, 99
  deliberate, 101, 115–116, 120
  electronic voice phenomena, 109–113
  equipment for, 115
  history of, 103–109
  hypothesized spirit participants in, 116–117
  images in, 108
  phenomena of, 113–117
  qualities of persons for, 114–115
  reflections on, 121–124
  research on, 70, 101–102, 121–124

Intelligence, 12, 129. *See also* Entities; Residue theories
　anomalous, 122, 145
　artificial, 5
　intelligent agents, 73–74
　military, 21, 142
　nonhuman, 140
Interactions with the deceased, 64. *See also* Instrumental Transcommunication; Mediumship
　in bereavement, 64–67
　in dreams, 60–61
　following EMDR, 65–66
　interventions to help, 58
　limits on, 219
　in mirror-gazing, 67–69
　objects moving on their own, 56
　in organ transplant cases, 70–71
　receiving correct information, 57, 60–61
　relatives "return" for the one dying, 32–34, 39–40
　as reported by hospice nurses, 37
　as reported by hospice residents, 37–39
　as sensed presence, 55–56
　in shared death experiences, 27–28, 43–44, 46–47
Intermission memories. *See* Interregnum
International Association for Near-Death Studies, 4
International Society for Catholic Parapsychologists, 105
Interregnum (between lives), 176, 178, 192–194, 201, 205. *See also* Prebirth memories
Irwin, H. J., 133–134
ITC. *See* Instrumental transcommunication

J

Jahn, D. R., 55
Jahn, R. G., 17
Janis, Irving, 19, 21
Journal of Near-Death Studies, 4
Journeying metaphor, 34–35
Jürgenson, Friedrich, 102, 105–106
"Just one of those things" (JOTT), 132

K

Kadiragha, Durra, 119–120
Kāmaloka, 205, 212, 217
Kaplan, W., 21

Kean, Leslie, 130–131, 146
Keen, Montague, 126–127, 136–139
Keil, H. H. J., 184
Kelleher, Colm A., ix
Kelley, P., 34
Kelly, E. W., 84
Kerr, C. W., 37–38, 49
Knapp, George, ix
Koedam, I., 28, 41, 47
Korchnoi, Victor, 81, 89–90
Kripal, J. J., 163–165
Krippner, S., 61
Krohn, Elizabeth, 150–151, 163–165, 169, 171–173
Kubis, P., 104–105
Kwilecki, Susan, 125

L

Lacatski, James T., ix
Lake, J., 158
Lang, Basil, 143
Lang, Lyndon, 143, 147
Lang, William, 143, 147
LAP. *See* Living agent psi
Lawrence, M., 35–37
Lee, R. L. M., 202
Lenzi, Giuseppe, 113
Levitation, 18, 129–130, 144, 146, 229
Life After Life (Moody), 4
Life reviews
　in the afterlife, 203
　during near-death experiences, 156, 167–168
Light(s)
　in the afterlife, 214
　at the deathbed, 28
　experience of, and delirium, 48
　limited sensory perception of, 62
　in near-death experiences, 150, 151
　in physical mediumship, 127
　in shared death experiences, 43–44
Lilly, John, 66
Lily Dale (NY), 91
Lindbergh, Charles, 54
Living agent psi (LAP), x, 16, 24
　arguments for, 52
　dead agent psi vs., 228
　distinguishing between survival hypothesis and, 88–91, 122–124
　materialist–LAP–survival dial, x. *See also* Materialist–LAP–survival dial

and mediumship, 87–91
and near-death experiences, 16
as source of information for mediums, 77
in transplant cases, 71
versions of, for mediumship, 88
Lorimer, D., 206–207
Love, in the afterlife, 216
Lucid dreams, 59–60
Lucidity
　paradoxical, 39
　terminal, 38–40, 50, 215
Lumping, in explaining pathological ADCs, 62–63

M

Macy, M., 104–105
Magic wand hypothesis (LAP), 88, 123. *See also* Living agent psi
Ma Htwe Win, 183–185
Manifestation
　in the afterlife, 209–210
　physical. *See* Physical manifestation
Ma Oh Tin, 183
Marconi, Guglielmo, 103
Marks, A. D., 41
Maróczy, Géza, 81, 89–91
Martial, C., 153
Martin, M., 25
Marvell, 117–118
Master teachers, 140. *See also* Entities
Materialism, ix, x
　academic bias toward, 12–13
　arguments against survival in, 24–25
　in explaining near-death experiences, 156–162
　neutralizing, 226–227
　as normative idea, 19
　science differentiated from, 13–14
　scientific, 14
Materialist–LAP–survival dial, x
　and afterdeath communication, 73–74
　and the afterlife, 199
　and anomalous physical phenomena, 147–148
　and instrumental transcommunication, 99–100
　and mediumship, 81
　and near-death experiences, 149–150, 174
　and past-life experiences, 194–197
　physical phenomena on, 127–128

Materialists, 10, 102
Materializations, 127, 135, 146, 211. *See also* Anomalous physical phenomena
Matlock, J. G., 192–193
Mattingley, Annie, 225
McCarthy, Karen, 51–54, 56, 65, 216, 218–219
McLuhan, R., 82
Meaning. *See also* Meaning fields; Self-transformation
　and beliefs, 11, 28
　and afterdeath communication, 64, 69, 72
　and deathbed phenomena, 8, 49
　assessing degree of, 45, 47, 63, 71, 79, 115, 150, 181
　attributed to ambiguous stimuli, 99
　and the brain, 159, 166
　in coincidences, 47
　in dying process, 38, 49
　of experienced phenomena, 71, 72
　in grief process, 63
　in near-death experiences, 154, 169
　interpretation in EVP and ITC, 99, 109, 124
　interpretation in mediumship, 80, 83, 85, 93
　interpretation in past-life phenomena, 185, 189–190
　in personal experience, 11, 29, 38, 49, 52, 63, 96, 154, 189
　preserved after death, 222
　of psychomanteum experiences, 69
　and self-transformation, 96, 229
　and synchronicities, 8, 222
　in terminal lucidity, 215
Meaning fields, 197, 219, 229. *See also* Exosomatic theory
Medhus, Elisa, 140, 147, 230
Medhus, Erik, 90–91, 139–140, 147, 200–201, 209, 216–219, 230
Meditation, 11, 170, 216. *See also* Insights; Self-transformation
　and NDE-like experiences, 151–153
Mediums
　academics' reputation with, 92
　accuracy of, 83–87
　defined, 78
　embodiment of entities by, 127
　incorporation of entities by, 79
　information conveyed by, 76–77, 81–82

interaction with entities by, 79, 123
mental health of, 91–95
unique challenges faced by, 95
Mediumship, 75–97
as afterdeath communications, 53
artistic mediumship, 80
Beischel's protocol for studying, 85–86
and channeling, 78
contexts for examining, 81–83
and conventional view of death, 81–82
defined, 78
development of, 95–97
developmental hypothesis, 96
historical context for, 82–83
incorporation of entities in, 79. *See also* Physical mediumship
lack of psychophysical/neurophysiological markers of, 92
living agent psi vs. survival explanations of, 87–91
mediumistic painting, 80
terminology associated with, 78–81
trance, 80, 82–83
veridicality of, 83–87
versions of living agent psi for, 88
without incorporation of entities, 79. *See also* Mental mediumship
Meek, George, 106–107, 124
Memory(-ies)
in the afterlife, 203, 215
in altered states of consciousness, 221
cellular memory theory, 71
in determining presence of deceased persons, 91
distortions of, 196
episodic, 194
future, 164
genetic, 196
interregnum, 176, 192–194
between lives, vehicle for, 185
of near-death experiences, 152, 160, 166–167
past-life, 178. *See also* Past-life experiences
and sleep, 158
storage of, 215
"Men in Black" (MIBs), 140
Mental clarity
with deathbed phenomena, 49
paradoxical lucidity, 39
terminal lucidity, 38–40, 50

Mental health. *See also* Pathomorphism
and mediumship, 78, 91–92, 94–96
professionals lacking informed approach, 63, 78, 92, 94–95, 227
Mental mediumship, 79–97
contexts for examining, 81–83
defined, 8, 79
development of, 95–97
living agent psi vs. survival explanations of, 87–91
and mental health of mediums, 91–95
terminology associated with, 78
and trance channeling, 80
Mental monists, 11
Mental plane, 211
Metacognition, 6, 221
Metaphysical issues, in studying death, 6, 10
Meyers, George, 117–118
Mindsight, 174, 217, 221, 223
defined, 152
implications of, 228–229
during near-death experiences, 166–170
Miron, S. G., 143
Mirror gazing, 65–69
Mishlove, J., 143
Mitchell-Yellin, B., 157
Modern Mechanix and Inventions, 103–104
Monastic Tibetans, 216
Moody, Raymond A. Jr., 156, 161
on being in the presence of death, 27, 50
on hallucinations, 68
on impact of near-death experiences, 18
and mirror gazing, 66–69
near-death experiences described by, 4
on shared death experiences, 43–44
Moon, C., 140
Moon, P., 140
Moore, R. J., 13
Moore, Robert, 10–13, 178–179
Moquin, David, 177, 185. *See also* Past-life experiences
Morse, Samuel F. B., 103
Mossbridge, Julia, 5, 17, 18, 38, 39, 65–66, 88, 164
Motivation on the part of deceased. *See also* Survival hypothesis
to console bereaved, 123
need to say goodbye, 72
preserved after death, 221
reasons for attributing, 72–73, 78

similar to while alive, 76
source difficult to judge, 148
as support for survival hypothesis, 73, 89
unfinished business, 72, 76
Movement of objects
　flowers jump out of basket, 56–57, 64, 144
　in physical mediumship, 127
　"Just one of those things" (JOTT), 132
　poltergeist activity, 131–135
Mueller, George, 106
Multiple-process hypothesis (LAP), 88. *See also* Living agent psi
Murray, C. D., 72
Myers, Frederic, 209

N

Nahm, M., 38
Nani, A., 24
NDE-C (Near-Death Experience Content) scale, 153
NDE-like experiences, 151–153, 157, 160
NDEs. *See* Near-death experiences
NDE scale, 152–153
Near-Death Experience Content (NDE-C) scale, 153
Near-death experiences (NDEs), 149–174
　aftereffects of, 162–166
　attenuated fear of death following, 30
　characteristics of, 152–156
　cognitive clarity with, 39
　defined, 151
　descriptions of, 150–151
　distressing, 153–154
　divorce rate with, 163
　Greyson's research on, 4
　inverted, 154
　materialist explanation for, 156–162
　mindsight during, 166–170
　Moody's descriptions of, 4
　NDE-like experiences vs., 151–153, 157, 160
　outside the context of death, 151–152
　premonitions of unborn children during, 177
　reflections on, 171–174
　secondhand effects of, 170–171
　self-transformation following, 170–171
　similarity of dying and, 207–208
　simulated, 171
　sudden conversion with, 22
　with temporal anchors, 14–18, 149, 152, 159–162, 227–229
　veridical, 14–16
　versus shared death experiences, 45
Near-Death Experience Scale, 208
Nees, M. A., 111
Nepp, V. M., 89–90
Neural activity
　as correlate of consciousness, 24–25
　and near-death experiences, 156–160
　with psychedelic drugs, 159–160
Noory, George, 99
Novotny, Karl, 206, 217

O

Ohkado, M., 193–194
O'Keeffe, C., 133, 140
Okonsky, Jennifer, 75
O'Neil, William, 102, 106, 115
Open-mindedness, dying supported by, 42
Ordinary waking state, 6, 172–173, 220
Organ transplant cases
　afterdeath communication in, 70–71
　near-death experiences in, 161
　possessing entities in, 140
　visions following transplants, 70
Oscar the cat, 33, 46
Osis, K., 40–41
Owen, George, 133–135

P

Pain, vicarious experience of, 46
Paradoxical lucidity, 39
Paramnesia, 196
Paraná, D., 84
Pareidolia, 99, 103, 106, 110–111, 113, 124, 146
Parker, A., 59–60
Past-life experiences, 175–197
　of adults, 185–188
　and birthmarks or congenital deformities, 175–176, 181–185
　of children, 175–176, 179–181
　context of, 176–179
　conventional explanations for, 196
　defined, 8, 178
　and interregnum memories, 192–194
　and past-life regression, 188–191
　reflections on, 194–197
　solved vs. unsolved cases, 178

Past-life regression, 176, 178, 188–192, 208
Past-life therapy, 190–191
Pathology
 afterdeath communication as, 61–63
 and mental health of mediums, 91–95
 separating anomalous phenomena and, 227
Pathomorphism, 61, 92. *See also* Mental health
 defined, 227
 neutralizing, 227
 and possession, 139
Pauli, Wolfgang, 145
Pauli effect, 163, 165, 229
Peak in Darien experience, 173
PEAR (Princeton Engineering Anomalies Research) laboratory, 121
Pearsall, P., 70–71
Pearson, P., 46–47
Perception
 in the afterlife, 217
 in altered states of consciousness, 221
 connected to death, 46, 50
 mindsight, 166–170
 during near-death experiences, 166–169
 remote, 17, 62, 170
 during sleep, 222
 synesthesia, 168–169
Percipient (term), 53, 55, 72–73
Pereira da Silva, José Roberto, 84
Peripheral shutdown, 31
Personality(-ies)
 in the afterlife, 215
 alternate, presence of, 128
 and beliefs about consciousness and reality, 12
 in determining presence of deceased persons, 91
 displacement of, 197
 previous, 178, 185, 215
 projected from timeless domain of consciousness, 197
Peyton, Bettina, 160–161
Phenomenal consciousness, 5–6, 10
 after death, 203–205
 in altered states of consciousness, 220–221
 in conservatively transcendent position, 11
 defined, 5
 as disembodied reality, 200
 and near-death experiences, 14–16, 159
 and neural processes, 24–25
 survival of, 214–215
Philip experiment, 134–135, 140, 148
Phillips, C., 111
Philosophical self-grasping, 216
Phone calls from the dead, 103, 119, 229. *See also* Anomalous telephone contacts
 prolonged calls, 118–119
Phone Calls From the Dead (Rogo & Bayless), 118
Physical contact, initiated by apparitions, 56
Physical events. *See also* Anomalous physical phenomena
 interpreted as messages, 56–57
 recurrent spontaneous psychokinesis, 128
Physical manifestation
 as crust of alterations of consciousness, 26
 in home circles, 129
 as meaningful deathbed coincidence, 47
 in near-death experiences, 173–174
 plasticity of, 229
 with terminal lucidity, 40
 of vicarious pain, 46
Physical mediumship, 127–131. *See also* Anomalous physical phenomena
 Alexander's experience with, 128–131
 beneficial effects of, 142–143
 characteristics of, 79–80
 defined, 8
 materialization during, 211
 poltergeist phenomena, 82
 as presence of alternate personality, 128
 and trance channeling, 80
Physical plane, 211
Physical suffering, deathbed phenomena and reduction of, 35–36
Physics, laws of, 144–145
Physiology
 in altered states of consciousness, 220
 during sleep, 222
PK. *See* Psychokinesis
Plasma globes, 116.
Plasticity of physical manifestation, 229
Plato, 18–19, 22, 226. *See also* Room allegory
 cave allegory, 18–19, 22, 24, 226

Poltergeist phenomena, 82, 133, 146.
Poltergeists, 82, 131–135, 146, 148, 213, 228
  in afterlife, 193
  characteristics of, 133
  defined, 127
  health issues with, 142
  in instrumental transcommunication, 114
  Philip experiment, 134–135
  as presence of alternate personality, 128
  Sauchie case, 133–134
  and seismic tremors, 144–145
  traveling objects, 131–132
Pope Paul VI, 105
Possession, 139–144
  beneficial effects of, 142–143
  classic signs of, 141
  in development of mediumship, 97
  entities in, 140–142
  as presence of alternate personality, 128
  and reincarnation, 197
  use of term, 79
Possession syndrome, 141
Postmaterialism, 25–26
Prebirth memories, 177–178, 192–193
Precognition
  defined, 17
  following near-death experiences, 163–164
Precognitive dreaming, 22
Premonitions, of unborn children, 177
Premonitory symptoms of death, 28
Presi, Paolo, 102, 111
Previous personality, 178, 185, 215.
  See also Past-life experiences
  accounts of, 180, 192–193
  identification of, 183, 185, 189–190
  study of, 181, 185, 191, 194–197
Price, Henry, 203–205, 211, 217, 220–221
Priming, 110–111
Prince, W. F., 126
Princeton Engineering Anomalies Research (PEAR) laboratory, 121
Pritchett, Alf, 206–207
Probability, 24
Problem solving, afterdeath communication for, 57
Protection, afterdeath communication for, 57–58

Proxy sitters, 80, 86
Psyche(s)
  alternate personalities as aspects of, 128, 130
  brain-independent aspect of, 39
  in different dimension of reality, 50
  of dying persons, 50
  hells during life created by, 212
  and mindsight, 170, 228–229
  shadow part of, 40
  survival of, 214–217
  of transplant donors/recipients, 71
Psychedelics
  endogenous, 92
  in inducing afterdeath communication, 65
  in palliative care, 42
  in shamanism, 81
  similarity of NDE content and effects of, 159–160
Psychography, 80
Psychokinesis, 71. See also Recurrent Spontaneous Psychokinesis (RSPK)
Psychological phenomena. See also Psyche(s)
  exosomatic theory of, 145–146
  possession, 139–144
Psychological well-being, deathbed phenomena and reduction of, 35–36
Psychomanteum, 69
Psychometric skill, 196–197
Psycho-phones, 118
Psychophores, 185, 194, 197, 223
Puhle, A., 59–60

Q

Qualia, 5, 203
Quantum theory, 227

R

Radio sweep EVP, 108
Random event generators (REGs), 103, 121–122, 173, 210
Raudive, Konstantīns, 105–106
Raudive voices, 105, 109
Readings (in mediumship), 80, 81
  accuracy of, 83–87
  cold, 81–85
  hot, 82

Reaffirmation, afterdeath communications for, 57
Reality
  beliefs about, 10–14, 29, 226
  deceased in close-earth-plane dimensions of, 202
  extra-sensory dimensions of, 78
  feelings of, 68, 172–173
  knowledge of, in shared death experiences, 44–45
  limited sensory processing of, 62
  mind's ability to manipulate, 215
  need for postmaterialist interpretation of, 25–26
  as production of the self's mind, 202
  psyche existing in different dimension of, 50
  radical reconceptualization of, 227–228
Reassurance, afterdeath communications for, 57
Recognizing dying stage, 30–31
Recurrent spontaneous psychokinesis (RSPK), 128, 133–134, 210
Regression, 176, 178, 188, 190–191. *See also* Past-life regression
REGs. *See* Random event generators
Reincarnation, 8, 155, 171, 178–179. *See also* Past-life experiences
  belief in, 12–13, 18, 29
  birthmarks as evidence of, 195
  criticisms of research on, 195–196
  defined, 178
  incidence of, 178–179
  and possession, 197
  research approaches to, 178
Reincarnation and Biology (Stevenson), 179
Release, afterdeath communication for, 57
Religion
  preparation for afterlife in, 202
  survival narratives conforming to, 194
Religiosity, in conservatively transcendent position, 11
Religious figures, end-of-life visions of, 48
Religious ideation, and dysphoric end-of-life feelings, 41
Remote influencing, 17, 228
Remote perception, 17, 62, 170
Remote viewing, 228
Renz, M., 42
Repede, E., 35–37

The Republic (Plato), 18–19
Requested afterdeath communications, 53–54
Residue theories (afterlife), 73, 229
  in possession, 71
  from previous lives, 185, 208, 213, 222
Resolution, afterdeath communication for, 57
Restricted environmental stimulation technique (REST), 66
Retrocognition, 17, 24
Reverse Pauli effect, 165. *See also* Pauli effect
Reynolds, Pam, 160
Rinaldi, Sonia, 108, 115
Ring, Kenneth, 166–170, 172
Rivas, T., 15
Roe, C. A., 13
Rogo, D. Scott, 118, 123
Rollans, Robert, 80, 89–90
Room allegory, 23–24. *See also* Plato
RSPK. *See* Recurrent spontaneous psychokinesis
Rudy, Lloyd, 15, 17, 24, 151, 160, 169
Runólfsson, Runólfur, 216–217
Ruth, Babe, 180
Ryff, Carol, 119

S

Sarraf, M., 87
Satan, 140
Sauchie case, 133–134
Schizotypal personality disorder, 94–95
Schmid, Leo, 105
Schwartz, Gary, 115–117, 124, 208
Science, x
  as antidote to groupthink, 21–22
  authentic, 5, 21, 226
  inauthentic mode of, 21
  materialism differentiated from, 13–14
  materialism imposed on, 226
  in studying death, 13
Scientific American, 102
Scientism, 5, 14, 21. *See also* Inauthenticity
Scientistic materialism, 14
Scole experiment, 126–127, 135–139, 142, 146–148, 211, 219
Seeing blindfolded, 170. *See also* Mindsight; Veridical immediate seeing

Self. *See also* Insights; Self-transformation
  after death, 202, 212, 215, 217, 221
  consciousness of, 93, 96
  core self, 215–216
  dissociation of, in mediumship, 79, 130
  fear of loss of, 216
  losing importance of, 42
  innate versus philosophical self-grasping, 216
  notion of, 215–216
  self-acceptance, 170
  self-hypnosis, 153
  self-identity, 42, 140
  self-improvement, 221
  self-worth, 170
  sense of, following NDEs, 153, 155, 166–167, 172
  survival of, 215–216
  trait self, 215–216
Self-deception, about past-life experiences, 196
Self-development, 95–97, 119, 202–203. *See also* Self-transformation
  and the afterlife, 202
  importance of, for those with extraordinarily transcendent beliefs, 11
  lack of training in, 22
  for mediumship, 96
Self-talk, in altered states of consciousness, 221
Self-transformation, xi, 22, 41–42, 220, 229
  following ADCs, 54, 72
  of caregivers, 30
  in developing mediumship, 96
  following near-death experiences, 149, 155, 170–171, 226
  that changes boggle thresholds, 226
Senkowski, E., 122–123
Sensed presence, 55–56, 62
  felt, 55
  in near-death experiences, 150–151
  and sensory restriction, 66
Senses
  in the afterlife, 217
  involved in sensed presence of deceased, 56
  during near-death experiences, 160
  in peripheral shutdown stage of dying, 31
  physical reality processed by, 62
Sensory deprivation, 66

Sensory restriction, 66
Sexena, Gainda Wati, 175, 179–180
Sexena, Hanumant, 175–176, 180, 185. *See also* Past-life experiences
Shadow (psyche), 40, 154, 229
Shamanic spirit guides, 140
Shamanism, 81, 104, 115, 140
Shared afterdeath experiences, 72, 73
  of apparitions, 58–59
  of sensed presences, 62
Shared Crossing Research Initiative, 44–45, 49
Shared death experiences, 43–45, 49
  beneficial effects of, 49
  facilitated, 45
  inadvertent, 44–45
  as perceptions connected to death, 46
Shared hallucinations, 62
Shermer, Michael, 10, 102
Shinar, Y. R., 41
Shroder, T., 189
Shushan, Gregory, 23, 149
Simple phone calls from the dead, 118
Simulated near-death experiences, 171
Simulation constraint, 194
Singh, Maha Ram, 175–176, 180
Sitters (in mediumship), 80–82, 84–88, 96, 129, 132, 136, 216
Sitting circles, 82
Sixth Mass Extinction, 20
Skill(s)
  in determining presence of deceased persons, 91
  of mediumship, development of, 96–97
  psychometric, 196–197
Sleep, 6
  in the afterlife, 202
  analogy of afterlife and, 203–205
  comparing death and, 222
  memory of, 158
  sensed presence during, 56
Sliders, 213. *See also* Entities
Smart, Billy, 206
Social recognition, and beliefs about consciousness and reality, 12
Society for Psychical Research, 70, 136
Solved cases (past lives), 178, 190, 193. *See also* Previous personality
Specialized knowledge. *See also* Mediumship; Scole experiment
  anomalous, 17, 33, 77, 141, 143, 228
  expanding limits of, 17, 227

from NDEs, 169, 171, 174
scientific expertise, 7, 10, 14
as support for survival hypothesis, 148
Spencer-Thomas, S., 55
Spiricom, 106–107
Spirit guides, 80, 130, 140, 203, 213
Spiritual effects
positive, at the time of death, 28
transformative, 54
Spiritualism, 82–83, 91, 128
Spirituality, beneficial effects of deathbed phenomena on, 49
Spiritual plane, 211
Spiritual transformation, 22
Splitting, in explaining pathological ADCs, 62
Spontaneous afterdeath communications, 53
Stavis, Rachel, 140, 142, 210–211
Steere House Nursing and Rehabilitation Center, 33
Stevenson, Ian, 27–28, 35, 175–176, 179, 180, 183, 185–186, 190–191
Strada, E. A., 28
Strieber, Anne, 140, 207, 216, 218, 230
Strieber, Whitley, 140, 207, 214, 218
Studying death, 3–26
academics' avoidance of, 7–9
and beliefs about consciousness and reality, 10–14
controversial nature of, 7
epistemological considerations in, 23–26
experiential framework for, 9–10
and groupthink, 18–22
methodological variances in, 35–36
and near-death experiences with temporal anchors, 14–18
and phenomenal vs. behavioral consciousness, 5–6
range of perspectives brought to, 7
source material for, 8–10
and states of consciousness, 6
Sudden awakenings, 46–47
Sudduth, M., 215
Sumption, Frank, 108
Super-psi hypothesis, 24. *See also* Living agent psi (LAP)
Supervenience thesis, 156–157, 205
Survival (of death). *See also* Survival Hypothesis; Studying death
difficulty in conceptualizing, 203
for all vs. just for some, 208–209
as fully functioning human being, 229
materialist–LAP–survival dial, x.
See also Materialist–LAP–survival dial
problem in studying, 23
of the psyche, 214–217
of the "self," 215–216
Survival hypothesis, x–xi, 70. *See also* Afterlife; Studying death
arguments in support of, 52, 81, 89
defined, 4
distinguishing between living agent psi and, 88–91, 122–124
empirical evidence for, 23–24, 203
imitation of gestures of deceased, 89, 123
materialist arguments against, 24–25
and mediumship, 87–91
motivation of the deceased as support for, 73, 76–77, 89
quality of interaction as support for, 148
skills unique to the deceased, 81, 89–91, 123, 143
specialized knowledge as support for, 89, 123, 148
strategies for proving, 89, 117
Surviving Death (Kean), 130
Synesthesia, 168–169, 217

T

Taylor, S. F., 55
Technologies
communication with discarnate entities via. *See* Instrumental transcommunication (ITC)
malfunction of, following near-death experiences, 163, 165
Telepathic communication, 71, 221, 223, 226
among the deceased, 217
between the living and the deceased, 218
Telephone Calls From the Dead (Cooper), 118
Telephone contacts
anomalous, 117–120
following near-death experiences, 165
Temporal anchor, 14
near-death experiences with, 14–18, 149, 152, 159–162, 227–229

Temporality, NDEs and alteration of, 154–156, 160
Terminal illness, fear of death with, 29
Terminal lucidity, 38–40, 50, 215
Terror management theory, 29–30
Tesla, Nikola, 103, 115, 116, 212
Thanatos TV EN, 191
Thoughts, shaping of environment by, 209–210, 219
Time
  in the afterlife, 213–214
  altered, in near-death experiences, 154–156, 160
  nature of, 213–214
  projection of personalities into, 197
  timeless domain of consciousness, 197
Time of death
  knowledge or control of, 32–35
  unknown, with afterdeath communication, 72
Time sense
  in altered states of consciousness, 221
  during sleep, 222
Tomlinson, M., 82–83
Toronto Society for Psychical Research, 134, 140
Trance, 80, 136, 143, 153
  cognitive, 153
  and dissociation, 93–94
  under EEG, 92
  hypnotic, 188
  light, 83
  and loss of memory, 143–144
  and personality scores, 94
  and possession, 139, 141
Trance channeling, 80, 94, 139, 143–144
Trance lecturing, 83
Trance mediumship, 80, 82–83, 143–144
Transcendental awareness, 169–170. *See also* Mindsight
  in NDEs, 173, 208
Transcendentalism, 11
Transcendent Mind (Baruss & Mossbridge), 17, 88
Transformation. *See also* Self-transformation
  by afterdeath communications, 54
  with anomalous telephone contacts, 120
  by near-death experiences, 162–163
  when approaching death, 41–42

Transplant cases. *See* Organ transplant cases
Trauma
  for mediums, 95–96
  and past-life therapy, 190–191
Traveling objects, 131–132
Tricksters, 140, 142, 213. *See also* Entities
Tucker, J. B., 184
Tulpas, 135, 140. *See also* Entities
Twaddle (in mediumship), 80, 83, 85
Twenty Cases Suggestive of Reincarnation (Stevenson), 179

U

Umbanda, 214
Understanding, and beliefs about consciousness and reality, 12
U Nga Than, 182–184
Universal consciousness, 11
Unsolved case, of previous personality, 178
U.S. Defense Intelligence Agency, 142

V

Van Quekelberghe, R., 171
Veridical immediate seeing, 170. *See also* Mindsight; Remote perception
Veridicality
  of hallucinations, 62
  of mediumistic activity, 83–87
  of temporal anchors, 160–161
Veridical NDEs, 14–16, 174
Veridical perception, 15–16, 160
Visible processes of dying, 29–31
Visions at end of life
  as comforting, 37–38, 49
  and delirium, 48
  of the devil, 41
  distressing, 37–38, 40–41
  of past life, 177
  of religious figures, 48
  in shared deathbed experiences, 43, 45
  terminal lucidity with, 39–40
  terminology around, 35
  of those already dead, 28, 32, 34–35, 37–41, 43, 45
Visions of the future, given by an apparent visit of a person who is dying, 46
Von Szalay, Attila, 105

W

Wahbeh, Helané, 75
"Walkabout JOTT", 132
Walters, Harry, 118
Wassie, N., 151
Wehrstein, K. M., 82
White Feather (spirit guide), 79, 130, 139
Wilde, D. J., 95–96
Williams, B. J., 25

Windbridge Certified Research Mediums, 86, 92, 96–97
"Windfall JOTT", 132
Winsper, A. R., 111
Wooffitt, R., 72
Woollacott, M., 56–57, 62, 161
Worth, Patience, 126

X

Xavier, Chico, 84

About the Author

Imants Baruss, PhD, is a professor in the Department of Psychology at King's University College at Western University, Canada, where he teaches courses about consciousness and altered states of consciousness. His current research includes mathematical modeling of consciousness and empirical investigation of apparent afterdeath communication with electronic devices. He is the author of seven books, more than 50 papers, and more than 100 presentations at conferences and universities around the world. He is an associate editor of the *Journal of Scientific Exploration* and consulting editor of *Psychology of Consciousness*. He is also a member of the New York Academy of Sciences, the Society for Consciousness Studies, and the Academy for the Advancement of Postmaterialist Sciences.